NORAGAMI
STRAY GOD

ADACHITOKA

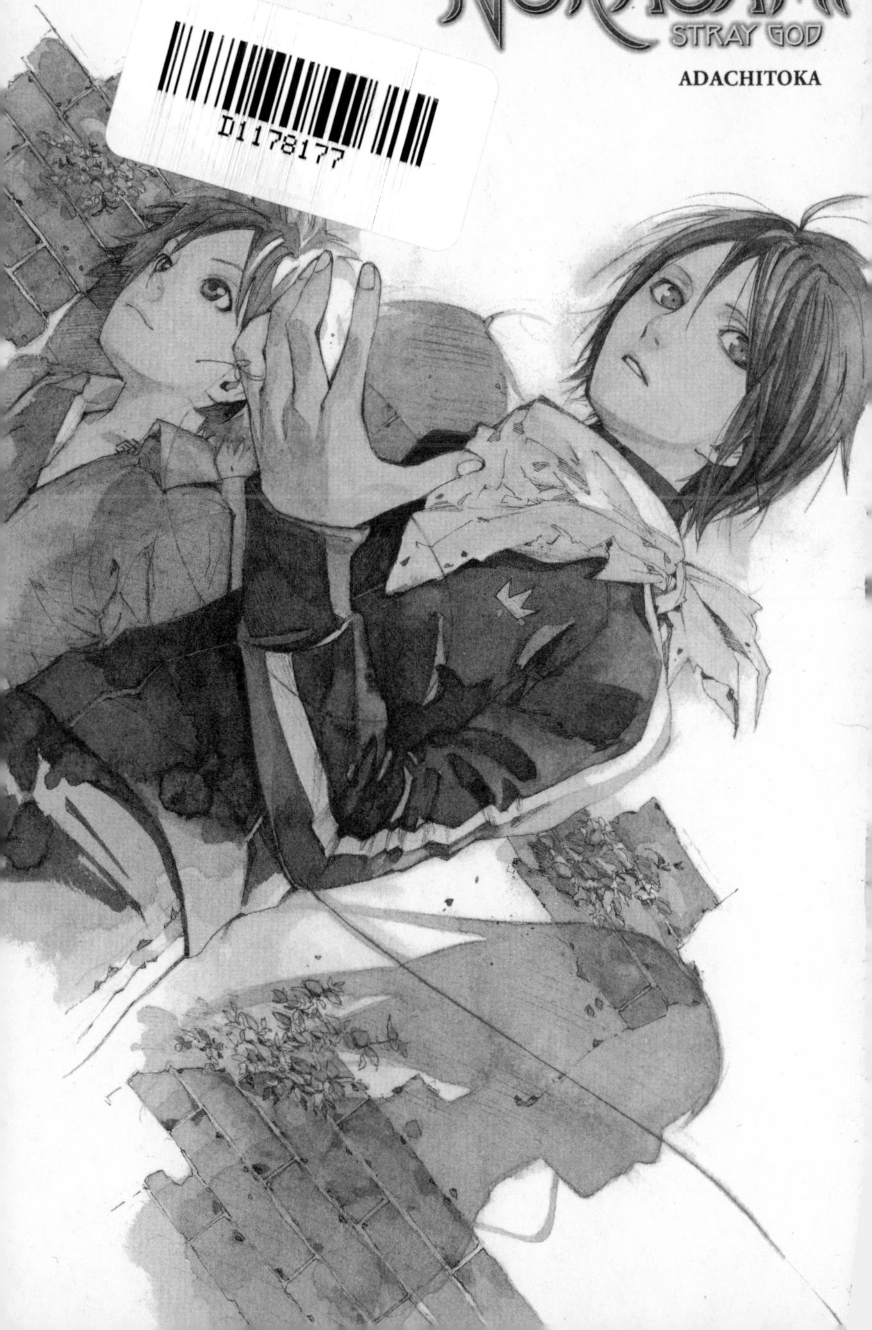

CHAPTER 20: PRAYERFUL OATH   5

CHAPTER 21: DON'T GO—STAY WITH ME   51

CHAPTER 22: WHAT MUST BE DONE   97

CHAPTER 23: GUIDING LIGHT   143

Characters

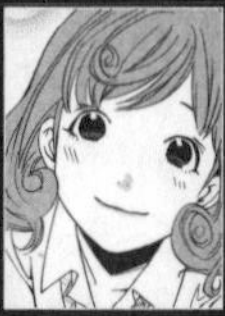

KOFUKU

A goddess of poverty who calls herself Ebisu after the god of fortune.

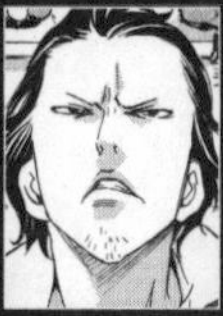

DAIKOKU

Kofuku's shinki who summons storms.

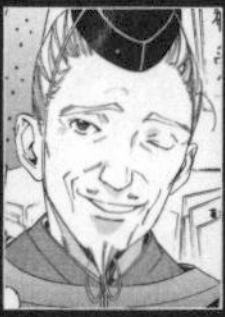

TENJIN

The God of Learning, Sugawara no Michizane.

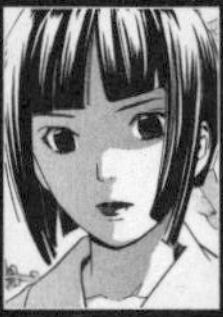

MAYU

Formerly Yato's shinki, now Tenjin's shinki.

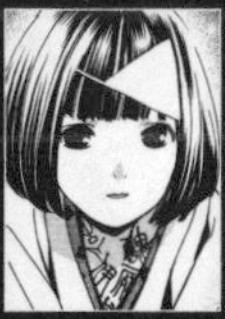

STRAY

A shinki who serves an unspecified number of deities

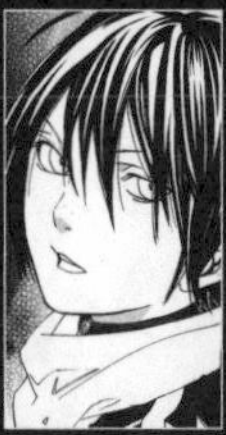

YATO

A minor deity who always wears a sweatsuit.

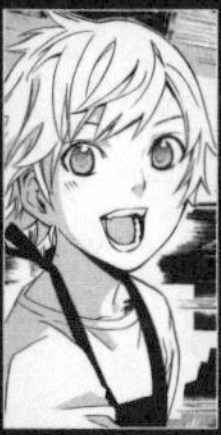

YUKINÉ

Yato's shinki who turns into a sword.

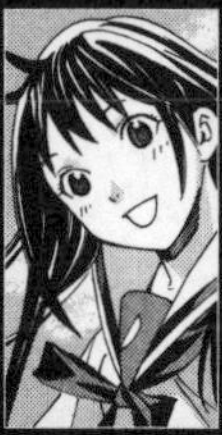

HIYORI IKI

A middle school student who has become half ayakashi.

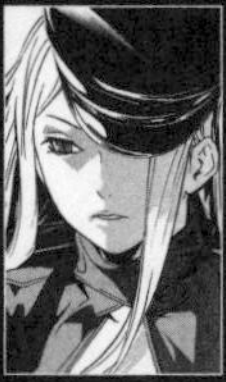

BISHAMONTEN

A powerful warrior god who seeks vengeance on Yato.

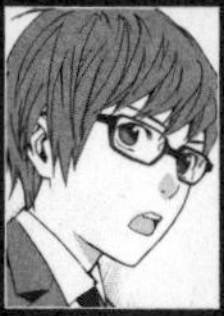

KAZUMA

A navigational shinki who serves as guide to Bishamon.

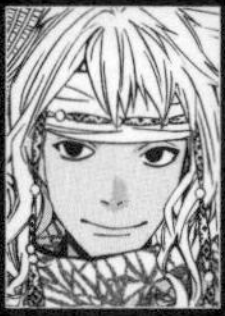

KUGAHA

A medicine man who is plotting to have Bishamon replaced.

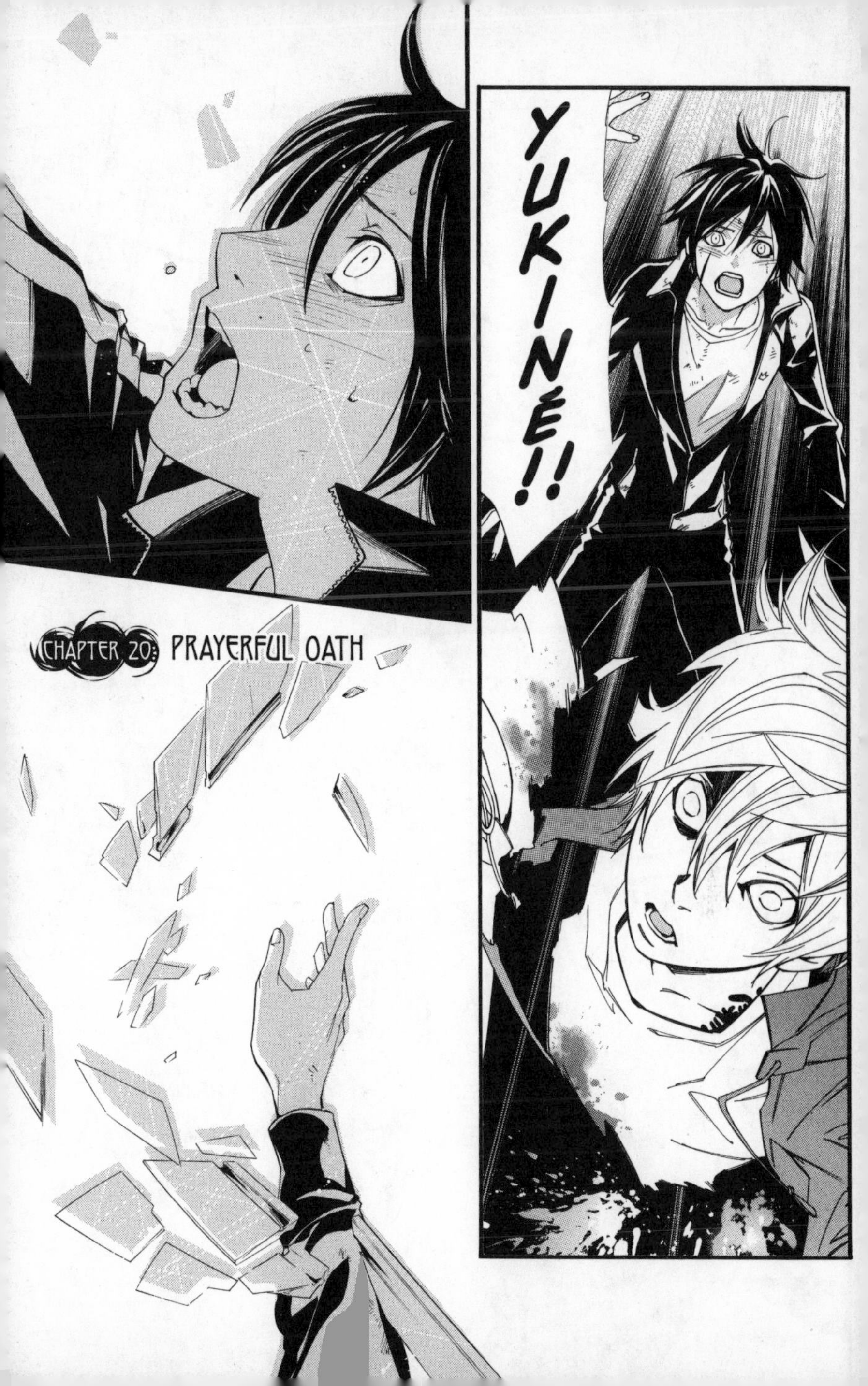
YUKINE!!
CHAPTER 20: PRAYERFUL OATH

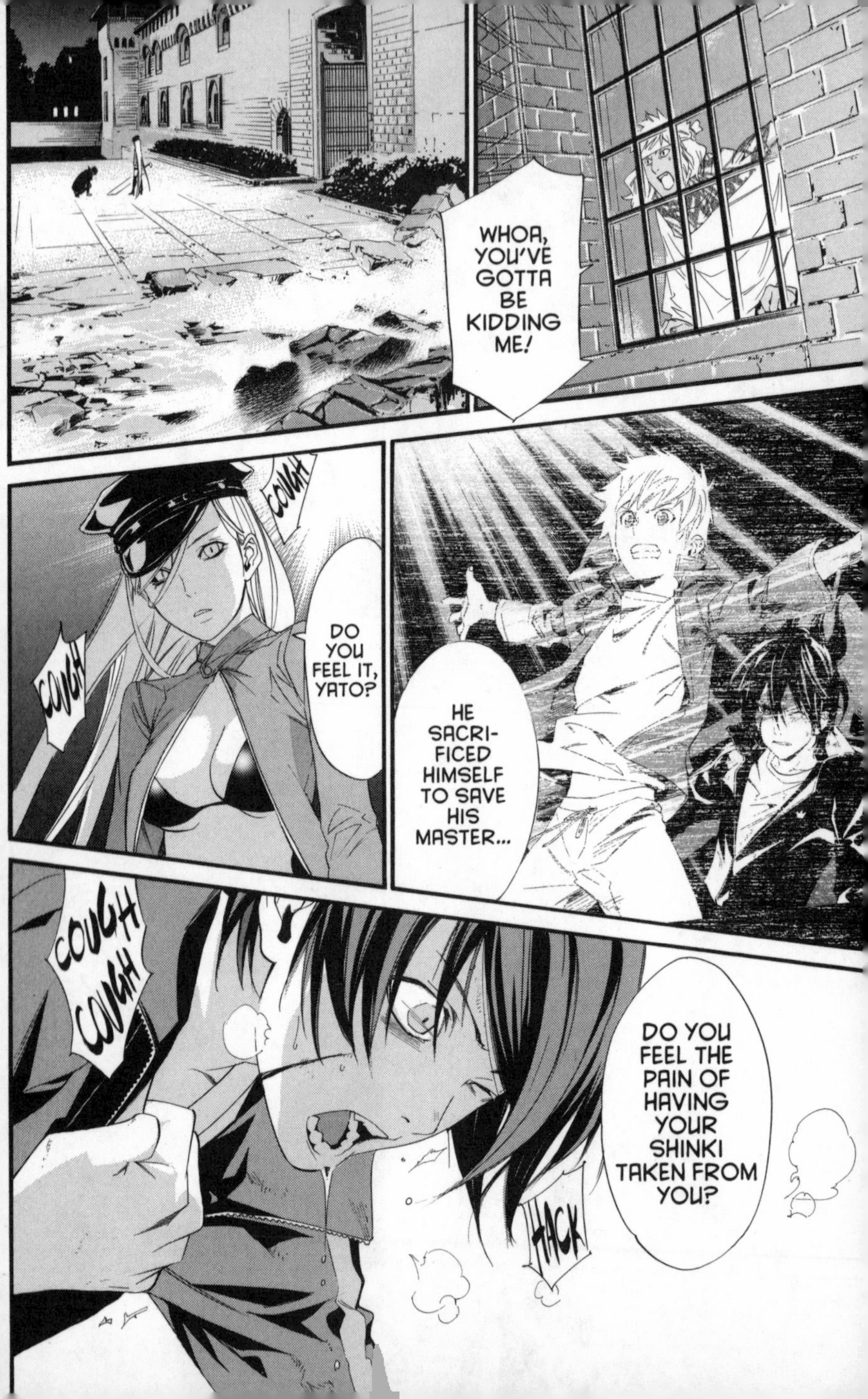
WHOA, YOU'VE GOTTA BE KIDDING ME!
HE SACRIFICED HIMSELF TO SAVE HIS MASTER...
COUGH
DO YOU FEEL IT, YATO?
COUGH
DO YOU FEEL THE PAIN OF HAVING YOUR SHINKI TAKEN FROM YOU?
COUGH COUGH
HACK

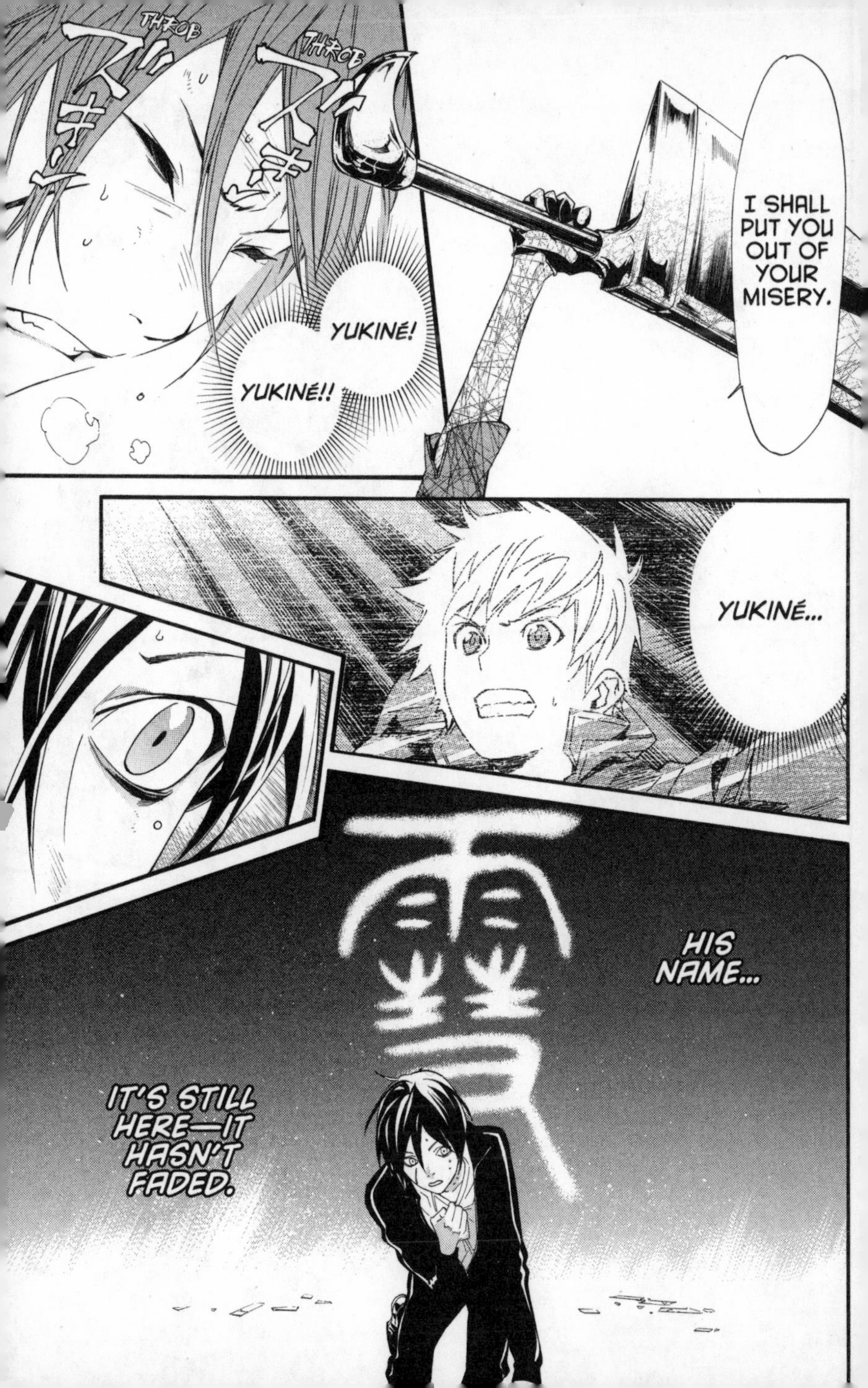
I SHALL PUT YOU OUT OF YOUR MISERY.
THROB
THROB
YUKINÉ!
YUKINÉ!!
YUKINÉ...
HIS NAME...
IT'S STILL HERE—IT HASN'T FADED.

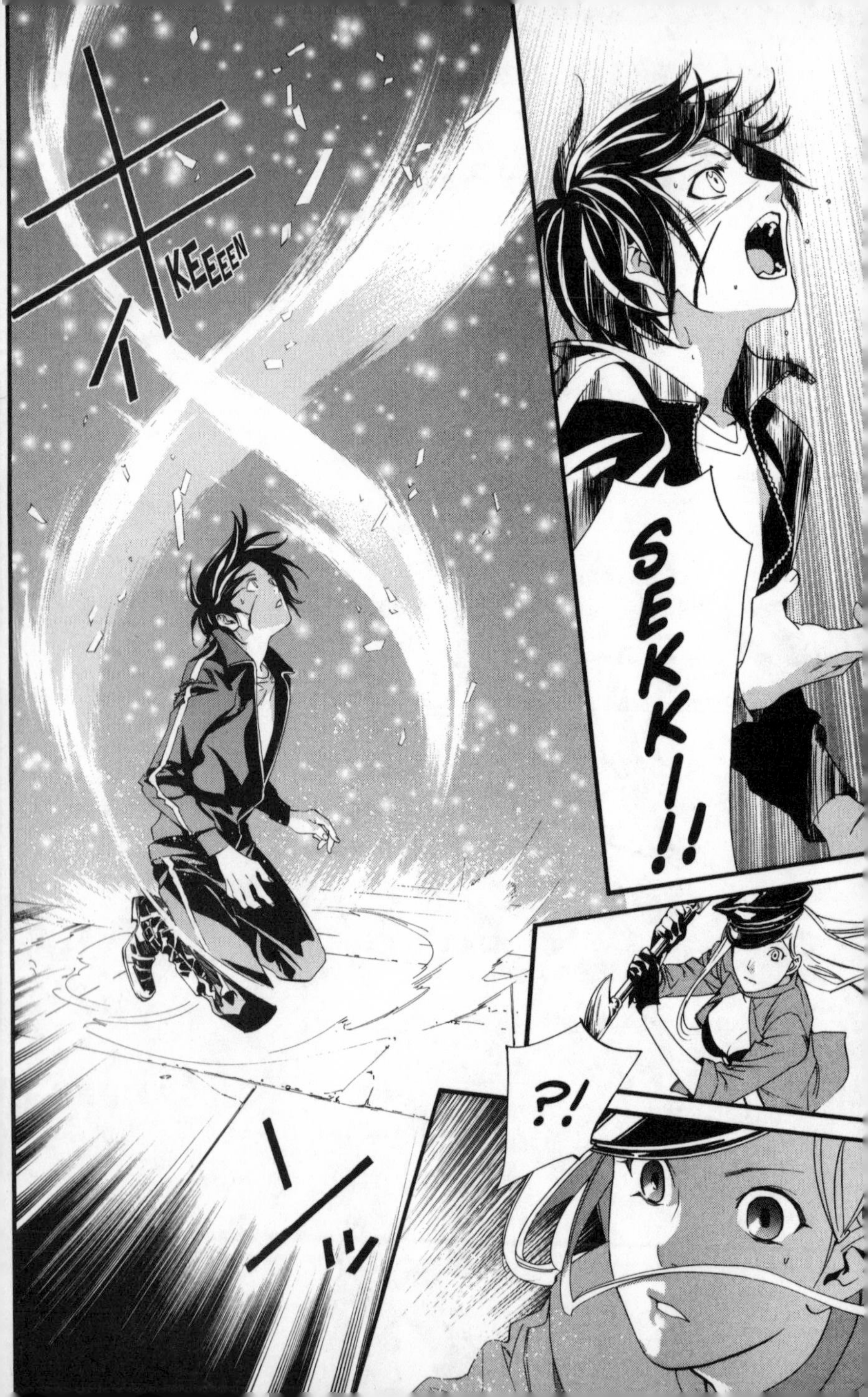
SEKKI!!
?!
KEEEEEN

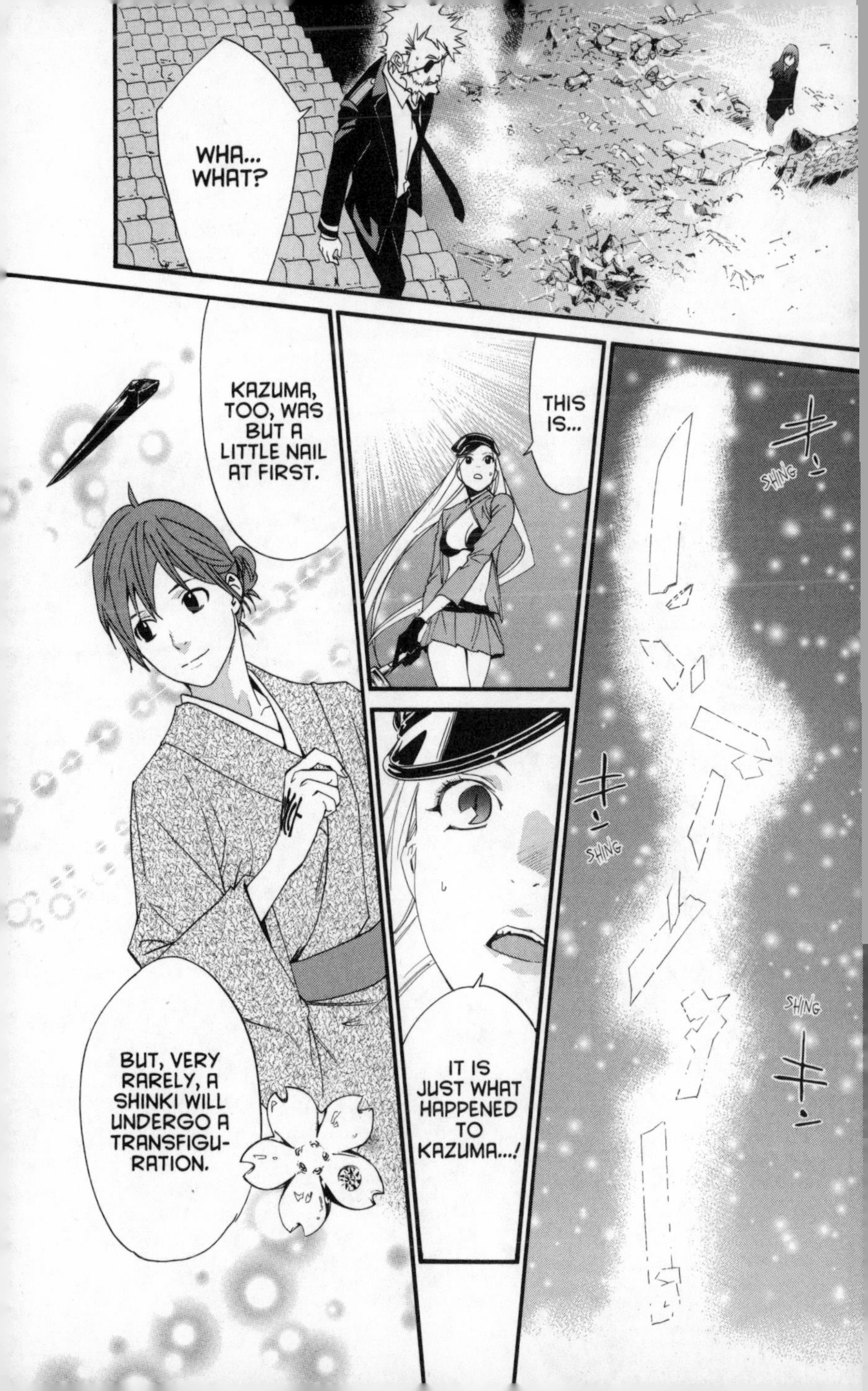
WHA... WHAT?
SHING
SHING
SHING
THIS IS...
IT IS JUST WHAT HAPPENED TO KAZUMA...!
KAZUMA, TOO, WAS BUT A LITTLE NAIL AT FIRST.
BUT, VERY RARELY, A SHINKI WILL UNDERGO A TRANSFIGU-RATION.

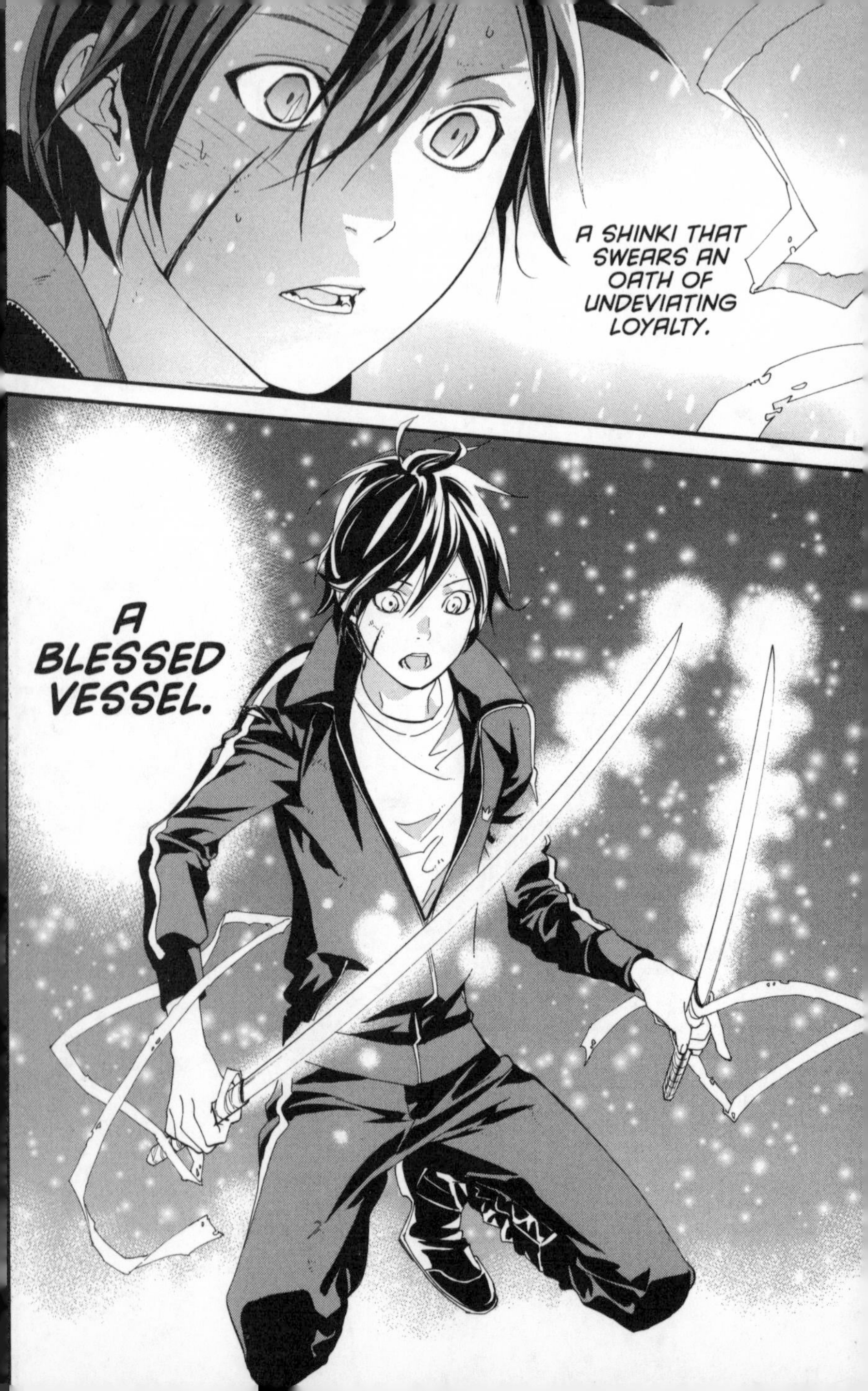
A SHINKI THAT SWEARS AN OATH OF UNDEVIATING LOYALTY.
A BLESSED VESSEL.

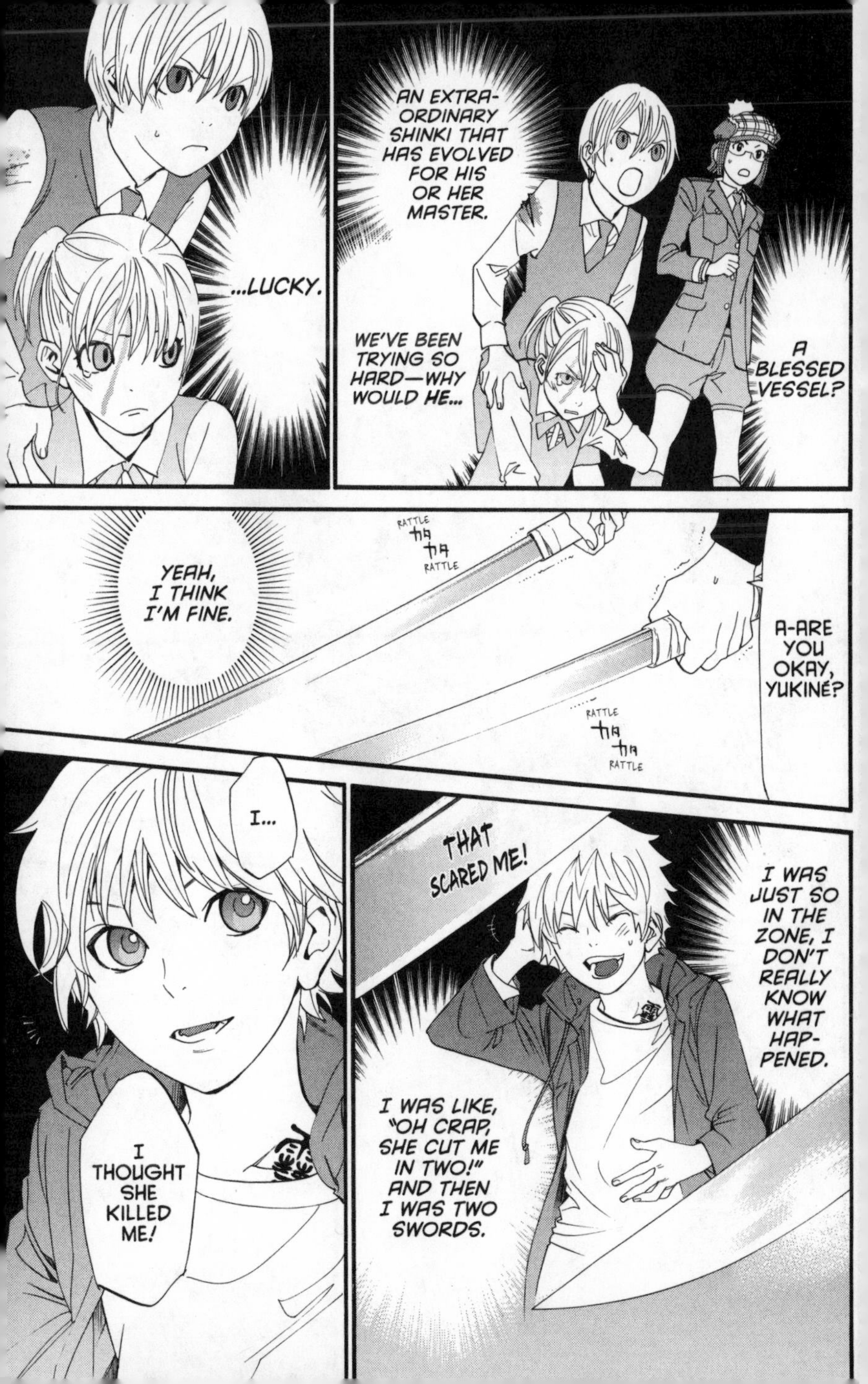

A BLESSED VESSEL?
AN EXTRA-ORDINARY SHINKI THAT HAS EVOLVED FOR HIS OR HER MASTER.
WE'VE BEEN TRYING SO HARD—WHY WOULD HE...
...LUCKY.
A-ARE YOU OKAY, YUKINE?
RATTLE カタ カタ RATTLE
RATTLE カタ カタ RATTLE
YEAH, I THINK I'M FINE.
I WAS JUST SO IN THE ZONE, I DON'T REALLY KNOW WHAT HAP-PENED.
THAT SCARED ME!
I WAS LIKE, "OH CRAP, SHE CUT ME IN TWO!" AND THEN I WAS TWO SWORDS.
I...
I THOUGHT SHE KILLED ME!

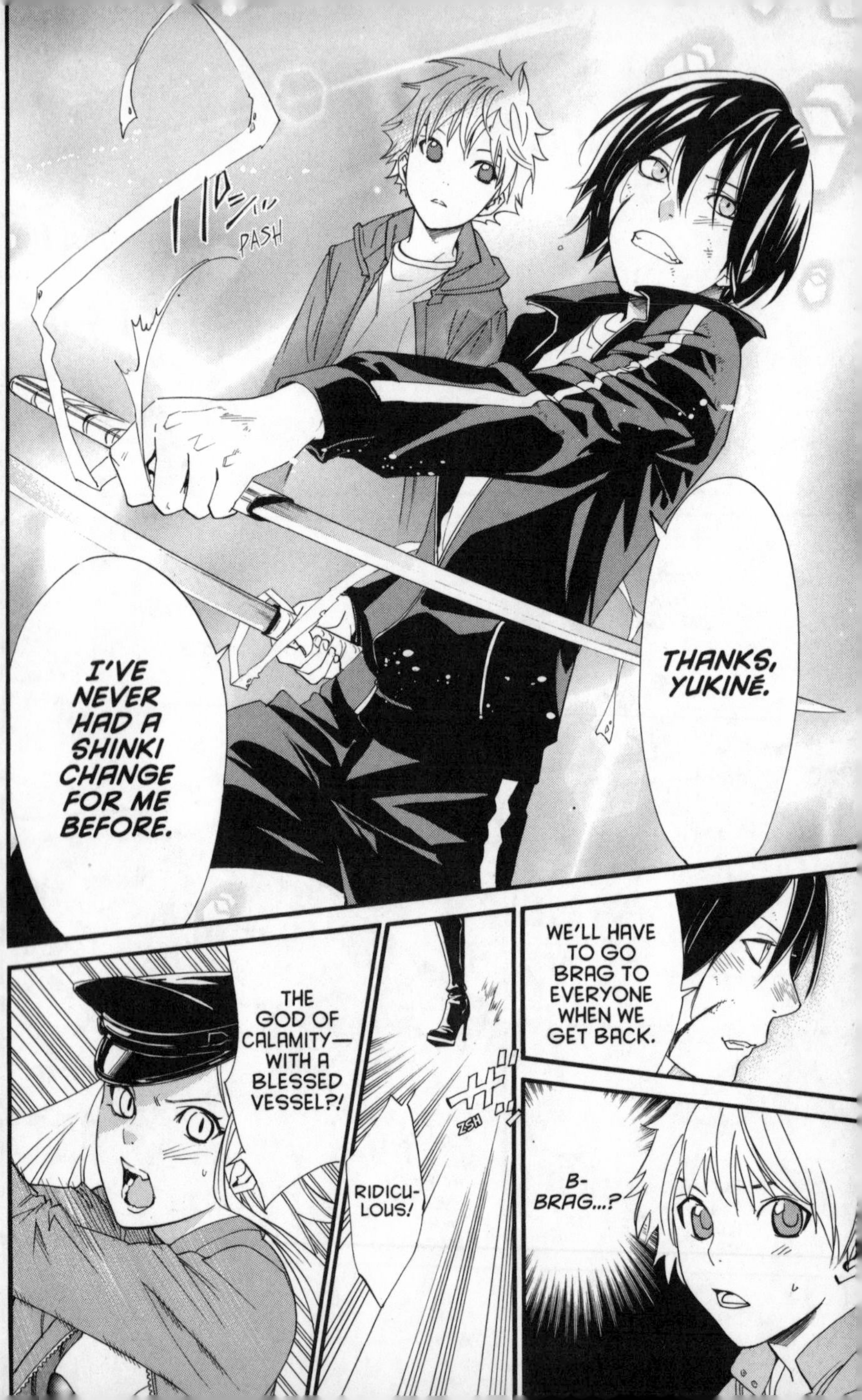

PASH
THANKS, YUKINÉ.
I'VE NEVER HAD A SHINKI CHANGE FOR ME BEFORE.
WE'LL HAVE TO GO BRAG TO EVERYONE WHEN WE GET BACK.
B- BRAG...?
THE GOD OF CALAMITY—WITH A BLESSED VESSEL?!
ZSH
RIDICU-LOUS!

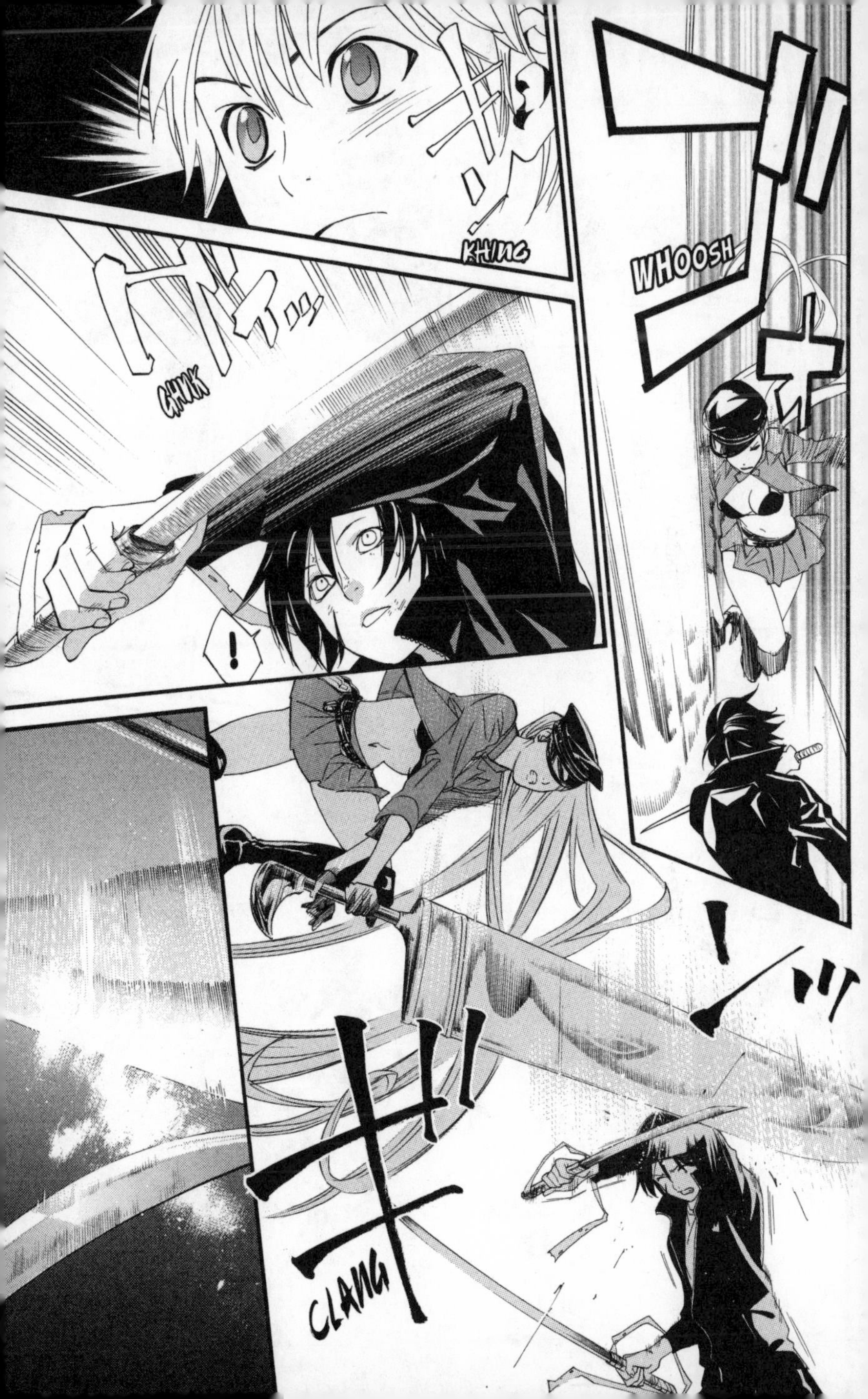
WHOOSH
KHING
CHINK
!
CLANG

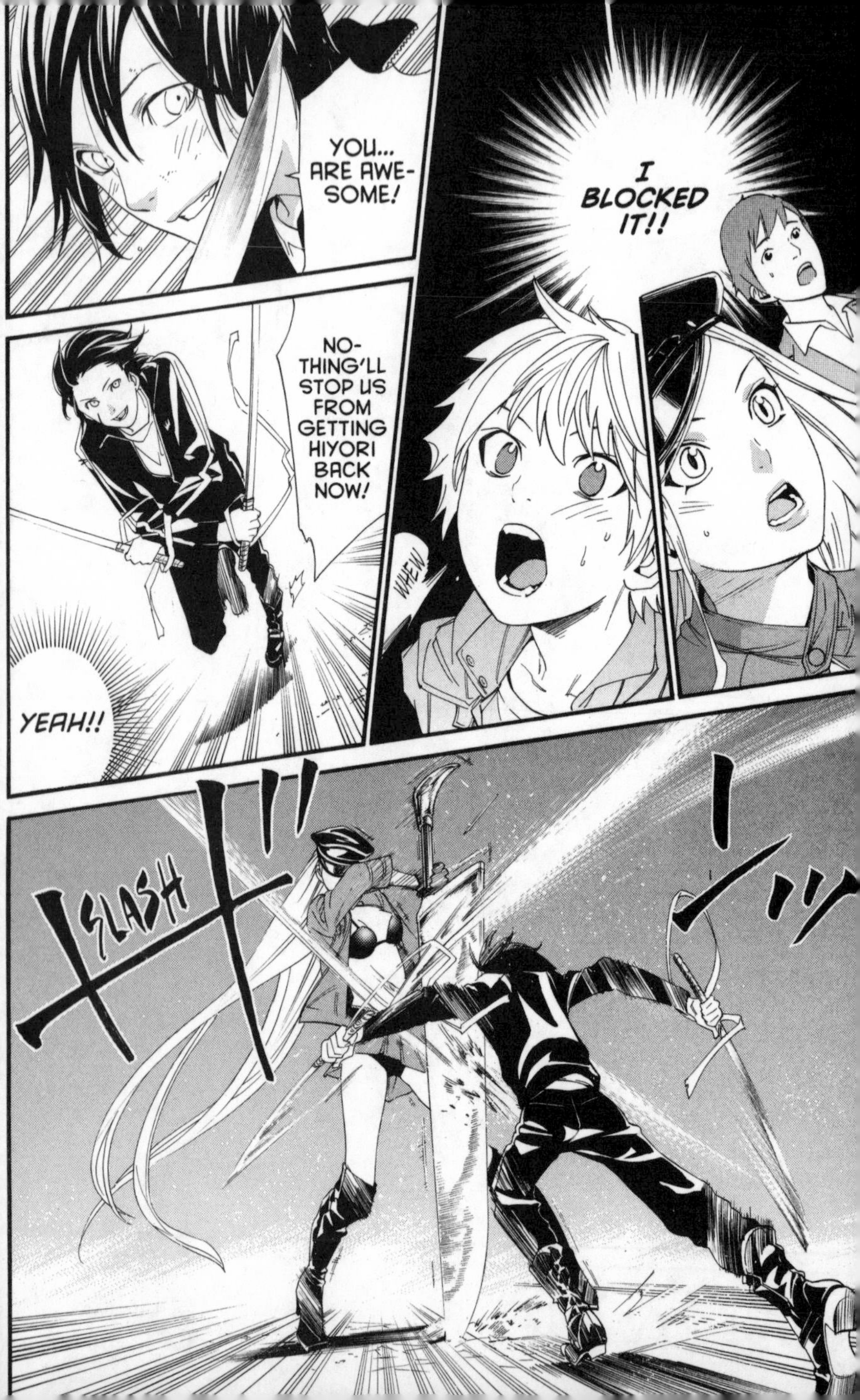
I BLOCKED IT!!
WHEW
YOU... ARE AWE-SOME!
NO-THING'LL STOP US FROM GETTING HIYORI BACK NOW!
YEAH!!
SLASH

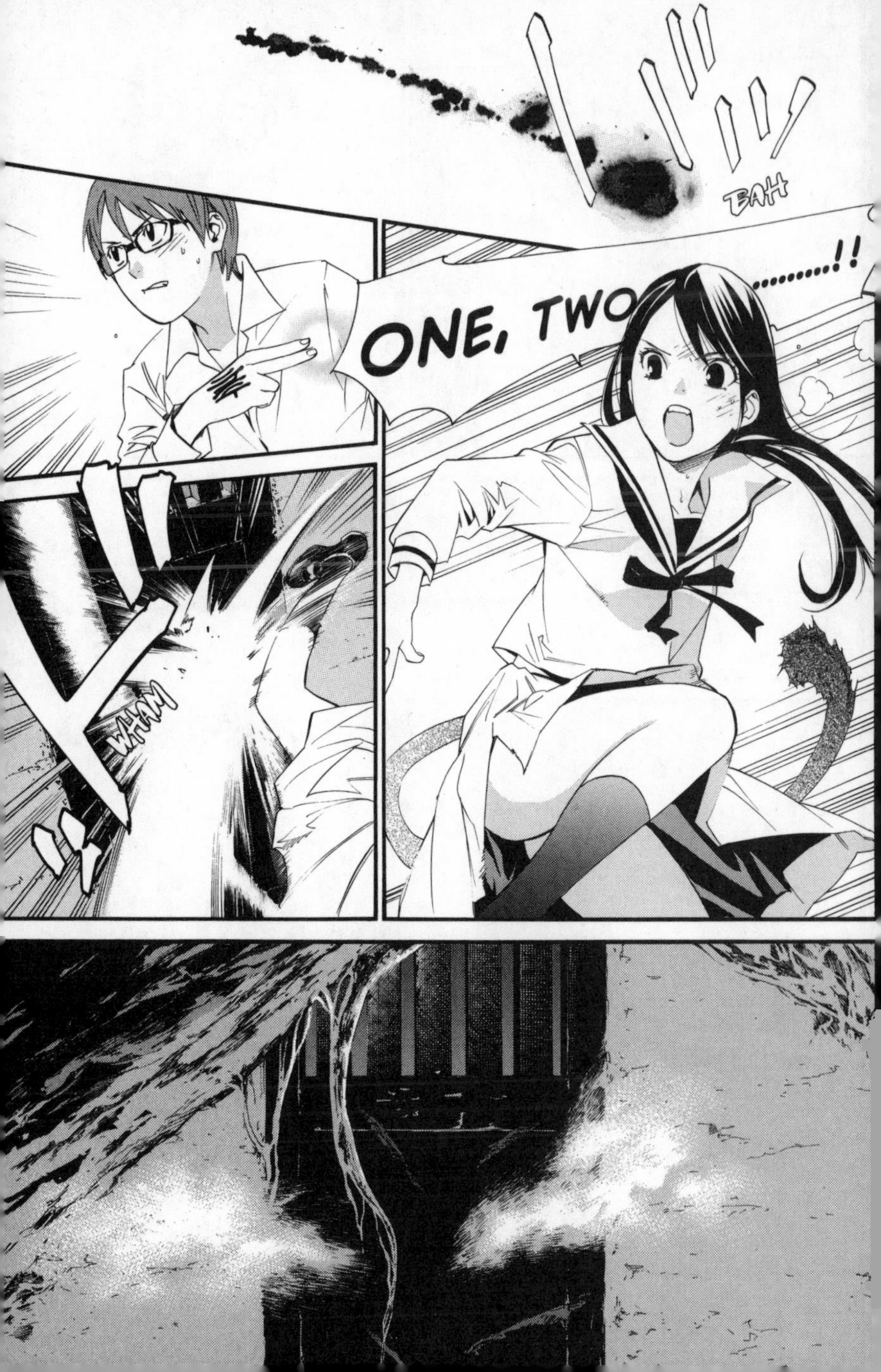
BAH
ONE, TWO..........!!
WHAM

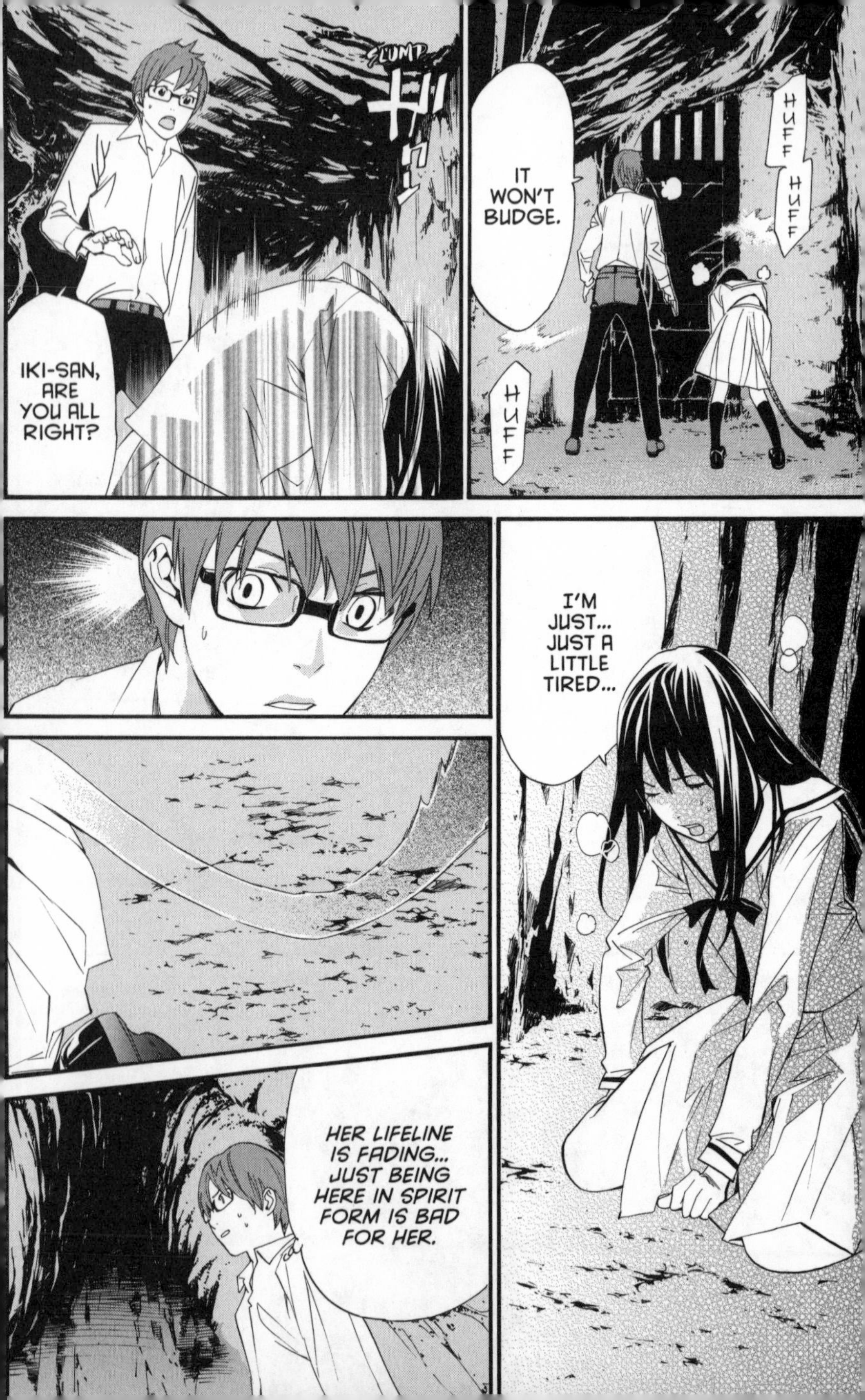
IT WON'T BUDGE.
HUFF HUFF HUFF
HUFF
SLUMP
IKI-SAN, ARE YOU ALL RIGHT?
I'M JUST... JUST A LITTLE TIRED...
HER LIFELINE IS FADING... JUST BEING HERE IN SPIRIT FORM IS BAD FOR HER.

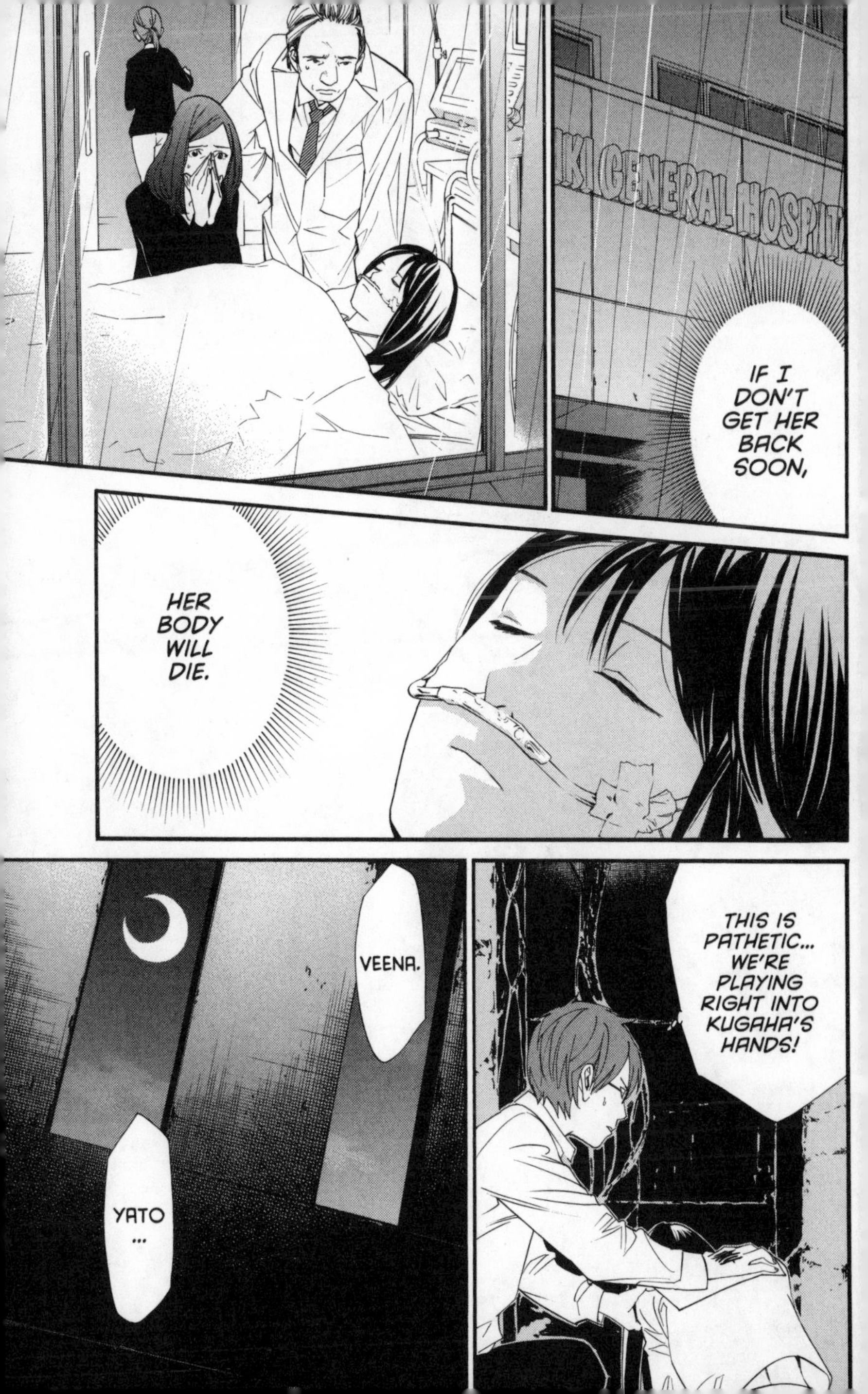
KI GENERAL HOSPIT
IF I DON'T GET HER BACK SOON,
HER BODY WILL DIE.
THIS IS PATHETIC... WE'RE PLAYING RIGHT INTO KUGAHA'S HANDS!
VEENA.
YATO ...

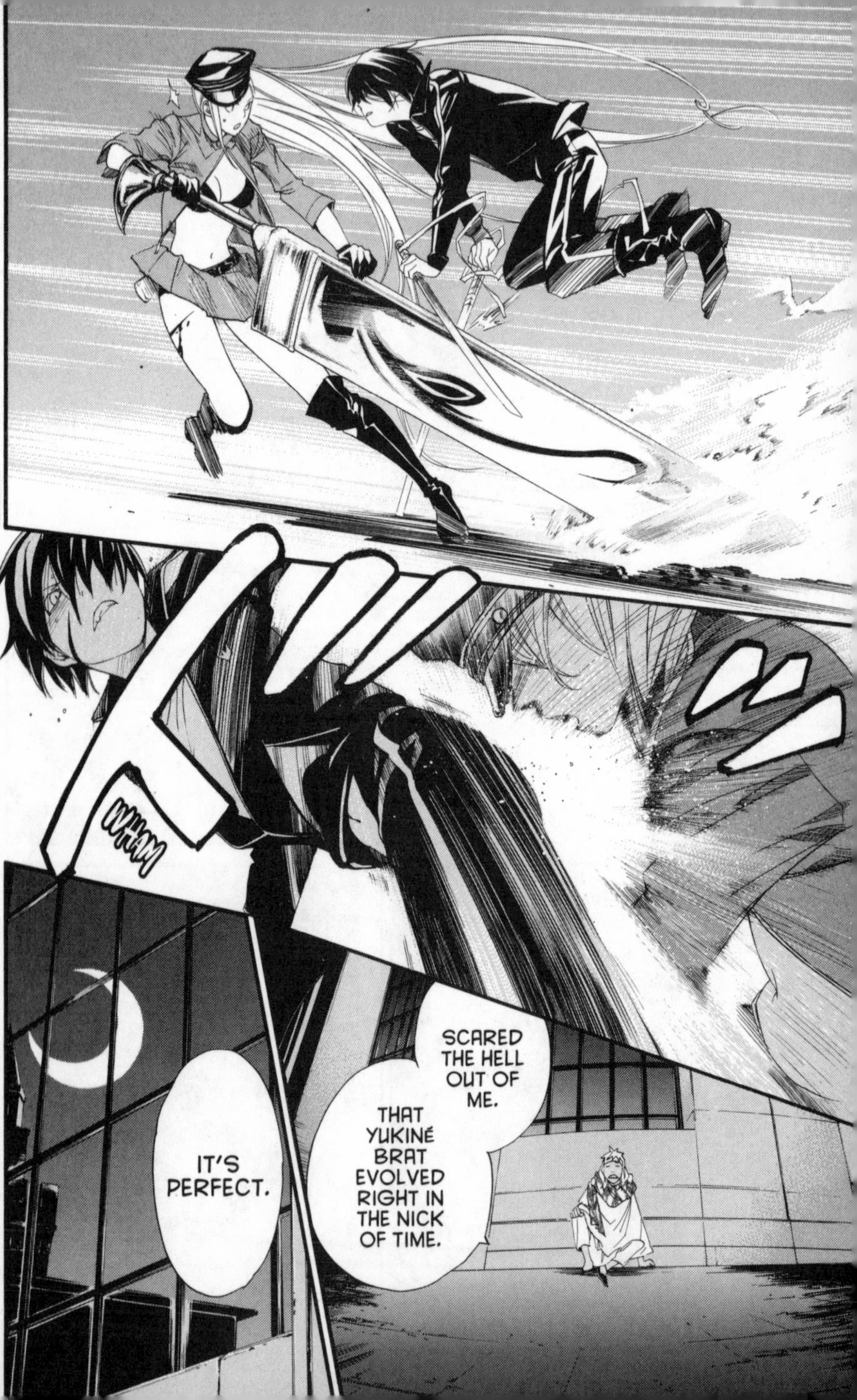
WHAM
SCARED THE HELL OUT OF ME.
THAT YUKINÉ BRAT EVOLVED RIGHT IN THE NICK OF TIME.
IT'S PERFECT.

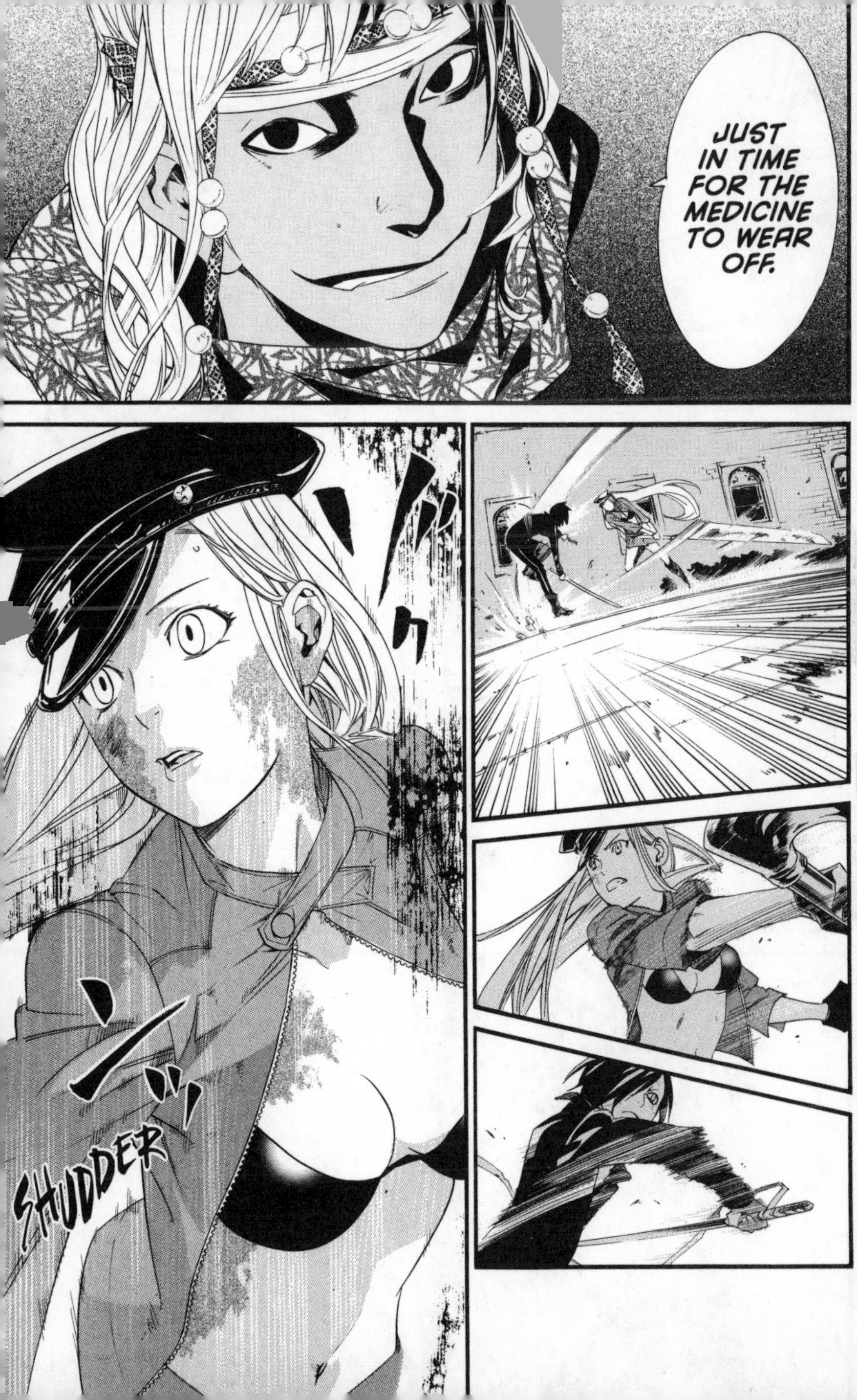
JUST IN TIME FOR THE MEDICINE TO WEAR OFF.
SHUDDER

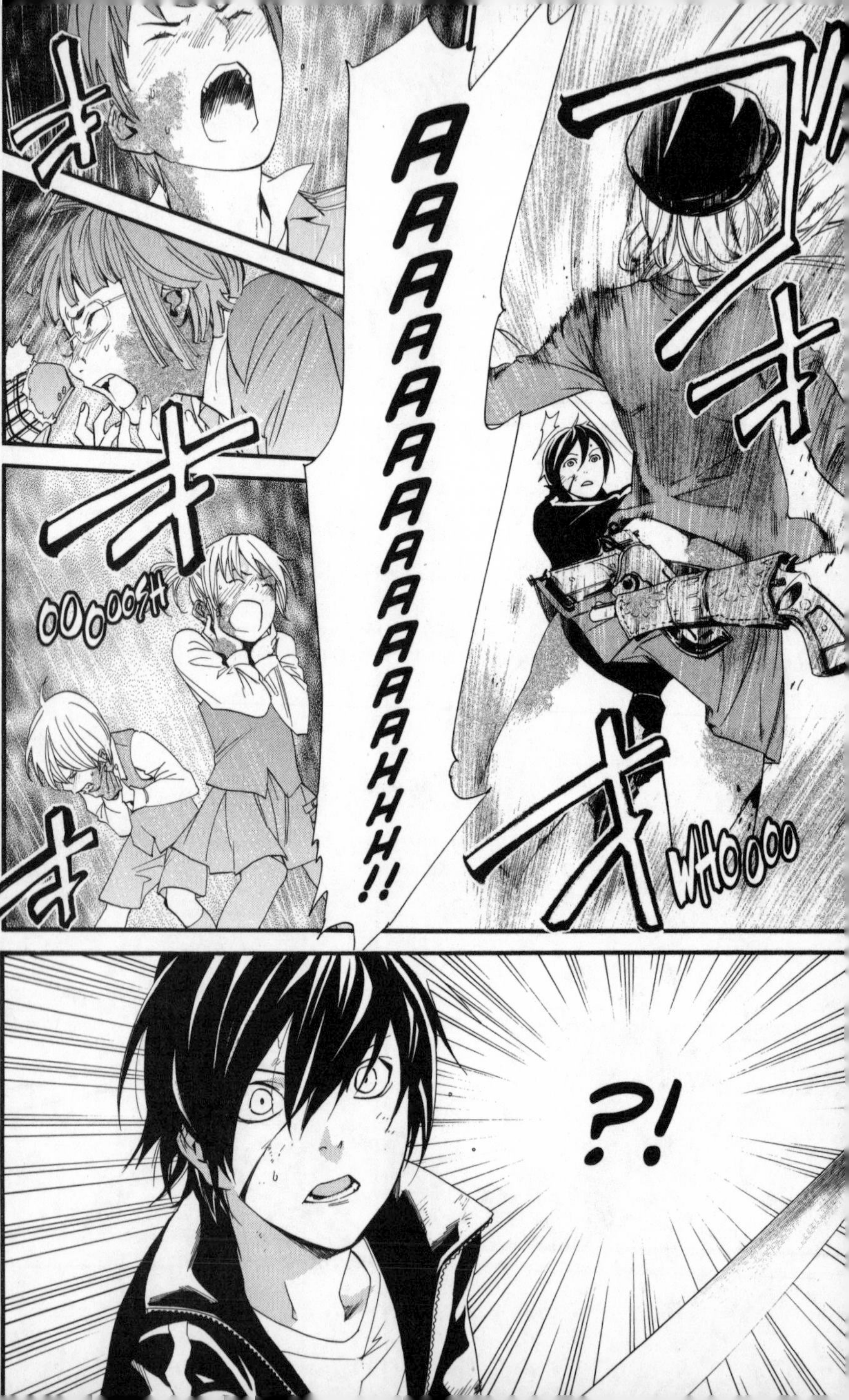
WHOOOO
AAAAAAAAAAAAAAAAAAHHHH!!
OOOOOSH
?!

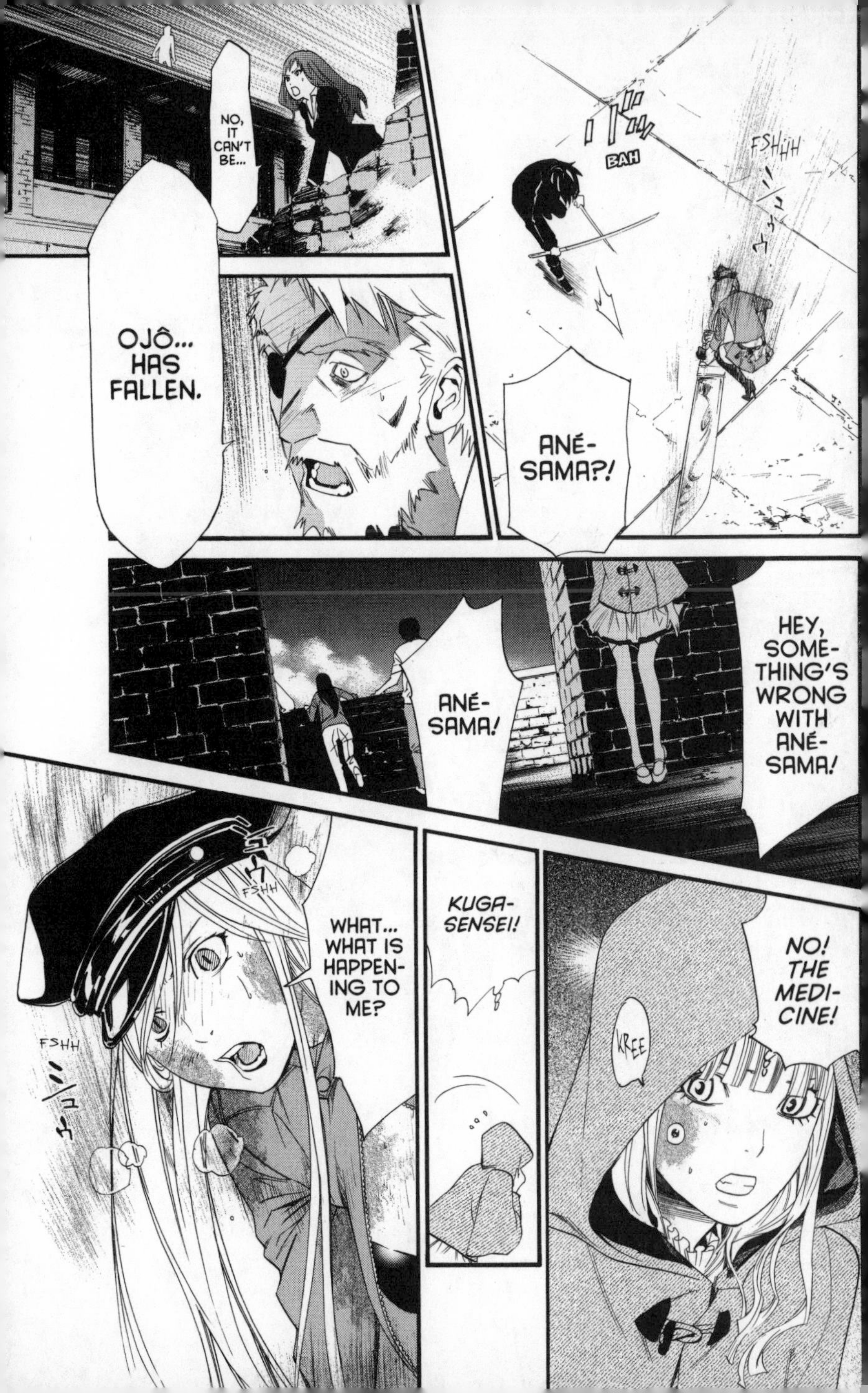
BAH
FSHHH
ANÉ-SAMA?!
NO, IT CAN'T BE...
OJÔ... HAS FALLEN.
HEY, SOMETHING'S WRONG WITH ANÉ-SAMA!
ANÉ-SAMA!
KREE
NO! THE MEDICINE!
KUGA-SENSEI!
FSHH
WHAT... WHAT IS HAPPENING TO ME?
FSHH

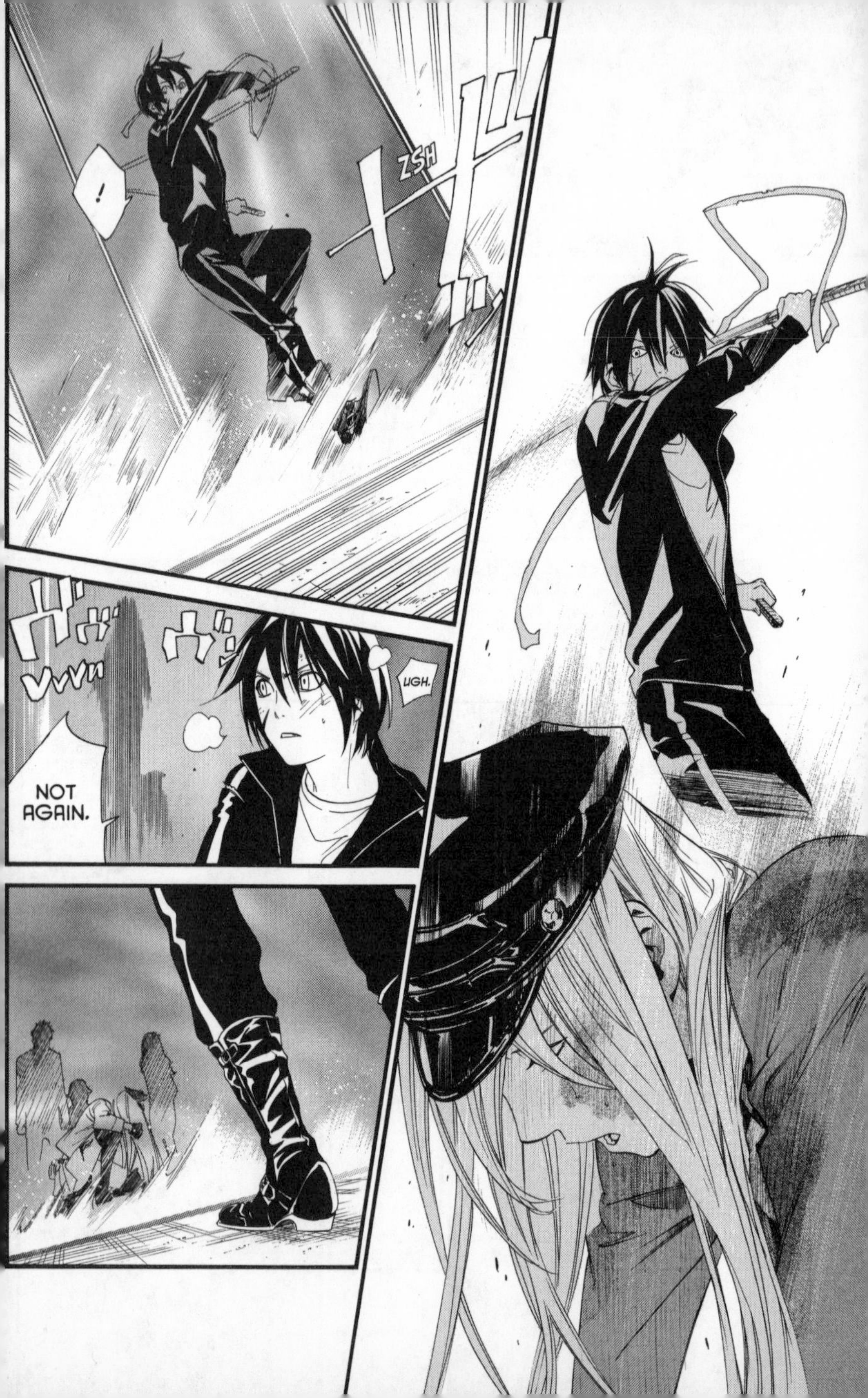
ZSH
!
UGH.
VVVN
NOT AGAIN.

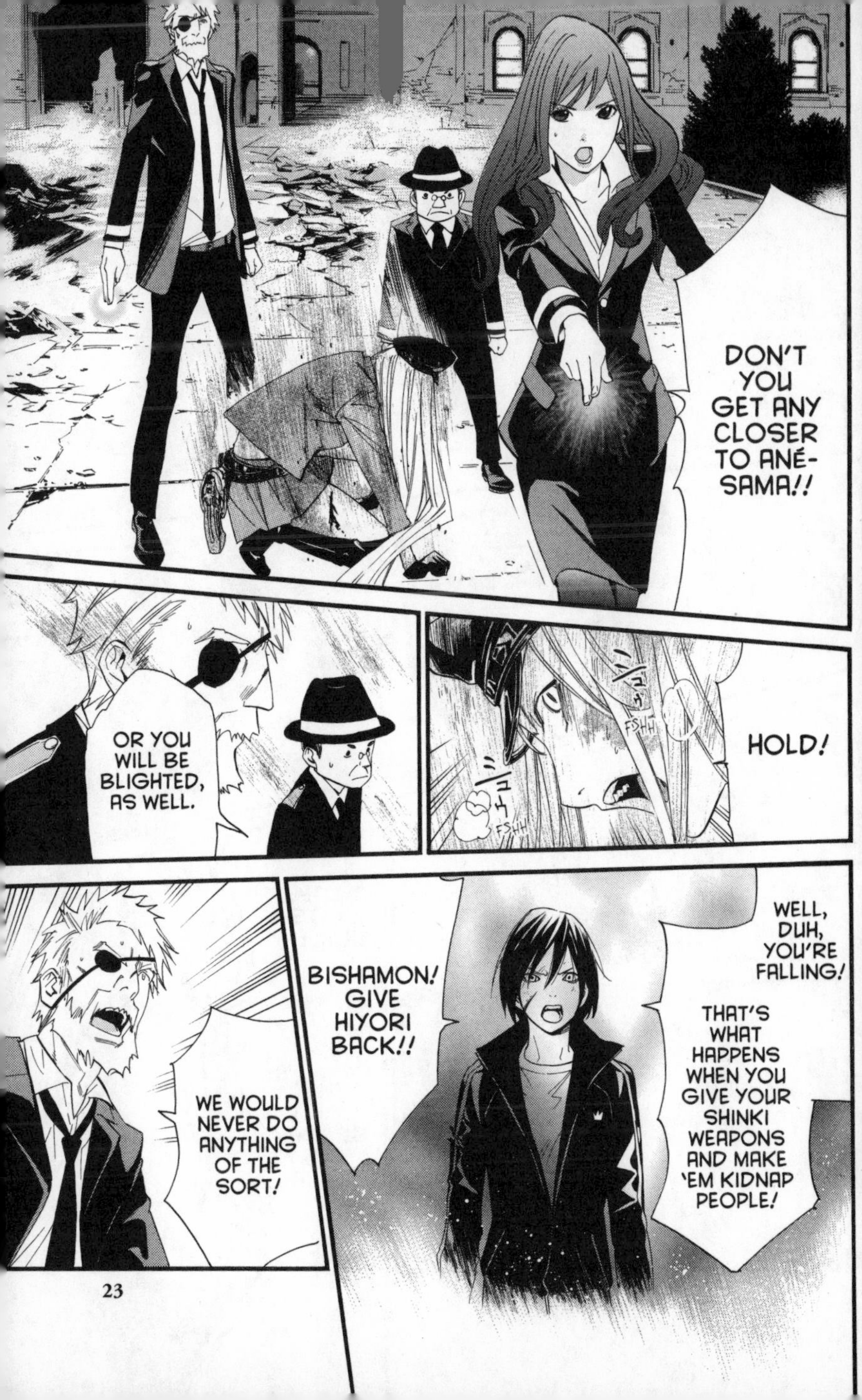
DON'T YOU GET ANY CLOSER TO ANÉ-SAMA!!
HOLD!
FSHH
FSHH
OR YOU WILL BE BLIGHTED, AS WELL.
WELL, DUH, YOU'RE FALLING!
THAT'S WHAT HAPPENS WHEN YOU GIVE YOUR SHINKI WEAPONS AND MAKE 'EM KIDNAP PEOPLE!
BISHAMON! GIVE HIYORI BACK!!
WE WOULD NEVER DO ANYTHING OF THE SORT!

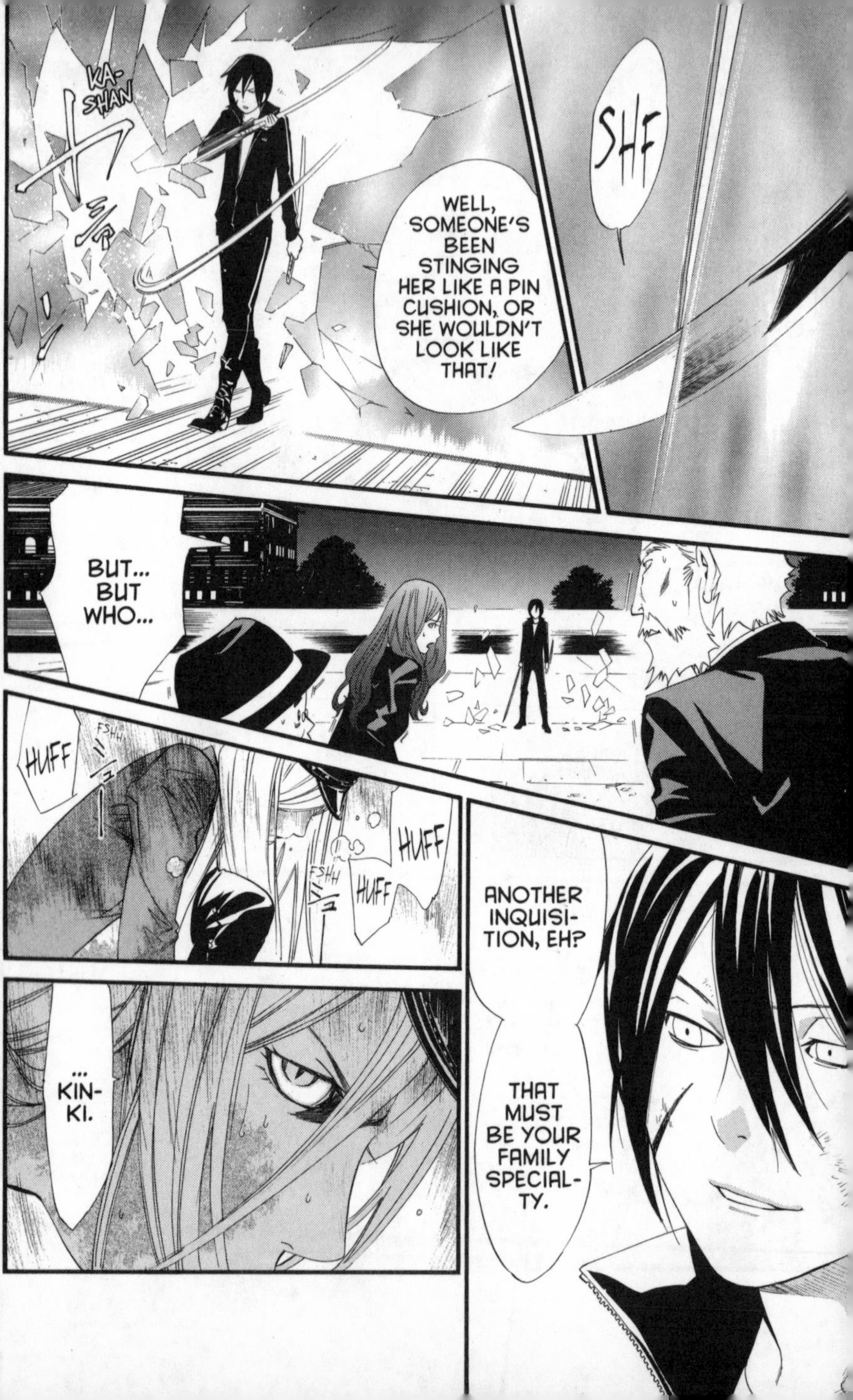
SHF
KA-SHAN
WELL, SOMEONE'S BEEN STINGING HER LIKE A PIN CUSHION, OR SHE WOULDN'T LOOK LIKE THAT!
BUT... BUT WHO...
ANOTHER INQUISITION, EH?
THAT MUST BE YOUR FAMILY SPECIALTY.
HUFF
FSHH
HUFF
FSHH
HUFF
...KINKI.

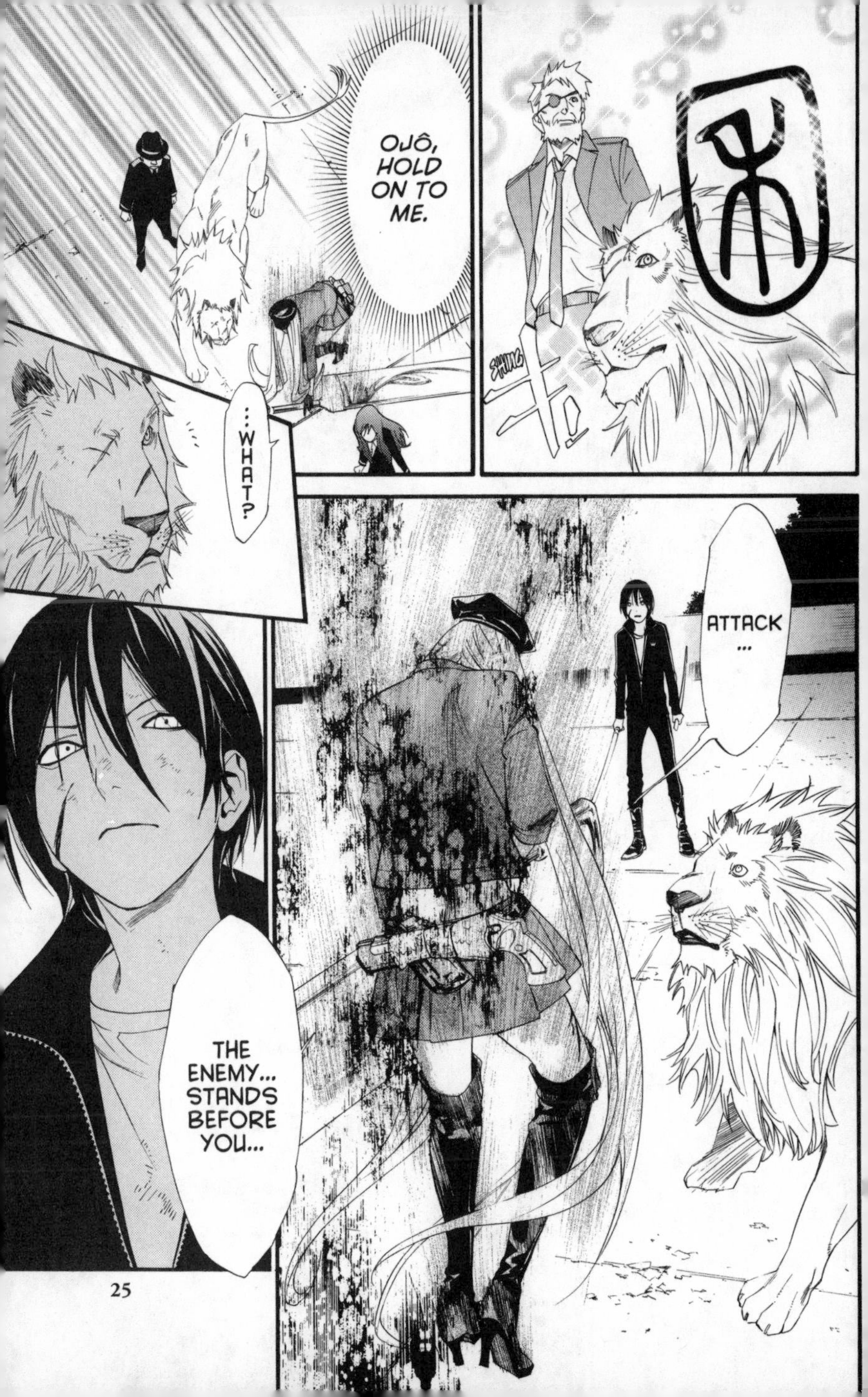
SHING
OJÔ, HOLD ON TO ME.
...WHAT?
ATTACK ...
THE ENEMY... STANDS BEFORE YOU...

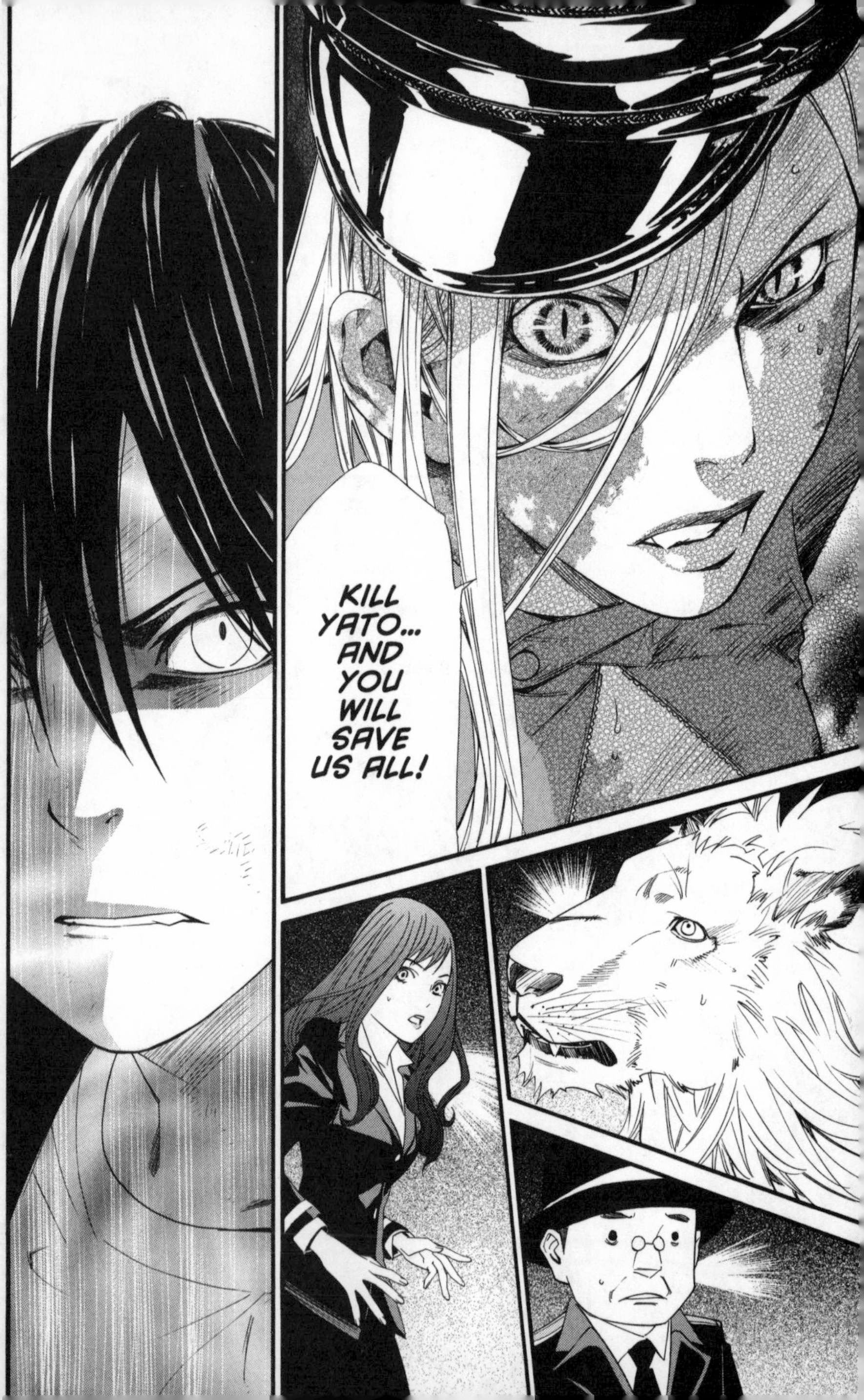
KILL YATO... AND YOU WILL SAVE US ALL!

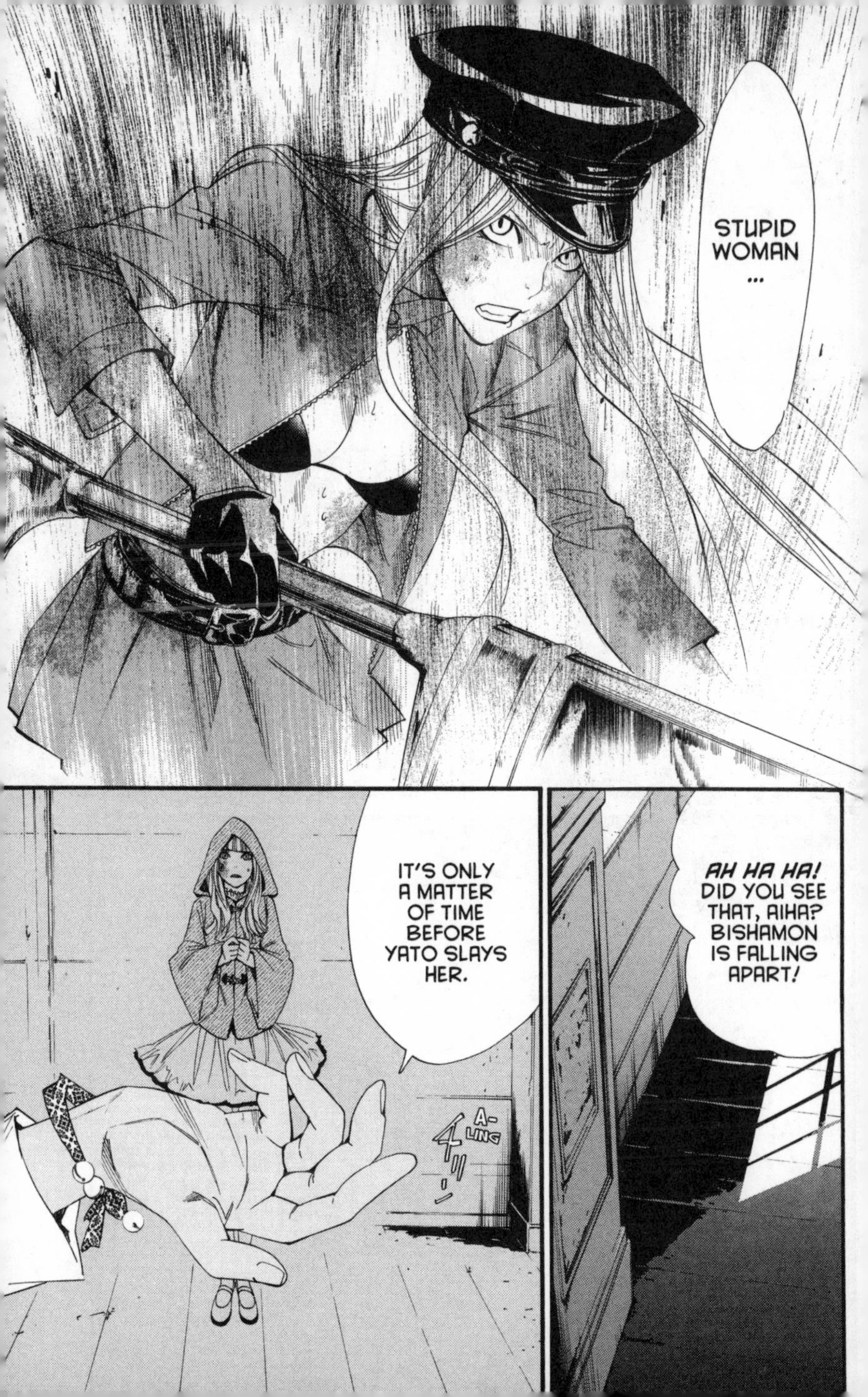
STUPID WOMAN ...
AH HA HA! DID YOU SEE THAT, AIHA? BISHAMON IS FALLING APART!
IT'S ONLY A MATTER OF TIME BEFORE YATO SLAYS HER.
A-LING

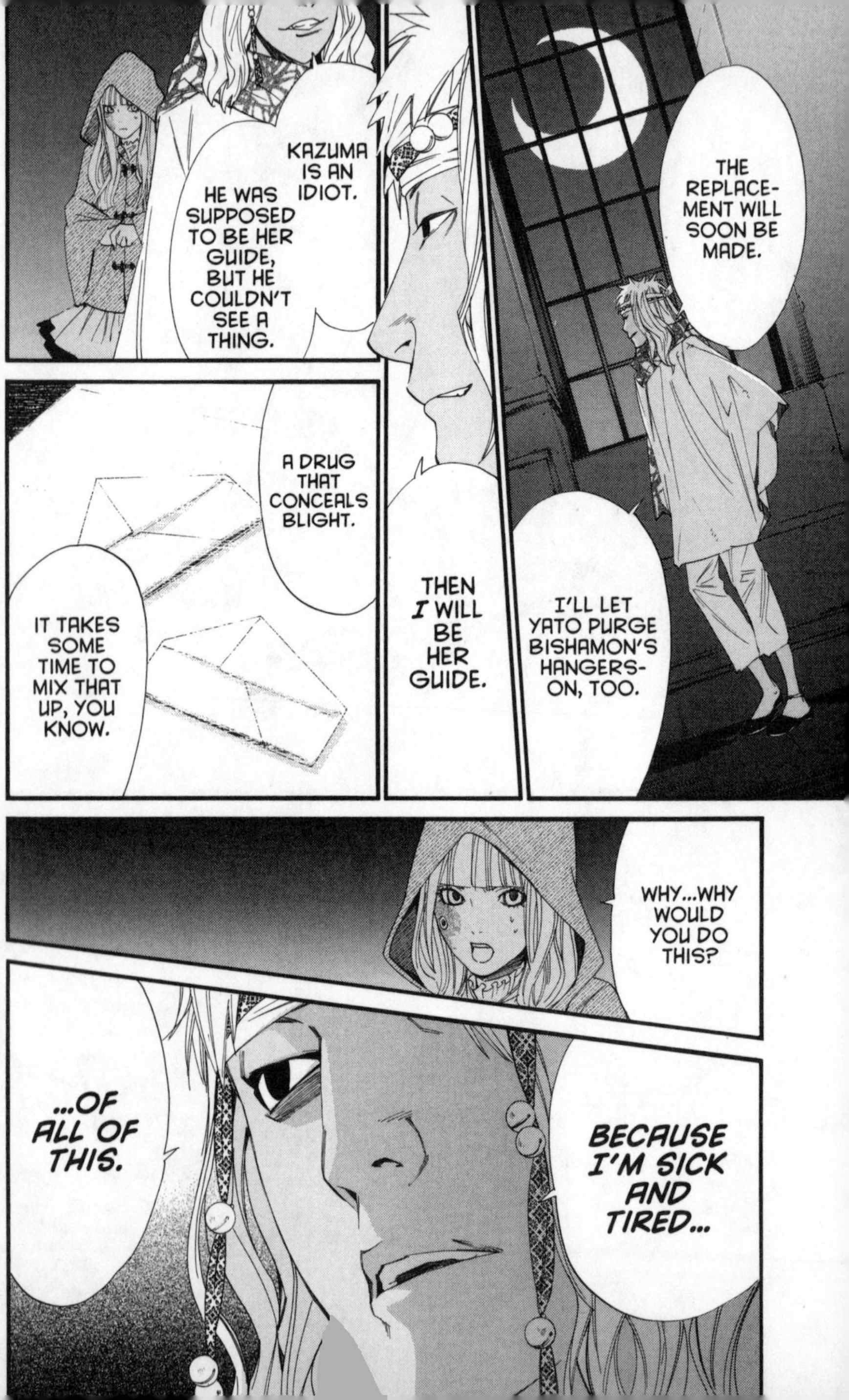
THE REPLACEMENT WILL SOON BE MADE.
I'LL LET YATO PURGE BISHAMON'S HANGERS-ON, TOO.
A DRUG THAT CONCEALS BLIGHT.
THEN *I* WILL BE HER GUIDE.
KAZUMA IS AN IDIOT.
HE WAS SUPPOSED TO BE HER GUIDE, BUT HE COULDN'T SEE A THING.
IT TAKES SOME TIME TO MIX THAT UP, YOU KNOW.
WHY...WHY WOULD YOU DO THIS?
BECAUSE I'M SICK AND TIRED...
...OF ALL OF THIS.

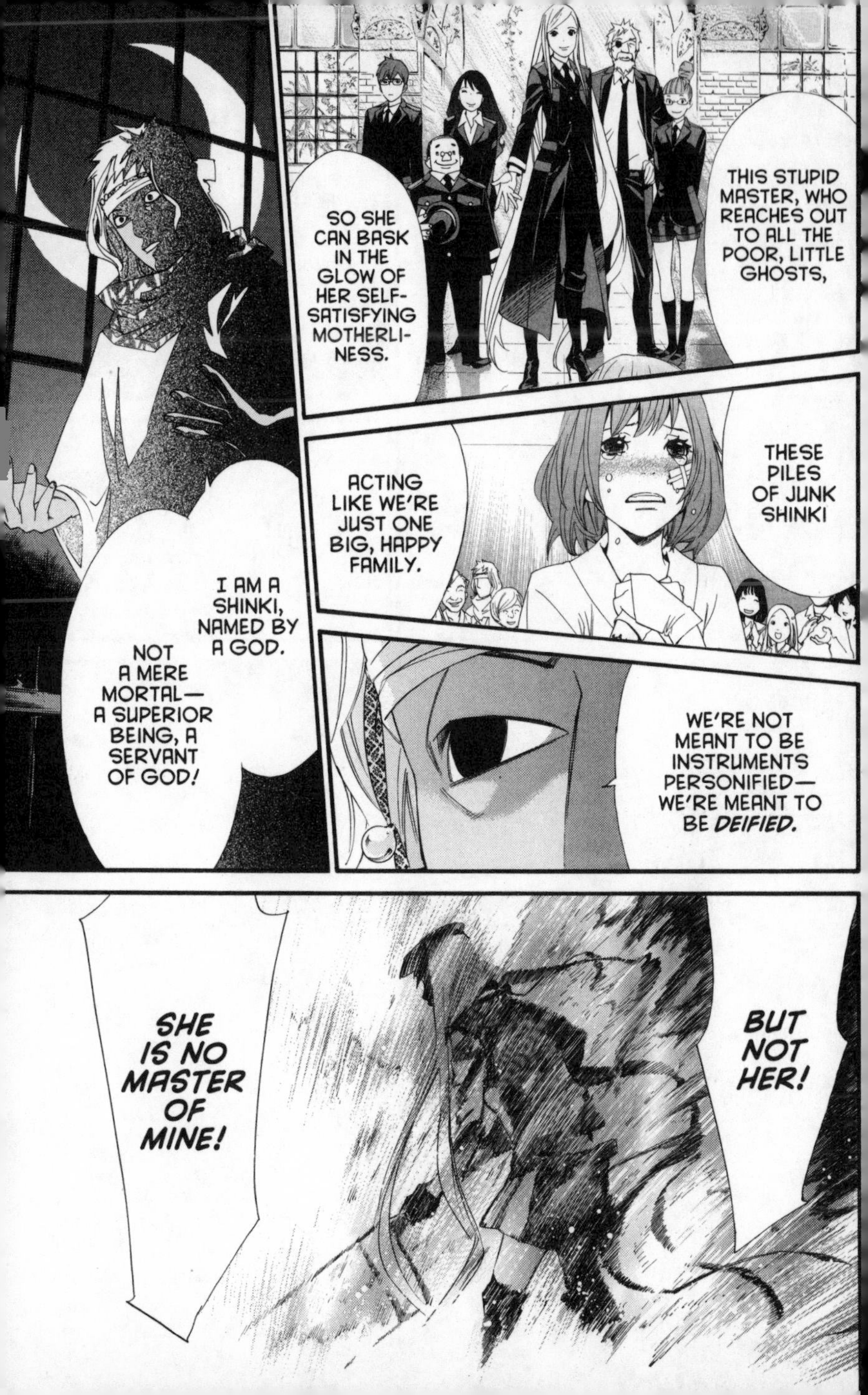
THIS STUPID MASTER, WHO REACHES OUT TO ALL THE POOR, LITTLE GHOSTS,
SO SHE CAN BASK IN THE GLOW OF HER SELF-SATISFYING MOTHERLINESS.
THESE PILES OF JUNK SHINKI
ACTING LIKE WE'RE JUST ONE BIG, HAPPY FAMILY.
WE'RE NOT MEANT TO BE INSTRUMENTS PERSONIFIED—WE'RE MEANT TO BE *DEIFIED.*
I AM A SHINKI, NAMED BY A GOD.
NOT A MERE MORTAL—A SUPERIOR BEING, A SERVANT OF GOD!
BUT NOT HER!
SHE IS NO MASTER OF MINE!

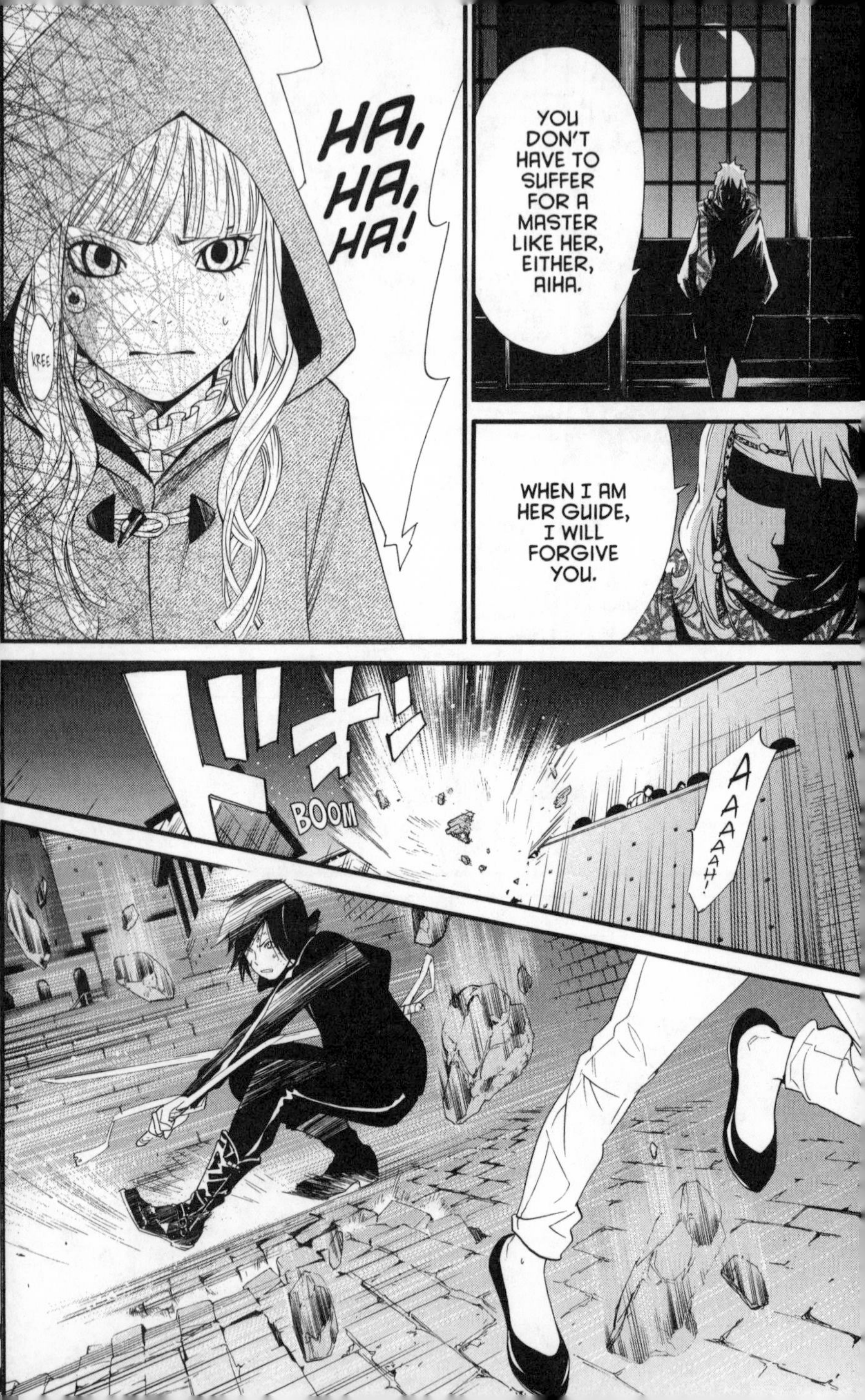
YOU DON'T HAVE TO SUFFER FOR A MASTER LIKE HER, EITHER, AIHA.
WHEN I AM HER GUIDE, I WILL FORGIVE YOU.
HA, HA, HA!
KREE
AAAAAH!
BOOM

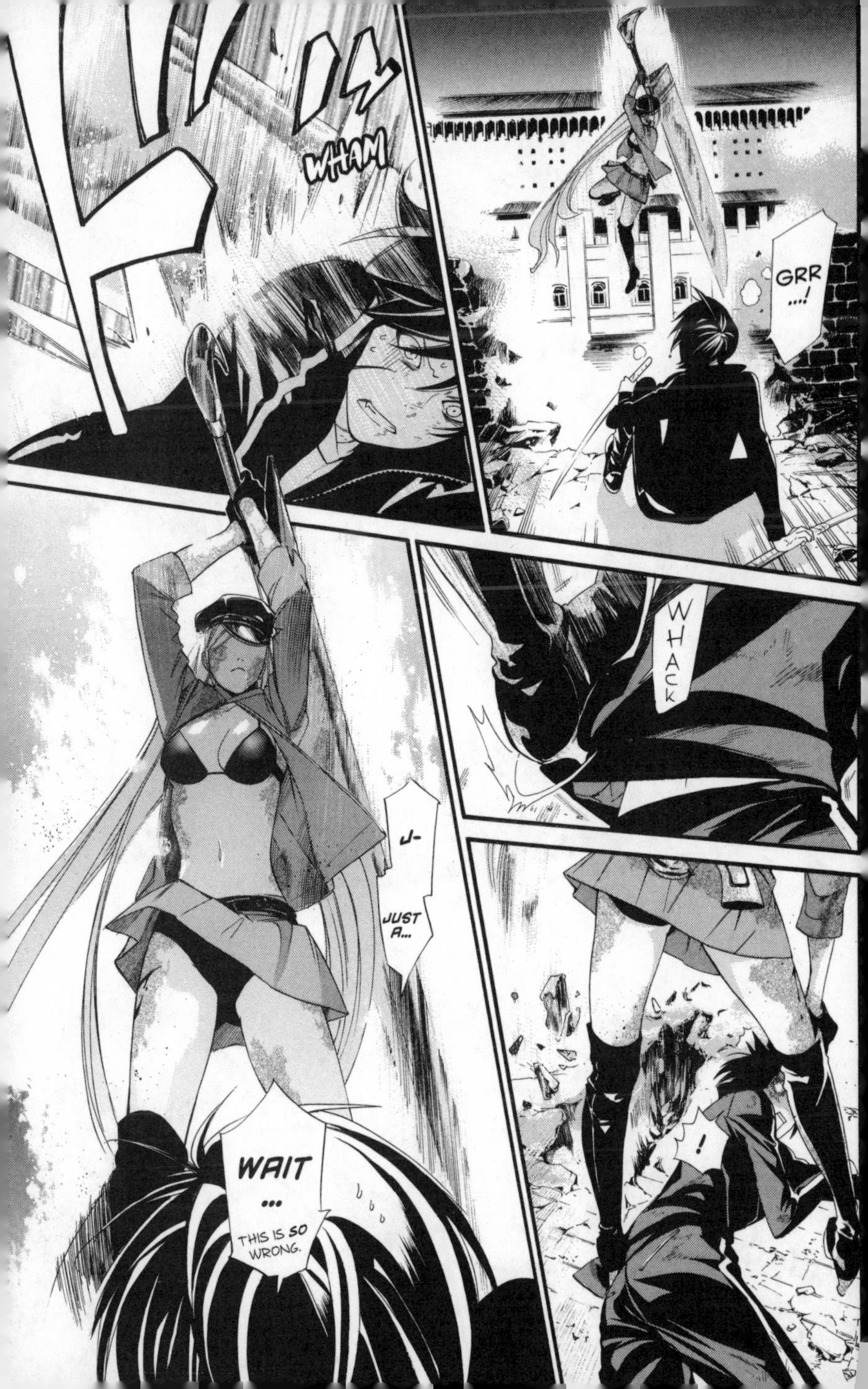
GRR ....!
WHAM
WHACK
!
J-
JUST A...
WAIT ...
THIS IS SO WRONG.

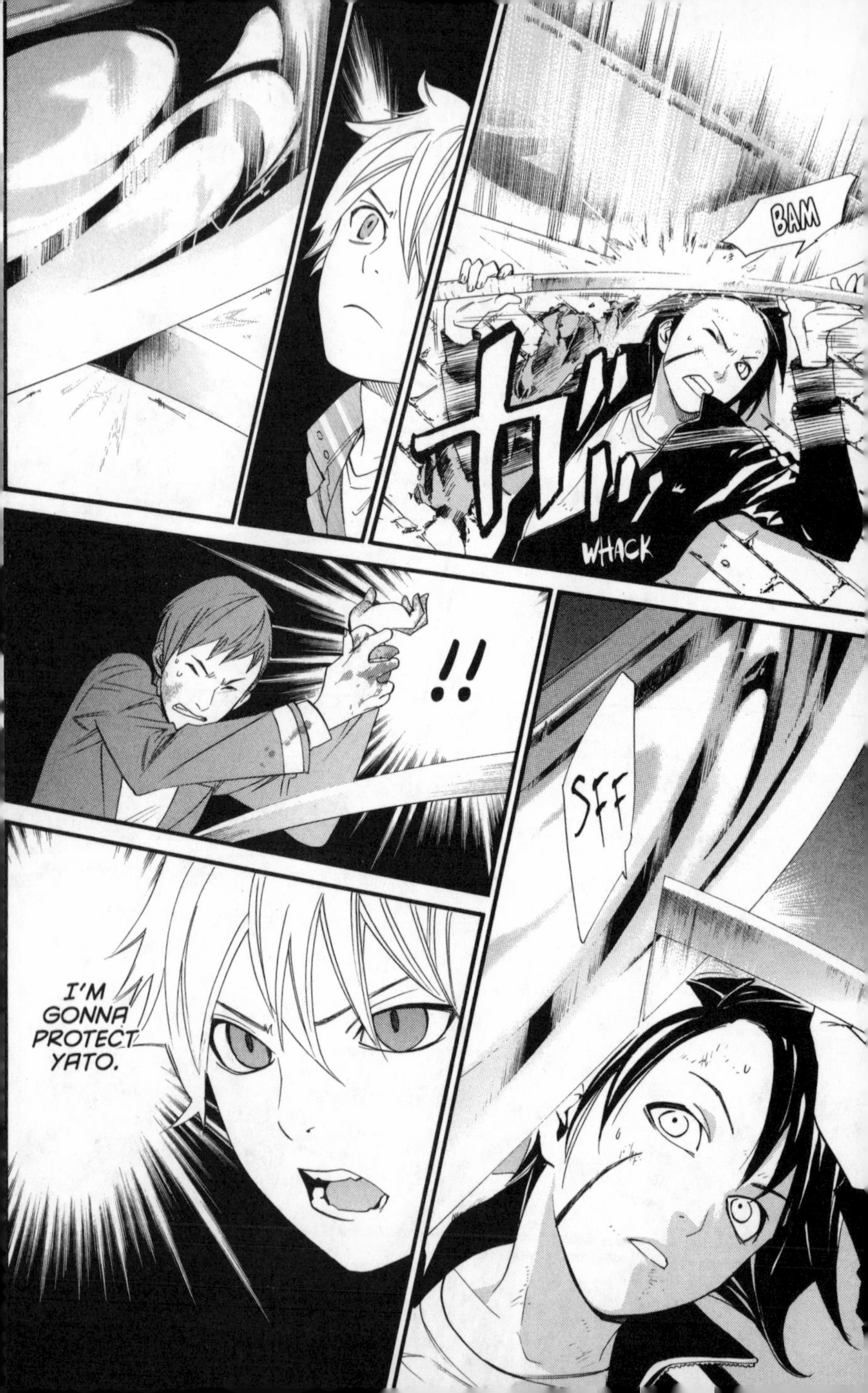
BAM
ガッ
WHACK
SFF
!!
I'M GONNA PROTECT YATO.

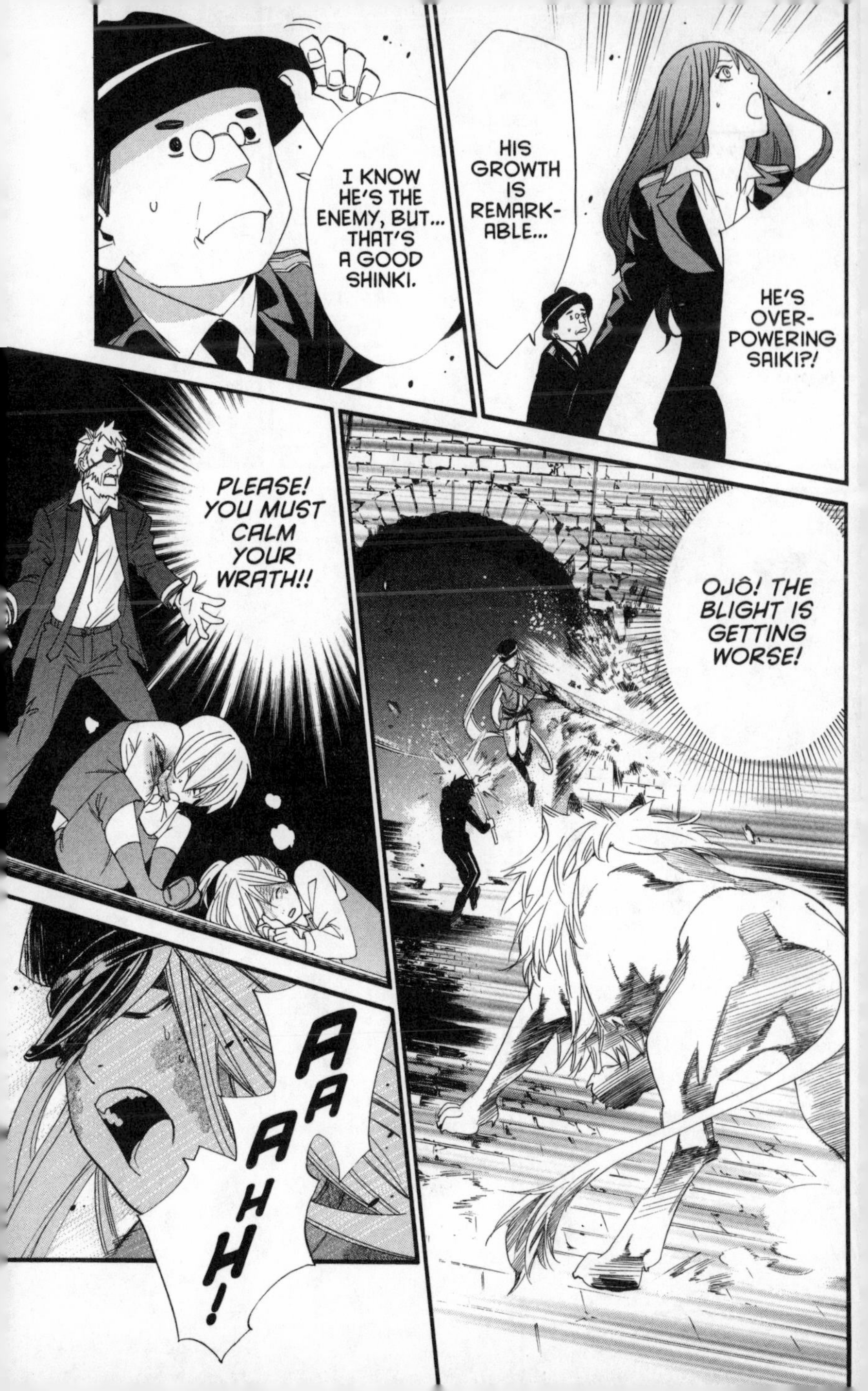
HE'S OVER-POWERING SAIKI?!
HIS GROWTH IS REMARK-ABLE...
I KNOW HE'S THE ENEMY, BUT... THAT'S A GOOD SHINKI.
OJÔ! THE BLIGHT IS GETTING WORSE!
PLEASE! YOU MUST CALM YOUR WRATH!!
AAAAHH!

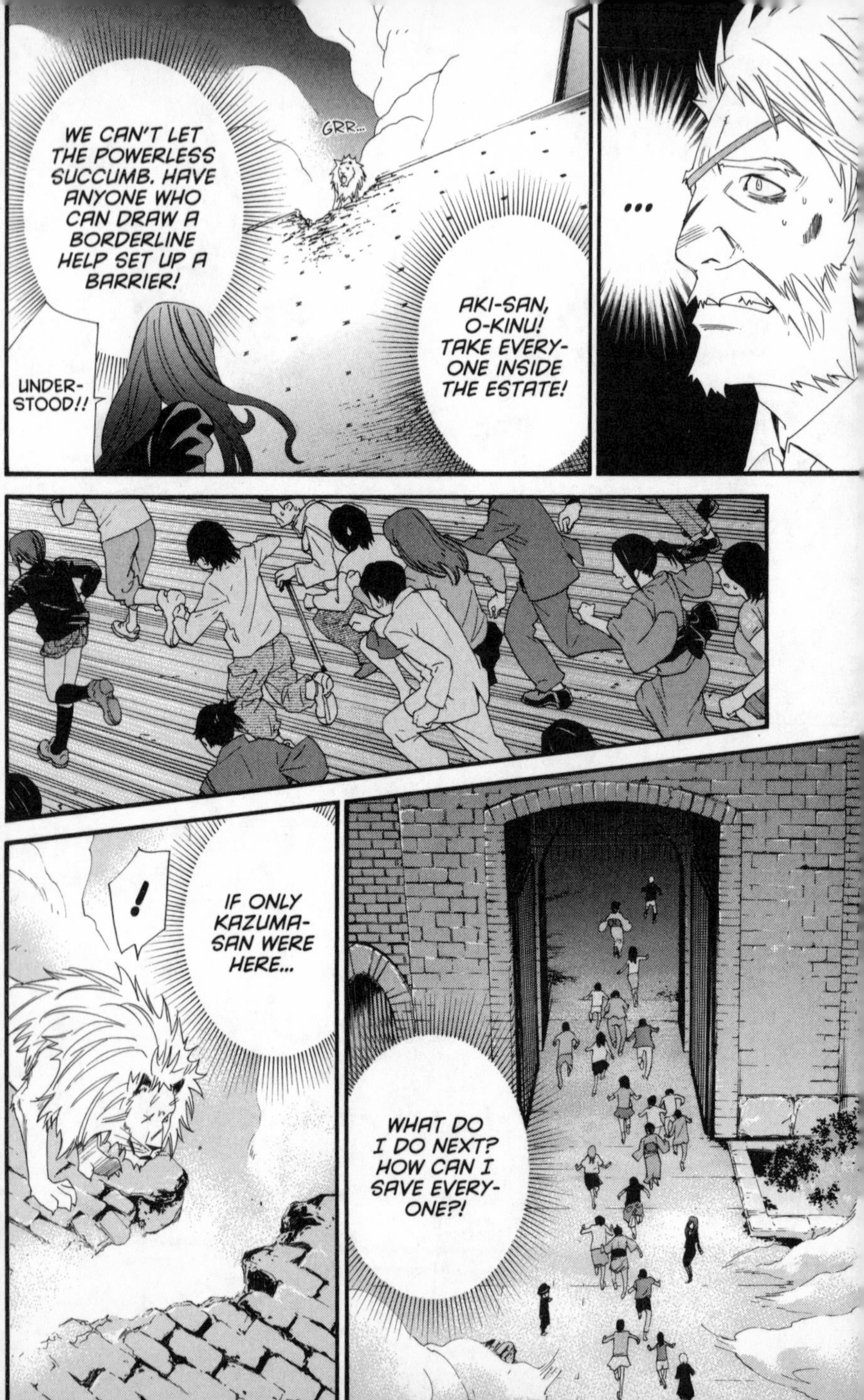
...
GRR...
AKI-SAN, O-KINU! TAKE EVERY-ONE INSIDE THE ESTATE!
WE CAN'T LET THE POWERLESS SUCCUMB. HAVE ANYONE WHO CAN DRAW A BORDERLINE HELP SET UP A BARRIER!
UNDER-STOOD!!
WHAT DO I DO NEXT? HOW CAN I SAVE EVERY-ONE?!
IF ONLY KAZUMA-SAN WERE HERE...
!

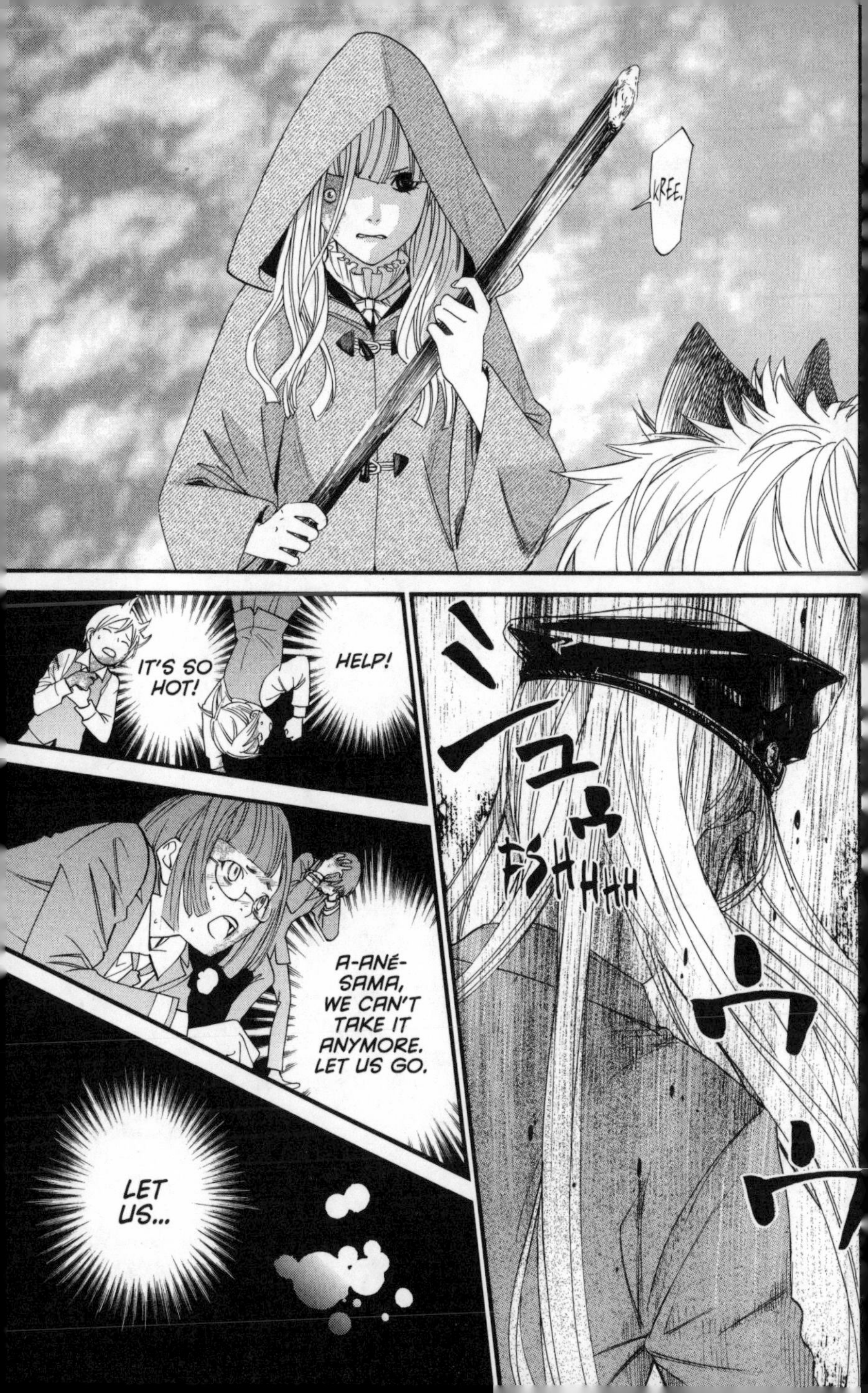
KREE.
FSHHHH
HELP!
IT'S SO HOT!
A-ANÉ-SAMA, WE CAN'T TAKE IT ANYMORE. LET US GO.
LET US...

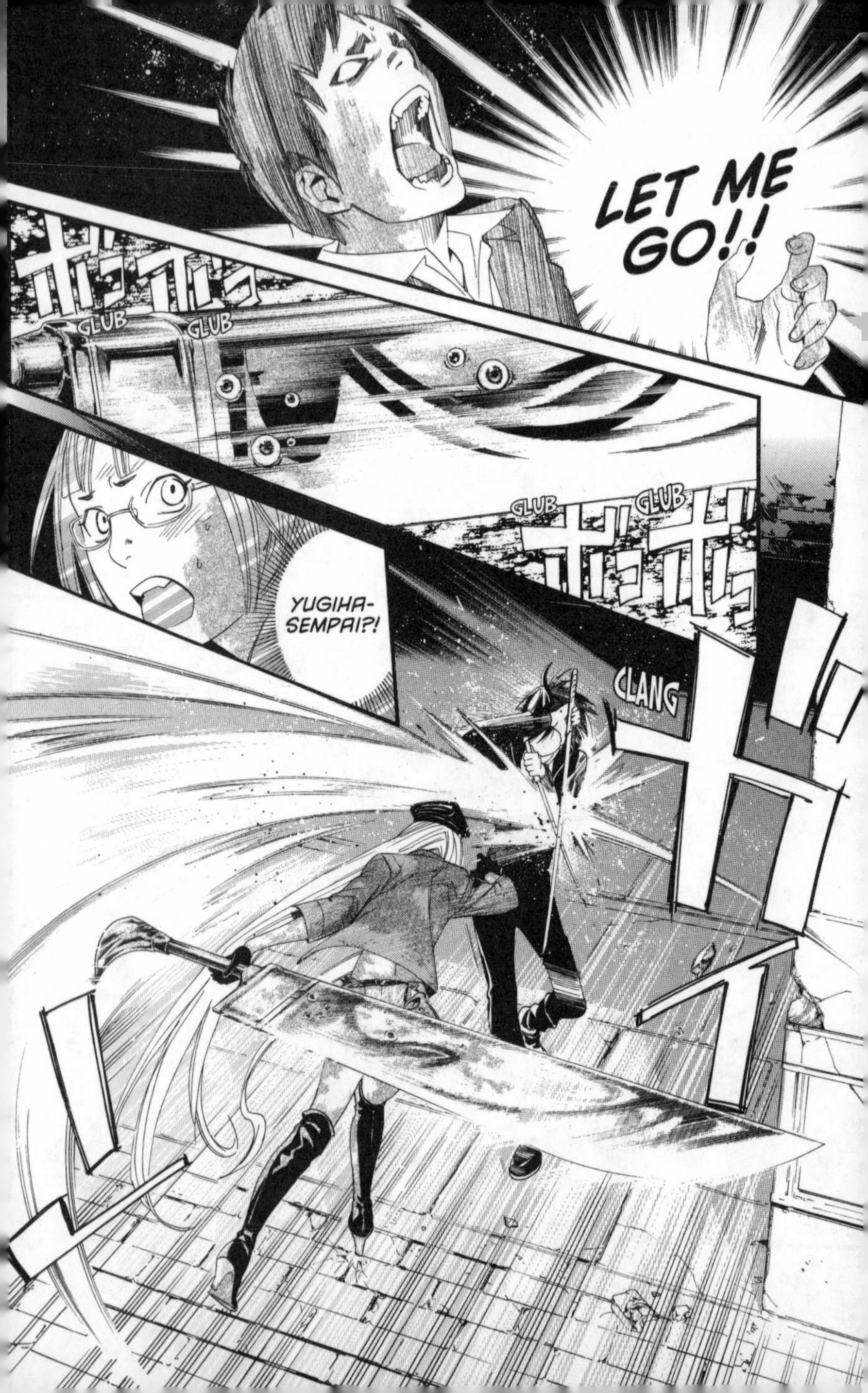
LET ME GO!!
GLUB GLUB
GLUB GLUB
YUGIHA-SEMPAI?!
CLANG

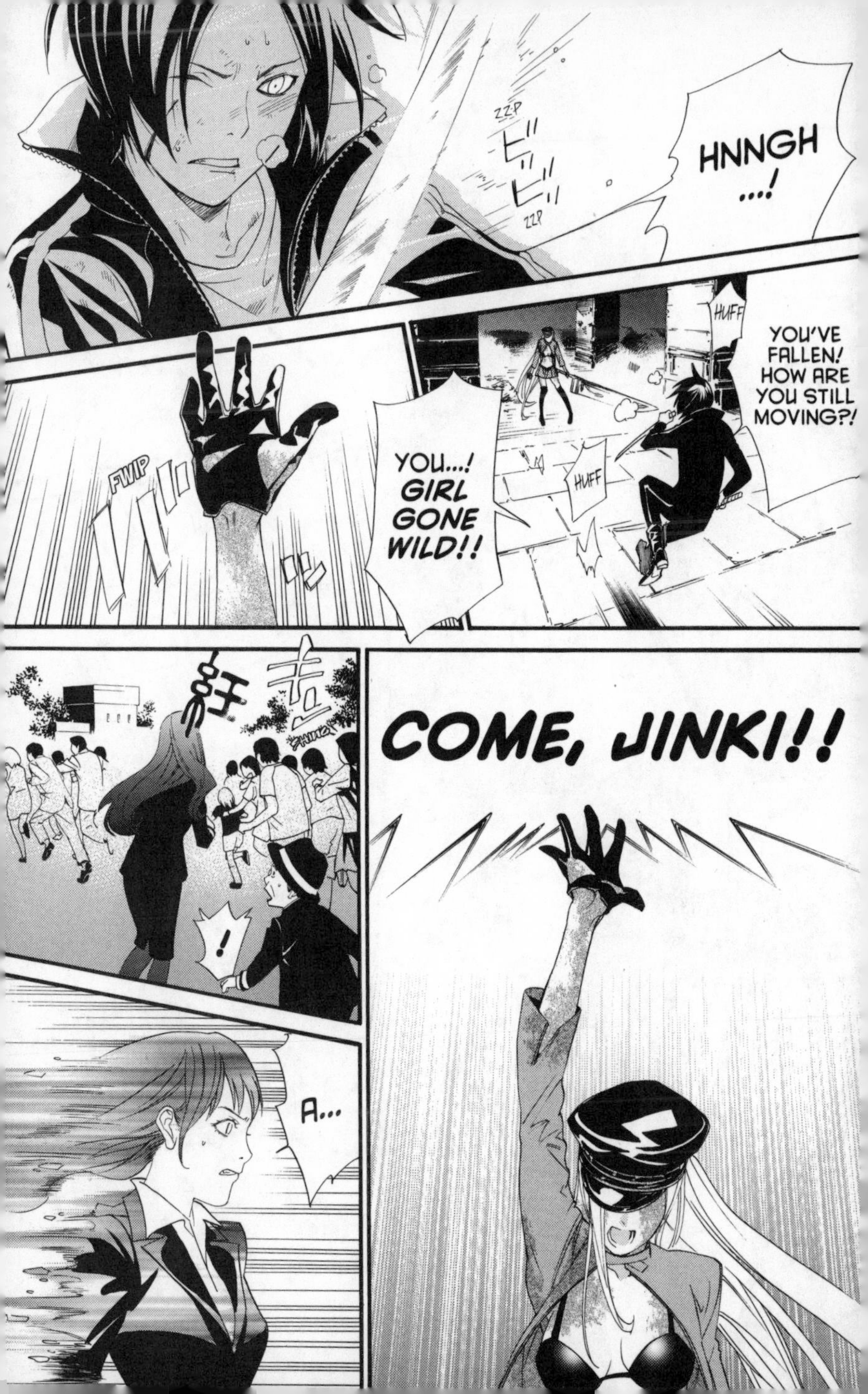
HNNGH ...!
ZZ-P
ZZP
HUFF
YOU'VE FALLEN! HOW ARE YOU STILL MOVING?!
HUFF
YOU...! GIRL GONE WILD!!
FWIP
COME, JINKI!!
!
A...

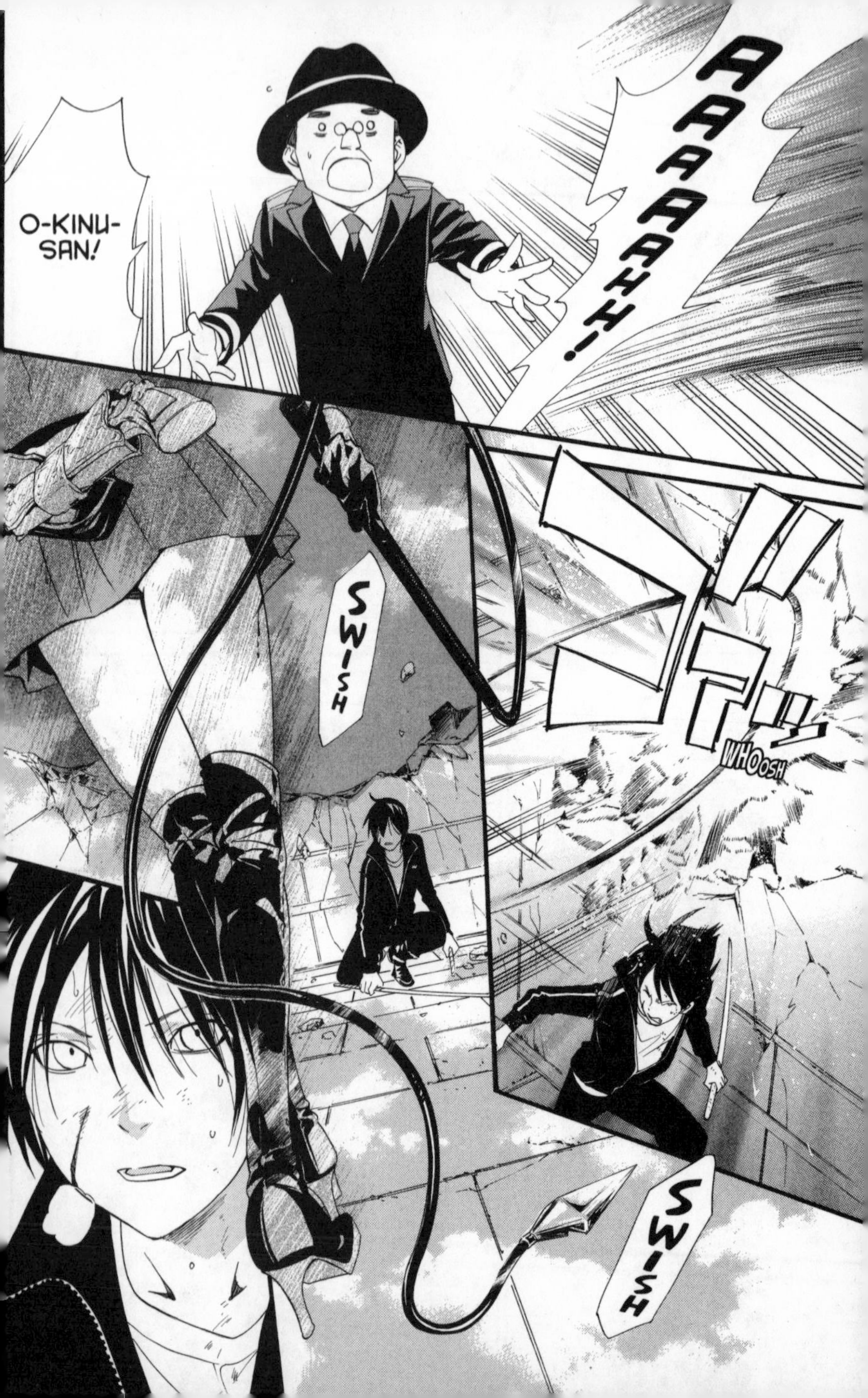
AAAAAAHH!
O-KINU-SAN!
WHOOSH
SWISH
SWISH

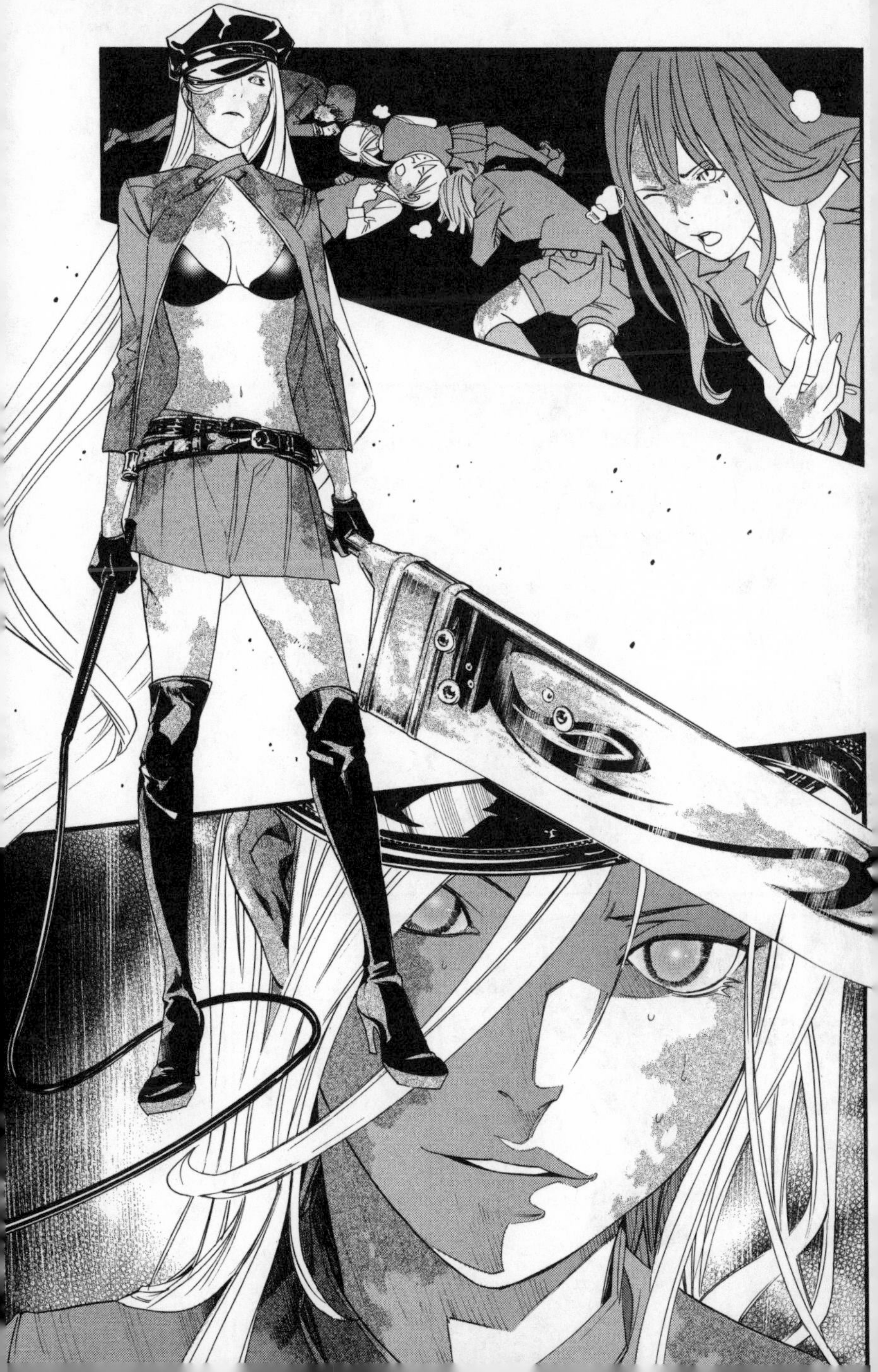

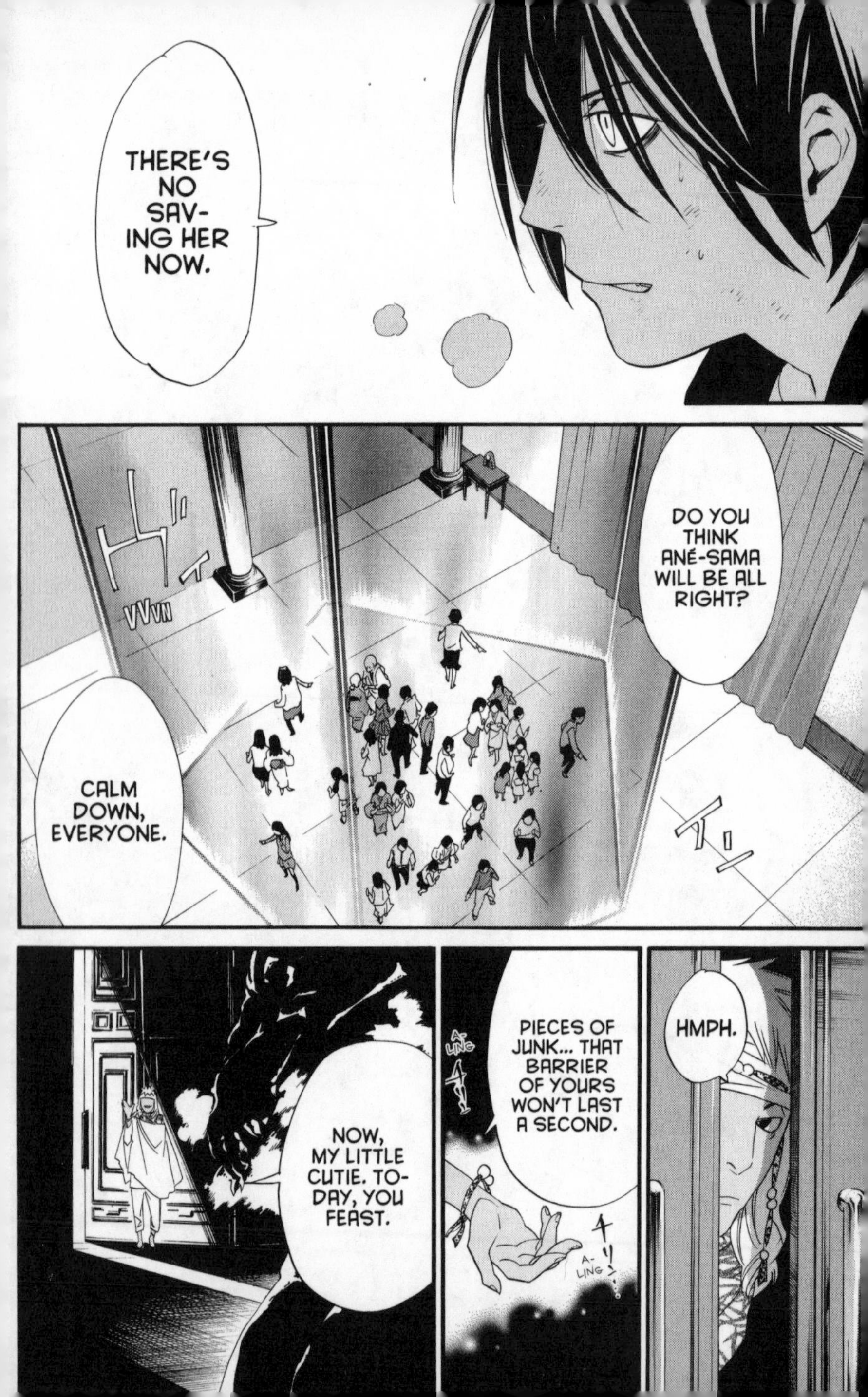
THERE'S NO SAV-ING HER NOW.
DO YOU THINK ANÉ-SAMA WILL BE ALL RIGHT?
VVVN
CALM DOWN, EVERYONE.
HMPH.
PIECES OF JUNK... THAT BARRIER OF YOURS WON'T LAST A SECOND.
A-LING
A-LING
NOW, MY LITTLE CUTIE. TO-DAY, YOU FEAST.

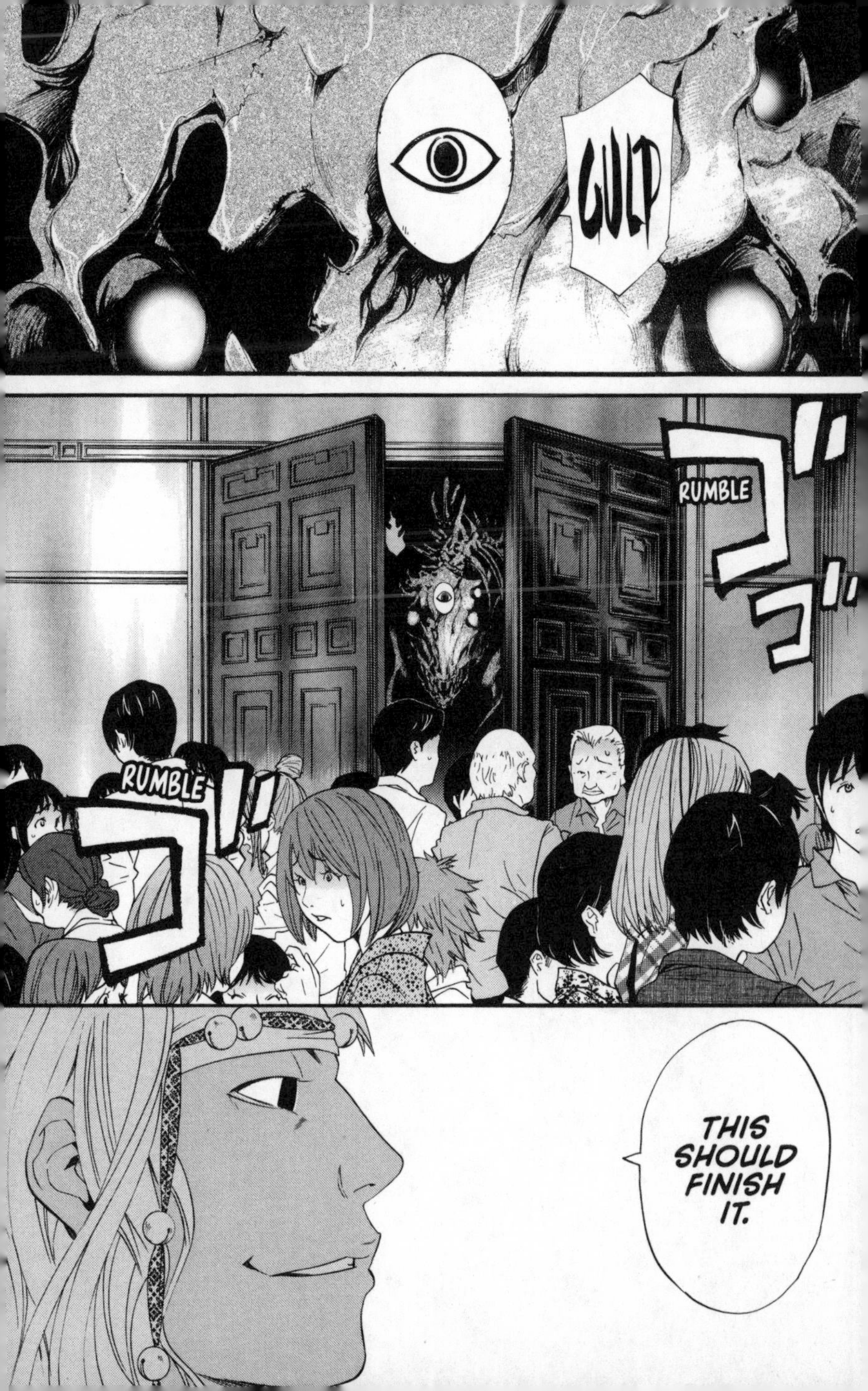
GULP
RUMBLE
RUMBLE
THIS SHOULD FINISH IT.

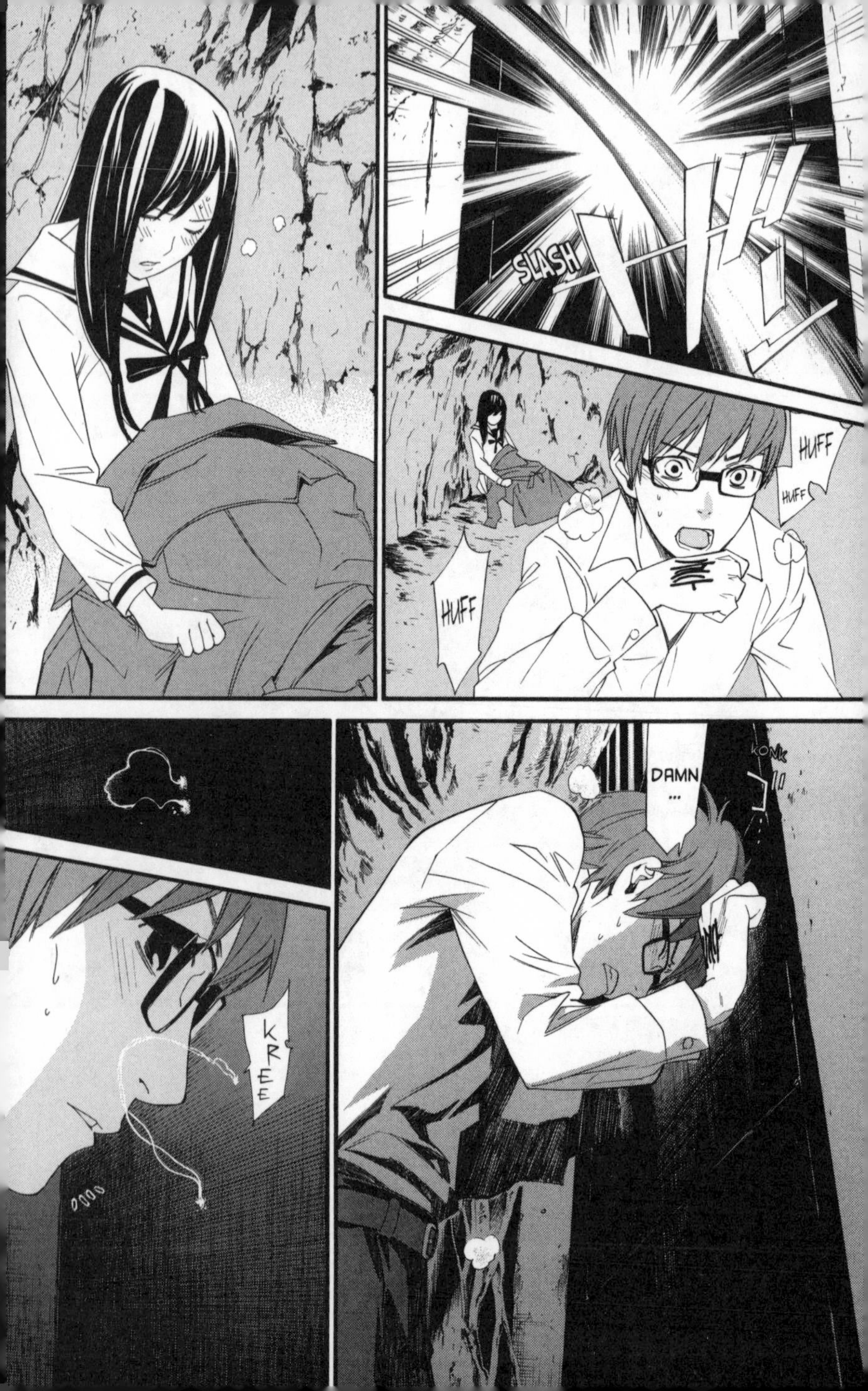
SLASH
HUFF
HUFF
HUFF
KONK
DAMN...
KREE

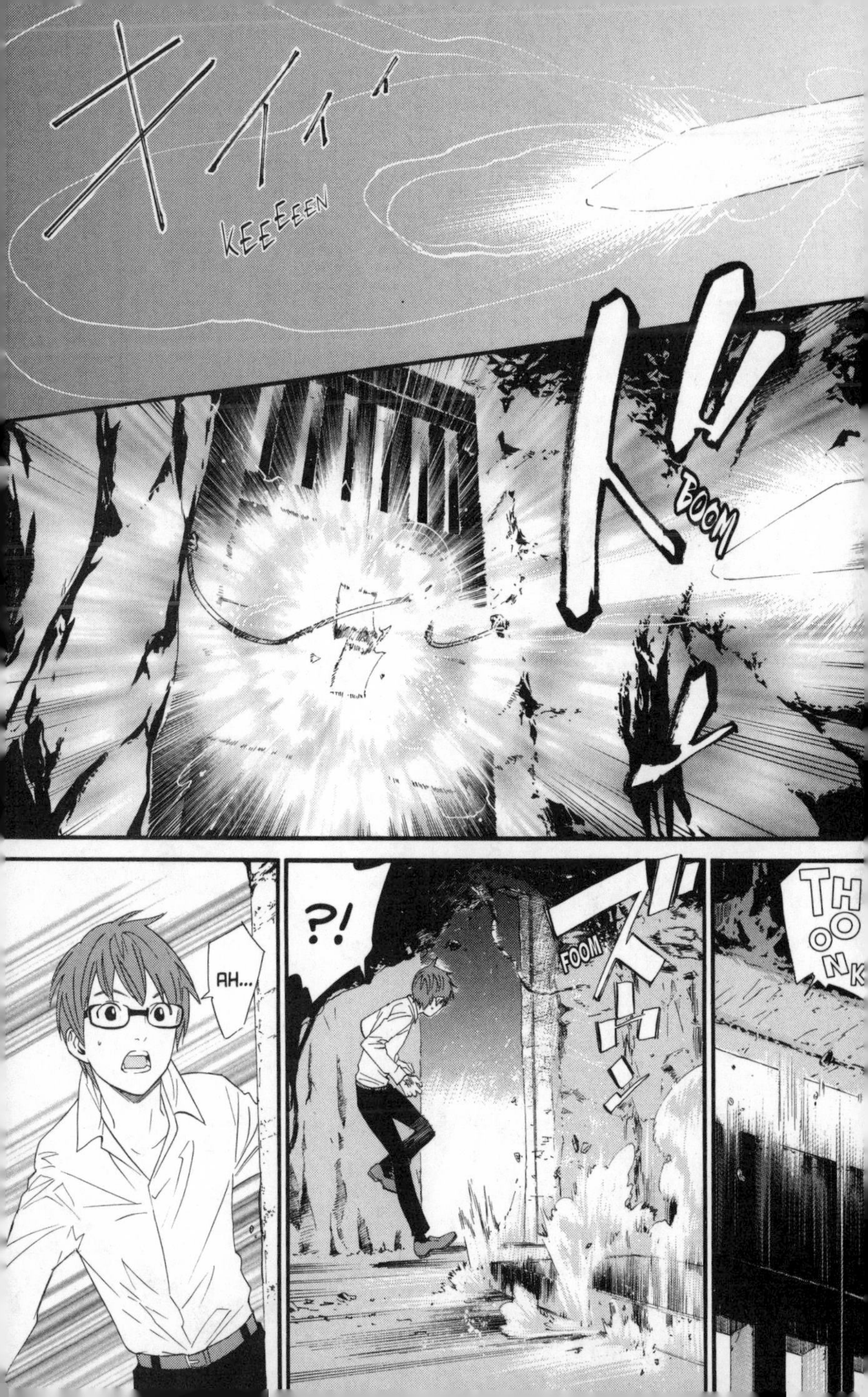
キィィィ
KEEEEEN
ド
BOOM
THOONK
ズ
FOOM
?!
AH...

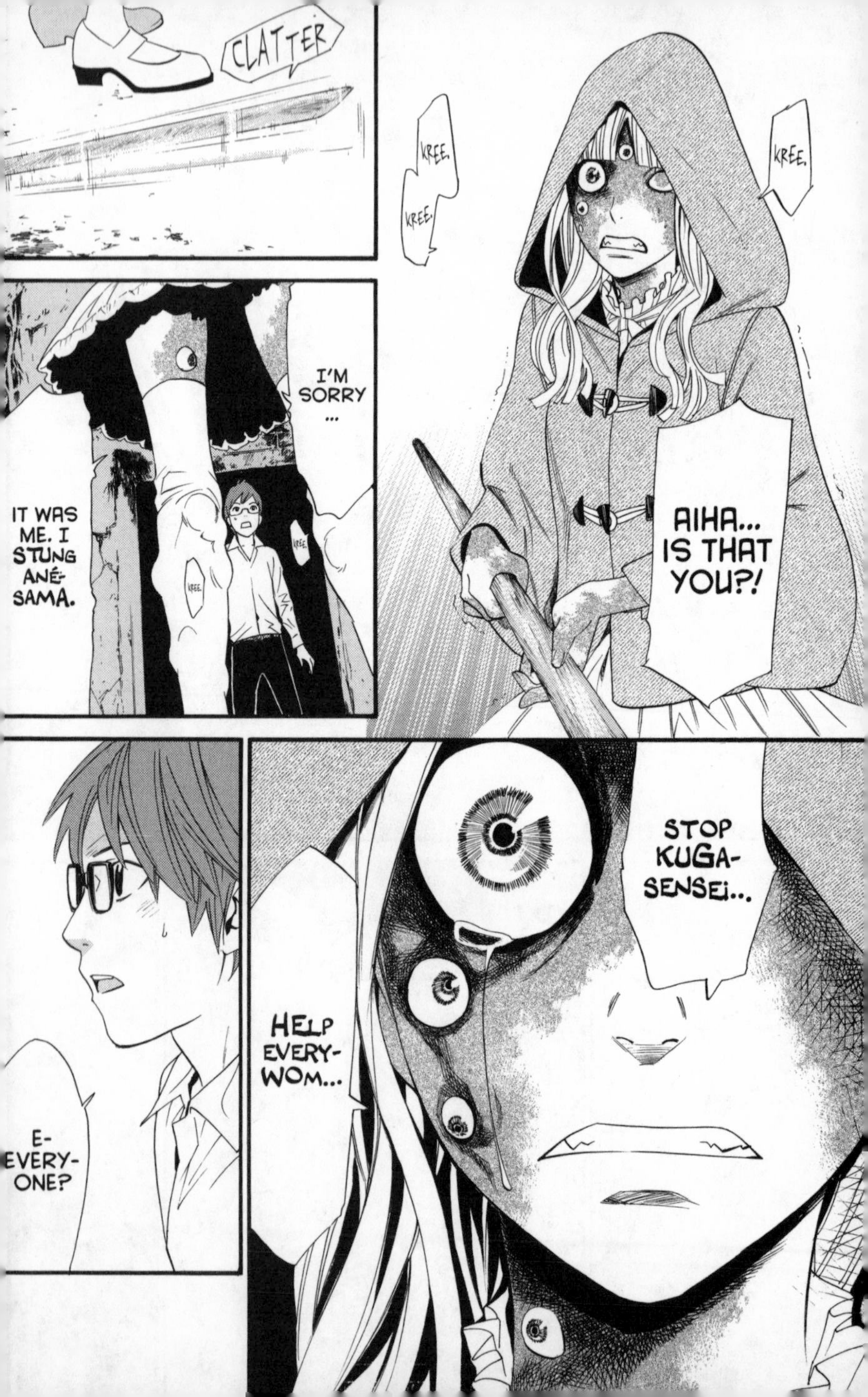
KREE.
KREE.
KREE.
AIHA... IS THAT YOU?!
CLATTER
I'M SORRY ...
KREE.
KREE.
IT WAS ME. I STUNG ANÉ-SAMA.
STOP KUGA-SENSEI...
HELP EVERY-WOM...
E-EVERY-ONE?

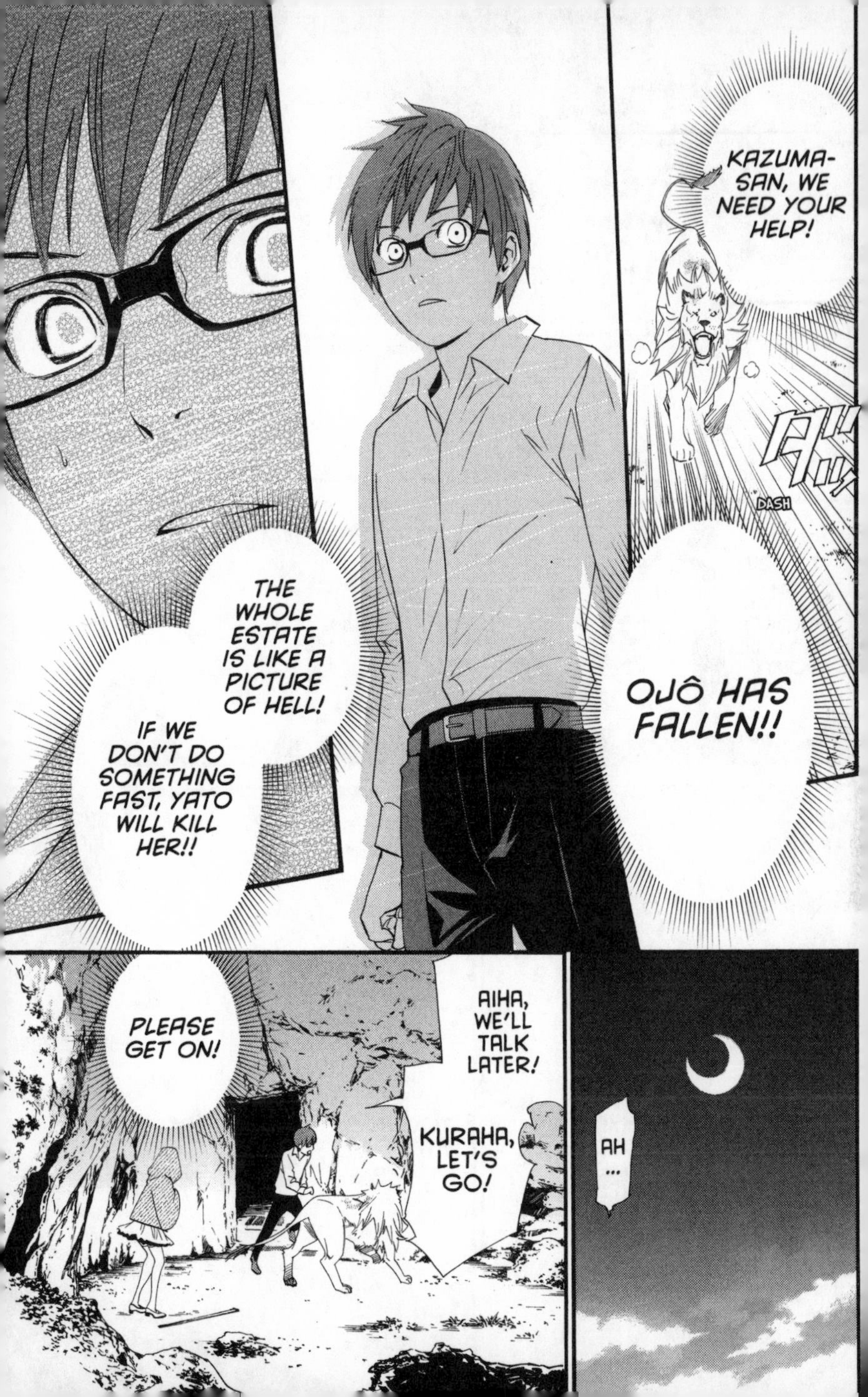
KAZUMA-SAN, WE NEED YOUR HELP!
DASH
OJÔ HAS FALLEN!!
THE WHOLE ESTATE IS LIKE A PICTURE OF HELL!
IF WE DON'T DO SOMETHING FAST, YATO WILL KILL HER!!
AH ...
AIHA, WE'LL TALK LATER!
KURAHA, LET'S GO!
PLEASE GET ON!

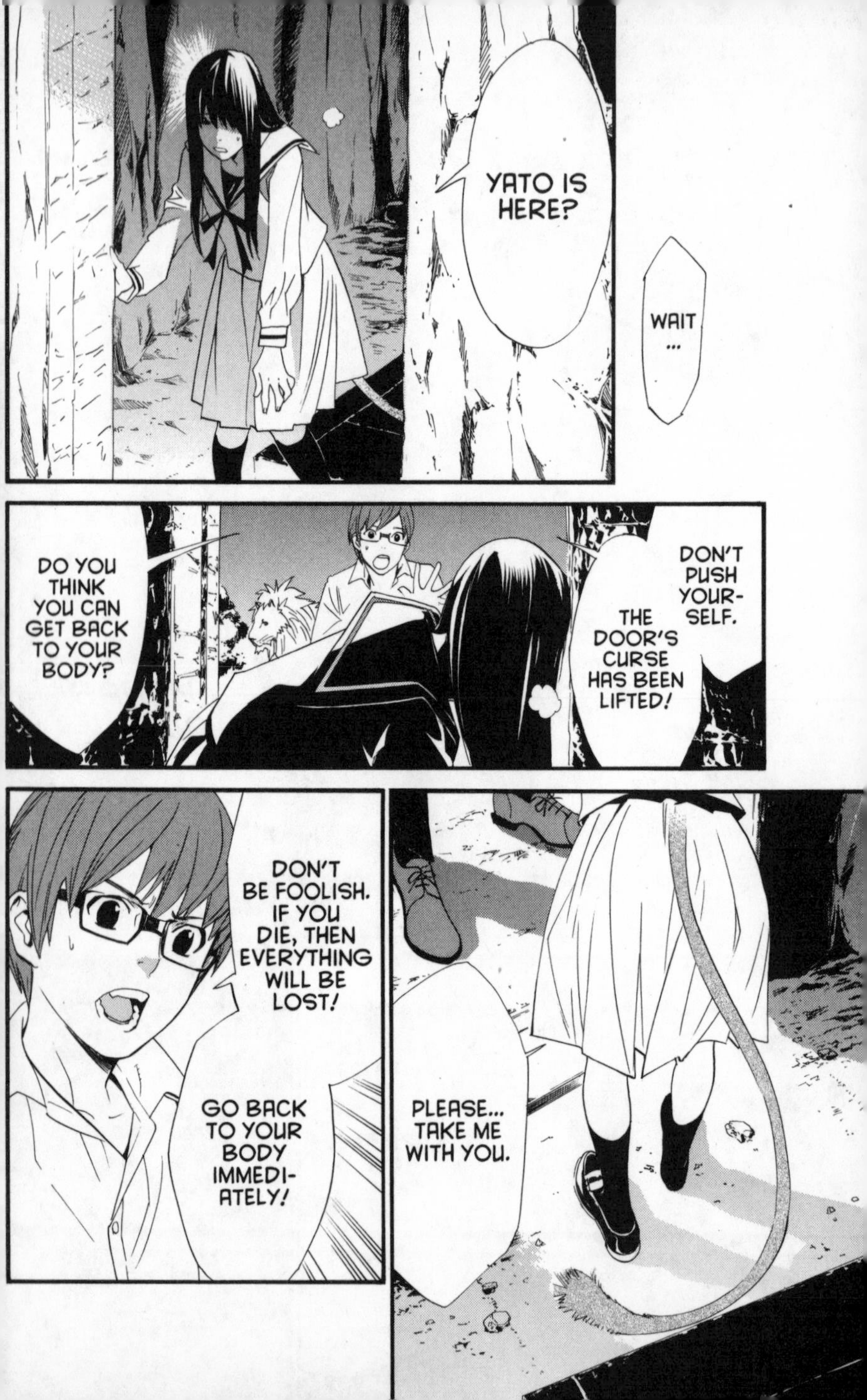
WAIT ...
YATO IS HERE?
DON'T PUSH YOURSELF.
THE DOOR'S CURSE HAS BEEN LIFTED!
DO YOU THINK YOU CAN GET BACK TO YOUR BODY?
PLEASE... TAKE ME WITH YOU.
DON'T BE FOOLISH. IF YOU DIE, THEN EVERYTHING WILL BE LOST!
GO BACK TO YOUR BODY IMMEDIATELY!

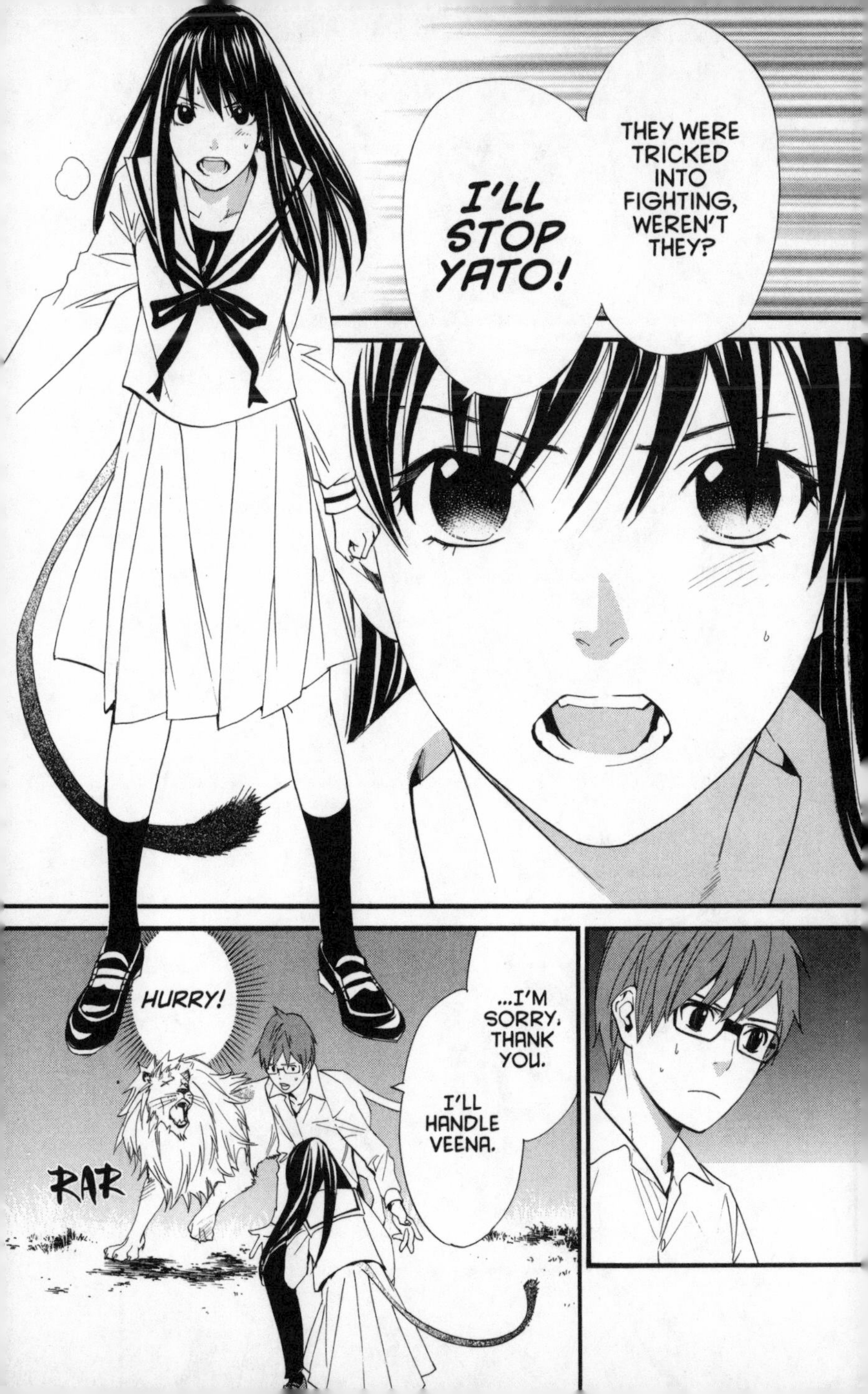
THEY WERE TRICKED INTO FIGHTING, WEREN'T THEY?
I'LL STOP YATO!
...I'M SORRY. THANK YOU.
I'LL HANDLE VEENA.
HURRY!
RAR

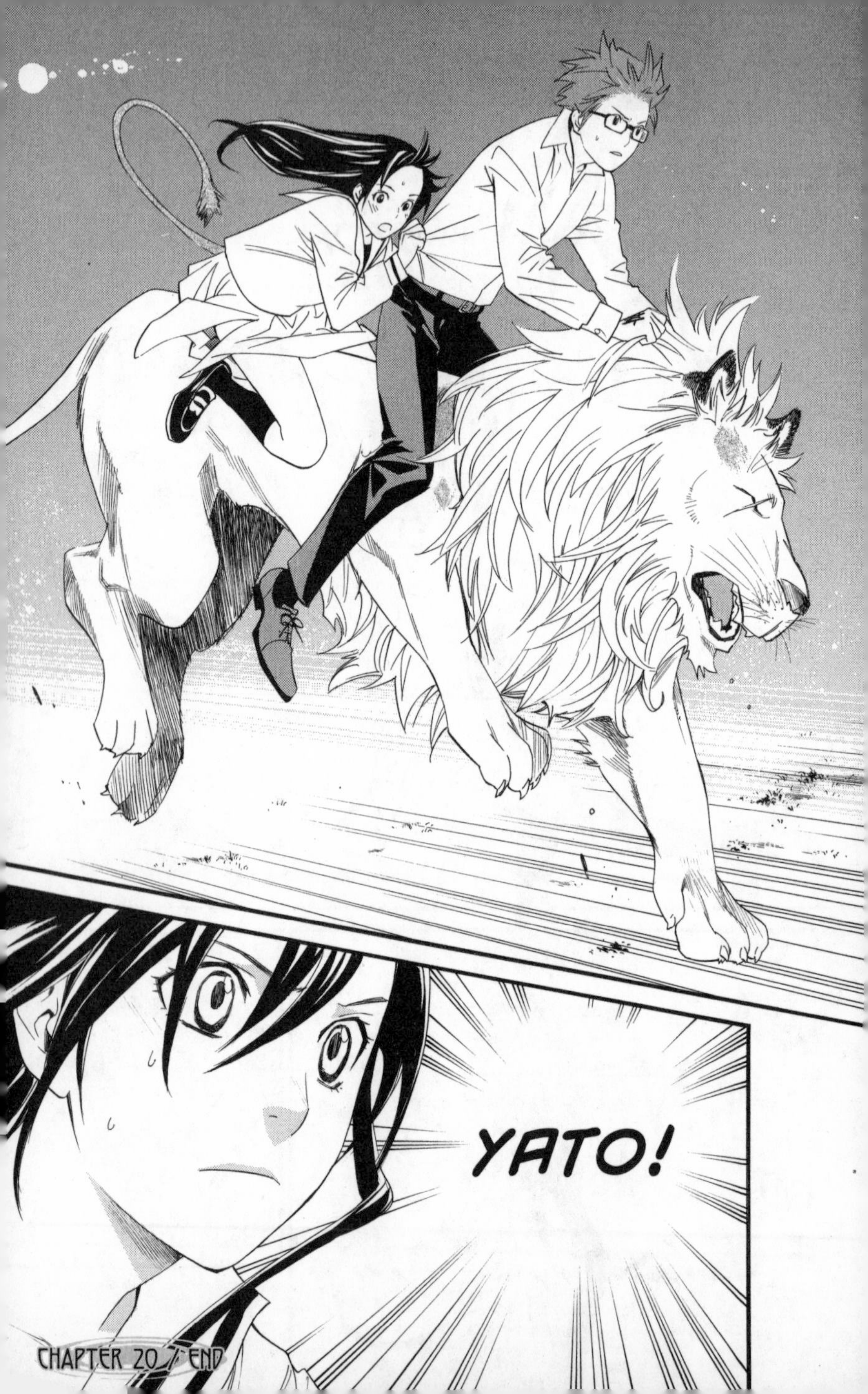
YATO!
CHAPTER 20 / END

野

亀

神

邏

首

祈

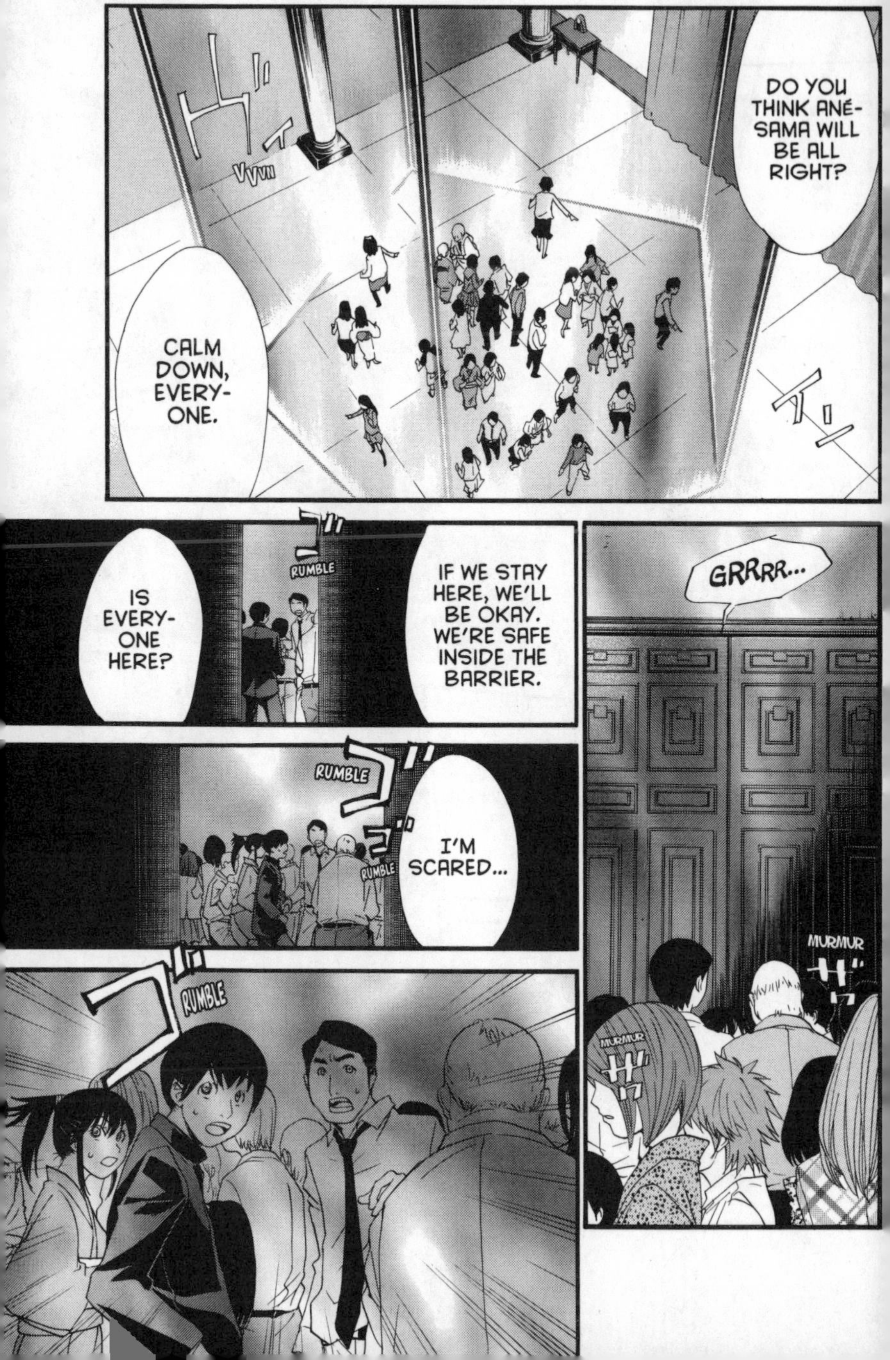
DO YOU THINK ANÉ-SAMA WILL BE ALL RIGHT?
VVVN
CALM DOWN, EVERYONE.
GRRRR...
MURMUR
MURMUR
IF WE STAY HERE, WE'LL BE OKAY. WE'RE SAFE INSIDE THE BARRIER.
RUMBLE
IS EVERYONE HERE?
I'M SCARED...
RUMBLE
RUMBLE
RUMBLE

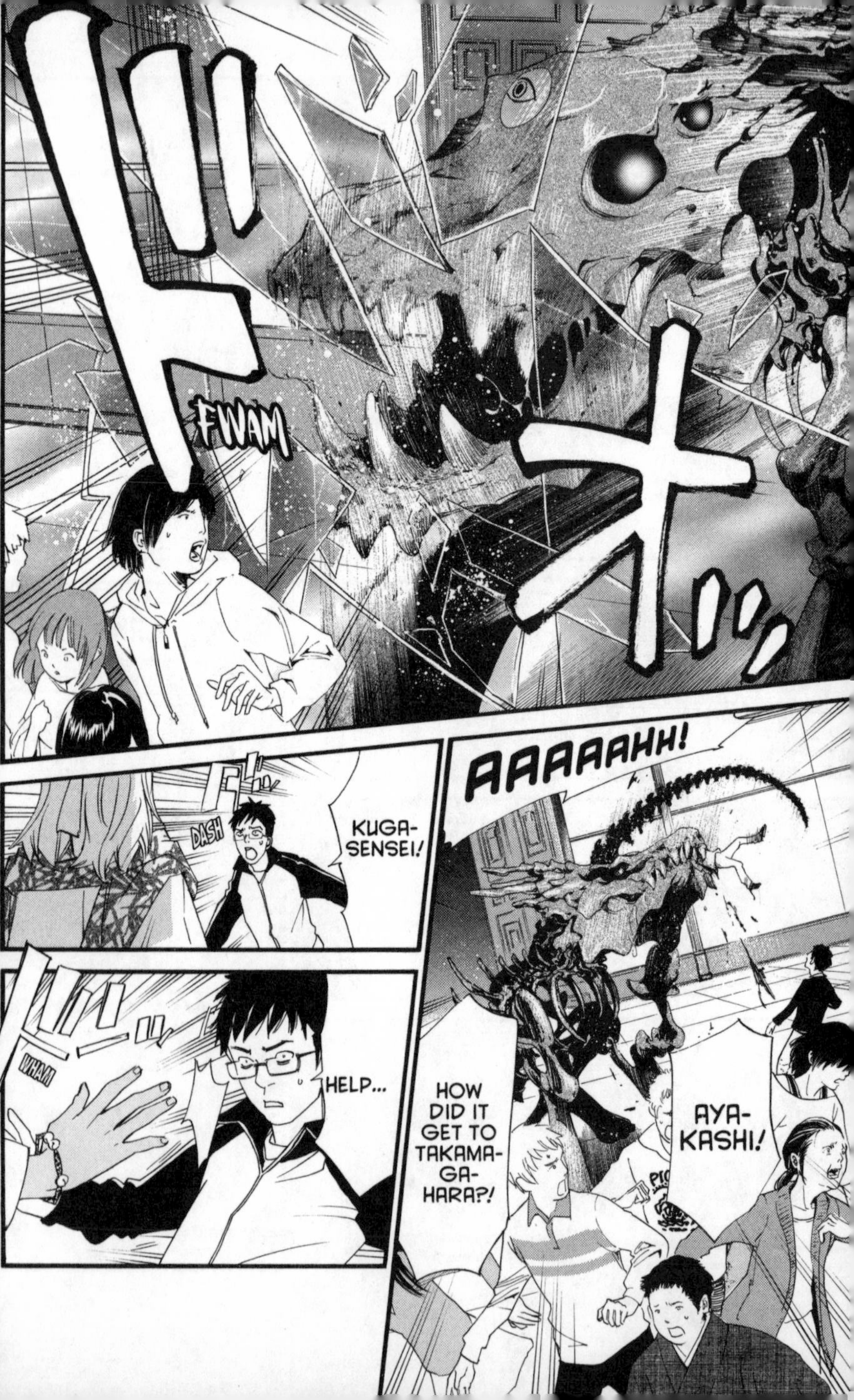
FWAM
AAAAAHH!
AYA-KASHI!
HOW DID IT GET TO TAKAMA-GA-HARA?!
DASH
KUGA-SENSEI!
WHAM
HELP...

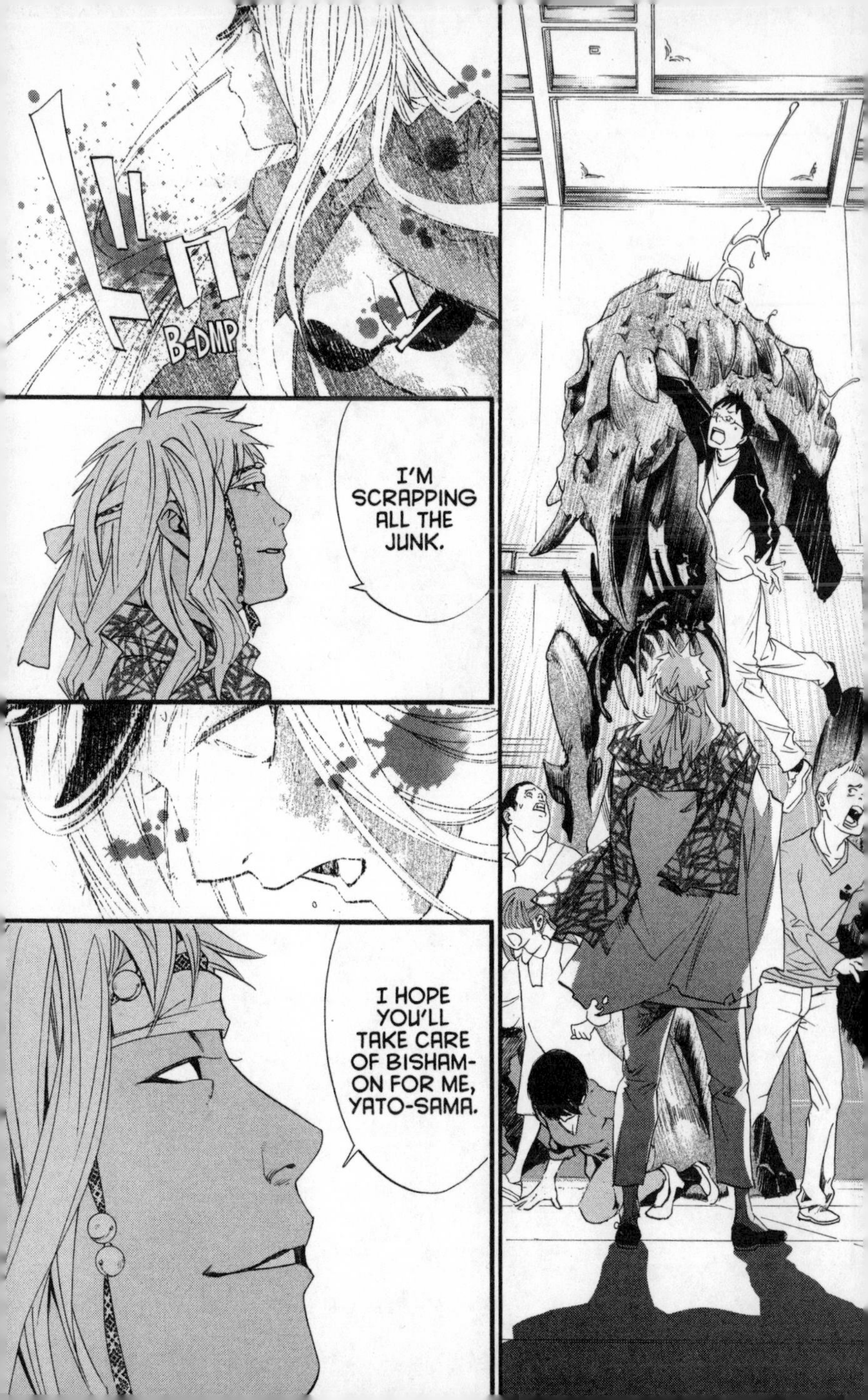
B-DMP
I'M SCRAPPING ALL THE JUNK.
I HOPE YOU'LL TAKE CARE OF BISHAM-ON FOR ME, YATO-SAMA.

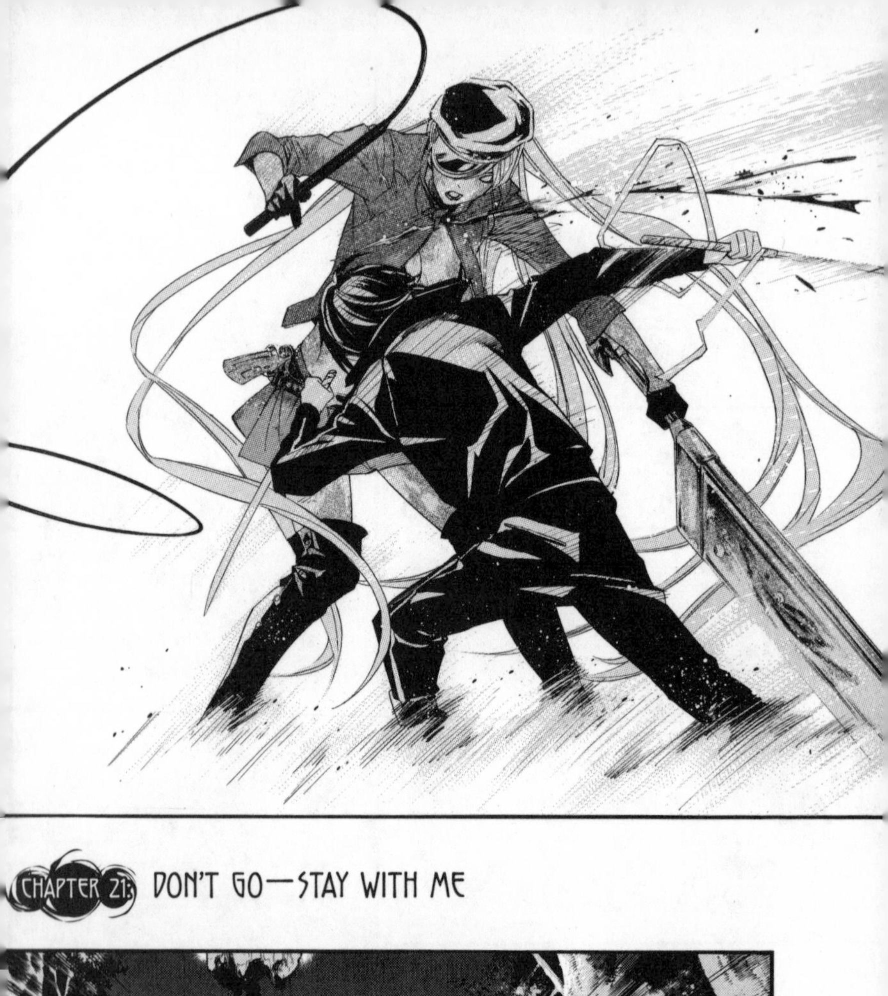

CHAPTER 21: DON'T GO—STAY WITH ME

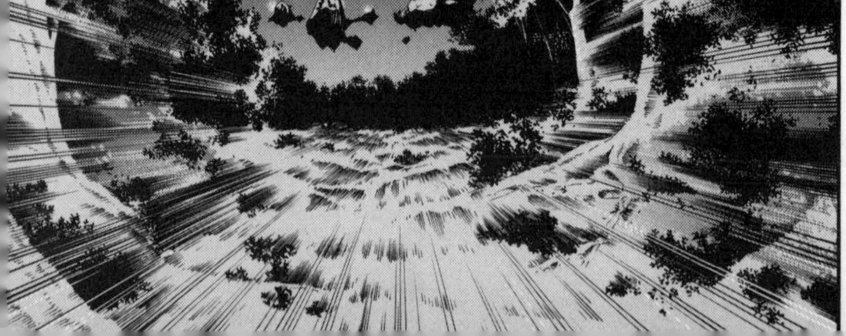

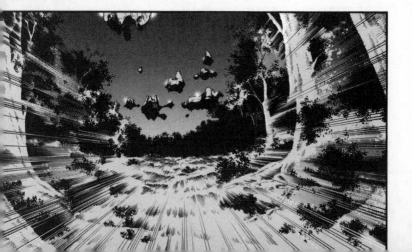

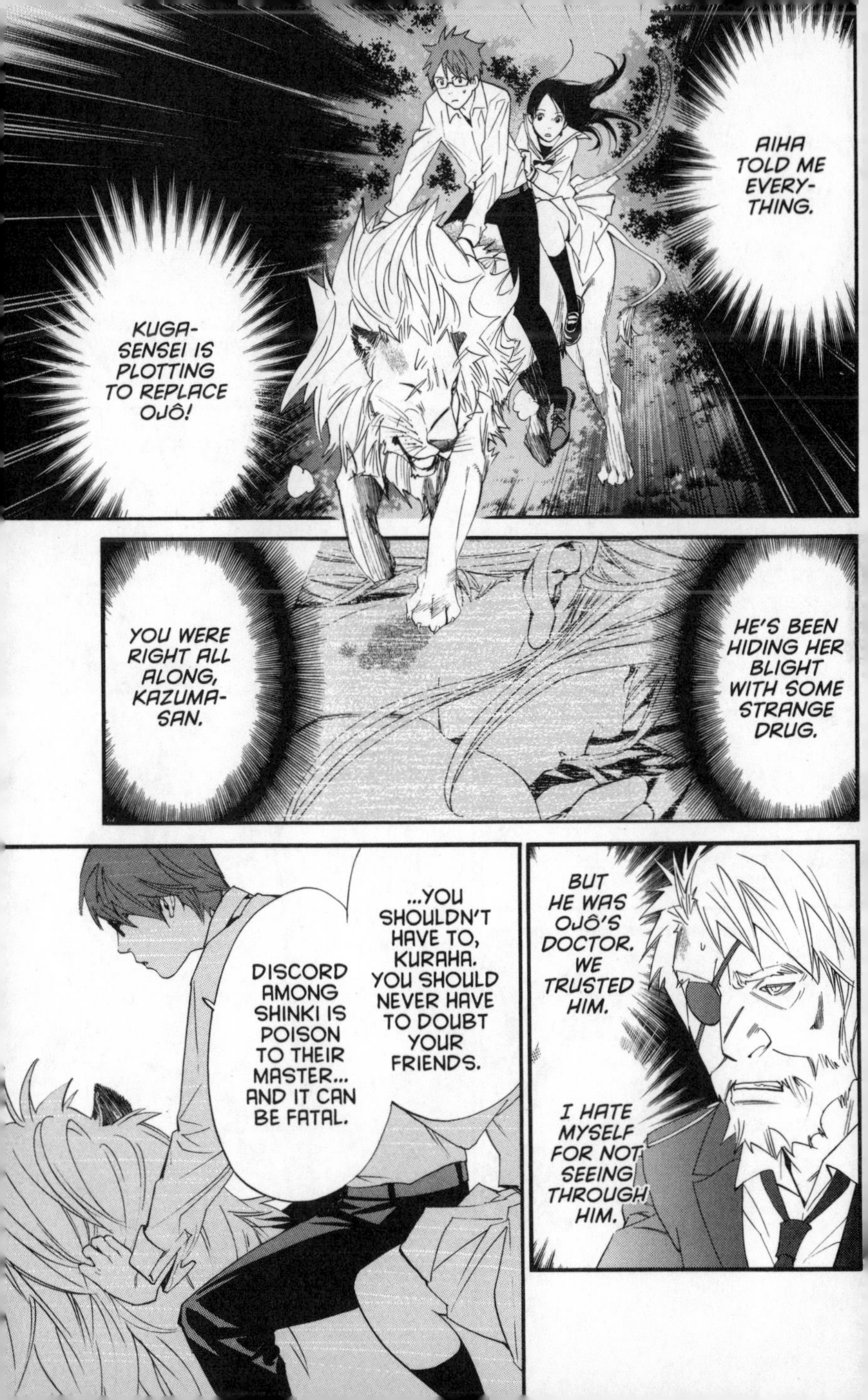
AIHA TOLD ME EVERYTHING.
KUGA-SENSEI IS PLOTTING TO REPLACE OJÔ!
HE'S BEEN HIDING HER BLIGHT WITH SOME STRANGE DRUG.
YOU WERE RIGHT ALL ALONG, KAZUMA-SAN.
BUT HE WAS OJÔ'S DOCTOR. WE TRUSTED HIM.
I HATE MYSELF FOR NOT SEEING THROUGH HIM.
...YOU SHOULDN'T HAVE TO, KURAHA. YOU SHOULD NEVER HAVE TO DOUBT YOUR FRIENDS.
DISCORD AMONG SHINKI IS POISON TO THEIR MASTER... AND IT CAN BE FATAL.

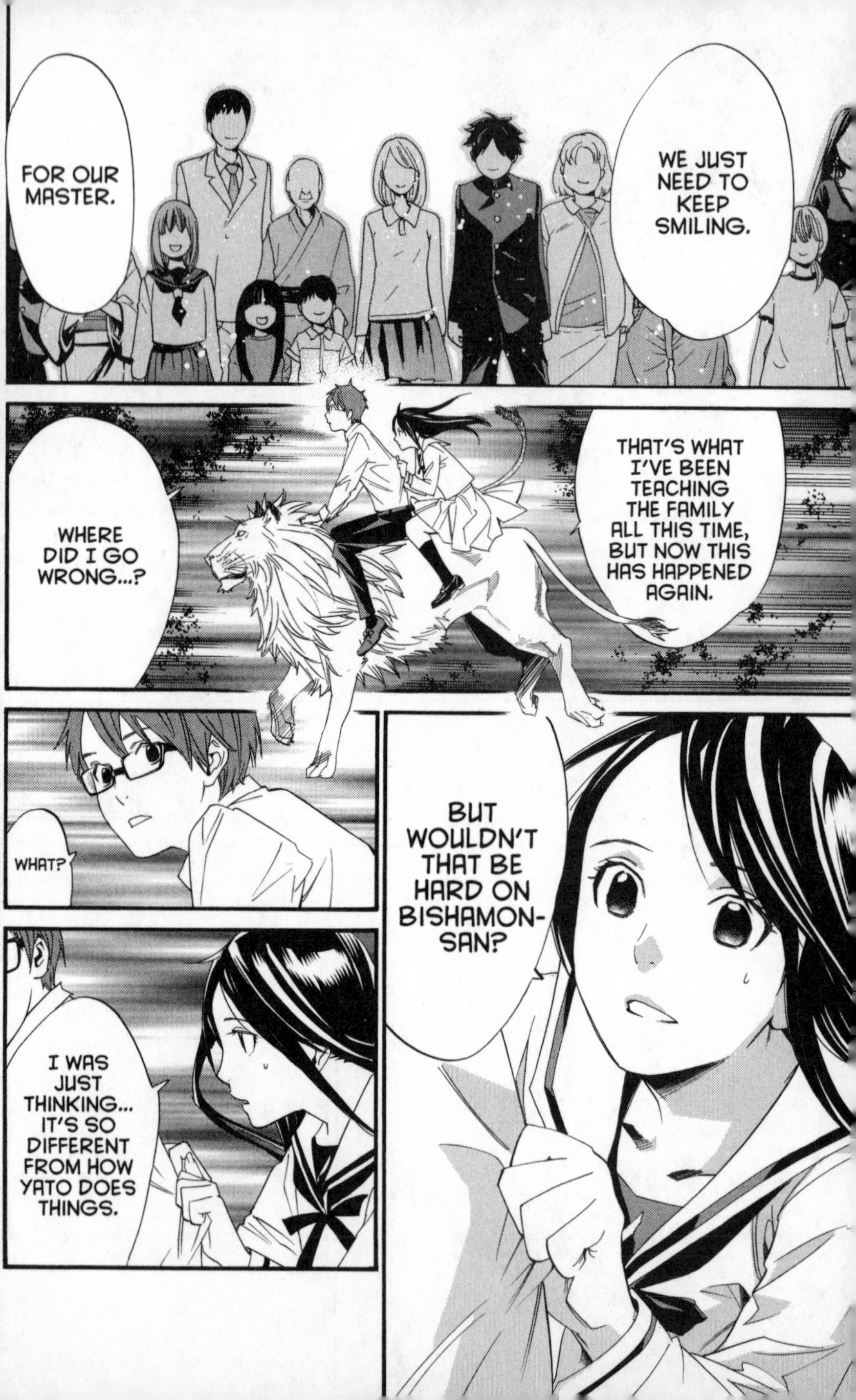
WE JUST NEED TO KEEP SMILING.
FOR OUR MASTER.
THAT'S WHAT I'VE BEEN TEACHING THE FAMILY ALL THIS TIME, BUT NOW THIS HAS HAPPENED AGAIN.
WHERE DID I GO WRONG...?
BUT WOULDN'T THAT BE HARD ON BISHAMON-SAN?
WHAT?
I WAS JUST THINKING... IT'S SO DIFFERENT FROM HOW YATO DOES THINGS.

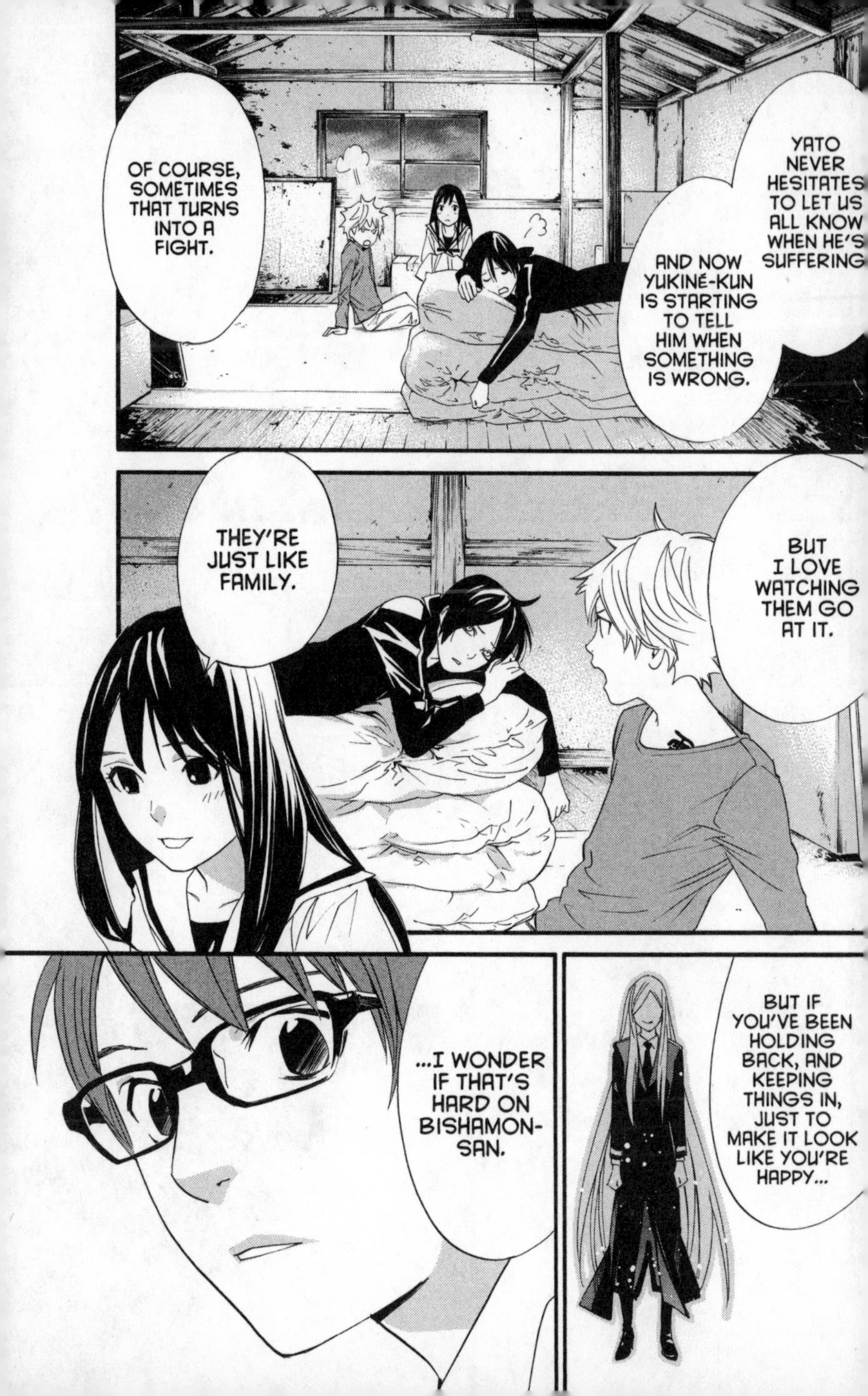
YATO NEVER HESITATES TO LET US ALL KNOW WHEN HE'S SUFFERING
AND NOW YUKINÉ-KUN IS STARTING TO TELL HIM WHEN SOMETHING IS WRONG.
OF COURSE, SOMETIMES THAT TURNS INTO A FIGHT.
BUT I LOVE WATCHING THEM GO AT IT.
THEY'RE JUST LIKE FAMILY.
BUT IF YOU'VE BEEN HOLDING BACK, AND KEEPING THINGS IN, JUST TO MAKE IT LOOK LIKE YOU'RE HAPPY...
...I WONDER IF THAT'S HARD ON BISHAMON-SAN.

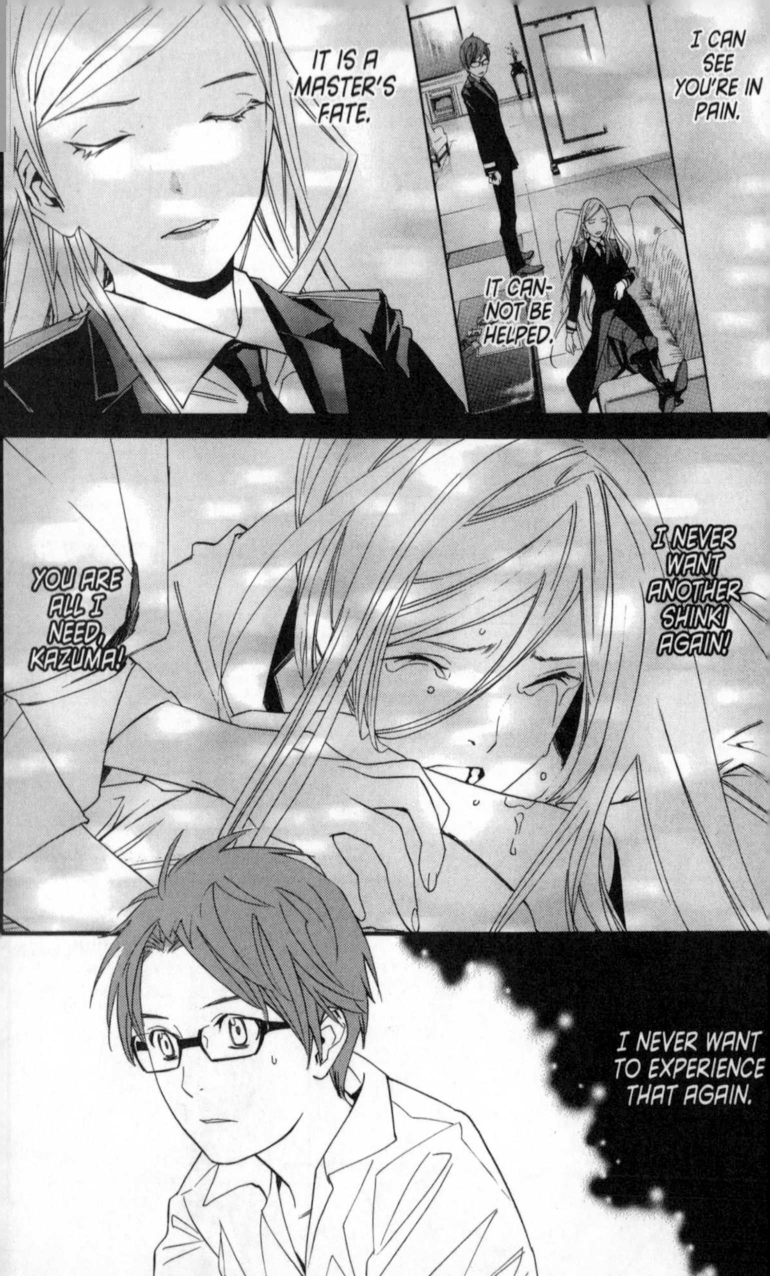
I CAN SEE YOU'RE IN PAIN.
IT CAN-NOT BE HELPED.
IT IS A MASTER'S FATE.
I NEVER WANT ANOTHER SHINKI AGAIN!
YOU ARE ALL I NEED, KAZUMA!
I NEVER WANT TO EXPERIENCE THAT AGAIN.

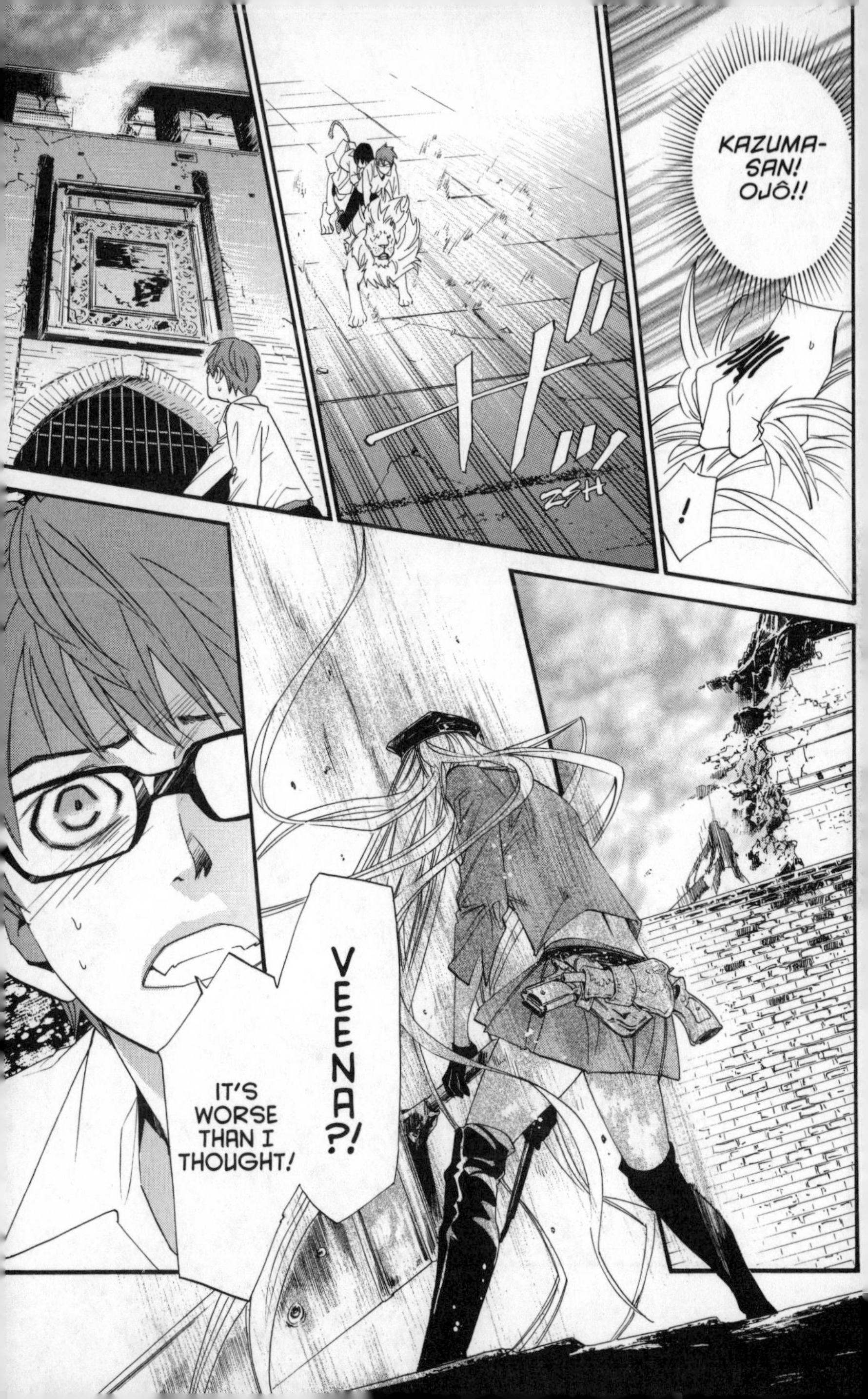
KAZUMA-SAN! OJÔ!!
ZSH
!
VEENA?!
IT'S WORSE THAN I THOUGHT!

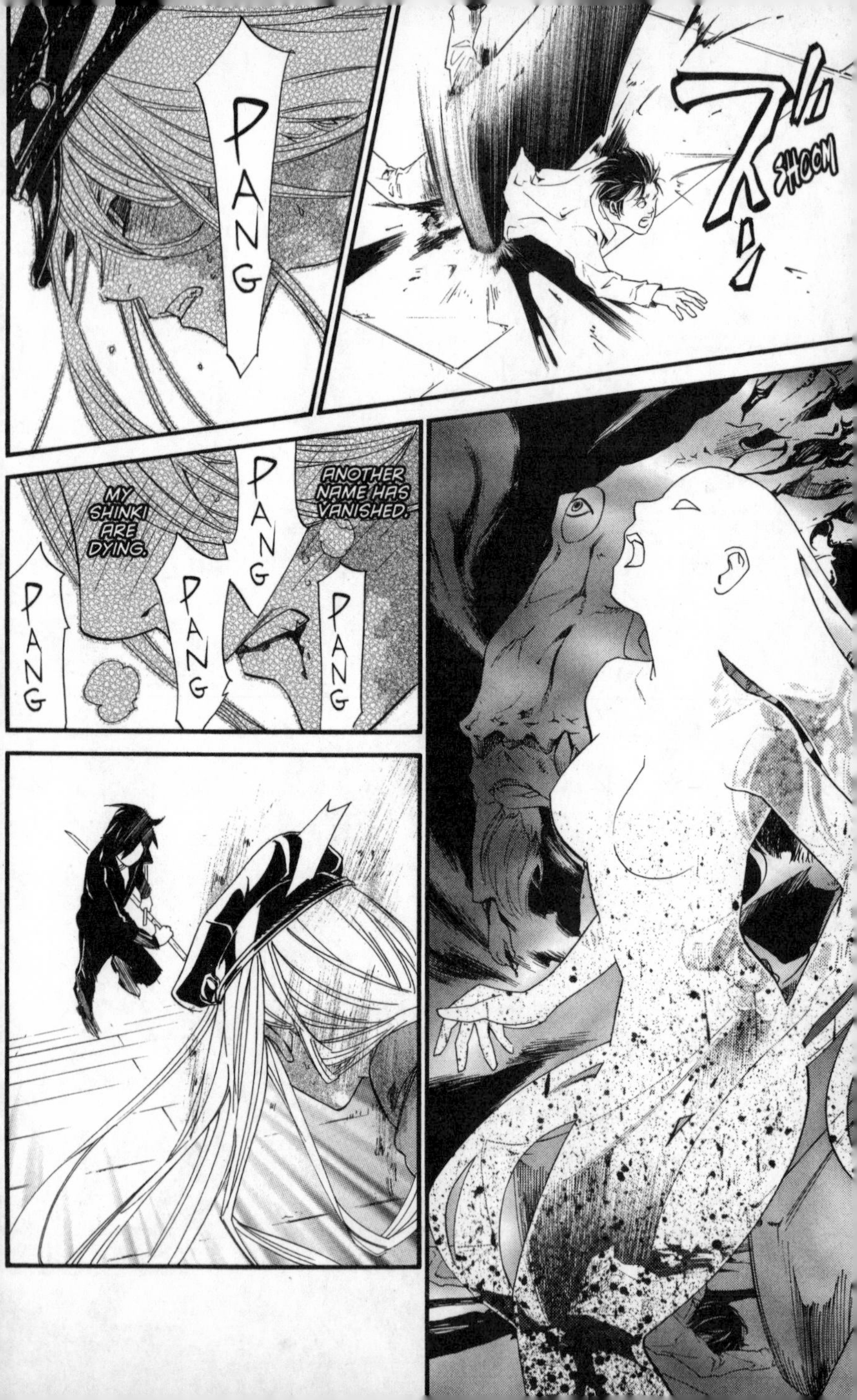
SHOOM
PANG
ANOTHER NAME HAS VANISHED.
PANG
PANG
MY SHINKI ARE DYING.
PANG
PANG

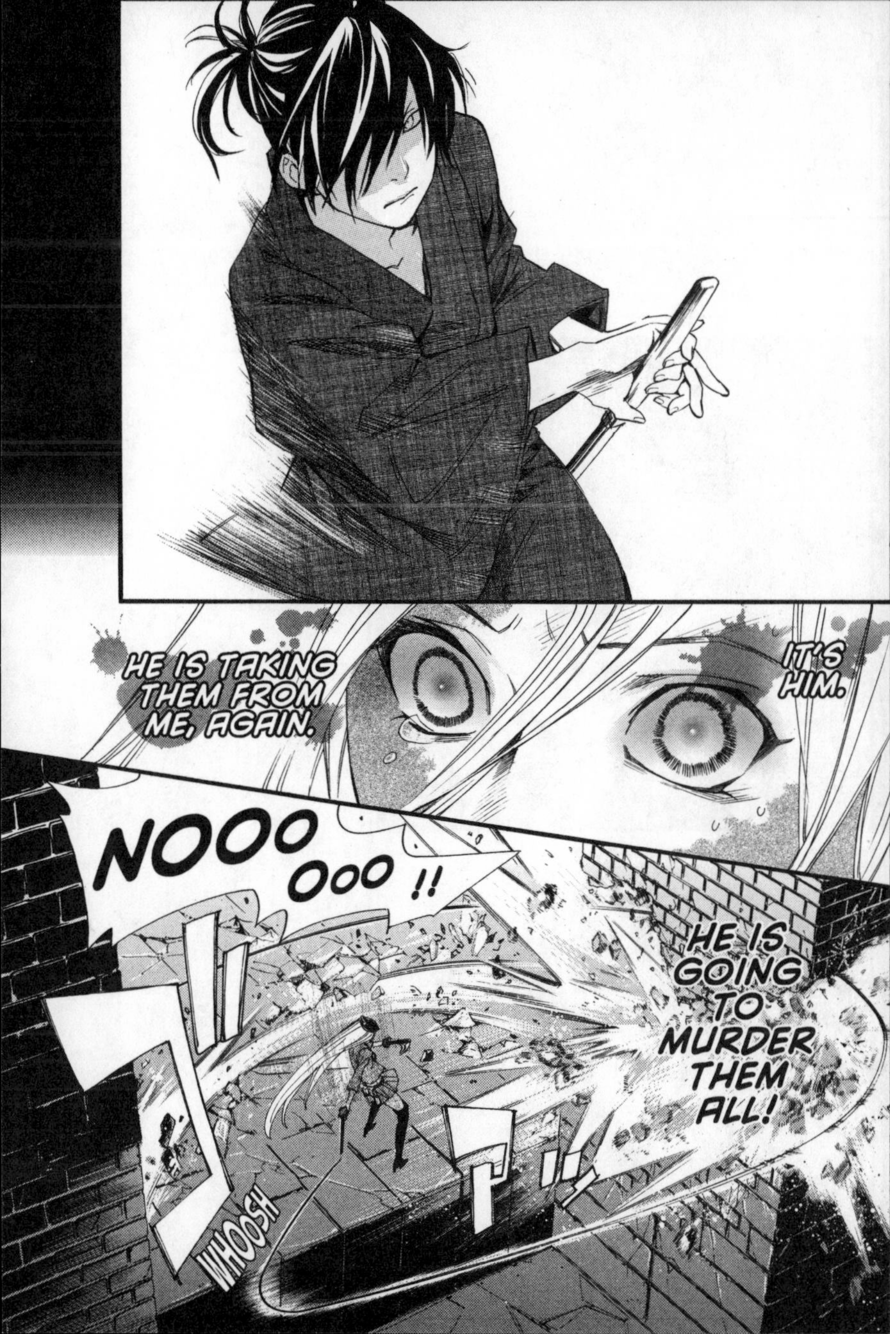
IT'S HIM.
HE IS TAKING THEM FROM ME, AGAIN.
NOOOOOO!!
HE IS GOING TO MURDER THEM ALL!
WHOOSH

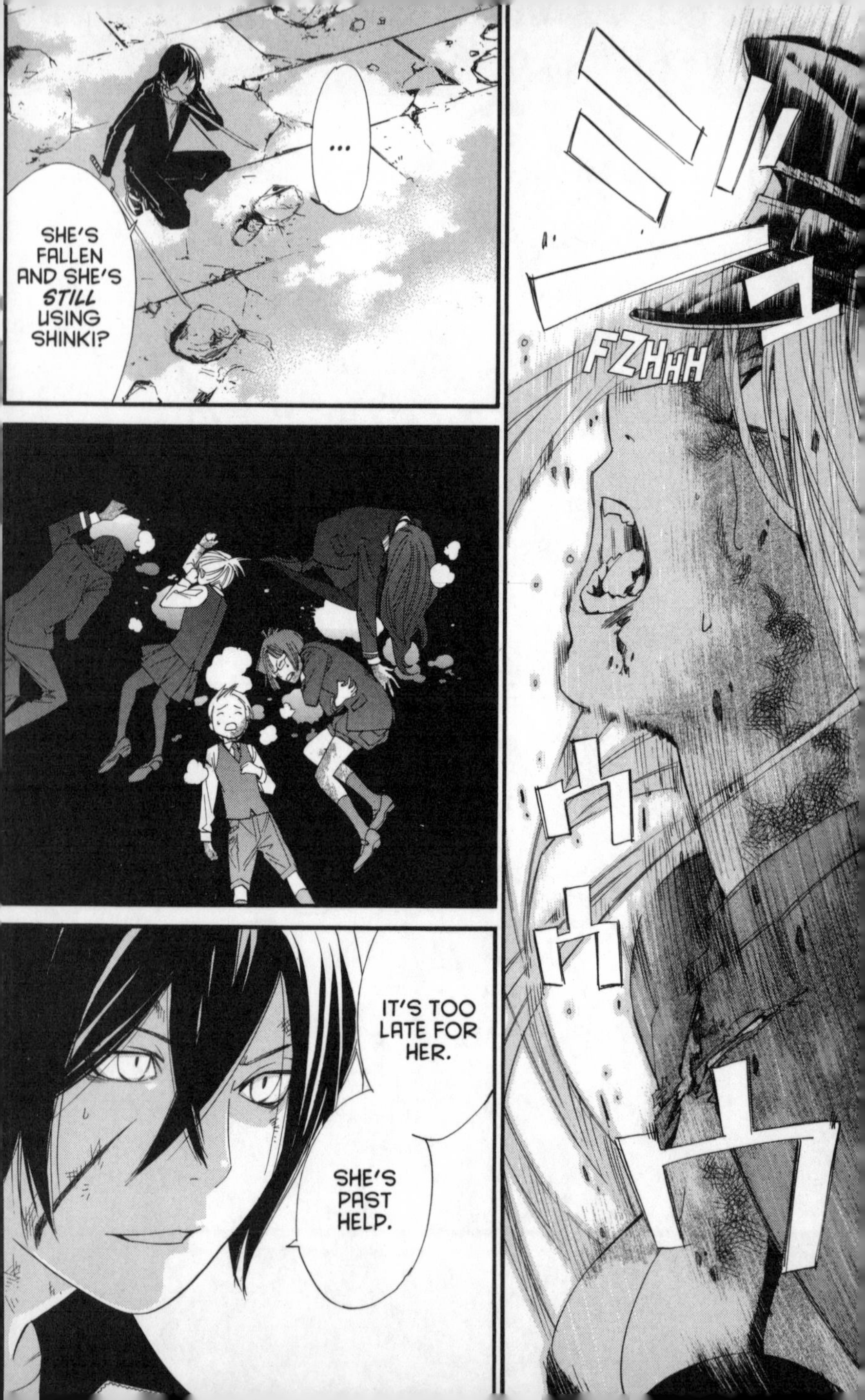
FZHHH
...
SHE'S FALLEN AND SHE'S *STILL* USING SHINKI?
IT'S TOO LATE FOR HER.
SHE'S PAST HELP.

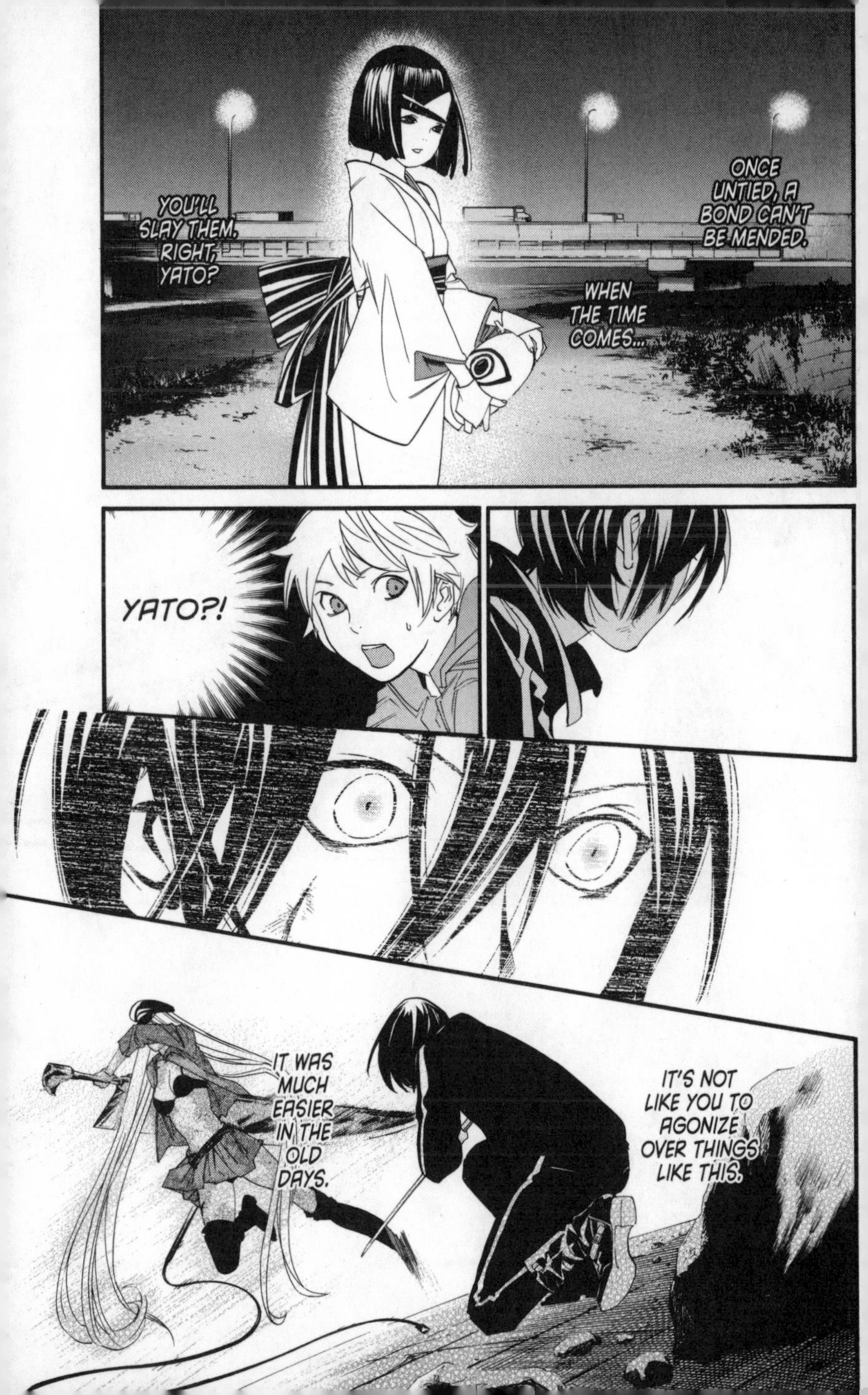
ONCE UNTIED, A BOND CAN'T BE MENDED.
WHEN THE TIME COMES...
YOU'LL SLAY THEM, RIGHT, YATO?
YATO?!
IT'S NOT LIKE YOU TO AGONIZE OVER THINGS LIKE THIS.
IT WAS MUCH EASIER IN THE OLD DAYS.

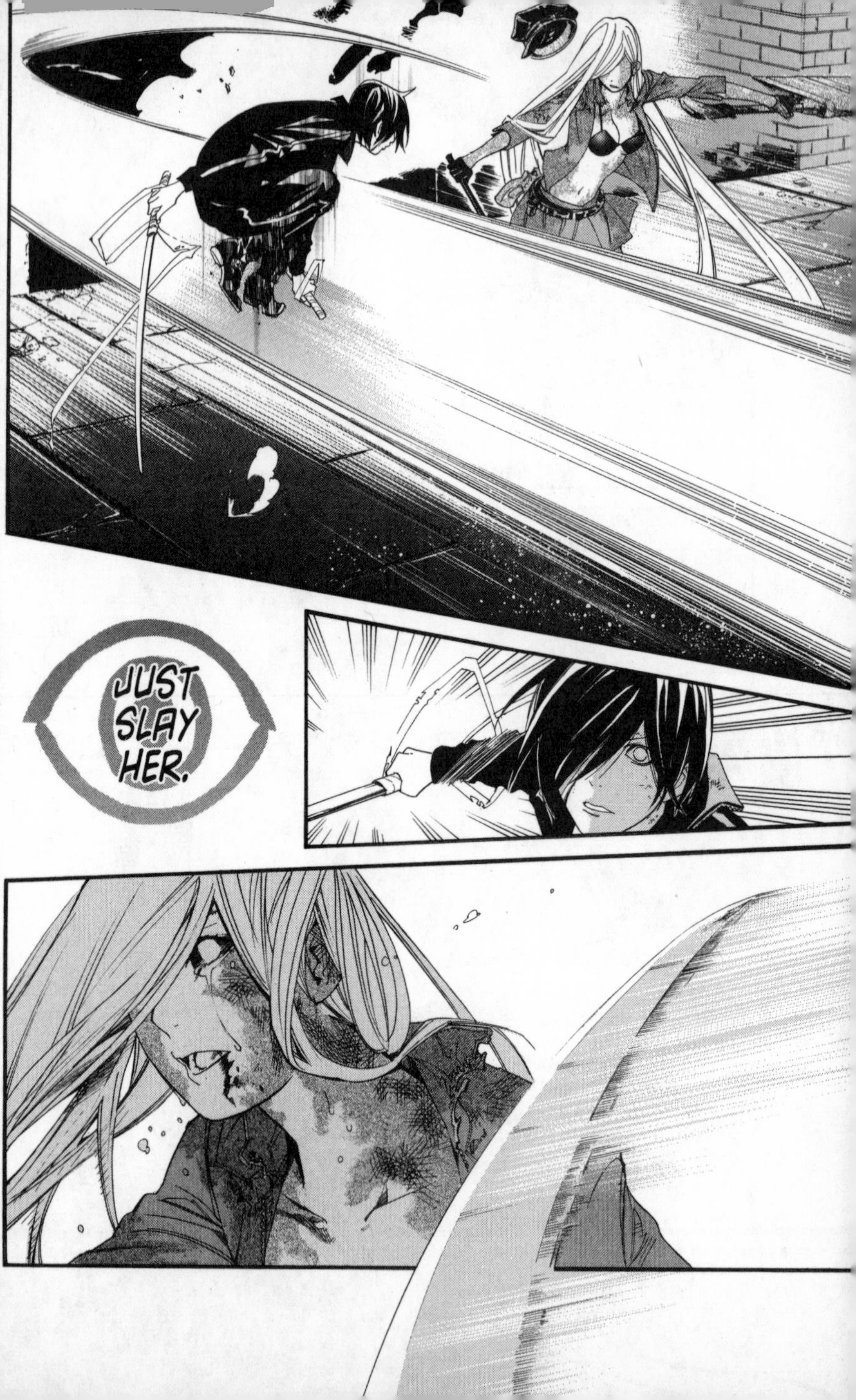
JUST SLAY HER.

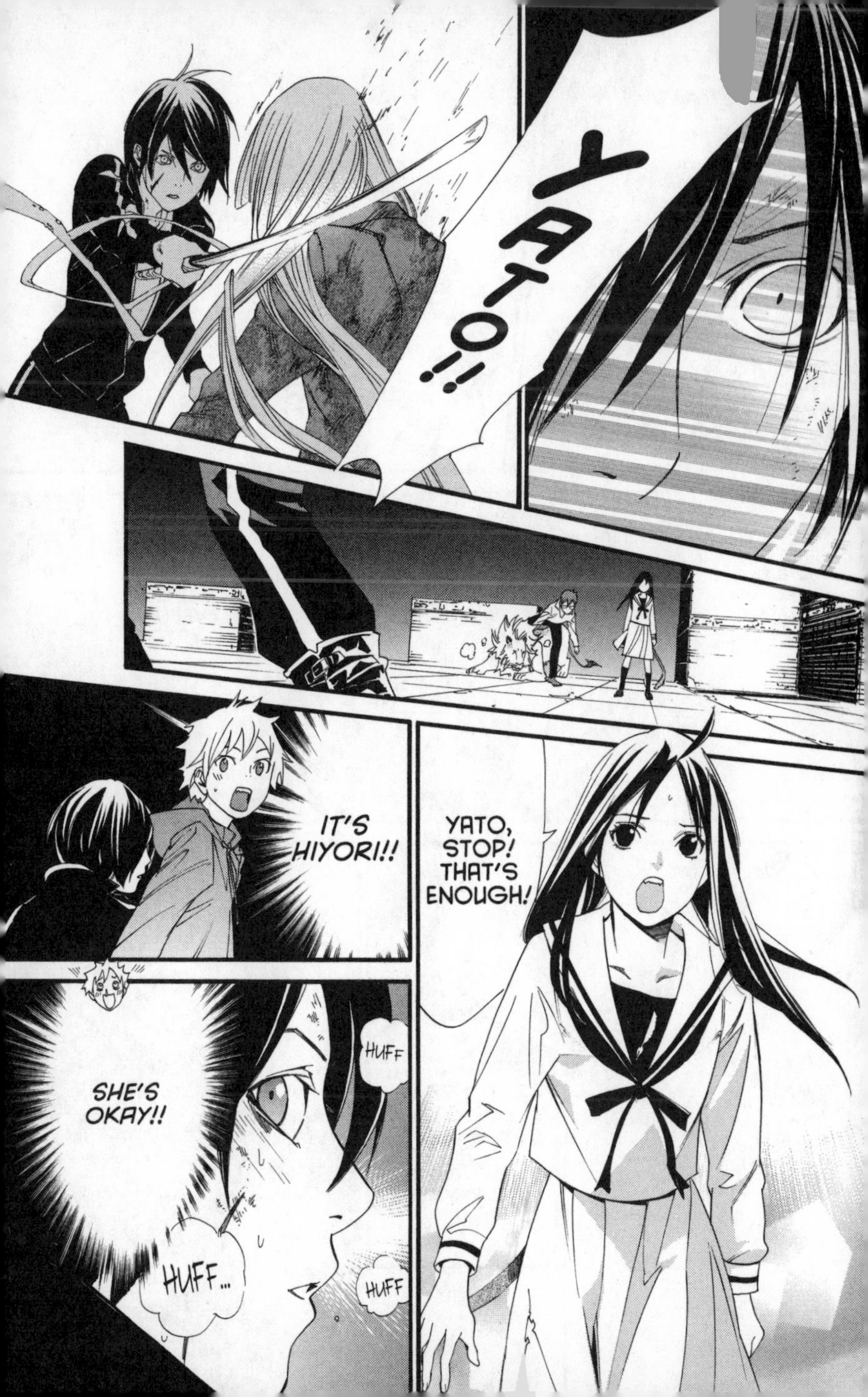
YATO!!
YATO, STOP! THAT'S ENOUGH!
IT'S HIYORI!!
HUFF
SHE'S OKAY!!
HUFF...
HUFF

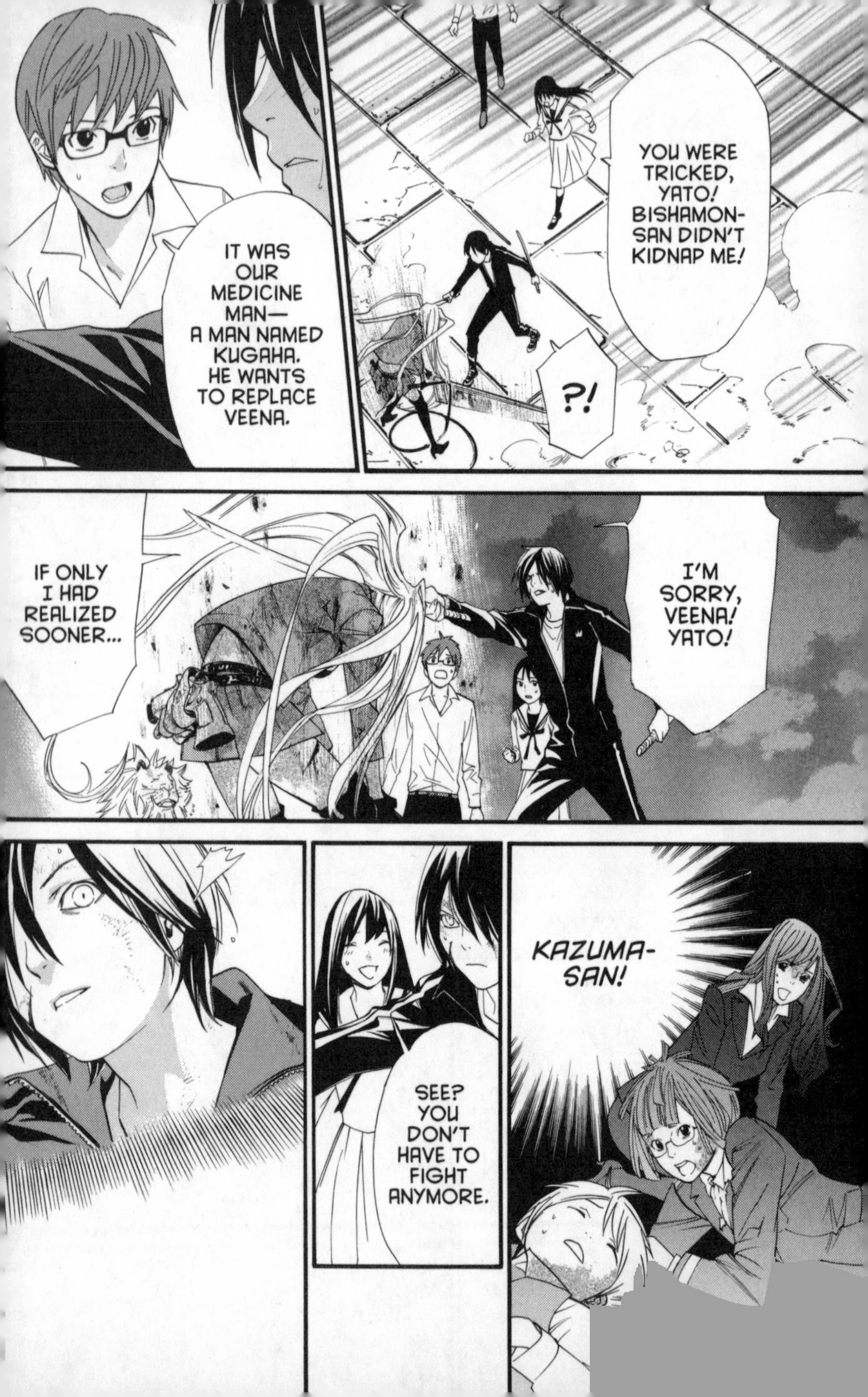
YOU WERE TRICKED, YATO! BISHAMON-SAN DIDN'T KIDNAP ME!
?!
IT WAS OUR MEDICINE MAN— A MAN NAMED KUGAHA. HE WANTS TO REPLACE VEENA.
I'M SORRY, VEENA! YATO!
IF ONLY I HAD REALIZED SOONER...
KAZUMA-SAN!
SEE? YOU DON'T HAVE TO FIGHT ANYMORE.

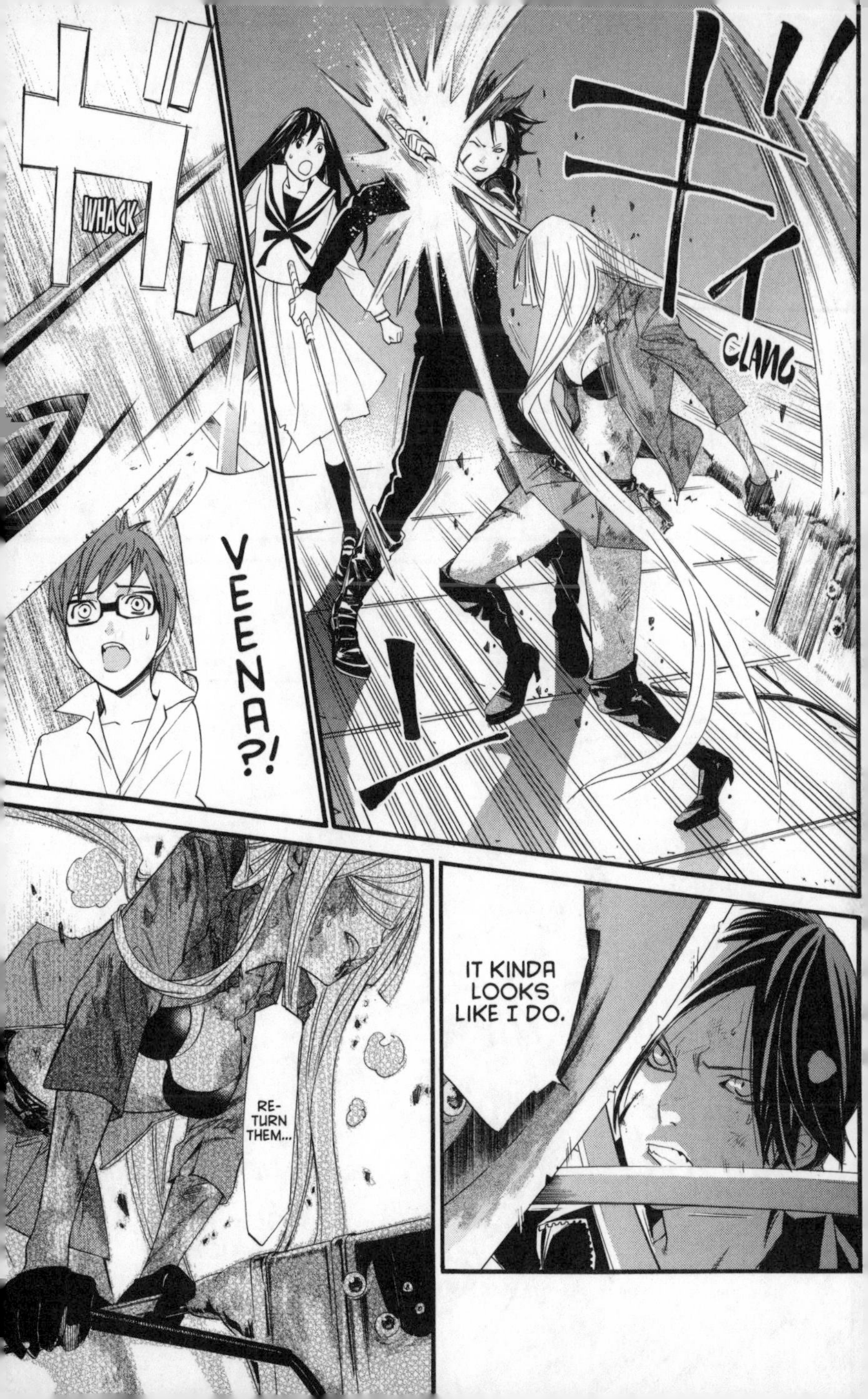
CLANG
WHACK
VEENA?!
IT KINDA LOOKS LIKE I DO.
RE-TURN THEM...

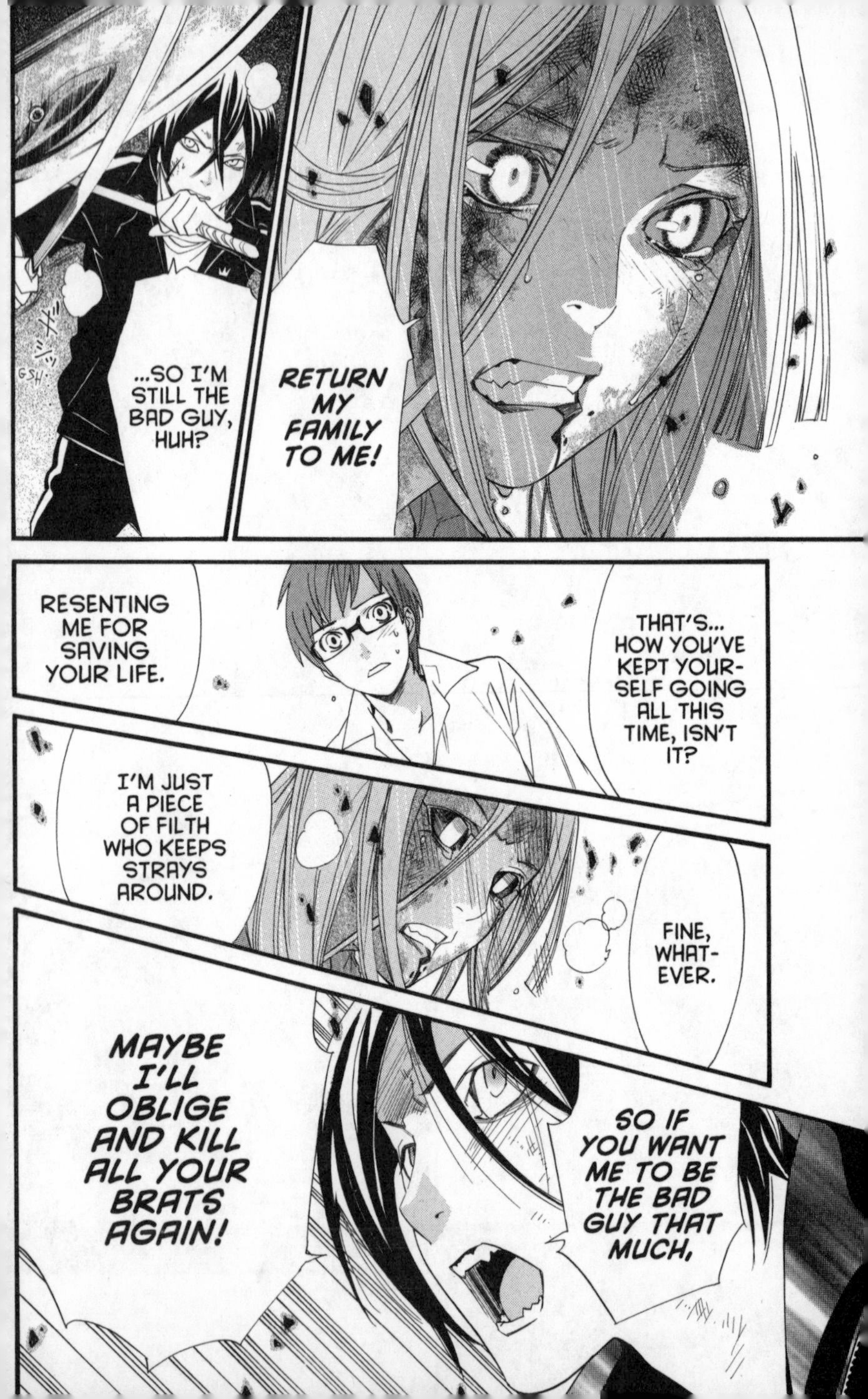
RETURN MY FAMILY TO ME!
...SO I'M STILL THE BAD GUY, HUH?
GSH
THAT'S... HOW YOU'VE KEPT YOURSELF GOING ALL THIS TIME, ISN'T IT?
RESENTING ME FOR SAVING YOUR LIFE.
I'M JUST A PIECE OF FILTH WHO KEEPS STRAYS AROUND.
FINE, WHATEVER.
SO IF YOU WANT ME TO BE THE BAD GUY THAT MUCH,
MAYBE I'LL OBLIGE AND KILL ALL YOUR BRATS AGAIN!

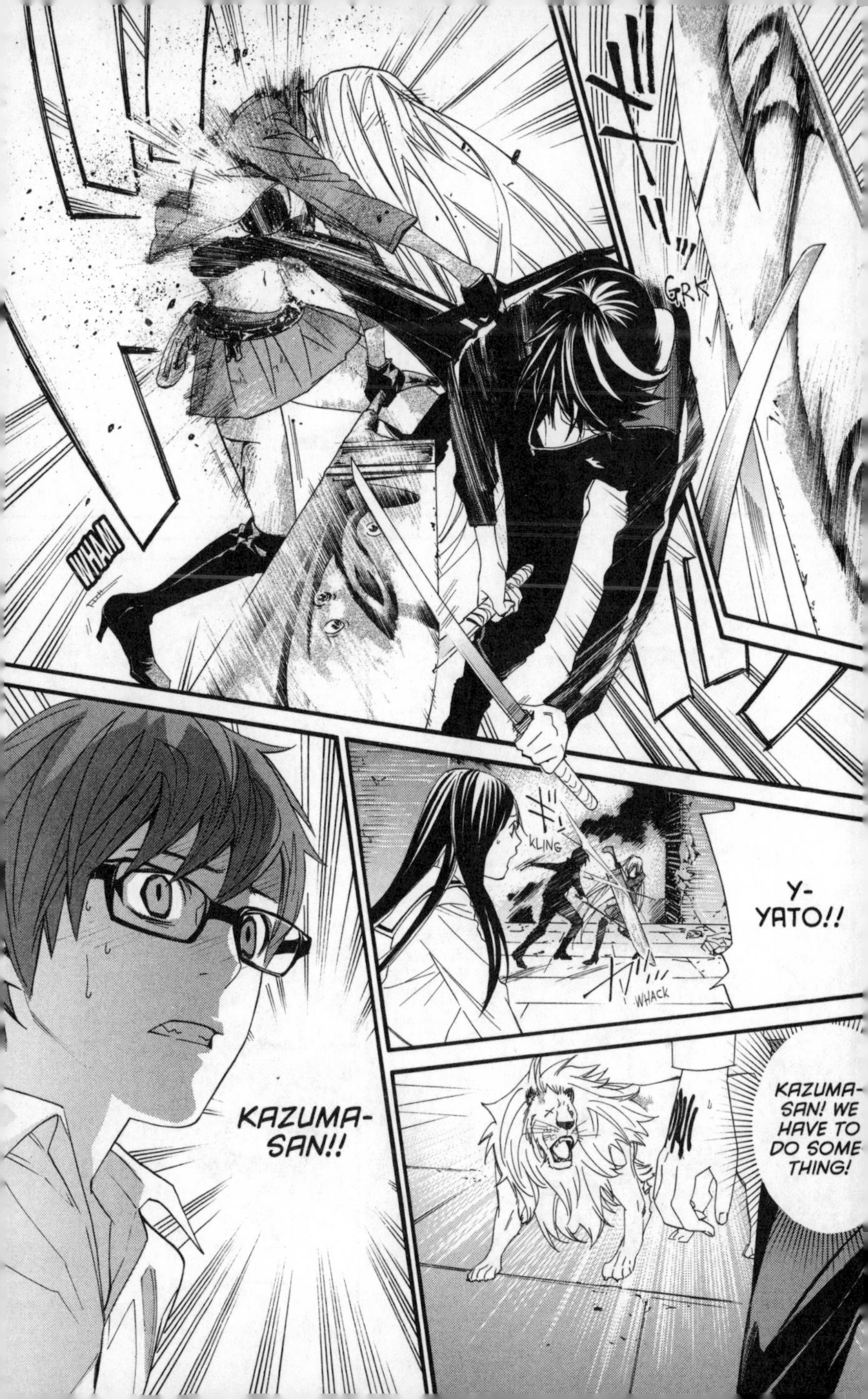
GRK
WHAM
Y-YATO!!
KLING
WHACK
KAZUMA-SAN! WE HAVE TO DO SOME THING!
KAZUMA-SAN!!

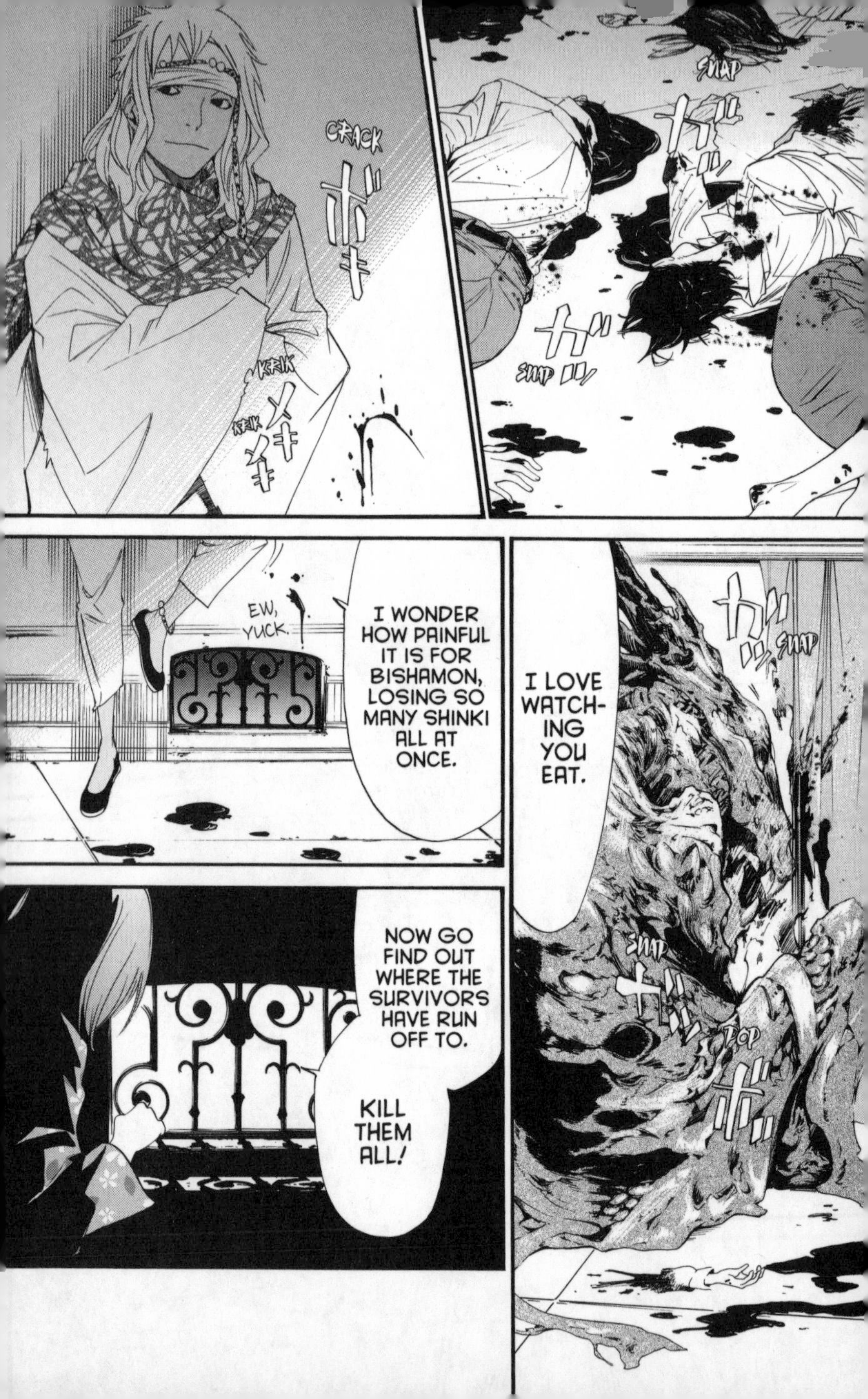
SNAP
SNAP
CRACK
KRIK
KRIK
I LOVE WATCHING YOU EAT.
SNAP
SNAP
POP
EW, YUCK.
I WONDER HOW PAINFUL IT IS FOR BISHAMON, LOSING SO MANY SHINKI ALL AT ONCE.
NOW GO FIND OUT WHERE THE SURVIVORS HAVE RUN OFF TO.
KILL THEM ALL!

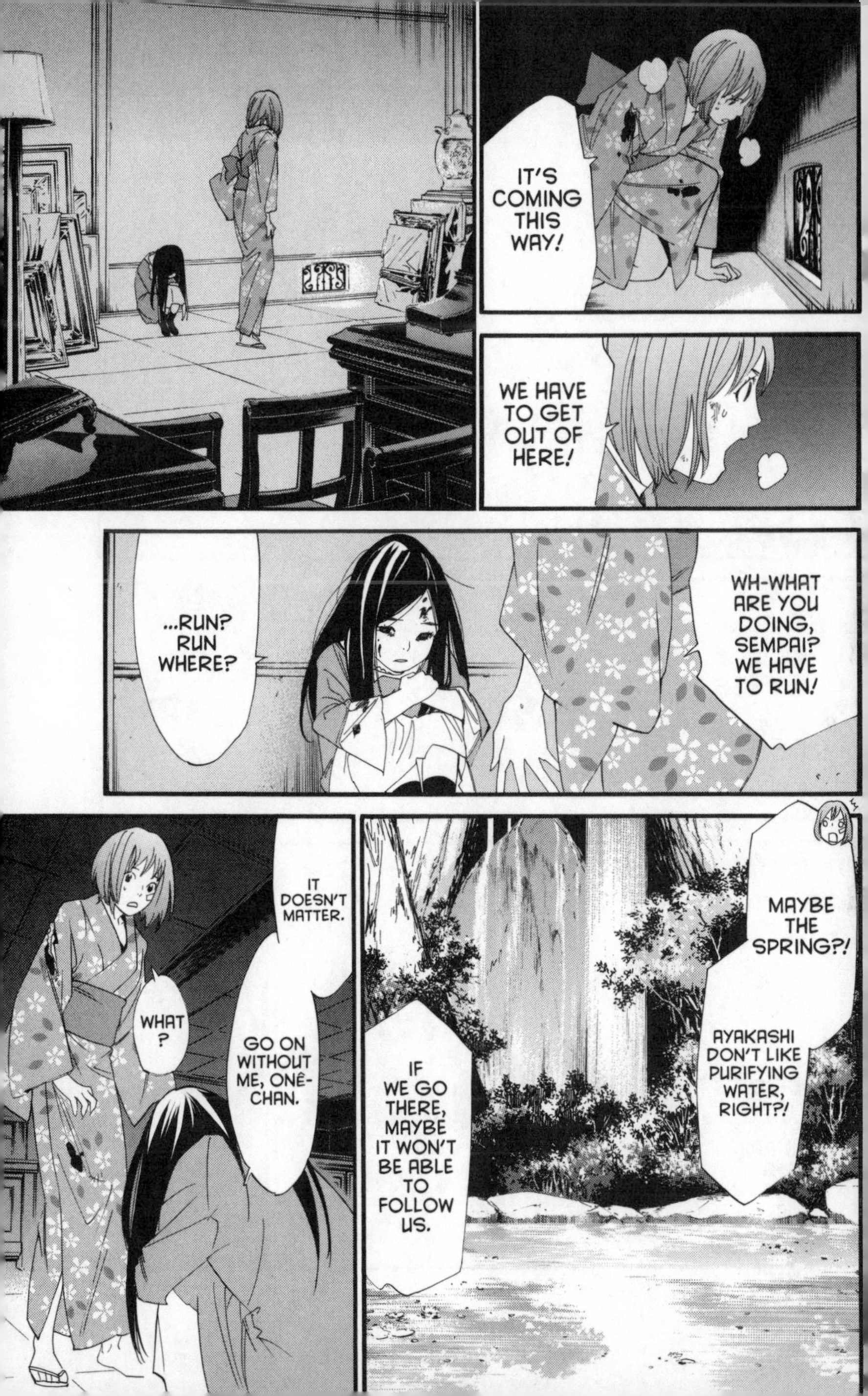
IT'S COMING THIS WAY!
WE HAVE TO GET OUT OF HERE!
WH-WHAT ARE YOU DOING, SEMPAI? WE HAVE TO RUN!
...RUN? RUN WHERE?
MAYBE THE SPRING?!
AYAKASHI DON'T LIKE PURIFYING WATER, RIGHT?!
IF WE GO THERE, MAYBE IT WON'T BE ABLE TO FOLLOW US.
IT DOESN'T MATTER.
WHAT?
GO ON WITHOUT ME, ONÊ-CHAN.

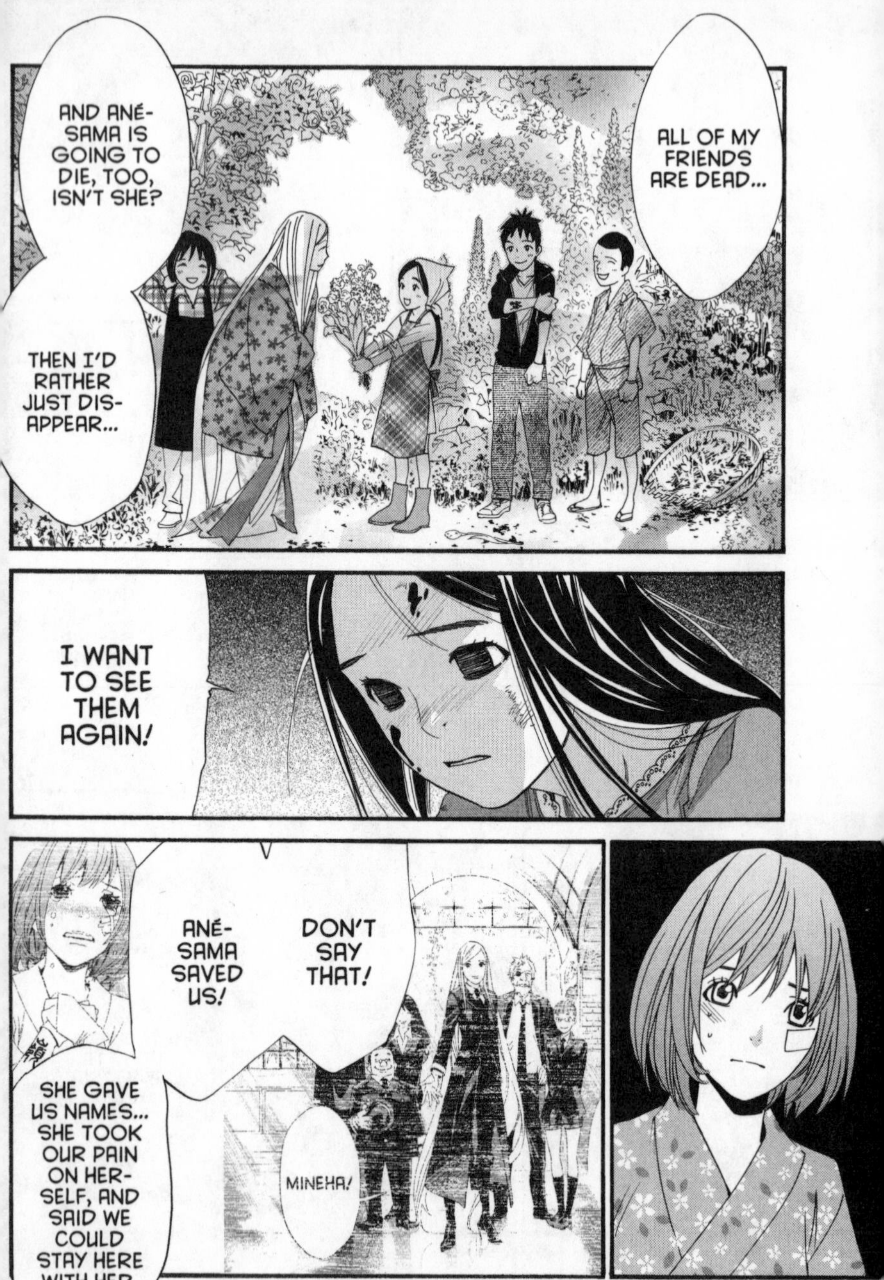
ALL OF MY FRIENDS ARE DEAD...
AND ANÉ-SAMA IS GOING TO DIE, TOO, ISN'T SHE?
THEN I'D RATHER JUST DIS-APPEAR...
I WANT TO SEE THEM AGAIN!
DON'T SAY THAT!
ANÉ-SAMA SAVED US!
SHE GAVE US NAMES... SHE TOOK OUR PAIN ON HER-SELF, AND SAID WE COULD STAY HERE WITH HER.
MINEHA!

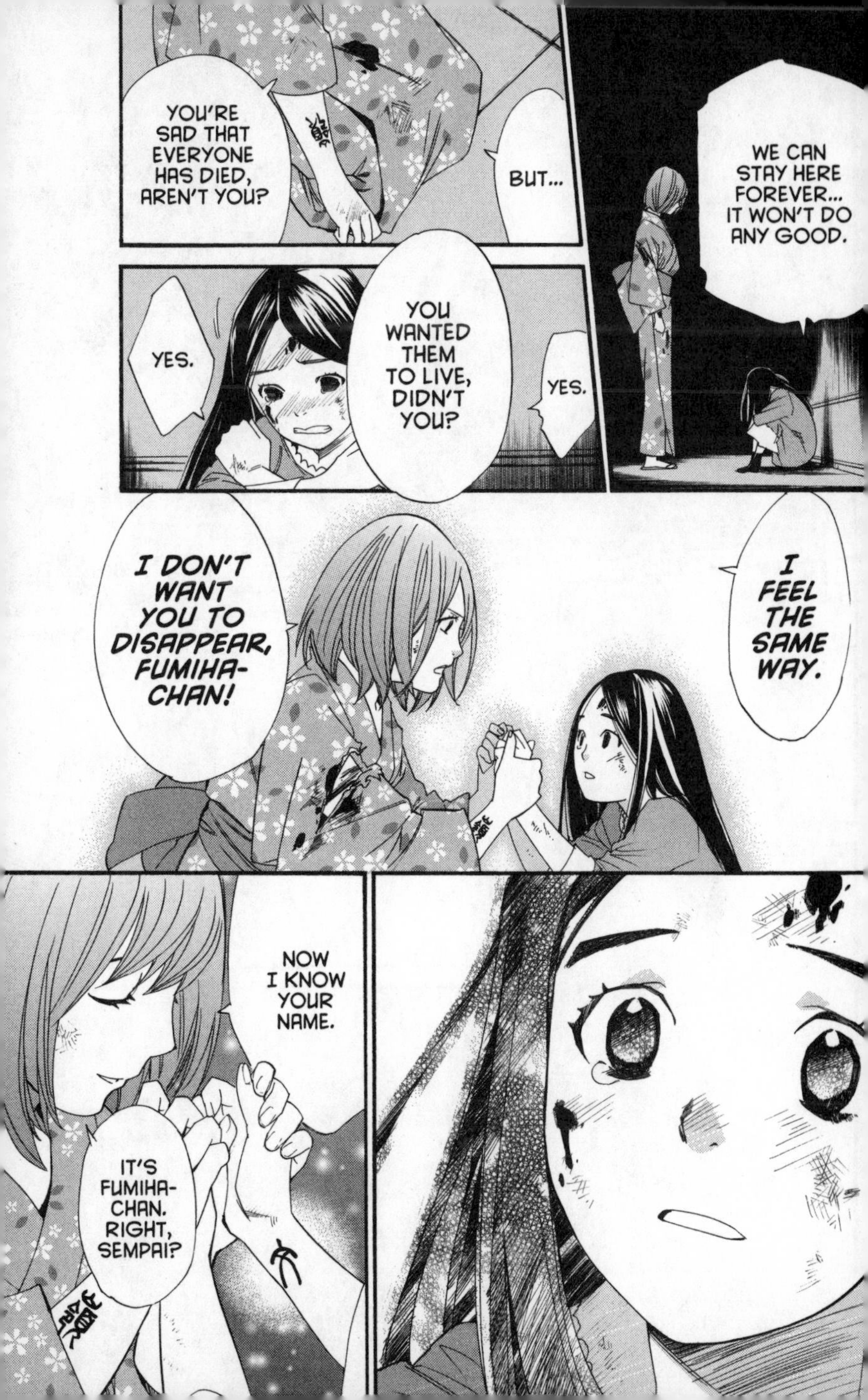
WE CAN STAY HERE FOREVER... IT WON'T DO ANY GOOD.
BUT...
YOU'RE SAD THAT EVERYONE HAS DIED, AREN'T YOU?
YES.
YOU WANTED THEM TO LIVE, DIDN'T YOU?
YES.
I FEEL THE SAME WAY.
I DON'T WANT YOU TO DISAPPEAR, FUMIHA-CHAN!
NOW I KNOW YOUR NAME.
IT'S FUMIHA-CHAN. RIGHT, SEMPAI?

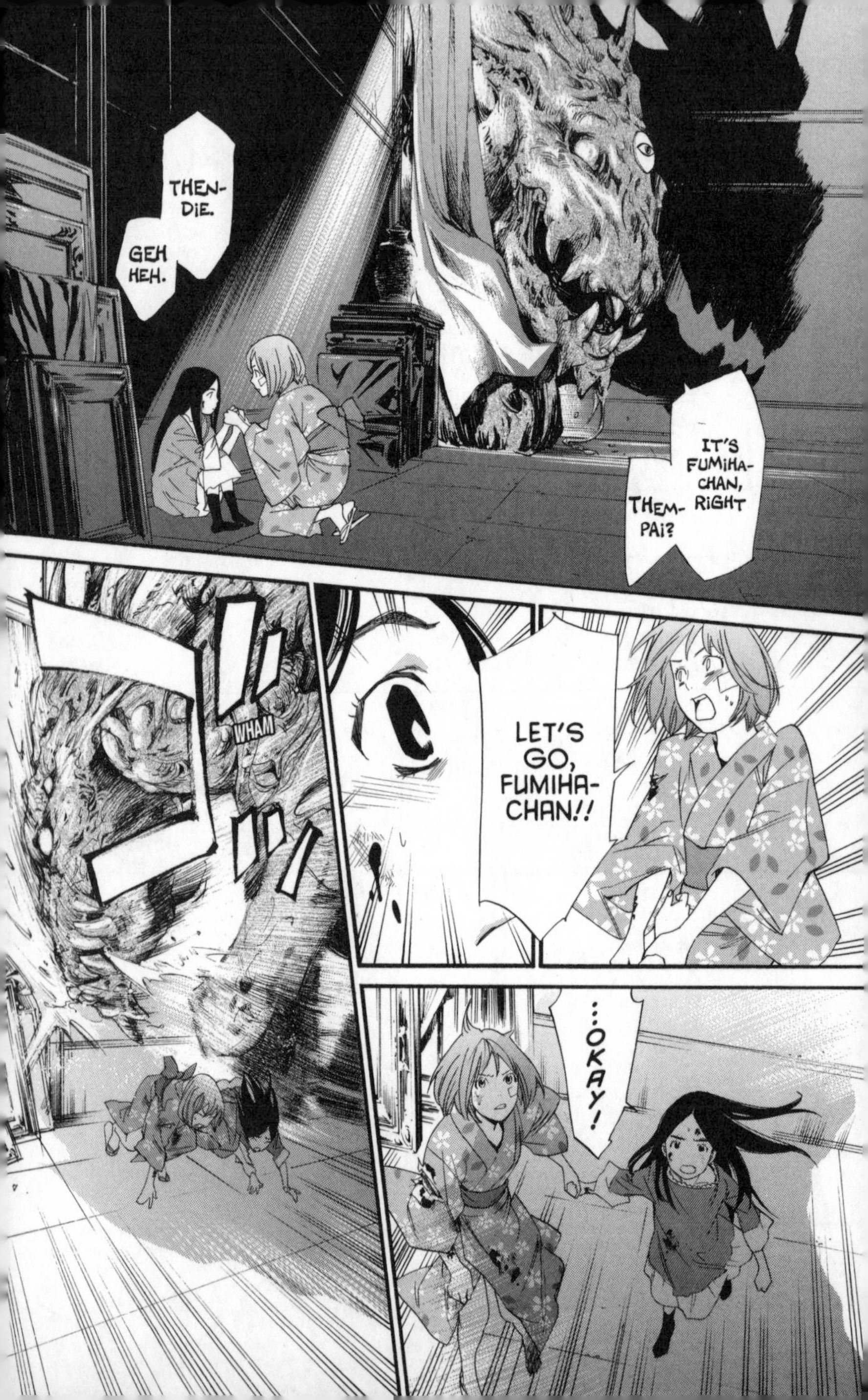
IT'S FUMIHA-CHAN, RIGHT
THEM-PAI?
THEN-DIE.
GEH HEH.
LET'S GO, FUMIHA-CHAN!!
...OKAY!
WHAM

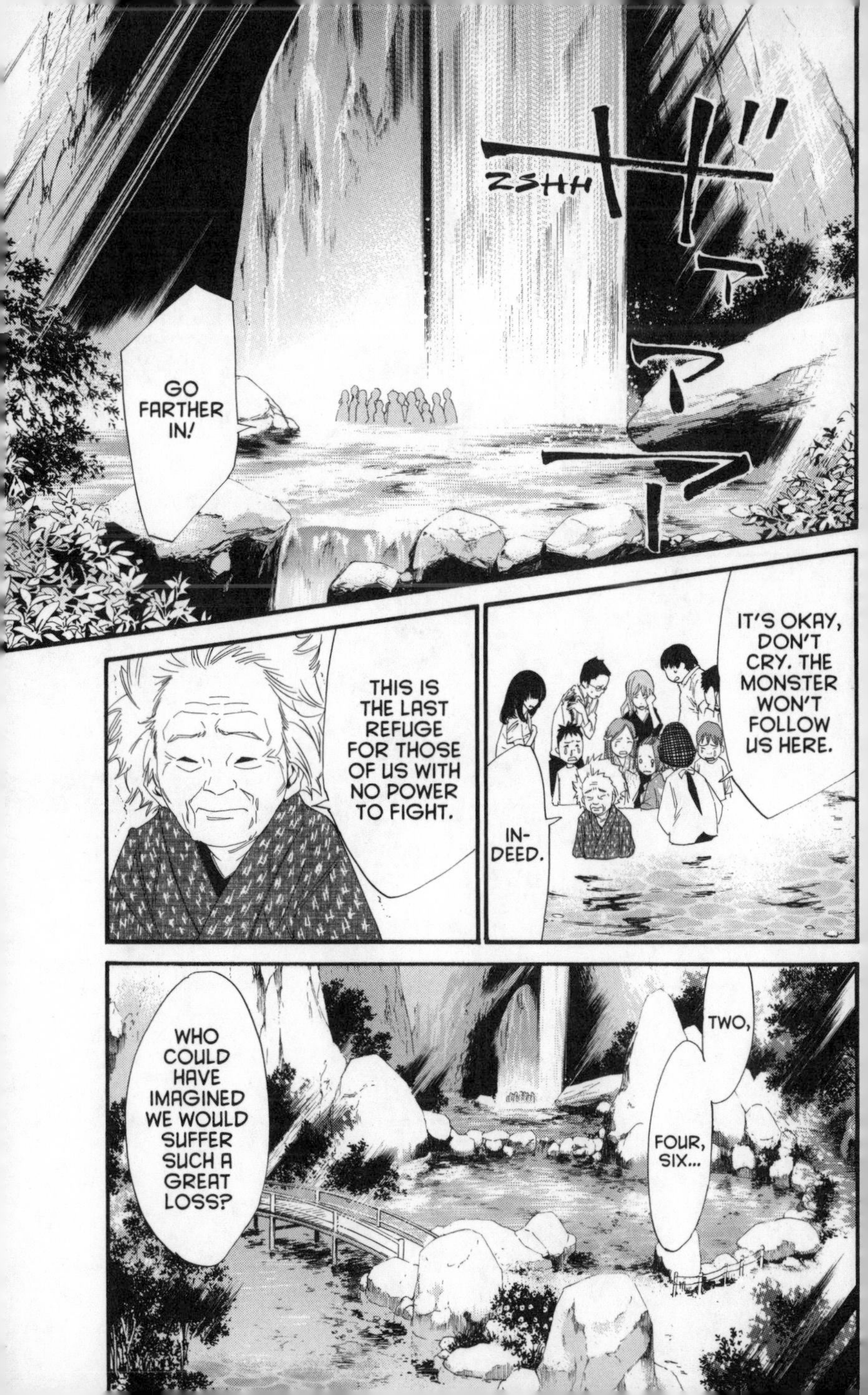
ZSHH
GO FARTHER IN!
IT'S OKAY, DON'T CRY. THE MONSTER WON'T FOLLOW US HERE.
IN-DEED.
THIS IS THE LAST REFUGE FOR THOSE OF US WITH NO POWER TO FIGHT.
TWO,
FOUR, SIX...
WHO COULD HAVE IMAGINED WE WOULD SUFFER SUCH A GREAT LOSS?

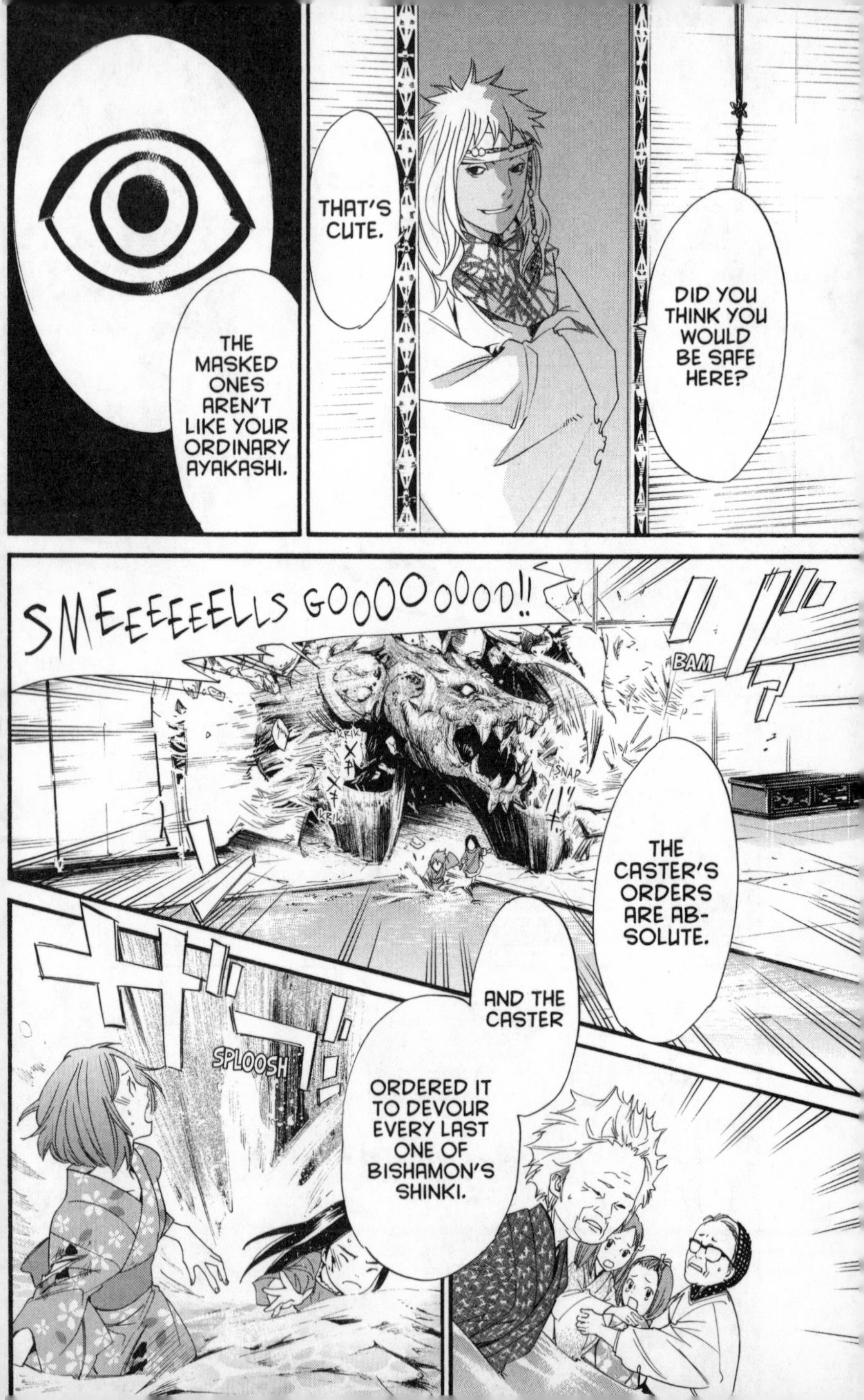
DID YOU THINK YOU WOULD BE SAFE HERE?
THAT'S CUTE.
THE MASKED ONES AREN'T LIKE YOUR ORDINARY AYAKASHI.
BAM
SMEEEEEELLS GOOOOOOOD!!
SNAP
KRIK
KRIK
THE CASTER'S ORDERS ARE AB-SOLUTE.
AND THE CASTER
ORDERED IT TO DEVOUR EVERY LAST ONE OF BISHAMON'S SHINKI.
SPLOOSH

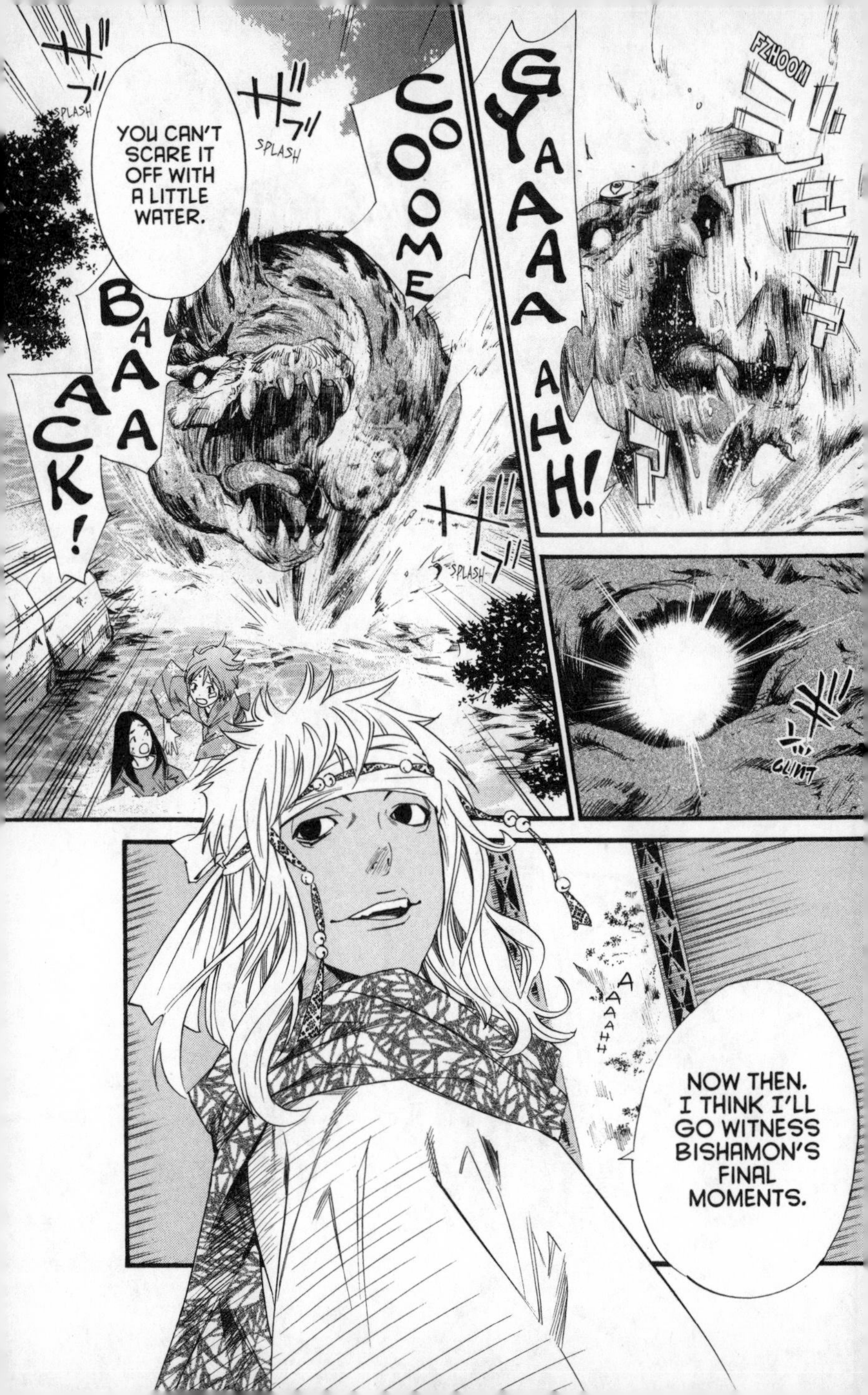
FZHOOM
GYAAAAAHH!
CLINT
SPLASH
YOU CAN'T SCARE IT OFF WITH A LITTLE WATER.
SPLASH
COOOME
BAAAACK!
SPLASH
AAAAHH
NOW THEN. I THINK I'LL GO WITNESS BISHAMON'S FINAL MOMENTS.

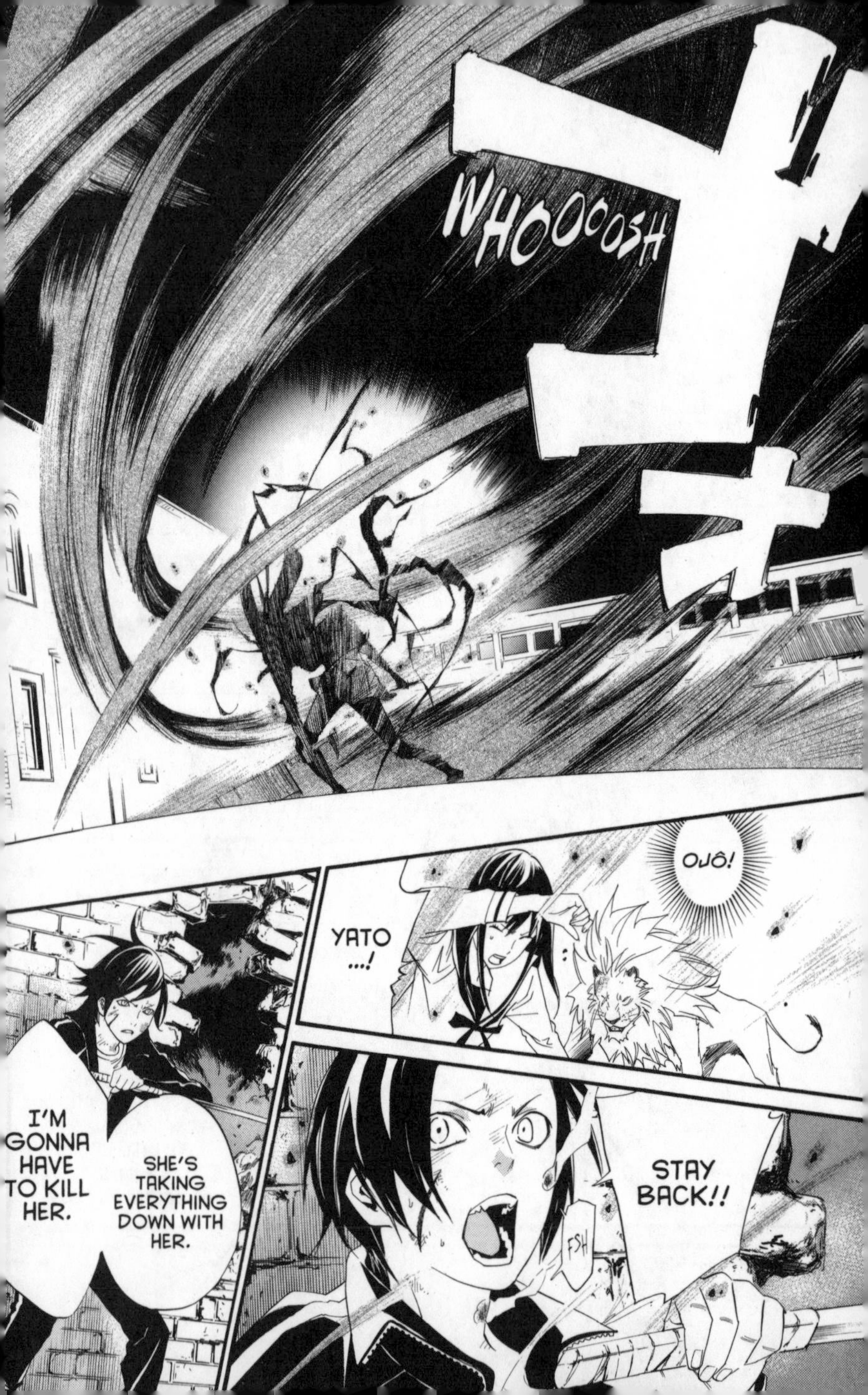
WHOOOOSH
OJÔ!
YATO ...!
STAY BACK!!
FSH
SHE'S TAKING EVERYTHING DOWN WITH HER.
I'M GONNA HAVE TO KILL HER.

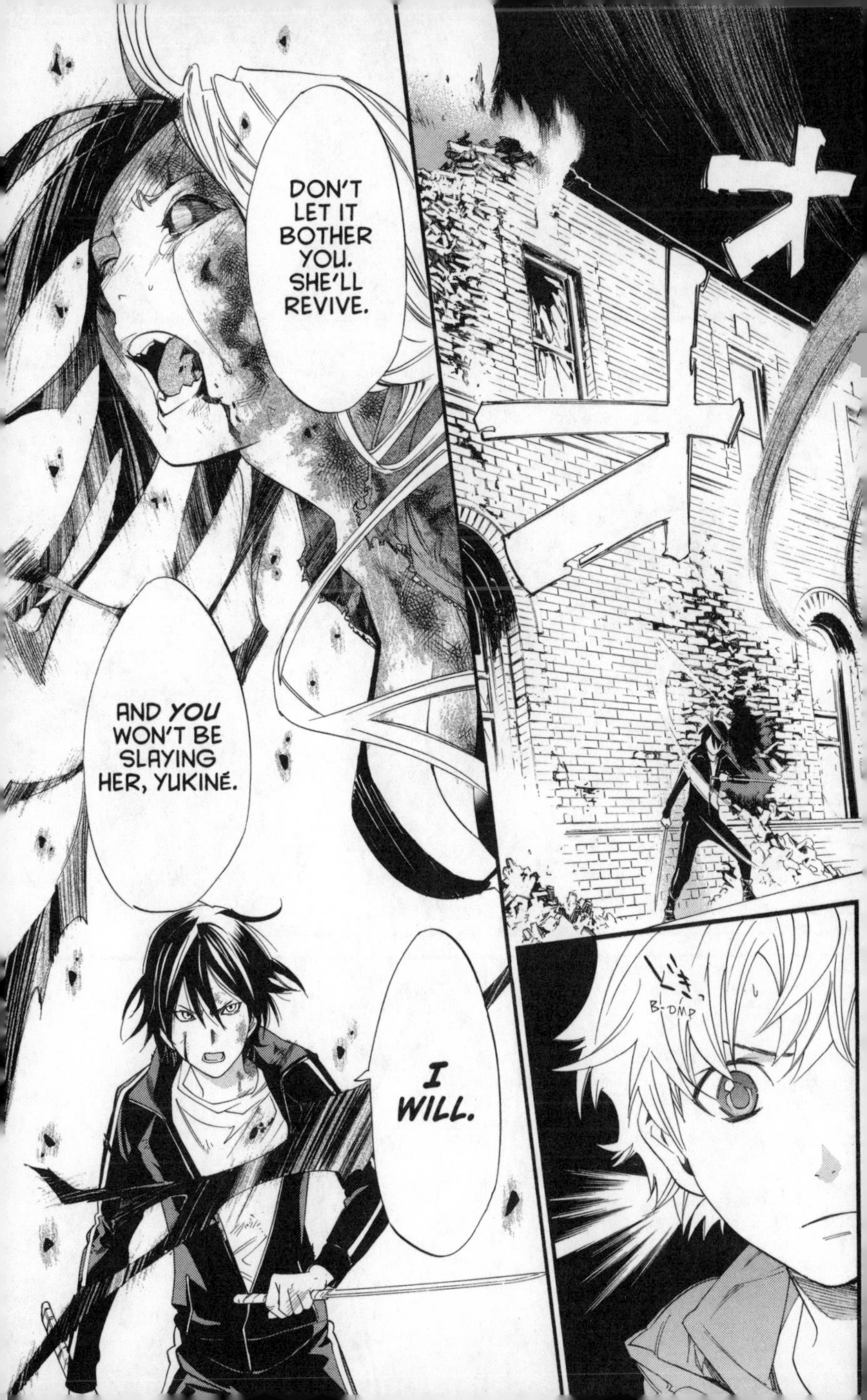
B-DMP
DON'T LET IT BOTHER YOU. SHE'LL REVIVE.
AND *YOU* WON'T BE SLAYING HER, YUKINÉ.
I WILL.

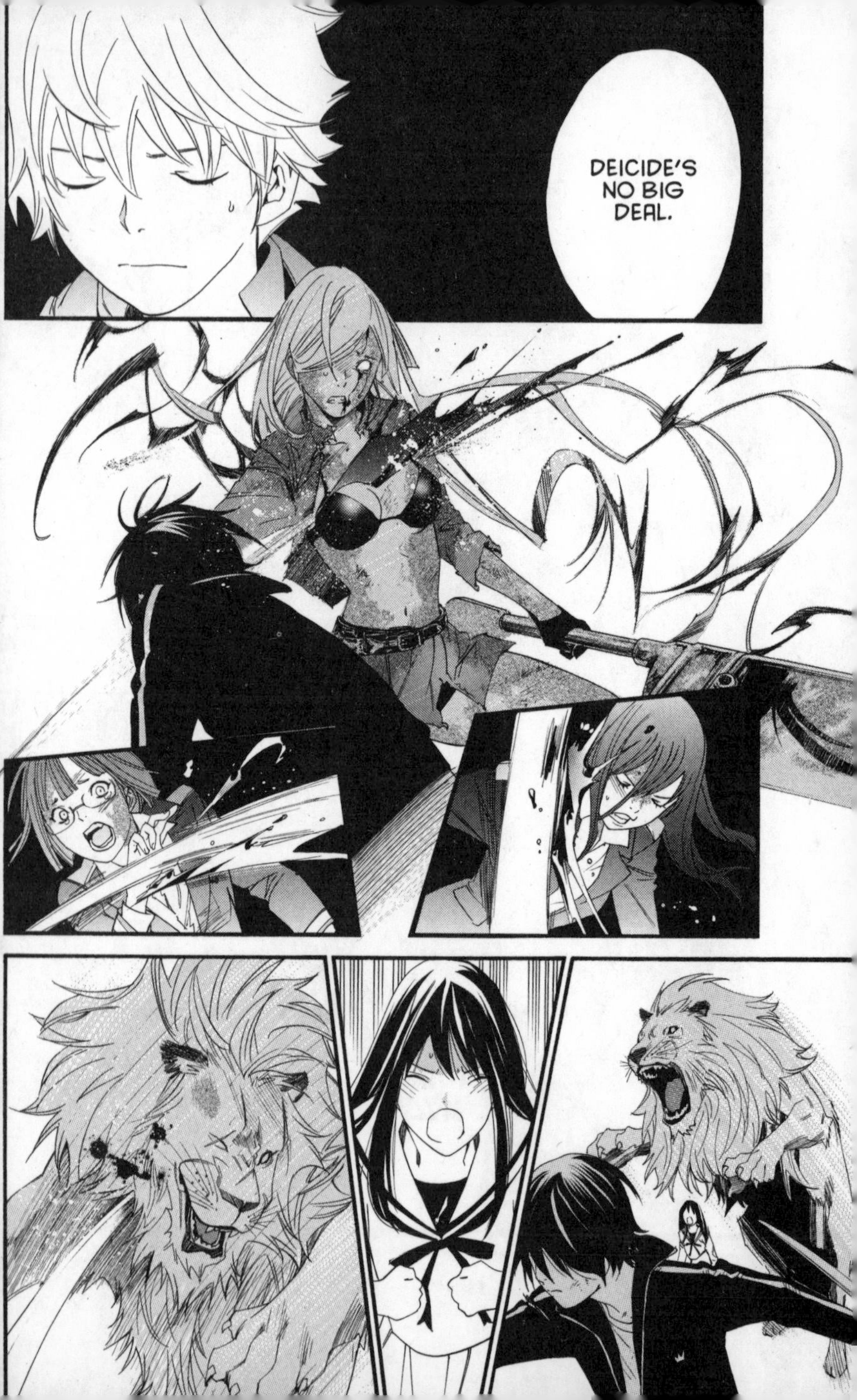
DEICIDE'S NO BIG DEAL.

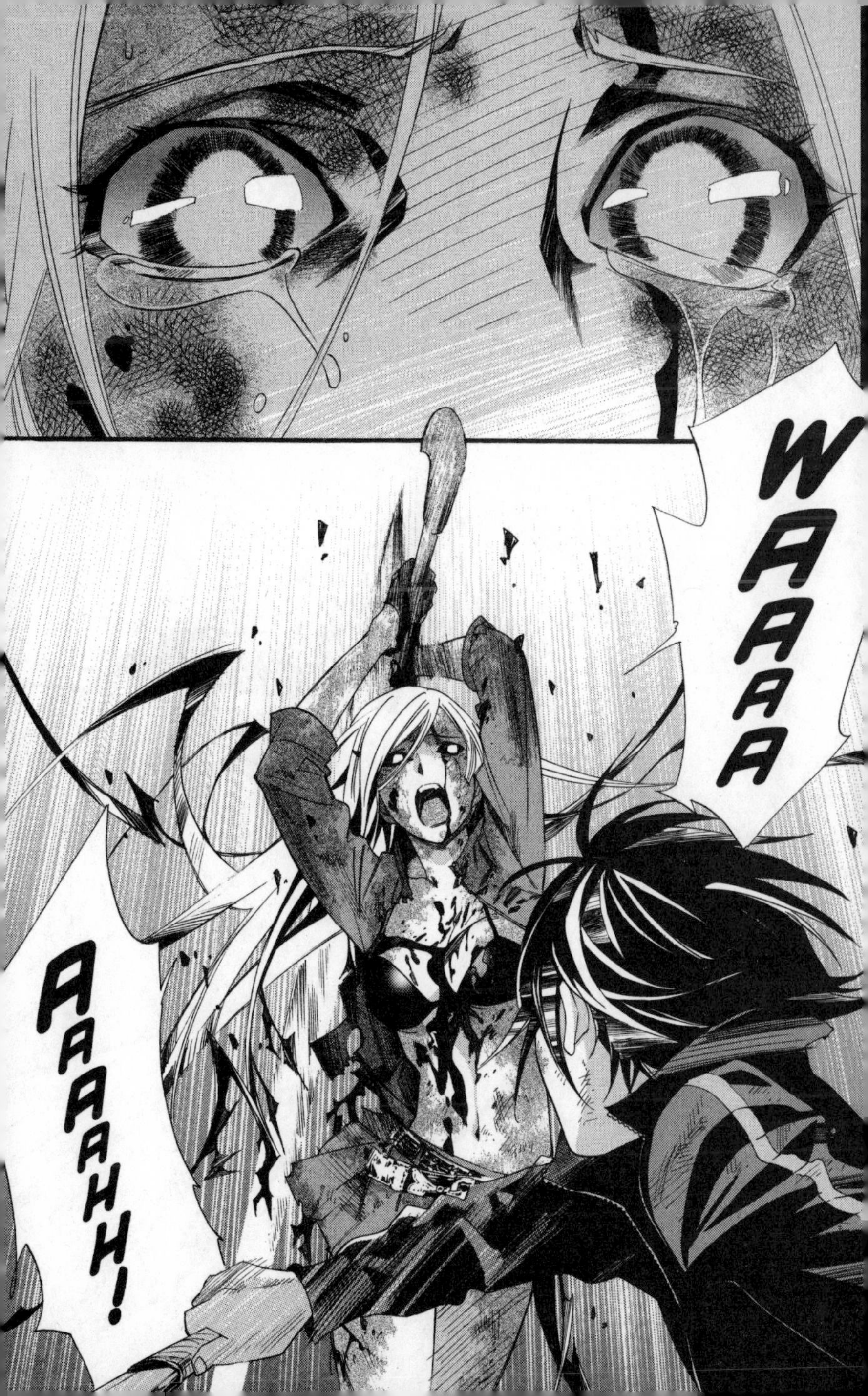
WAAAAA
AAAAAHH!

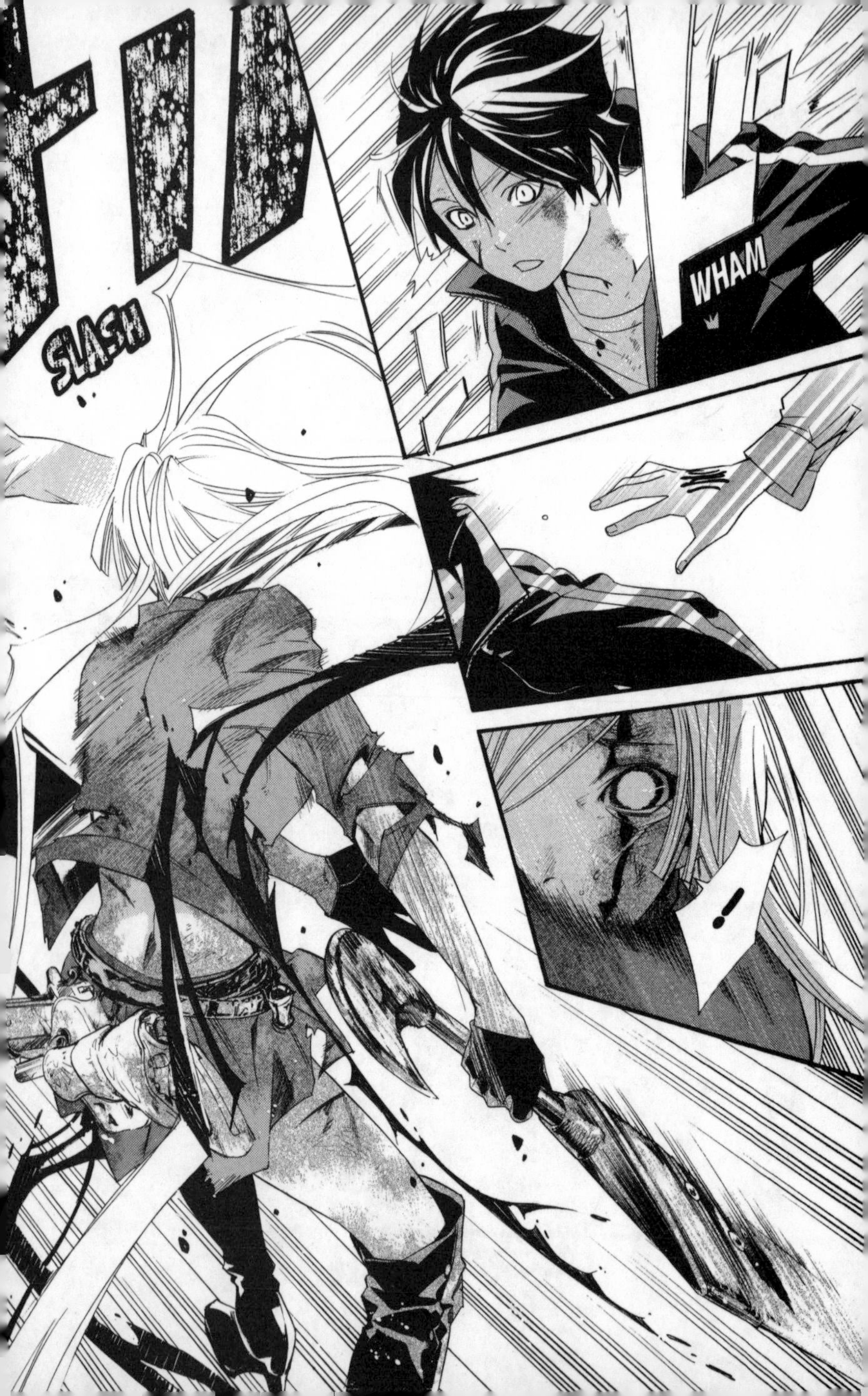
WHAM
SLASH

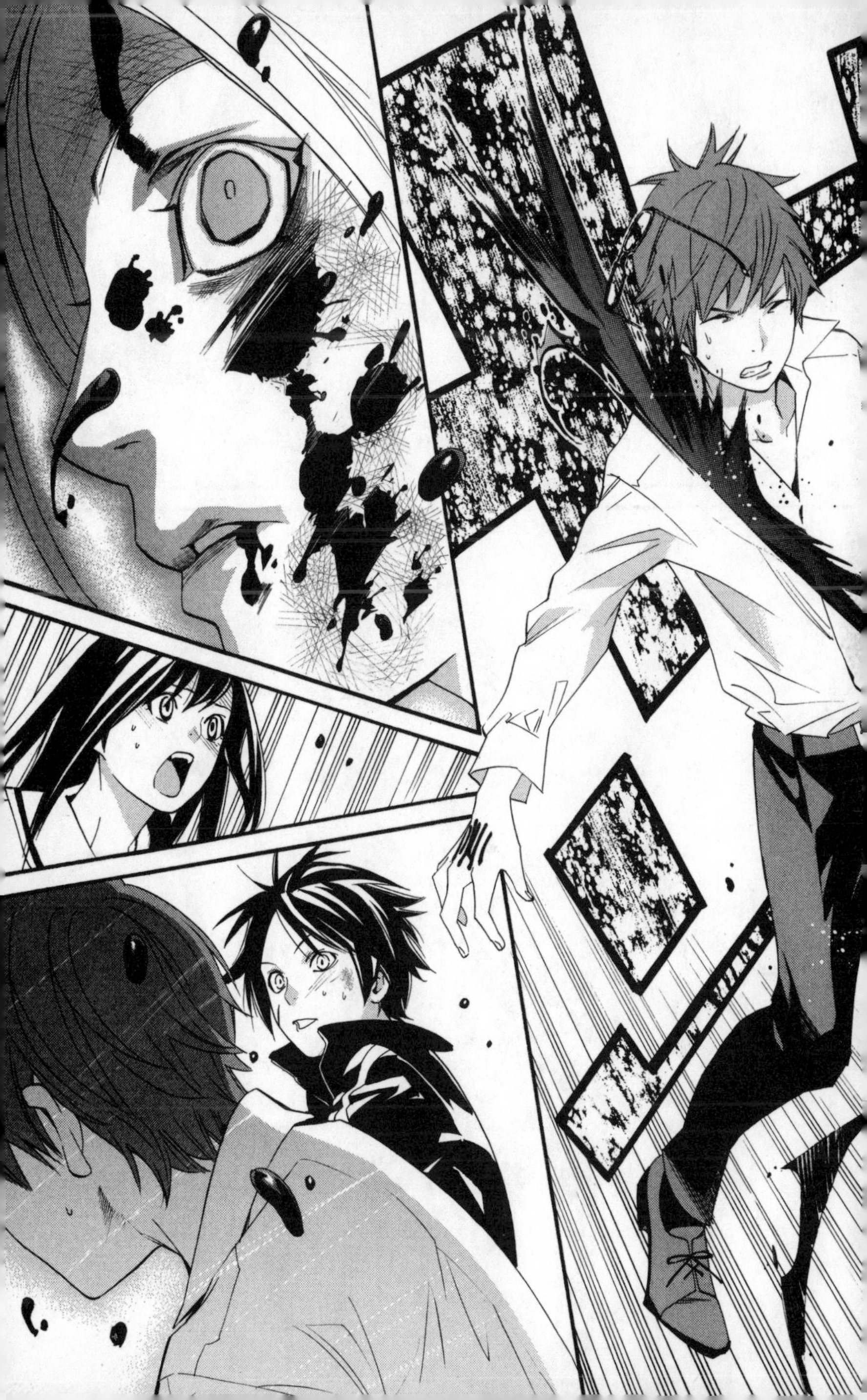

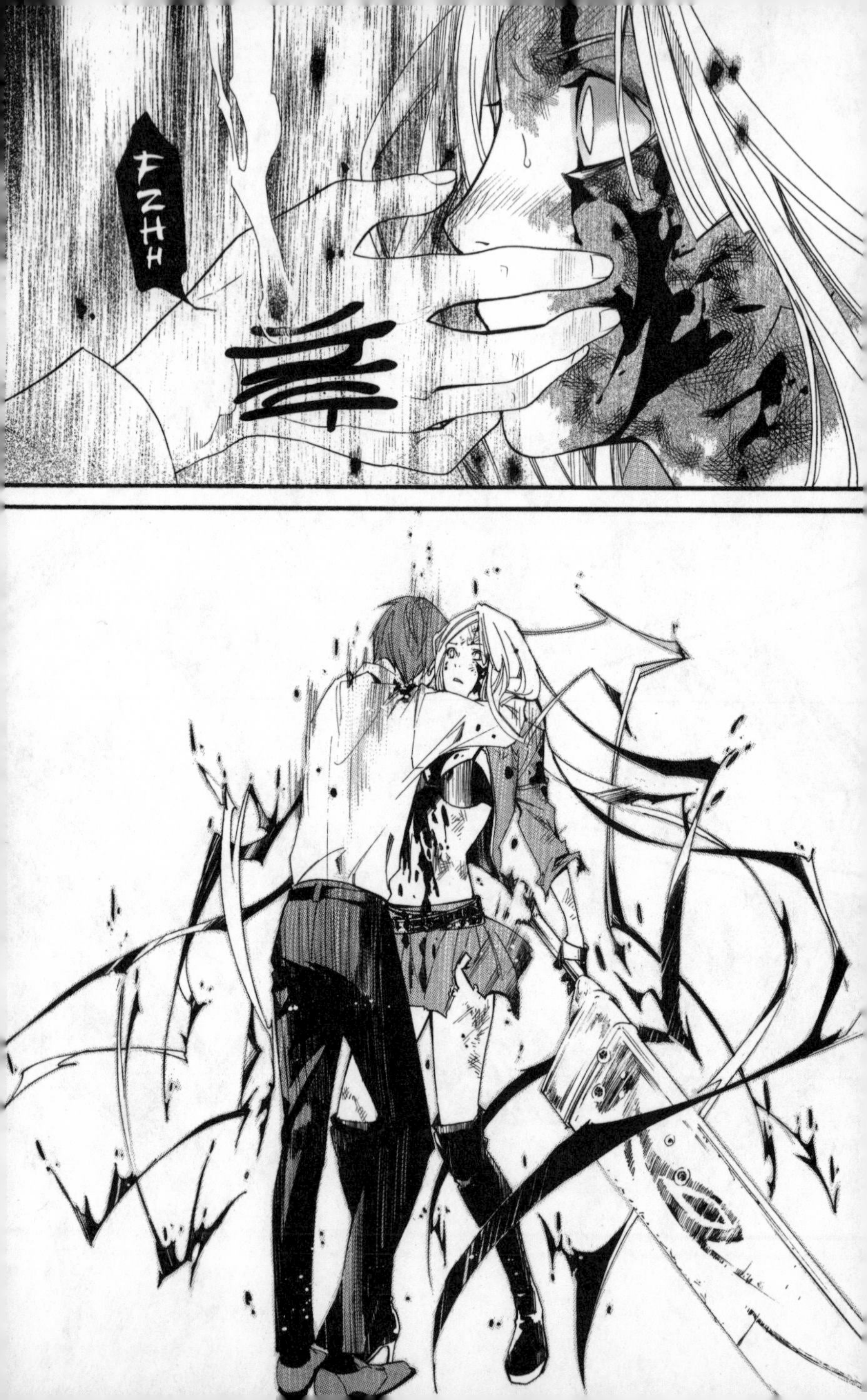
FZHH

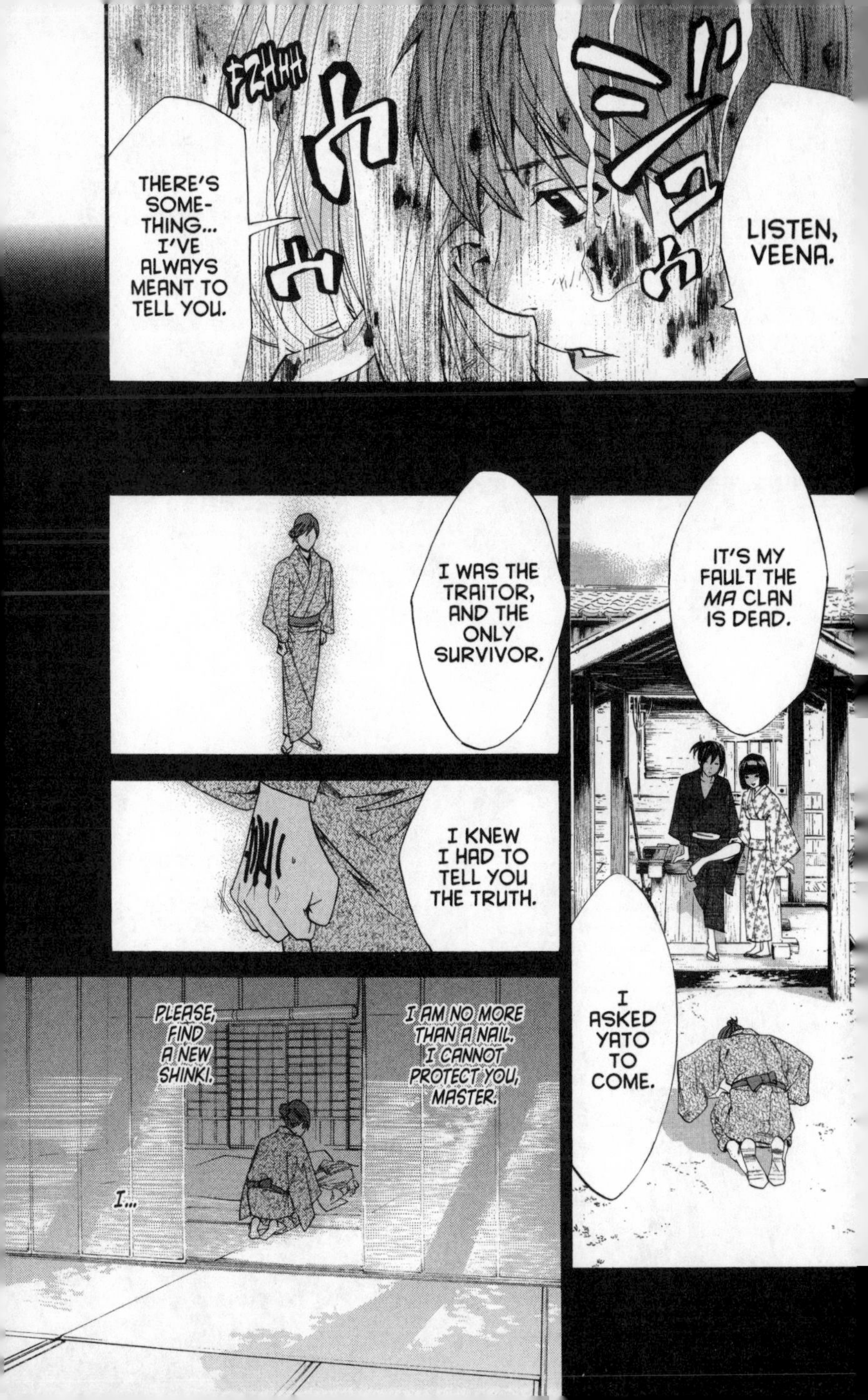
LISTEN, VEENA.
FZHHH
THERE'S SOME-THING... I'VE ALWAYS MEANT TO TELL YOU.
IT'S MY FAULT THE *MA* CLAN IS DEAD.
I ASKED YATO TO COME.
I WAS THE TRAITOR, AND THE ONLY SURVIVOR.
I KNEW I HAD TO TELL YOU THE TRUTH.
I AM NO MORE THAN A NAIL. I CANNOT PROTECT YOU, MASTER.
PLEASE, FIND A NEW SHINKI.
I...

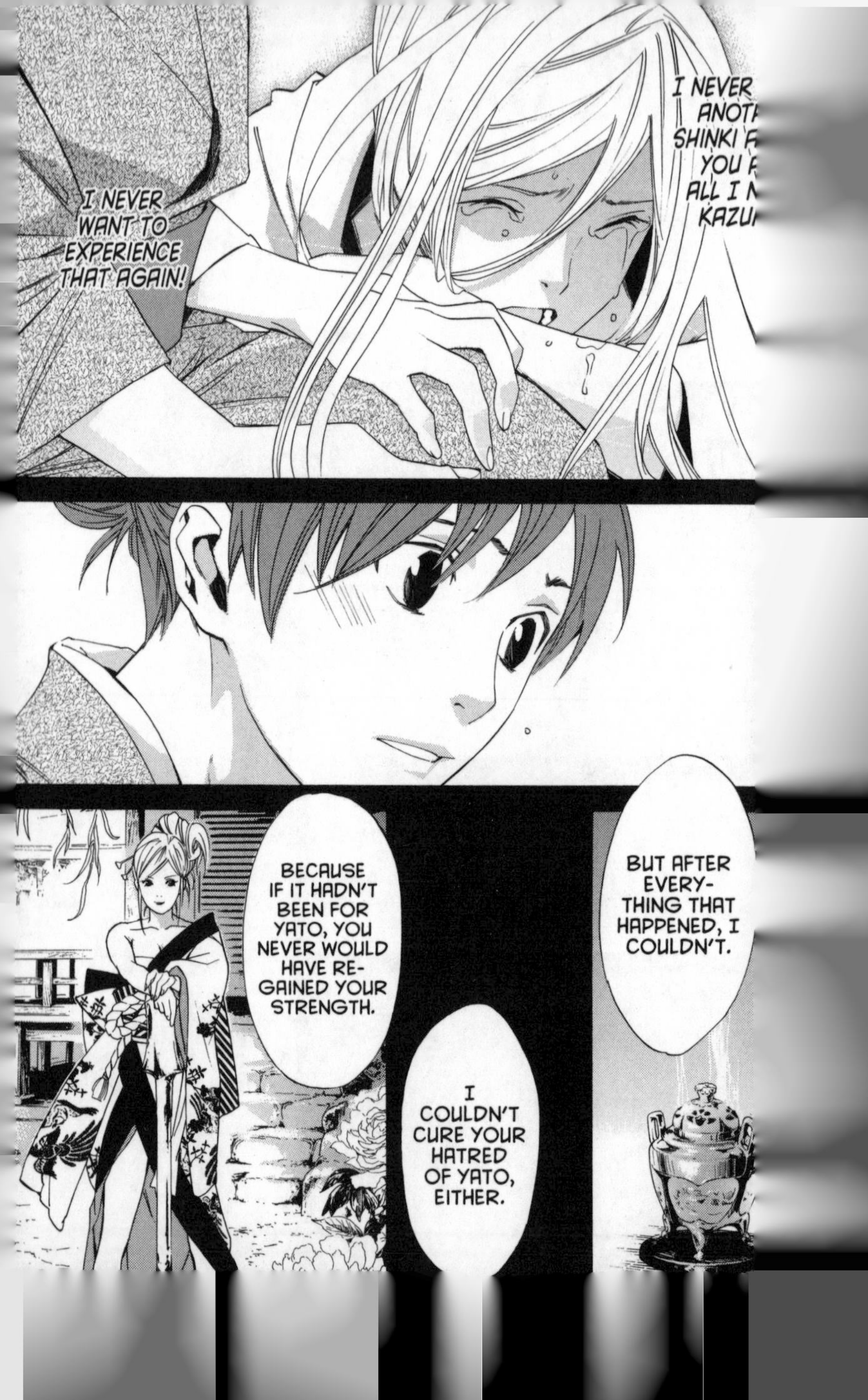
I NEVER ANOT SHINKI F YOU ALL I KAZU
I NEVER WANT TO EXPERIENCE THAT AGAIN!
BUT AFTER EVERY-THING THAT HAPPENED, I COULDN'T.
I COULDN'T CURE YOUR HATRED OF YATO, EITHER.
BECAUSE IF IT HADN'T BEEN FOR YATO, YOU NEVER WOULD HAVE RE-GAINED YOUR STRENGTH.

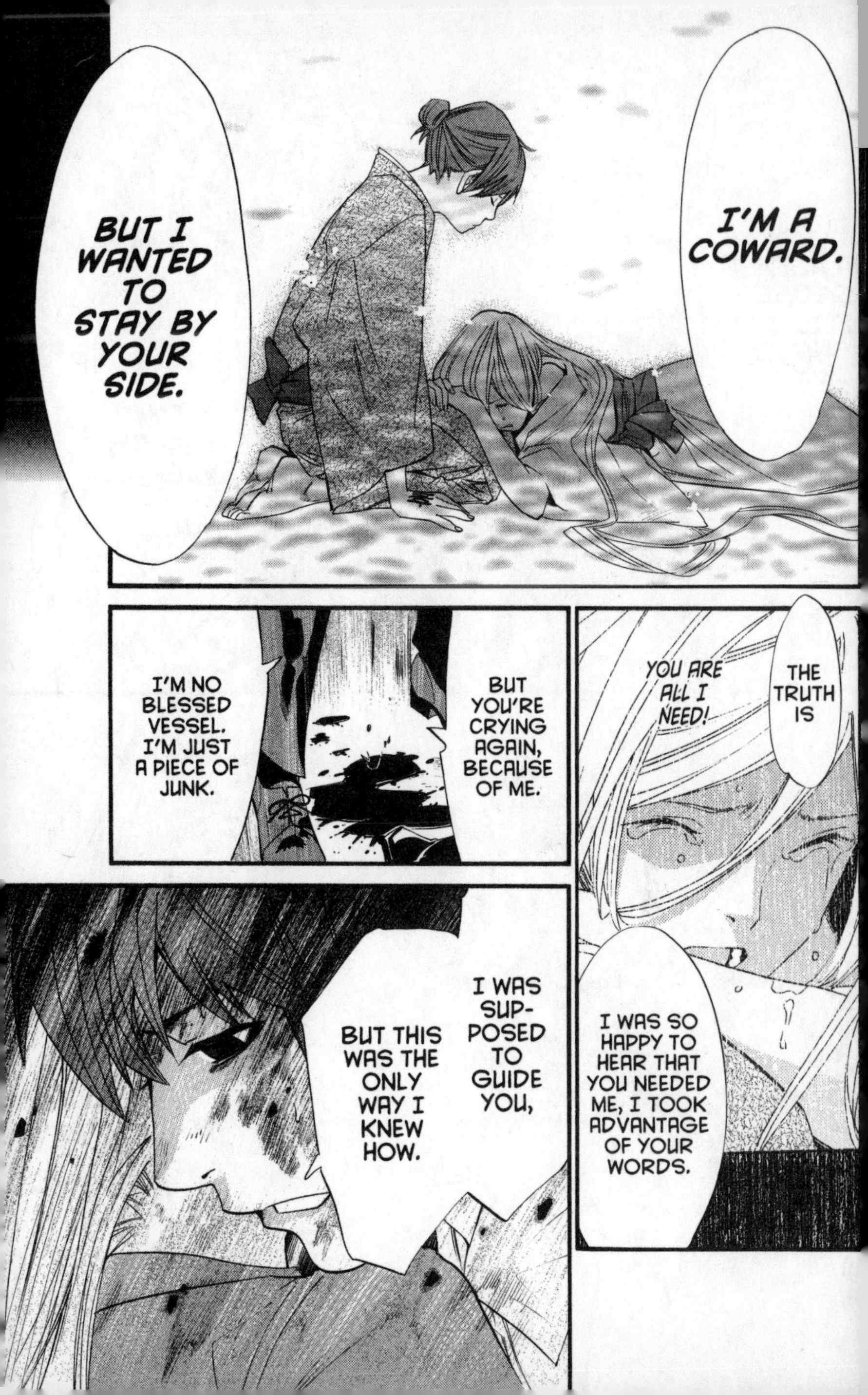
I'M A COWARD.
BUT I WANTED TO STAY BY YOUR SIDE.
THE TRUTH IS
YOU ARE ALL I NEED!
I WAS SO HAPPY TO HEAR THAT YOU NEEDED ME, I TOOK ADVANTAGE OF YOUR WORDS.
BUT YOU'RE CRYING AGAIN, BECAUSE OF ME.
I'M NO BLESSED VESSEL. I'M JUST A PIECE OF JUNK.
I WAS SUP-POSED TO GUIDE YOU,
BUT THIS WAS THE ONLY WAY I KNEW HOW.

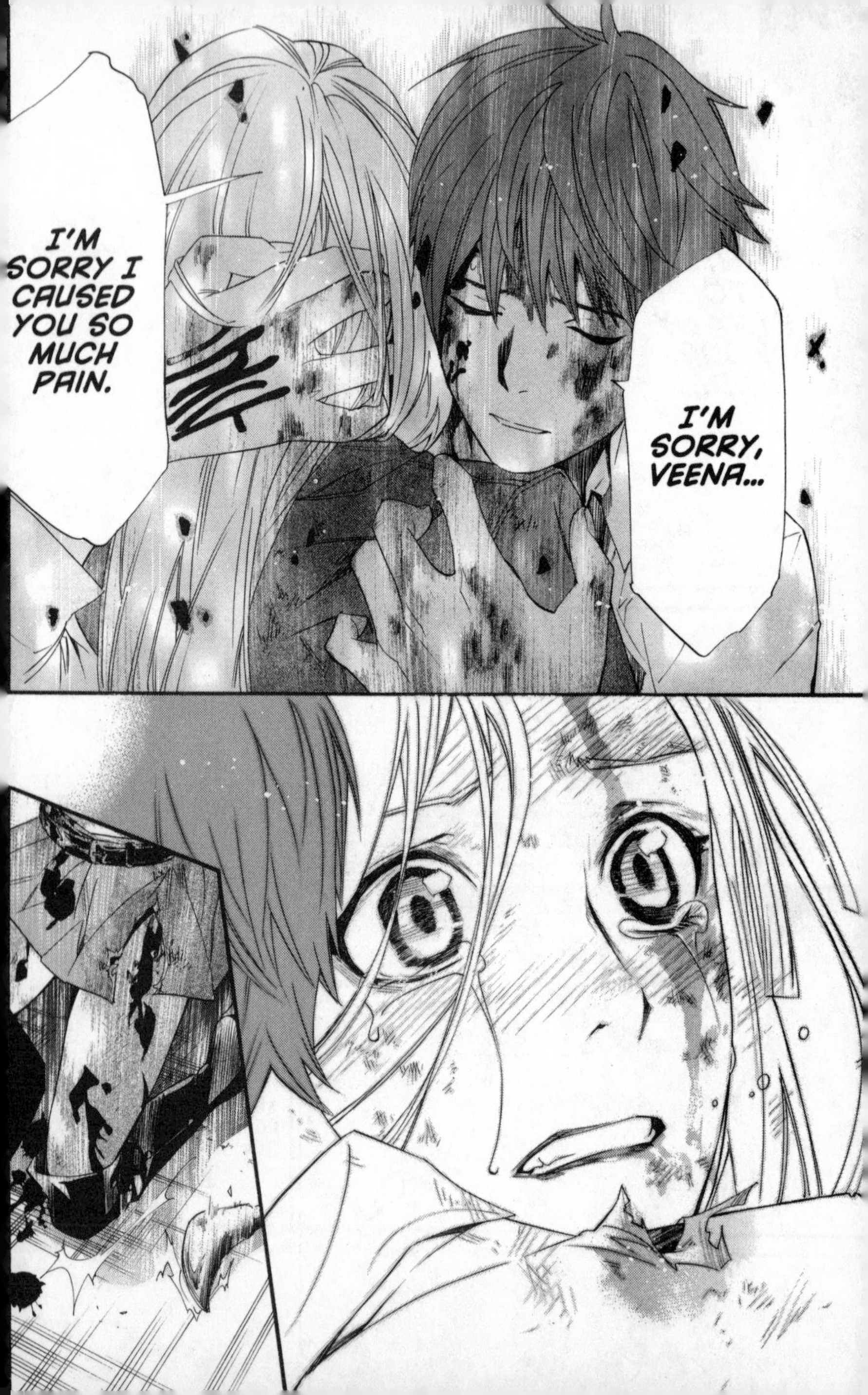
I'M SORRY, VEENA...
I'M SORRY I CAUSED YOU SO MUCH PAIN.

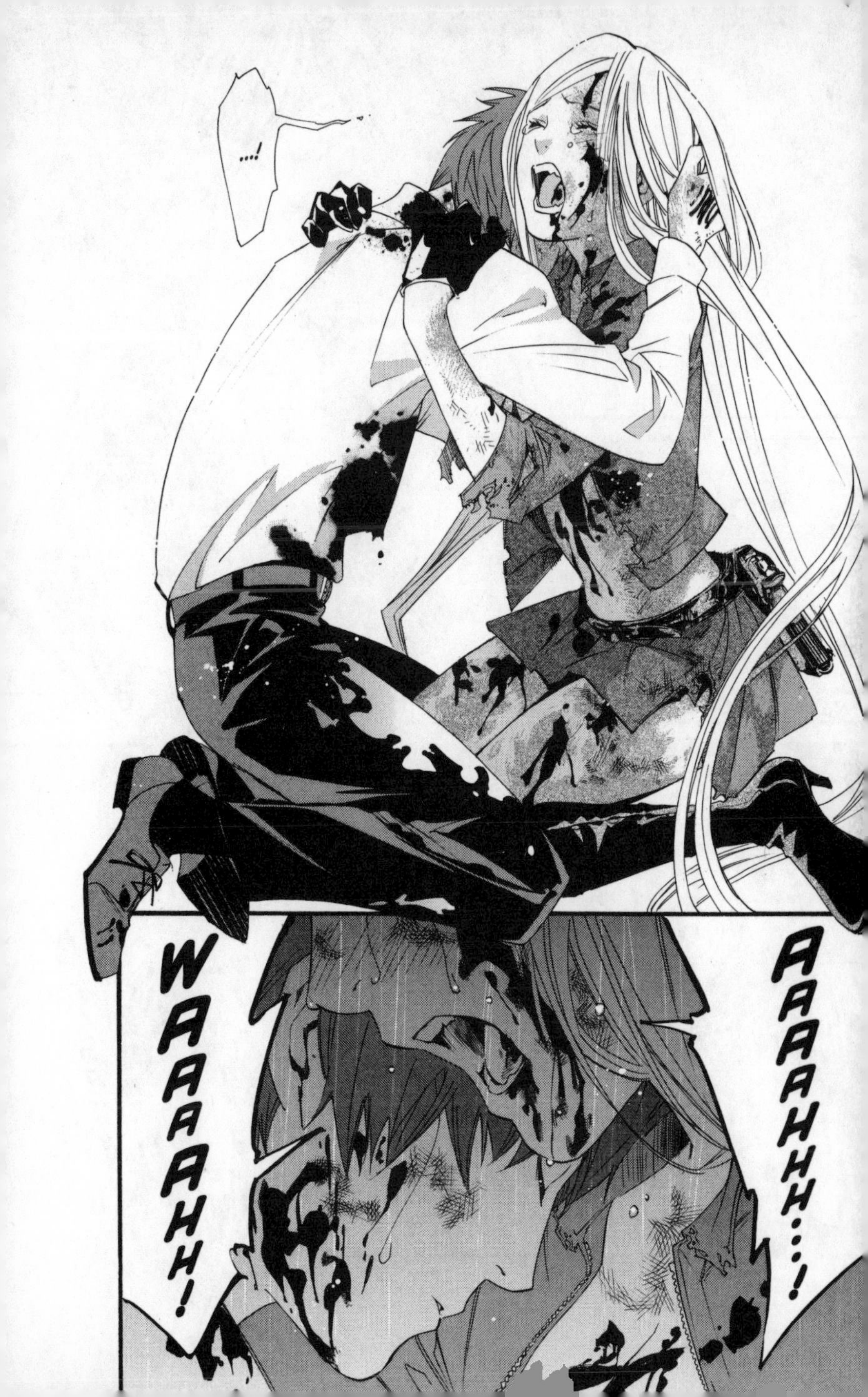
...!
AAAAAHHH...!
WAAAAAHH!

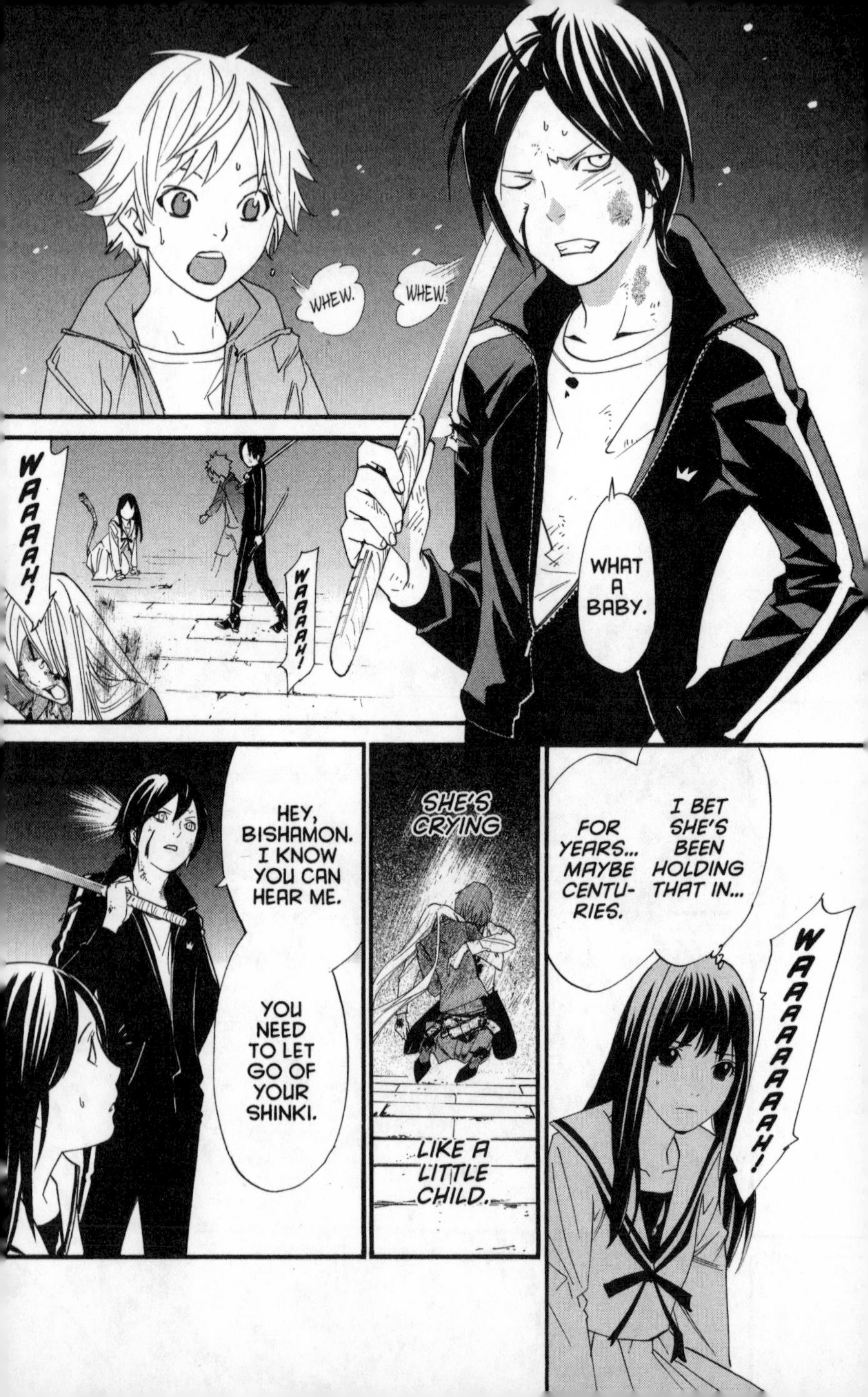
WHAT A BABY.
WHEW.
WHEW.
WAAAAAH!
WAAAAAH!
I BET SHE'S BEEN HOLDING THAT IN...
FOR YEARS... MAYBE CENTURIES.
WAAAAAAAAAH!
SHE'S CRYING
LIKE A LITTLE CHILD.
HEY, BISHAMON. I KNOW YOU CAN HEAR ME.
YOU NEED TO LET GO OF YOUR SHINKI.

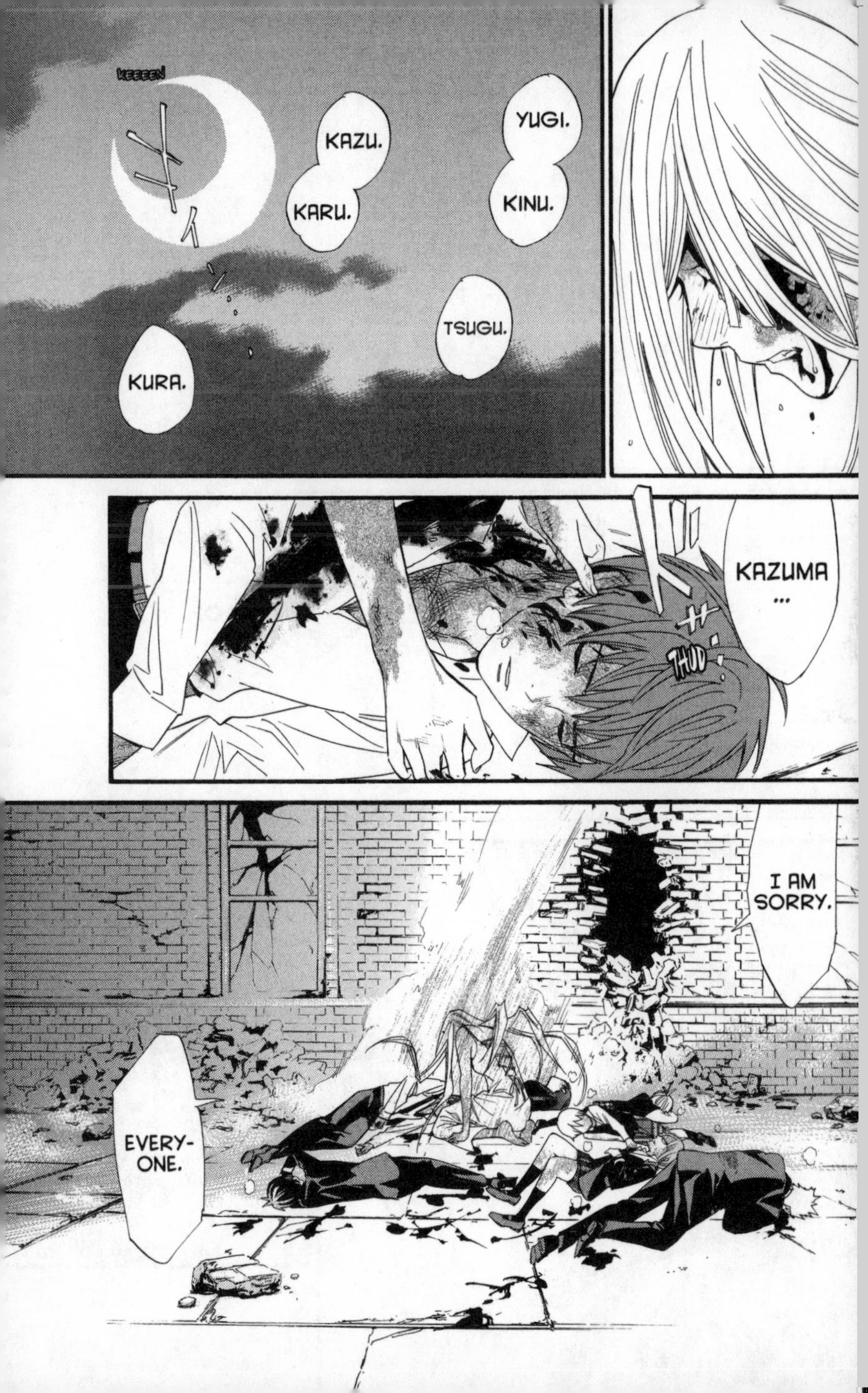
YUGI.
KINU.
KAZU.
KARU.
KEEEEN
TSUGU.
KURA.
KAZUMA ...
THUD
I AM SORRY.
EVERY-ONE.

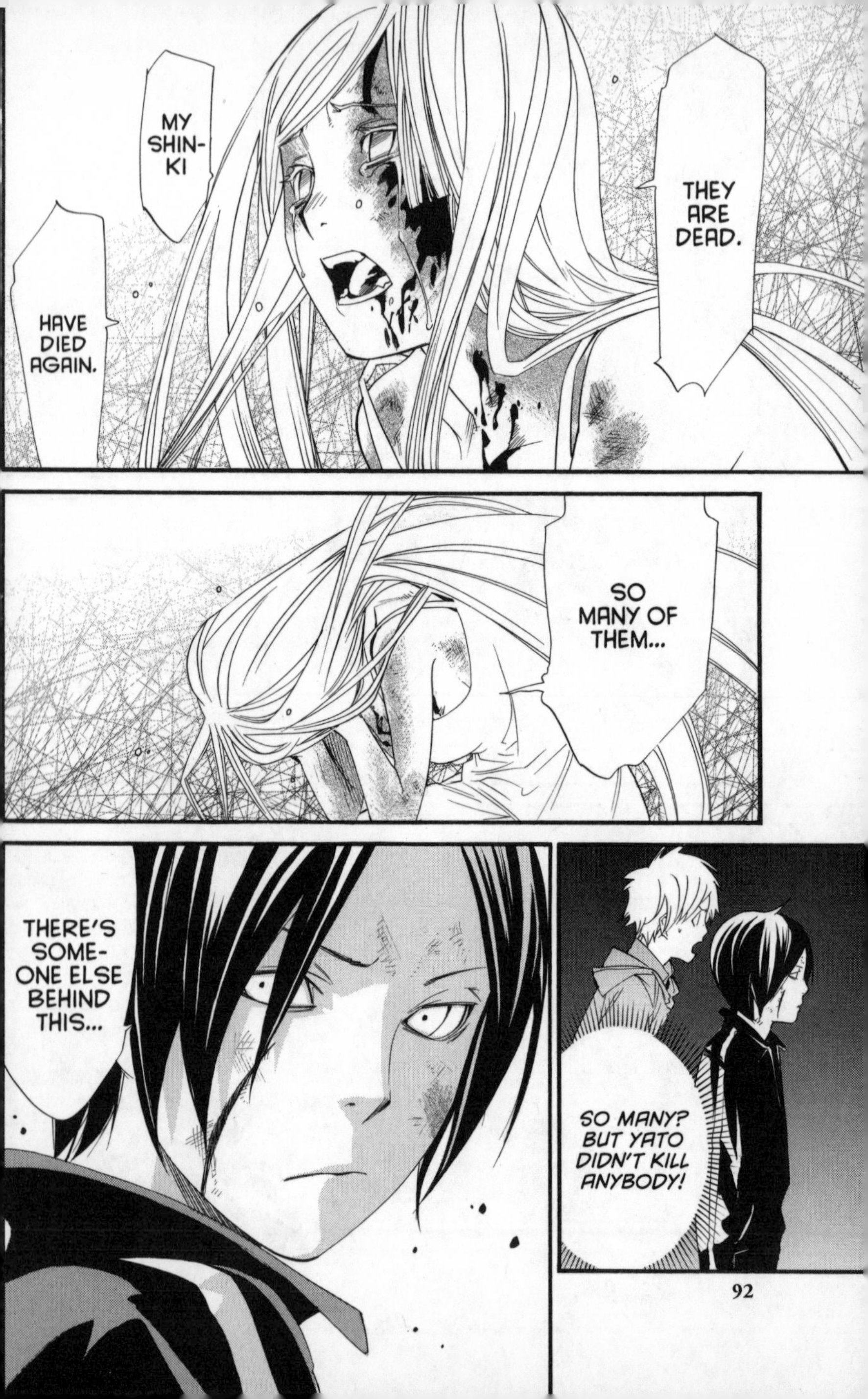
THEY ARE DEAD.
MY SHIN-KI
HAVE DIED AGAIN.
SO MANY OF THEM...
SO MANY? BUT YATO DIDN'T KILL ANYBODY!
THERE'S SOME-ONE ELSE BEHIND THIS...

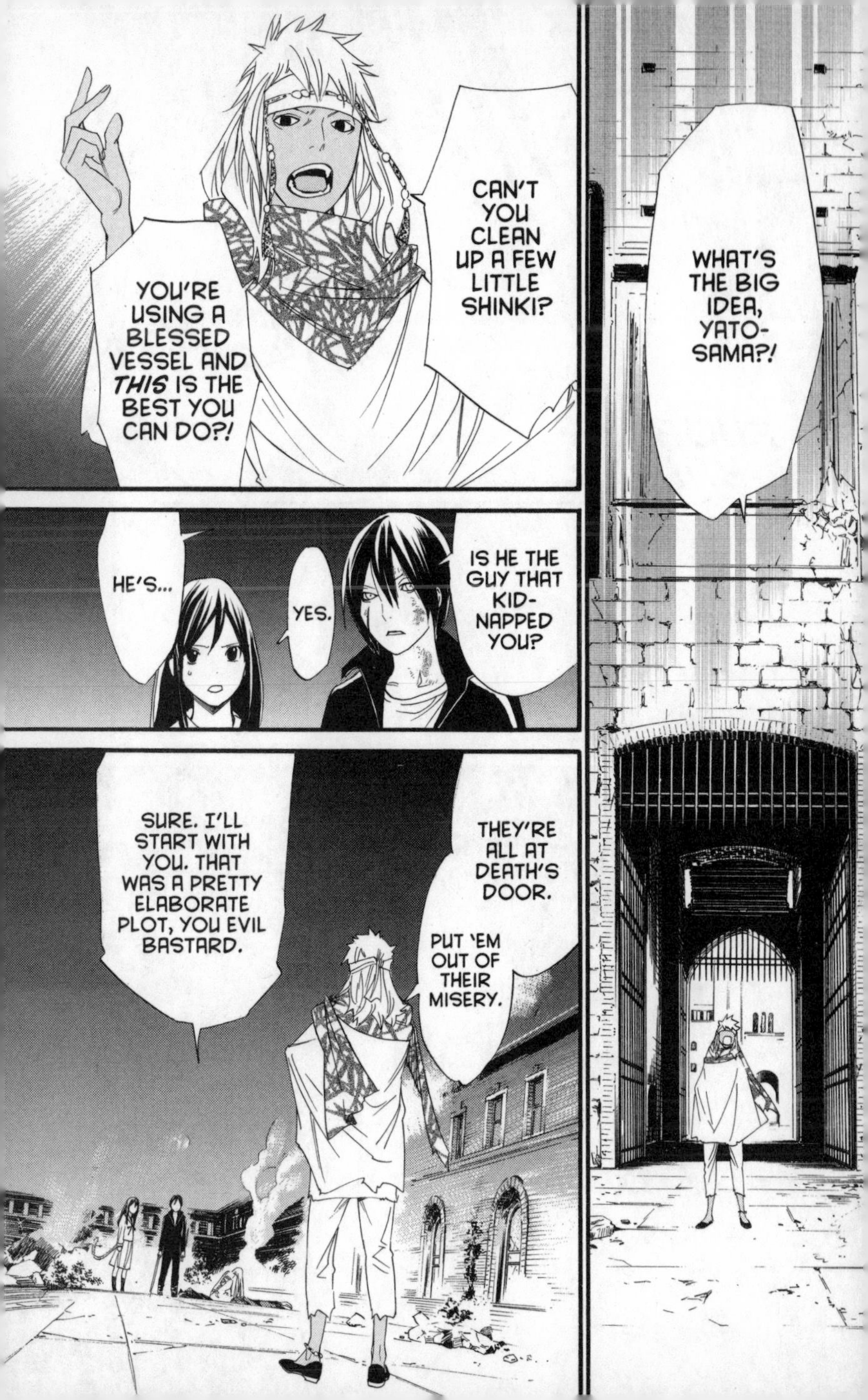
WHAT'S THE BIG IDEA, YATO-SAMA?!
CAN'T YOU CLEAN UP A FEW LITTLE SHINKI?
YOU'RE USING A BLESSED VESSEL AND *THIS* IS THE BEST YOU CAN DO?!
IS HE THE GUY THAT KID-NAPPED YOU?
YES.
HE'S...
THEY'RE ALL AT DEATH'S DOOR.
PUT 'EM OUT OF THEIR MISERY.
SURE. I'LL START WITH YOU. THAT WAS A PRETTY ELABORATE PLOT, YOU EVIL BASTARD.

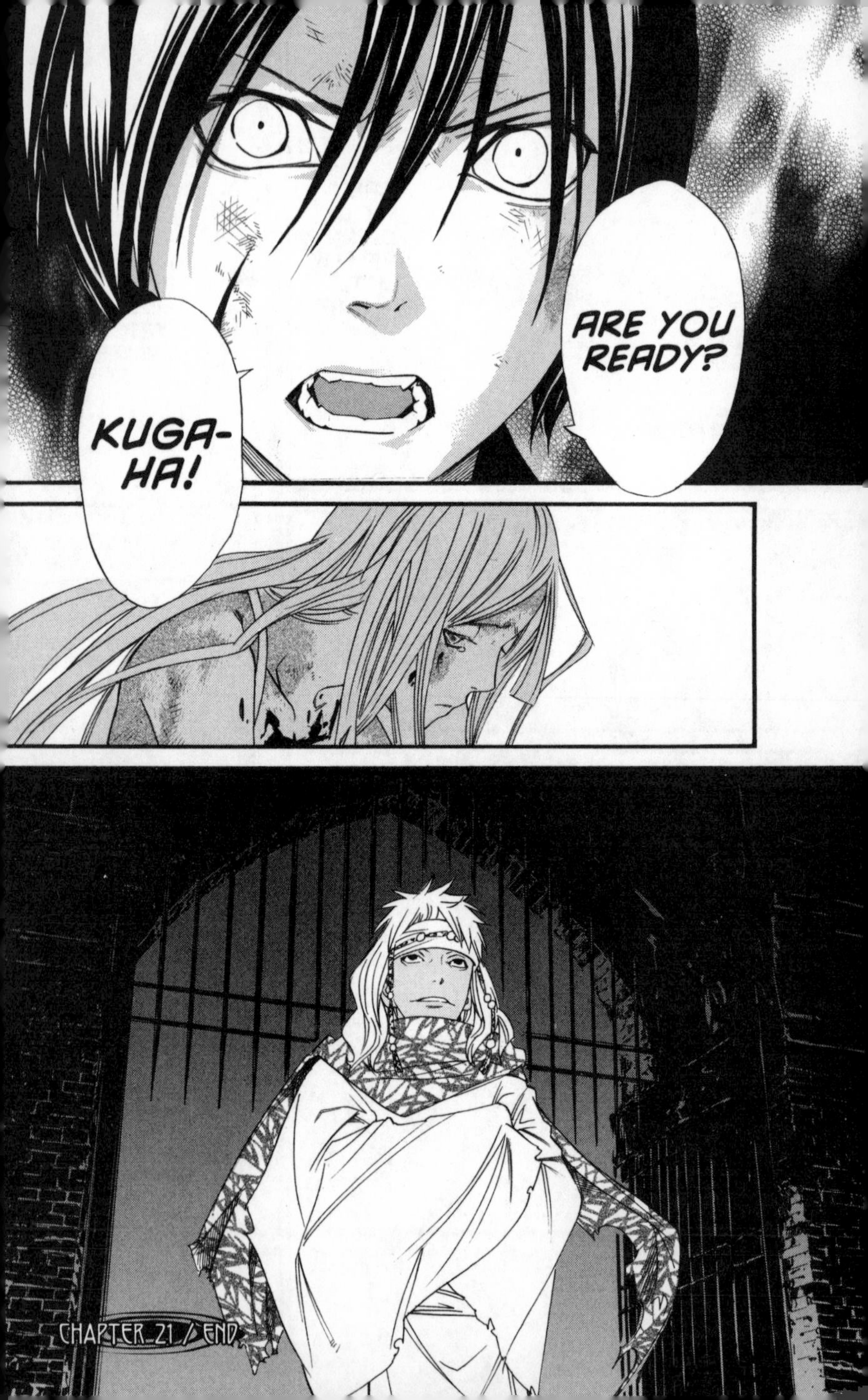
ARE YOU READY?
KUGA-HA!
CHAPTER 21 / END

野

良

神

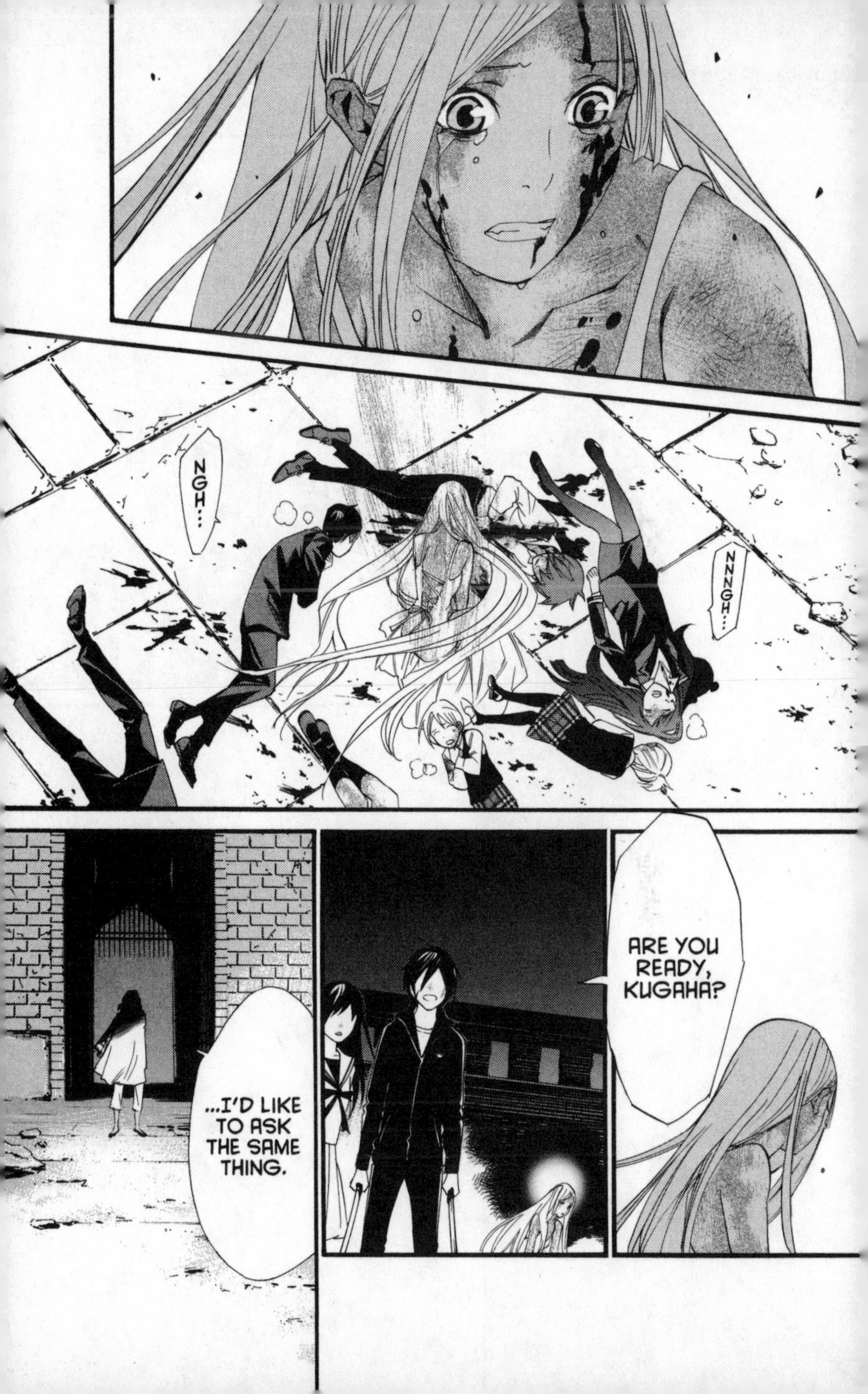
NNNGH...
NGH...
ARE YOU READY, KUGAHA?
...I'D LIKE TO ASK THE SAME THING.

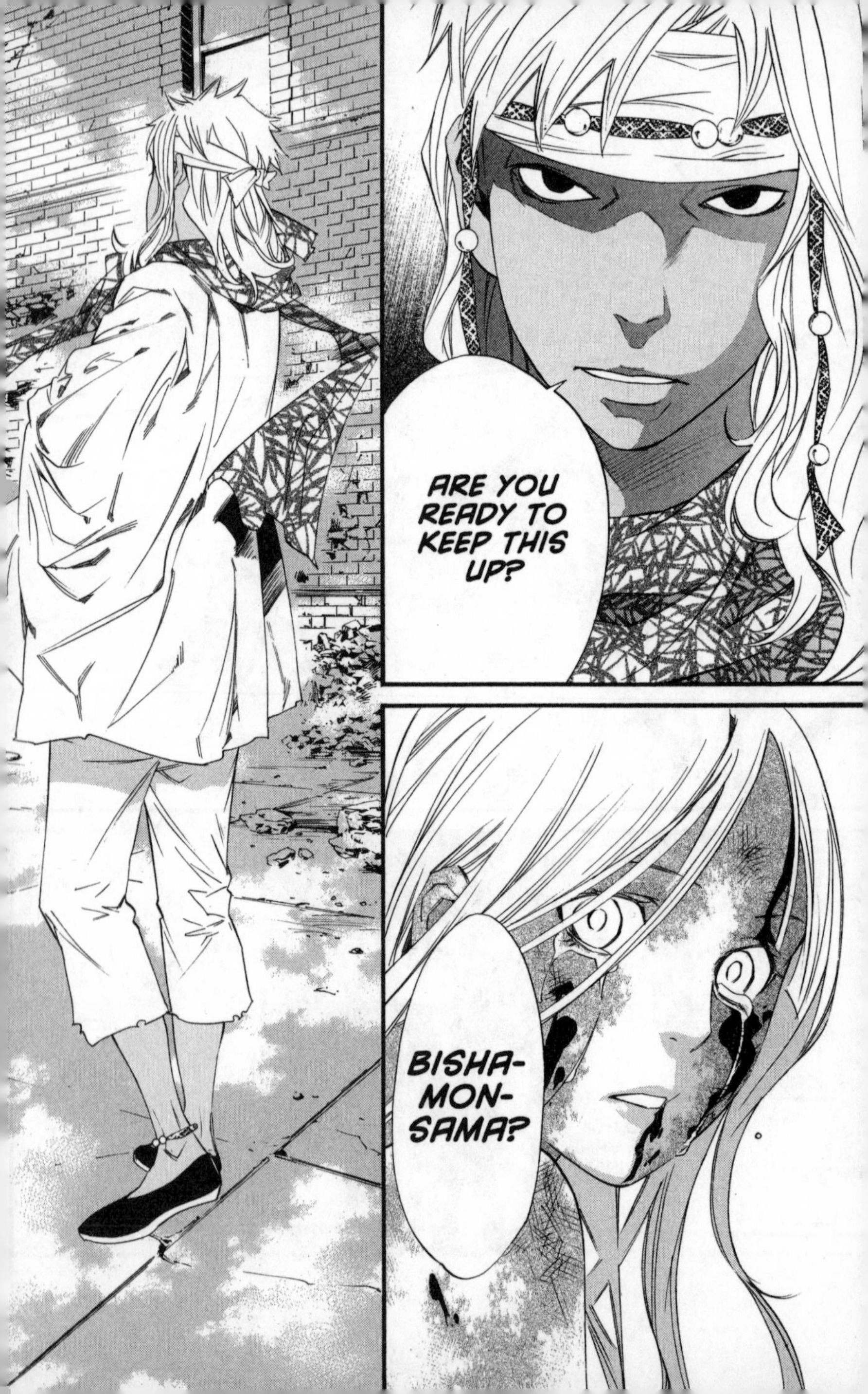
ARE YOU READY TO KEEP THIS UP?
BISHA-MON-SAMA?

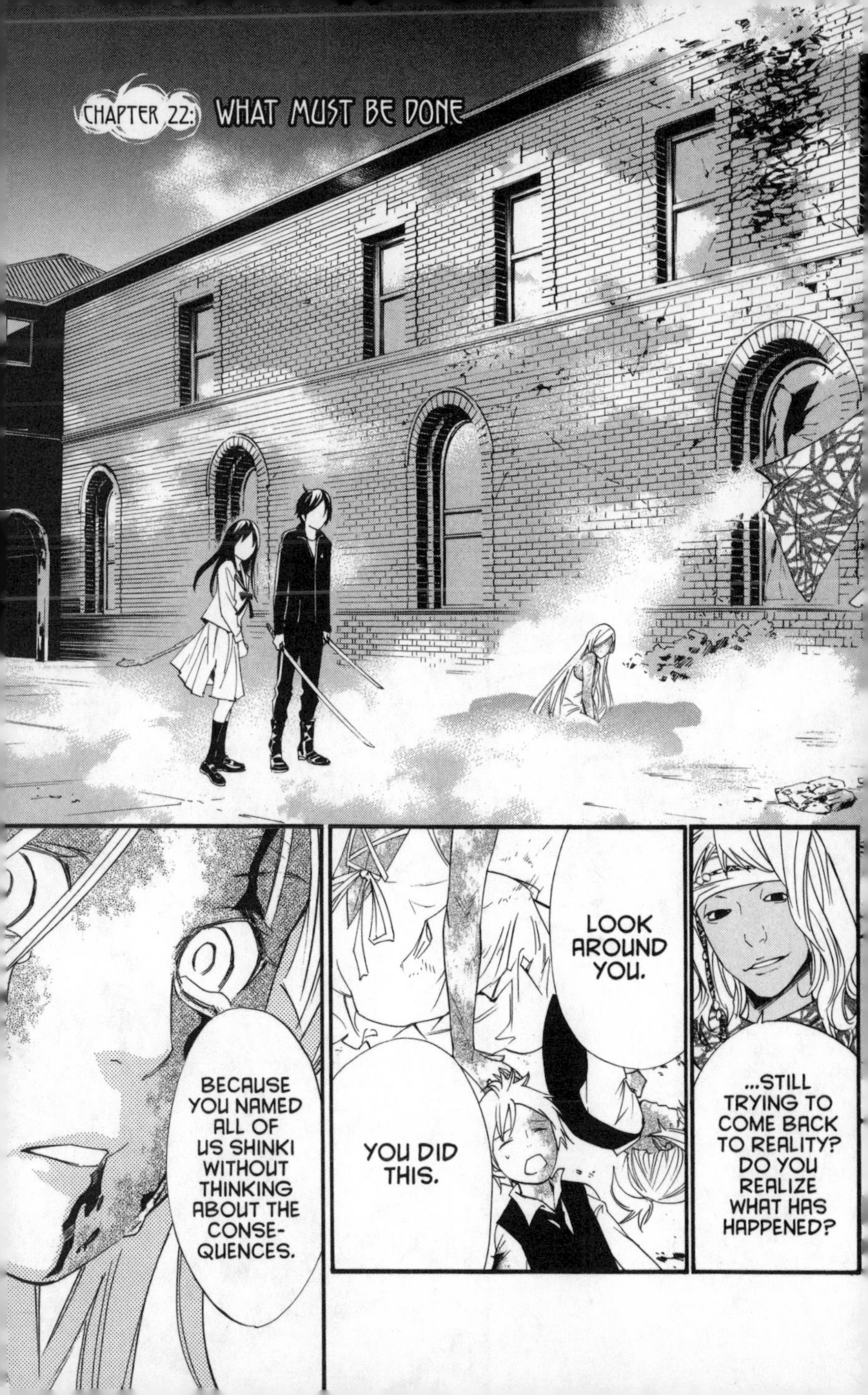
CHAPTER 22: WHAT MUST BE DONE
...STILL TRYING TO COME BACK TO REALITY? DO YOU REALIZE WHAT HAS HAPPENED?
LOOK AROUND YOU.
YOU DID THIS.
BECAUSE YOU NAMED ALL OF US SHINKI WITHOUT THINKING ABOUT THE CONSE-QUENCES.

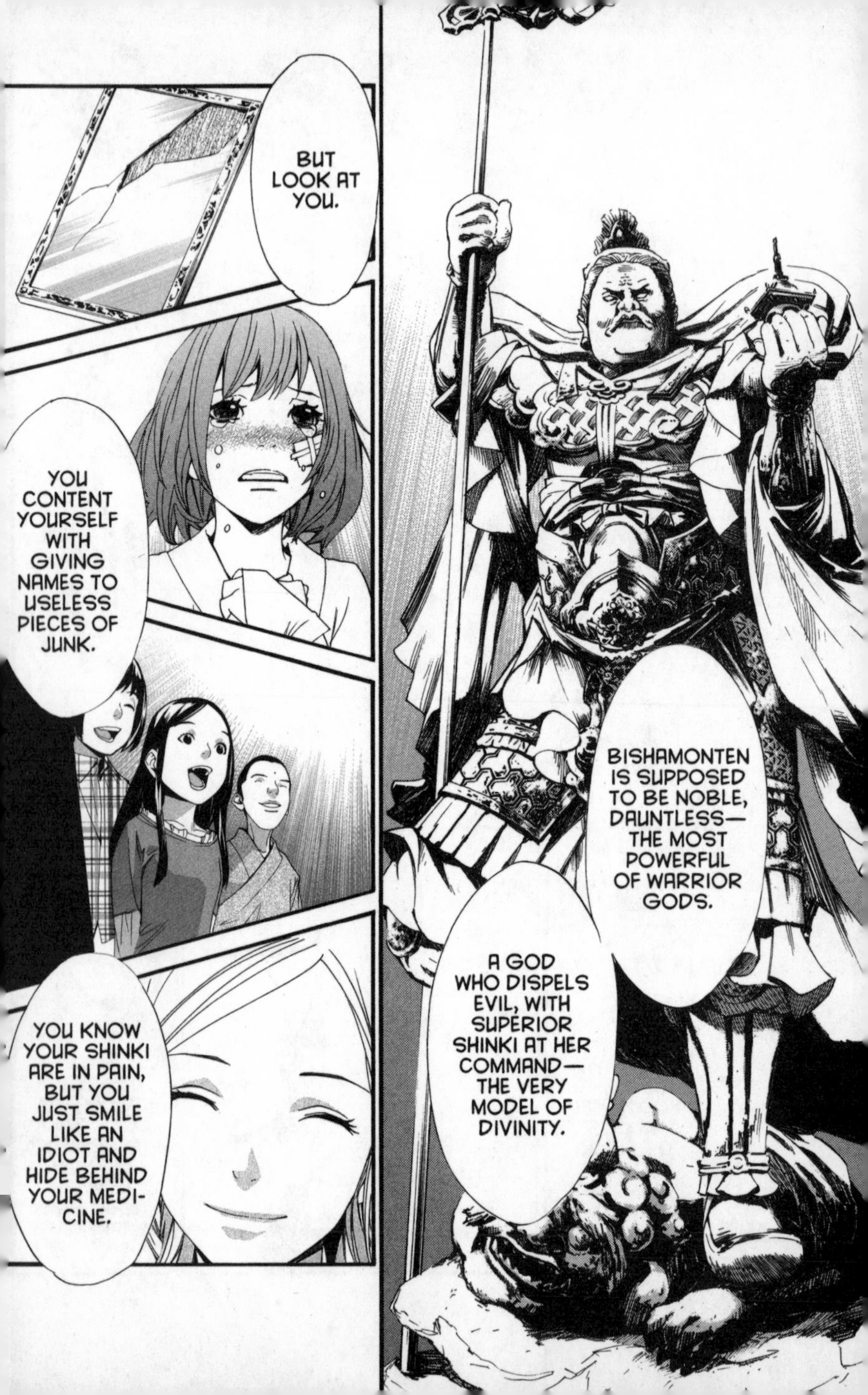
BISHAMONTEN IS SUPPOSED TO BE NOBLE, DAUNTLESS—THE MOST POWERFUL OF WARRIOR GODS.
A GOD WHO DISPELS EVIL, WITH SUPERIOR SHINKI AT HER COMMAND—THE VERY MODEL OF DIVINITY.
BUT LOOK AT YOU.
YOU CONTENT YOURSELF WITH GIVING NAMES TO USELESS PIECES OF JUNK.
YOU KNOW YOUR SHINKI ARE IN PAIN, BUT YOU JUST SMILE LIKE AN IDIOT AND HIDE BEHIND YOUR MEDI-CINE.

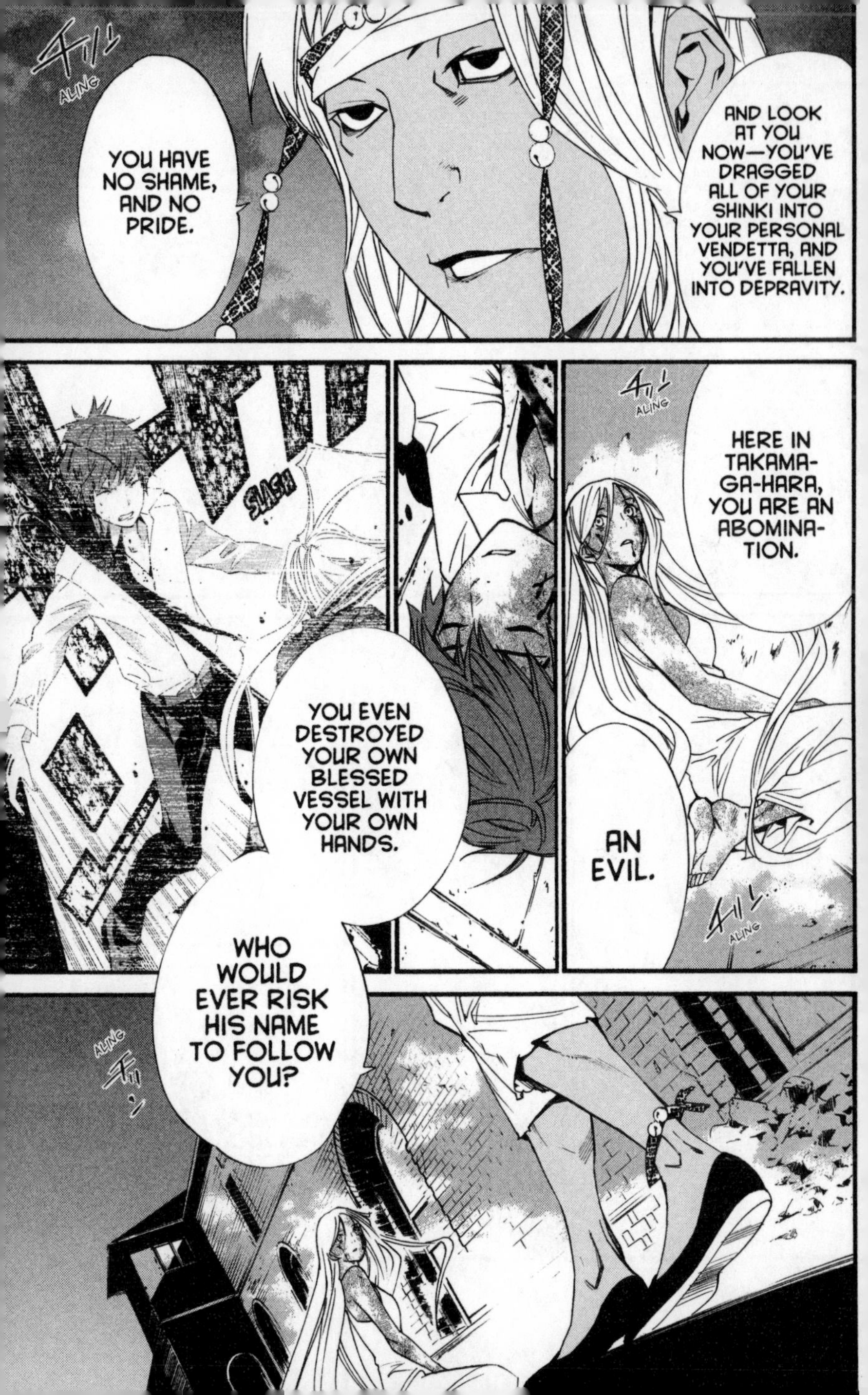
AND LOOK AT YOU NOW—YOU'VE DRAGGED ALL OF YOUR SHINKI INTO YOUR PERSONAL VENDETTA, AND YOU'VE FALLEN INTO DEPRAVITY.
ALING
YOU HAVE NO SHAME, AND NO PRIDE.
ALING
HERE IN TAKAMA-GA-HARA, YOU ARE AN ABOMINATION.
AN EVIL.
ALING
YOU EVEN DESTROYED YOUR OWN BLESSED VESSEL WITH YOUR OWN HANDS.
SLASH
WHO WOULD EVER RISK HIS NAME TO FOLLOW YOU?
ALING

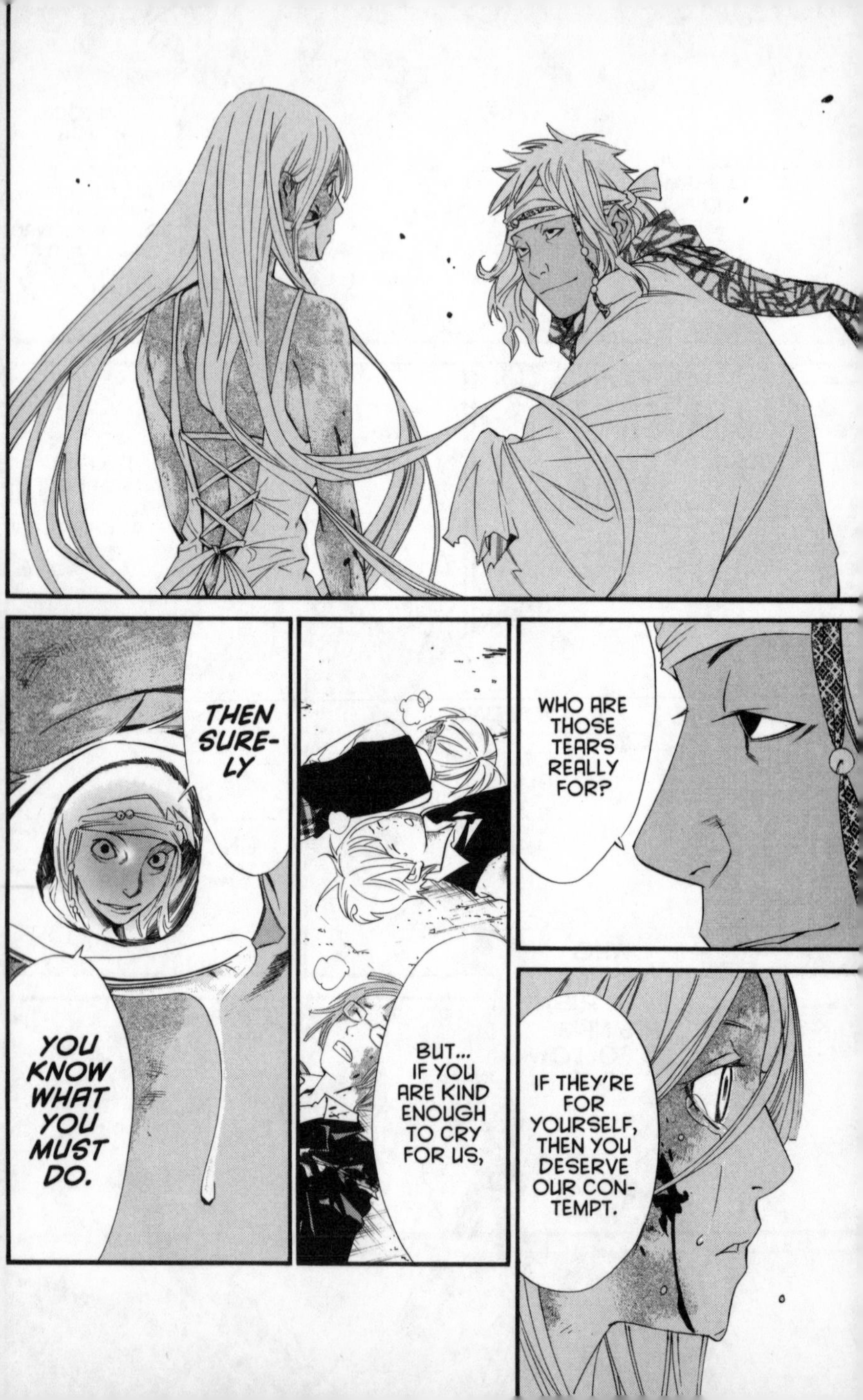
WHO ARE THOSE TEARS REALLY FOR?
IF THEY'RE FOR YOURSELF, THEN YOU DESERVE OUR CON-TEMPT.
BUT... IF YOU ARE KIND ENOUGH TO CRY FOR US,
THEN SURE-LY
YOU KNOW WHAT YOU MUST DO.

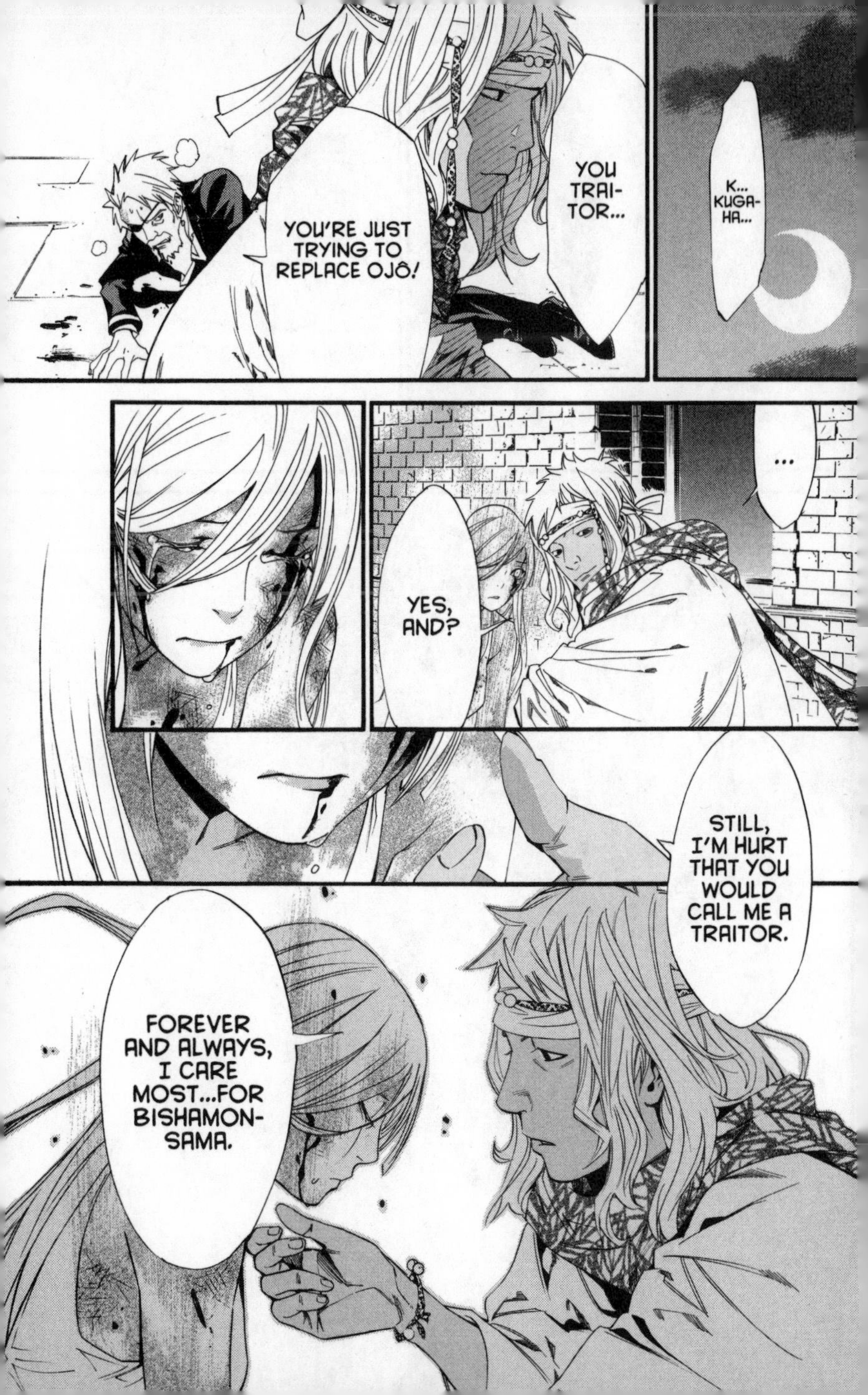
K... KUGAHA...
YOU TRAITOR...
YOU'RE JUST TRYING TO REPLACE OJÔ!
...
YES, AND?
STILL, I'M HURT THAT YOU WOULD CALL ME A TRAITOR.
FOREVER AND ALWAYS, I CARE MOST...FOR BISHAMON-SAMA.

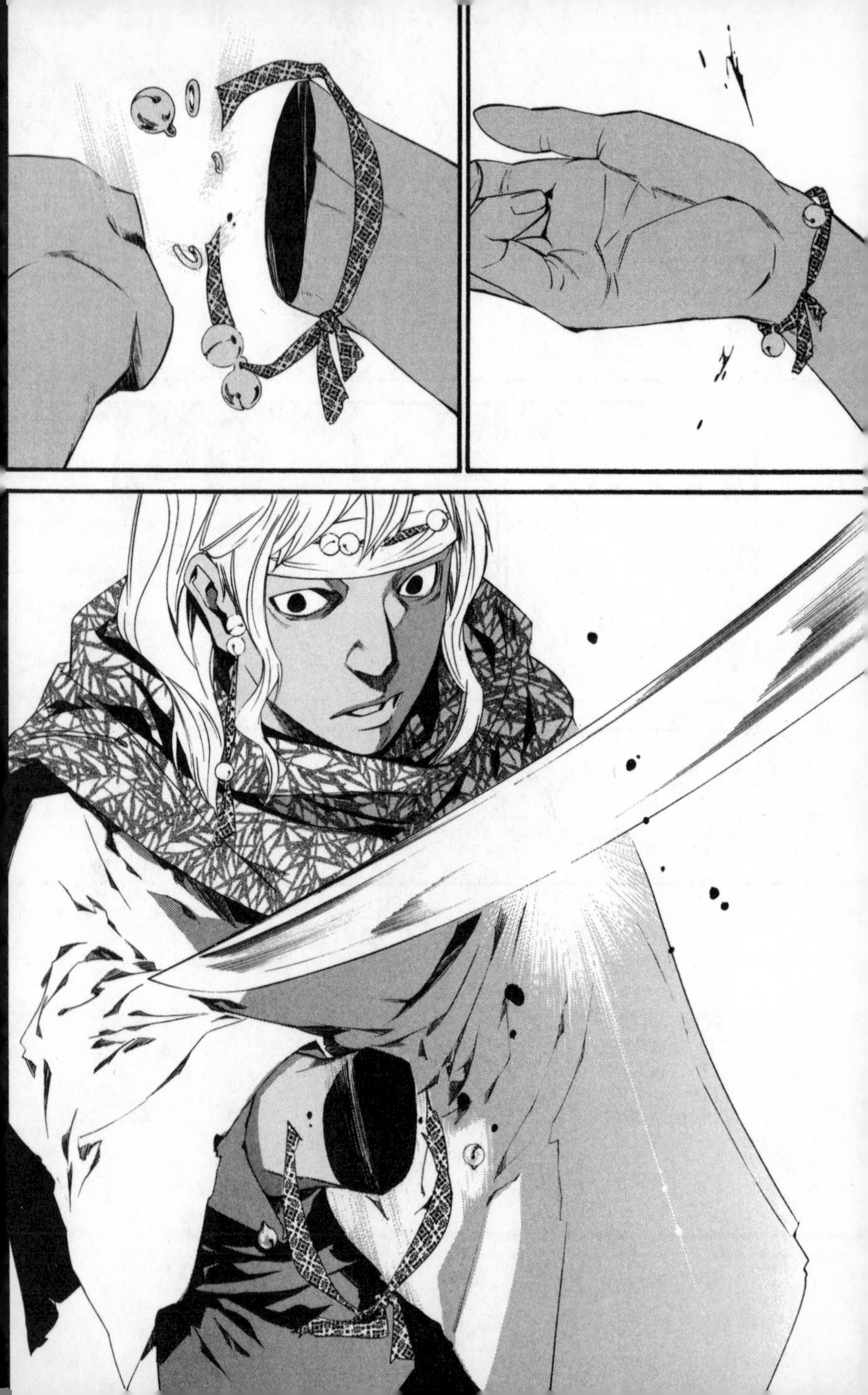

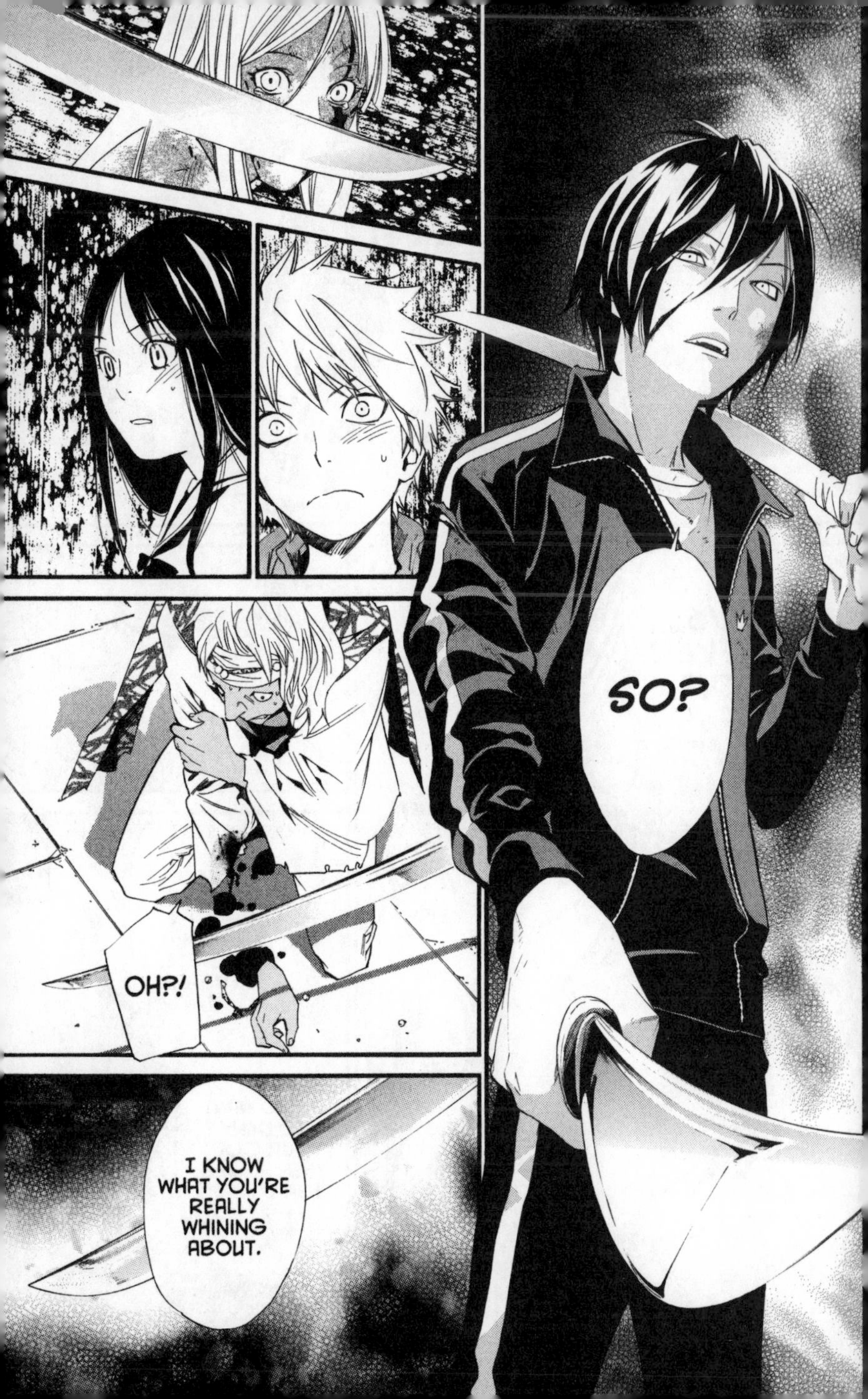
SO?
OH?!
I KNOW WHAT YOU'RE REALLY WHINING ABOUT.

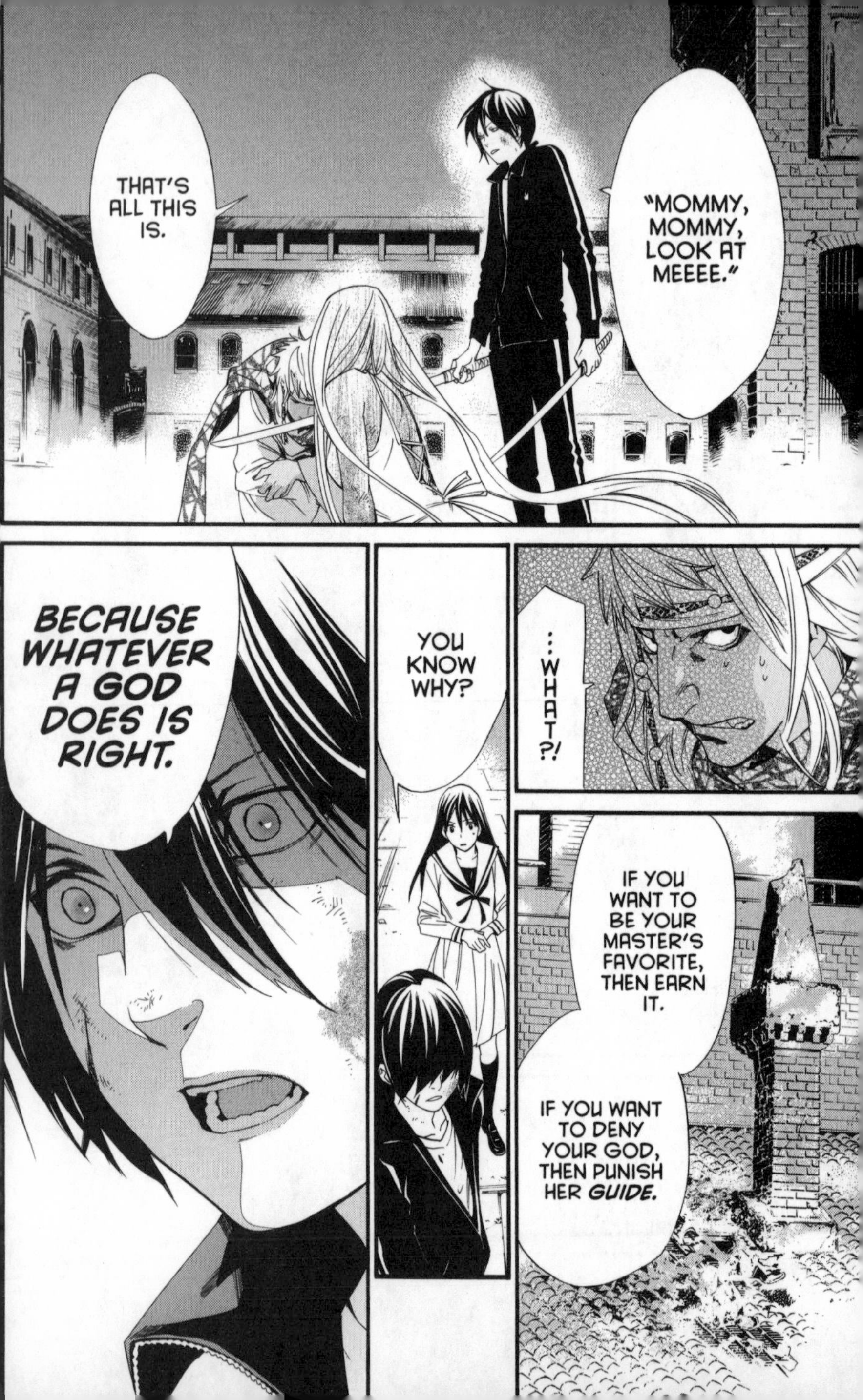
"MOMMY, MOMMY, LOOK AT MEEEE."
THAT'S ALL THIS IS.
...WHAT?!
IF YOU WANT TO BE YOUR MASTER'S FAVORITE, THEN EARN IT.
IF YOU WANT TO DENY YOUR GOD, THEN PUNISH HER *GUIDE*.
YOU KNOW WHY?
BECAUSE WHATEVER A GOD DOES IS RIGHT.

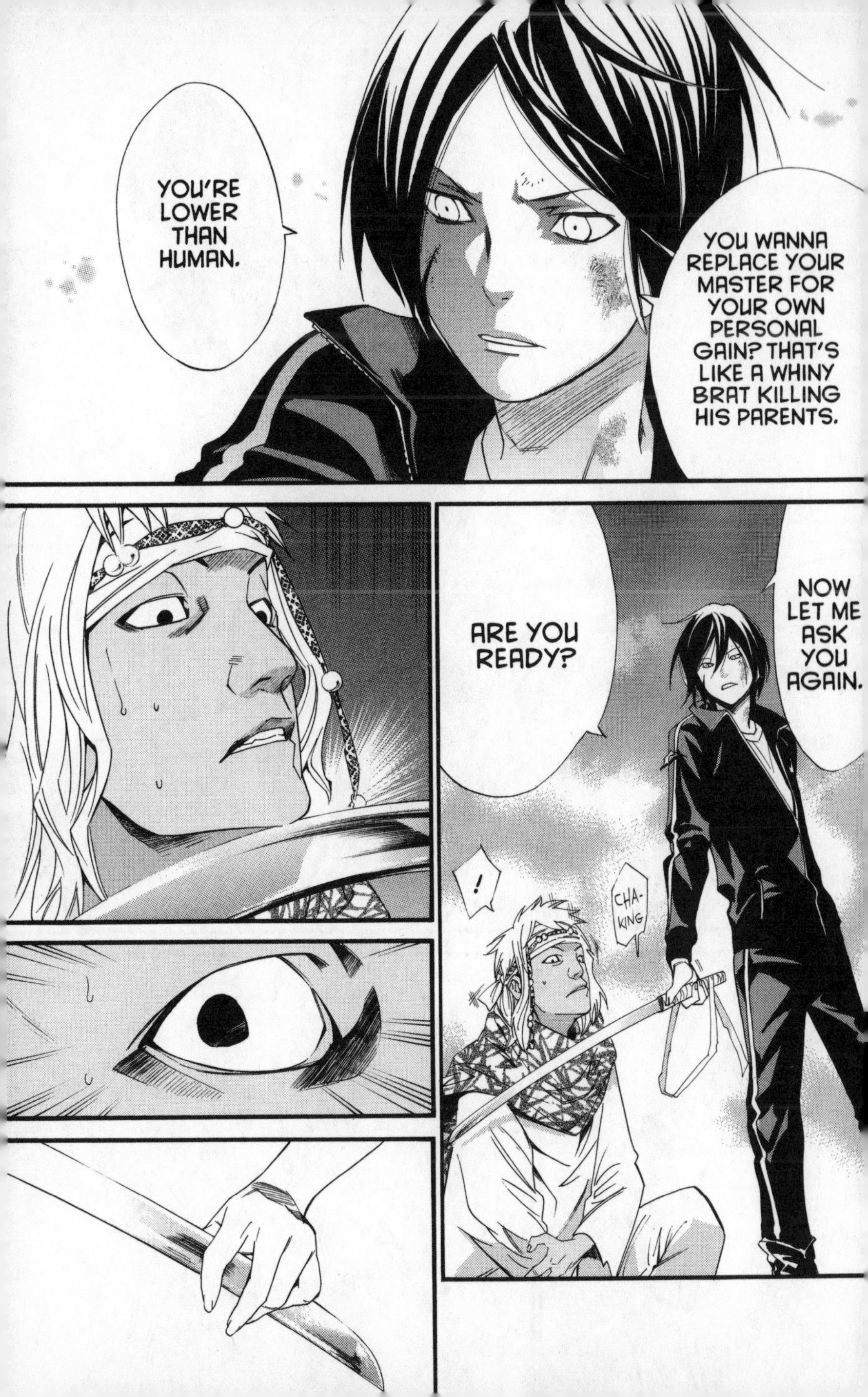
YOU WANNA REPLACE YOUR MASTER FOR YOUR OWN PERSONAL GAIN? THAT'S LIKE A WHINY BRAT KILLING HIS PARENTS.
YOU'RE LOWER THAN HUMAN.
NOW LET ME ASK YOU AGAIN.
ARE YOU READY?
CHA-KING
!

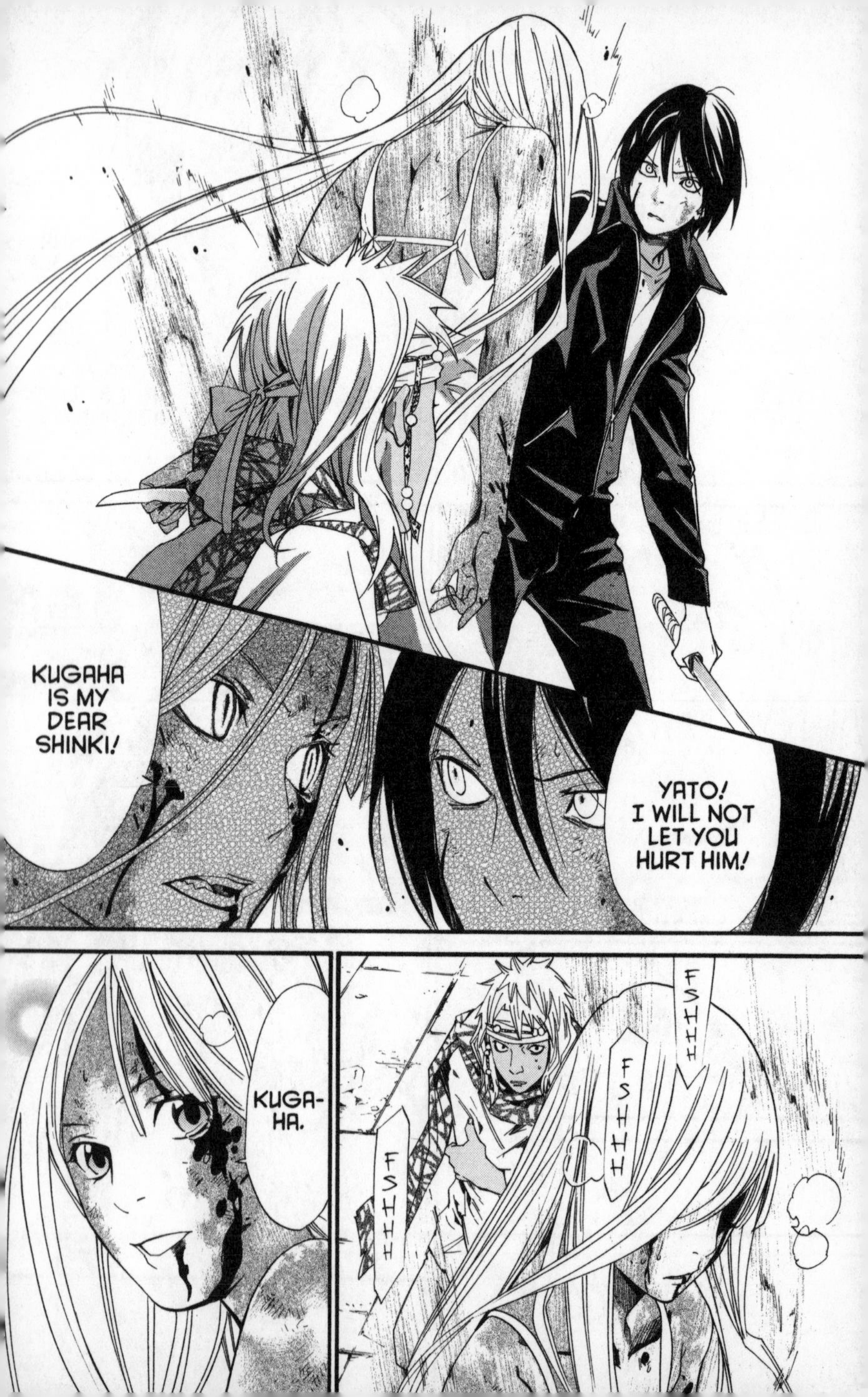
YATO! I WILL NOT LET YOU HURT HIM!
KUGAHA IS MY DEAR SHINKI!
FSHHH
FSHHH
FSHHH
KUGA-HA.

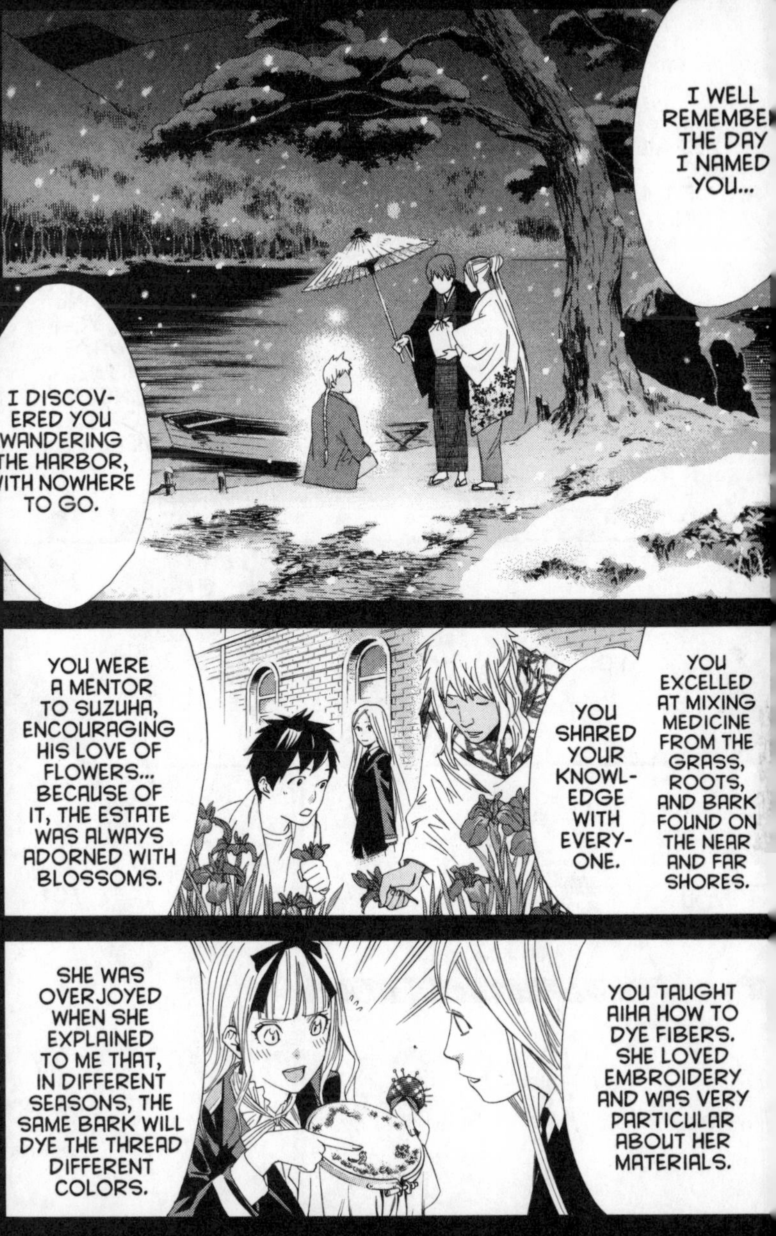
I WELL REMEMBE THE DAY I NAMED YOU...
I DISCOVERED YOU WANDERING THE HARBOR, WITH NOWHERE TO GO.
YOU EXCELLED AT MIXING MEDICINE FROM THE GRASS, ROOTS, AND BARK FOUND ON THE NEAR AND FAR SHORES.
YOU SHARED YOUR KNOWLEDGE WITH EVERYONE.
YOU WERE A MENTOR TO SUZUHA, ENCOURAGING HIS LOVE OF FLOWERS... BECAUSE OF IT, THE ESTATE WAS ALWAYS ADORNED WITH BLOSSOMS.
YOU TAUGHT AIHA HOW TO DYE FIBERS. SHE LOVED EMBROIDERY AND WAS VERY PARTICULAR ABOUT HER MATERIALS.
SHE WAS OVERJOYED WHEN SHE EXPLAINED TO ME THAT, IN DIFFERENT SEASONS, THE SAME BARK WILL DYE THE THREAD DIFFERENT COLORS.

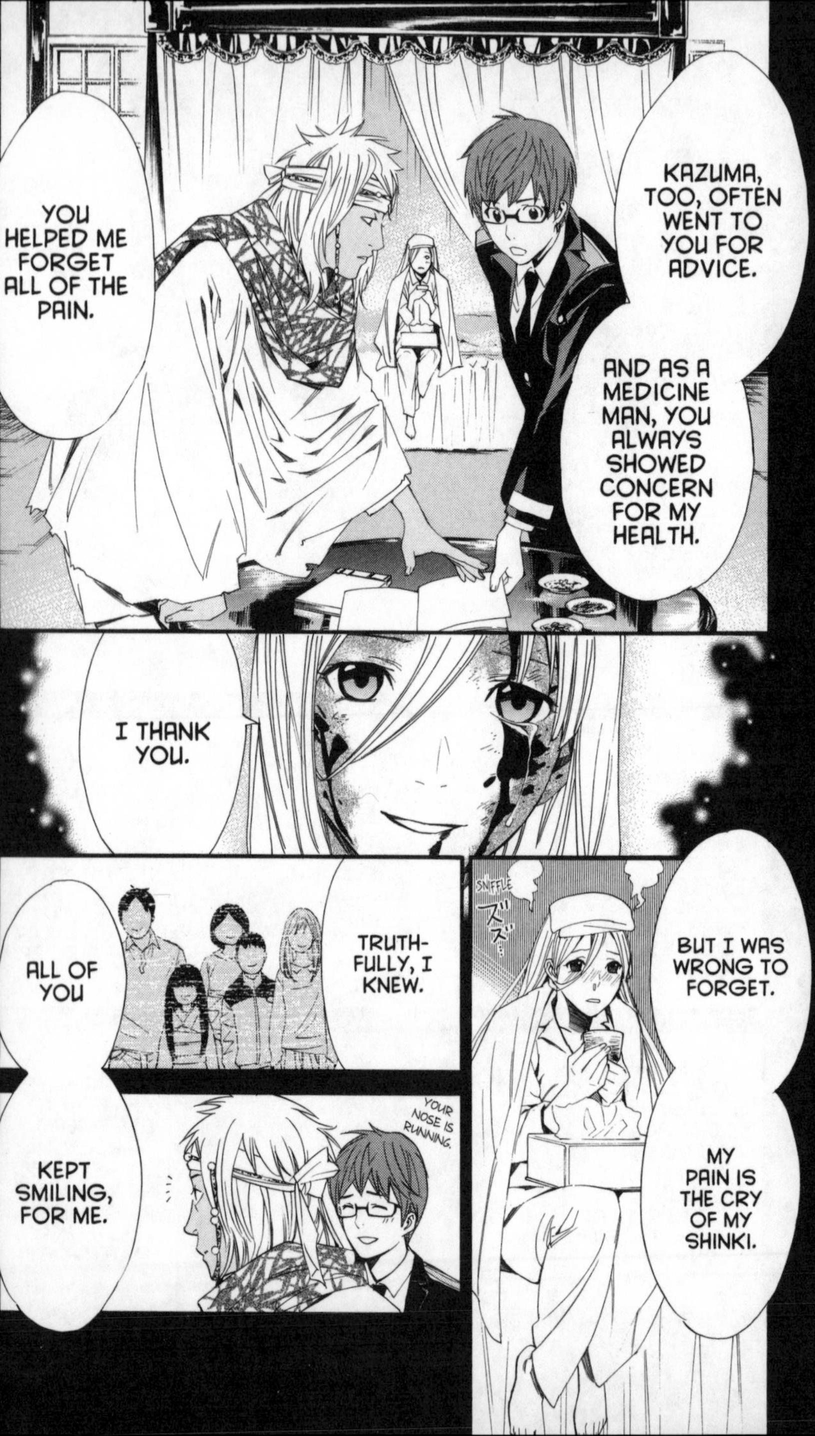
KAZUMA, TOO, OFTEN WENT TO YOU FOR ADVICE.
AND AS A MEDICINE MAN, YOU ALWAYS SHOWED CONCERN FOR MY HEALTH.
YOU HELPED ME FORGET ALL OF THE PAIN.
I THANK YOU.
SNIFFLE
BUT I WAS WRONG TO FORGET.
MY PAIN IS THE CRY OF MY SHINKI.
TRUTH-FULLY, I KNEW.
ALL OF YOU
YOUR NOSE IS RUNNING.
KEPT SMILING, FOR ME.

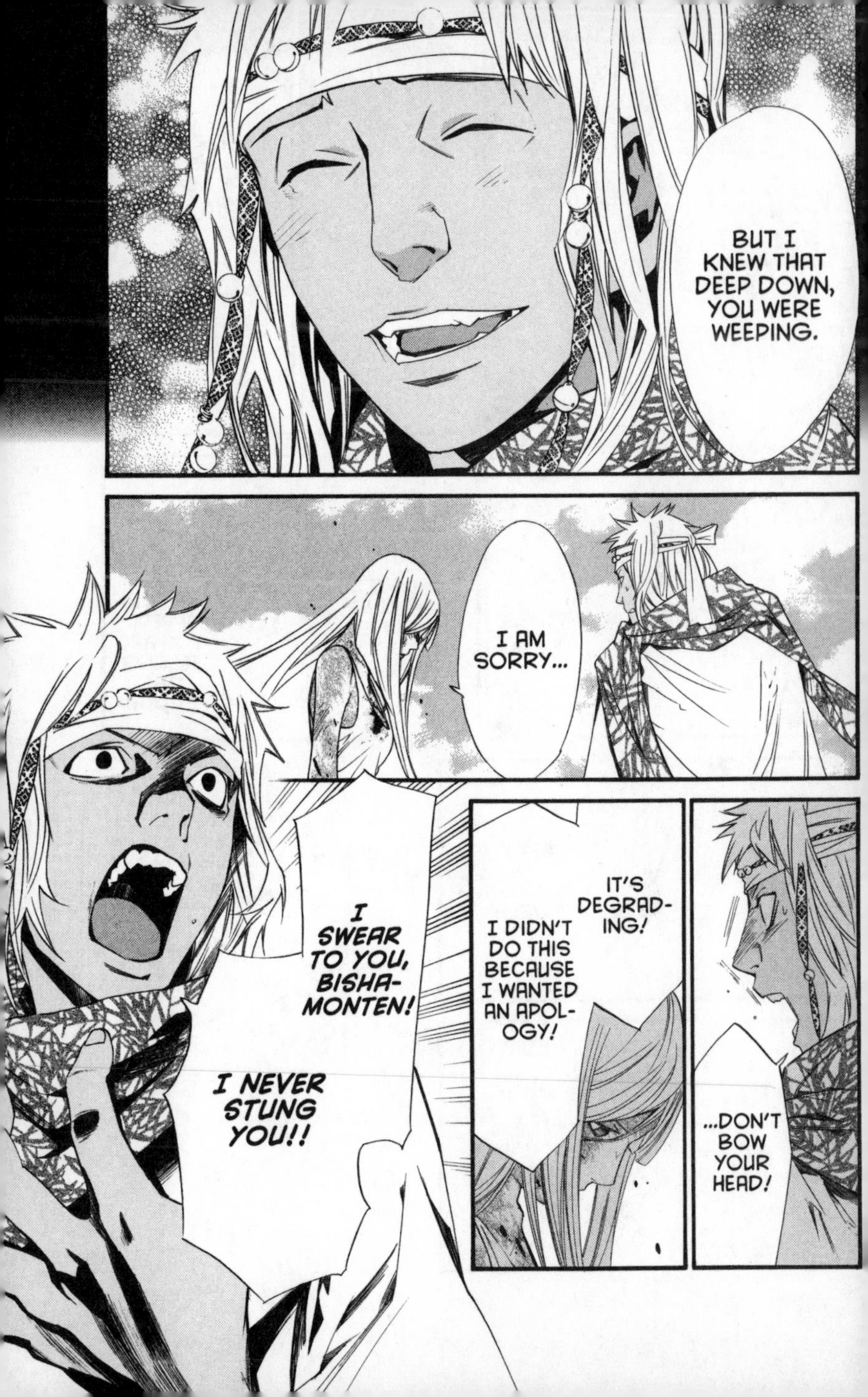
BUT I KNEW THAT DEEP DOWN, YOU WERE WEEPING.
I AM SORRY...
...DON'T BOW YOUR HEAD!
IT'S DEGRAD-ING!
I DIDN'T DO THIS BECAUSE I WANTED AN APOLOGY!
I SWEAR TO YOU, BISHAMONTEN!
I NEVER STUNG YOU!!

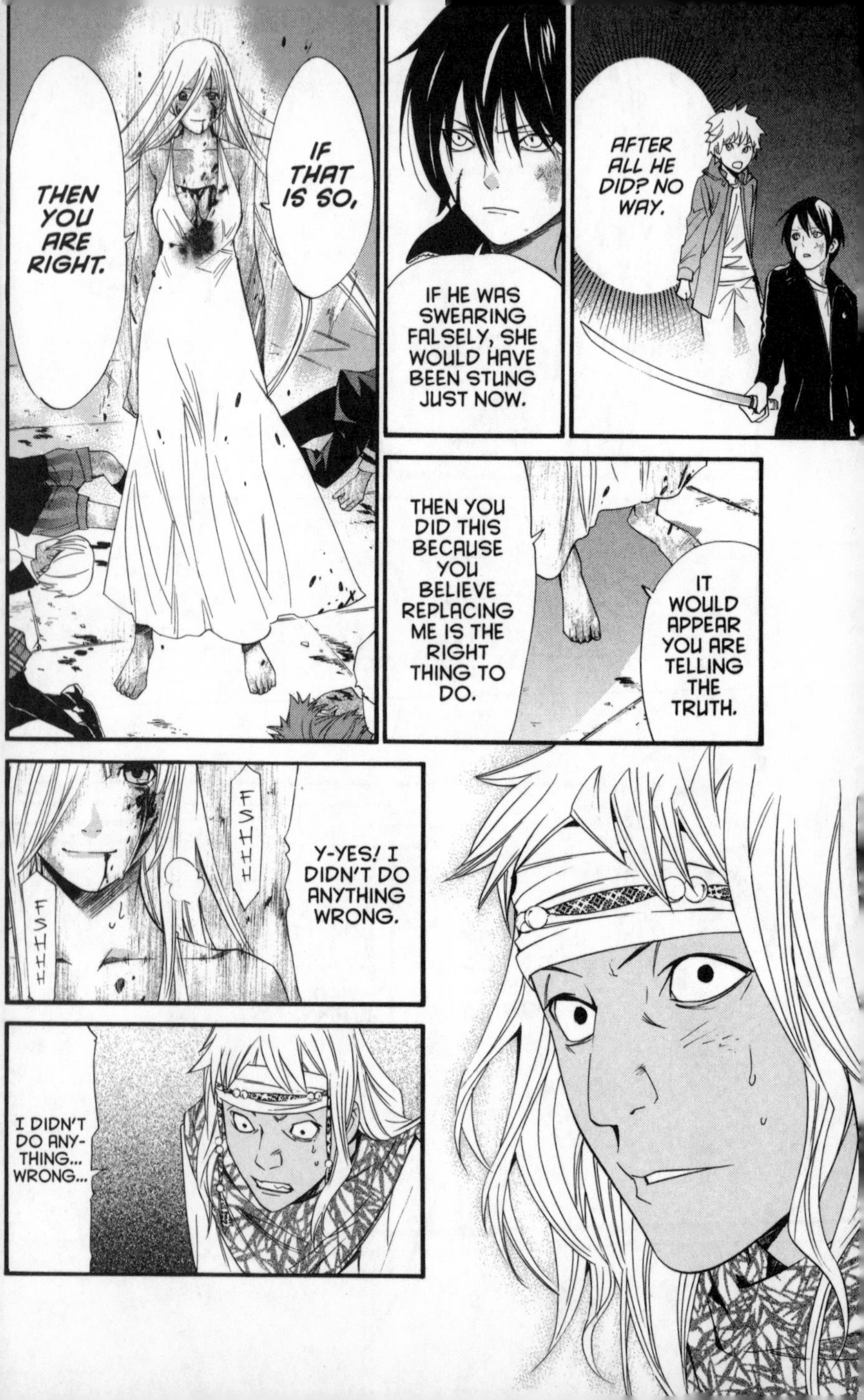
AFTER ALL HE DID? NO WAY.
IF HE WAS SWEARING FALSELY, SHE WOULD HAVE BEEN STUNG JUST NOW.
IT WOULD APPEAR YOU ARE TELLING THE TRUTH.
THEN YOU DID THIS BECAUSE YOU BELIEVE REPLACING ME IS THE RIGHT THING TO DO.
IF THAT IS SO,
THEN YOU ARE RIGHT.
Y-YES! I DIDN'T DO ANYTHING WRONG.
FSHHH
FSHHH
I DIDN'T DO ANY-THING... WRONG...

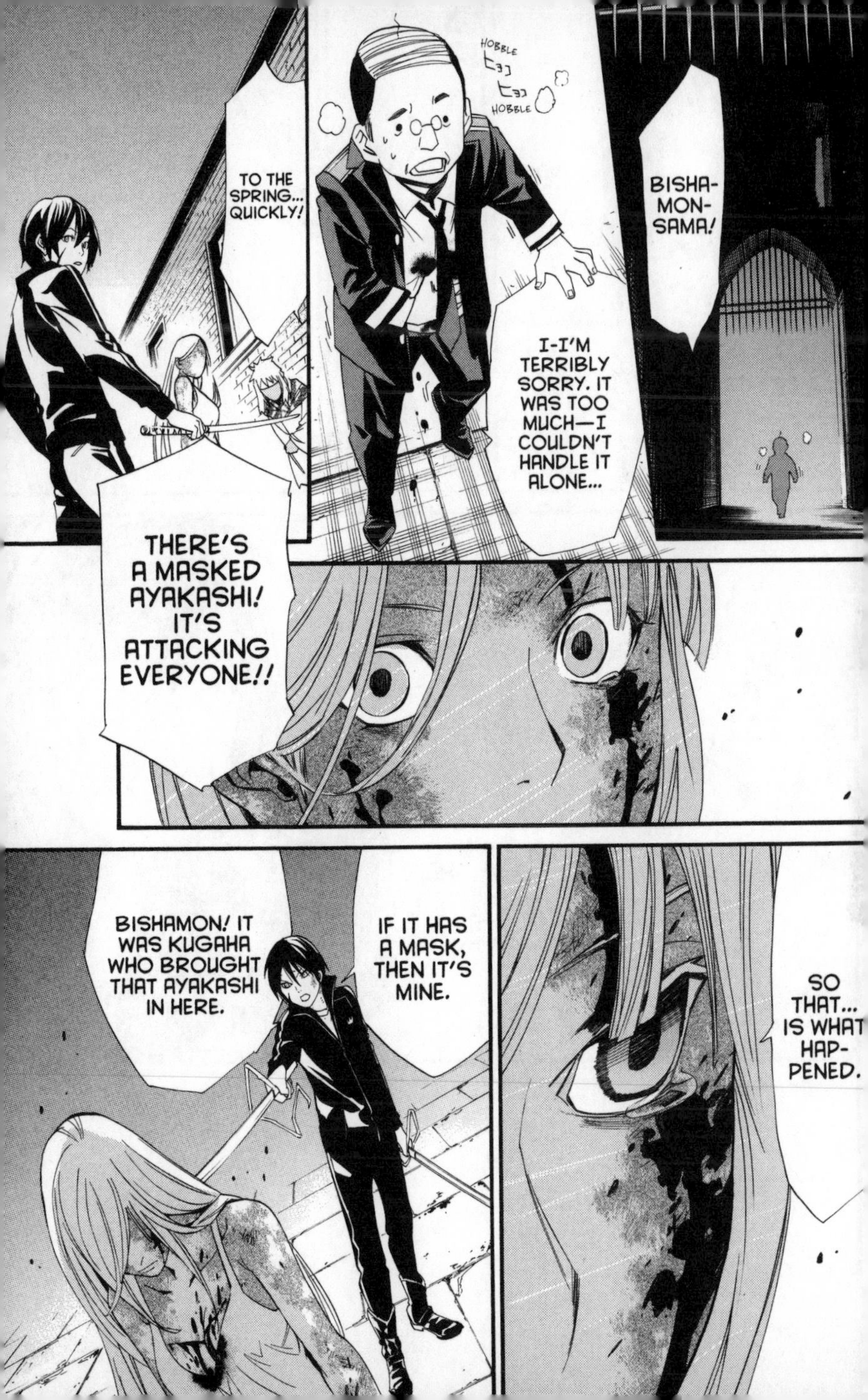
BISHAMON-SAMA!
HOBBLE
HOBBLE
I-I'M TERRIBLY SORRY. IT WAS TOO MUCH—I COULDN'T HANDLE IT ALONE...
TO THE SPRING... QUICKLY!
THERE'S A MASKED AYAKASHI! IT'S ATTACKING EVERYONE!!
SO THAT... IS WHAT HAPPENED.
IF IT HAS A MASK, THEN IT'S MINE.
BISHAMON! IT WAS KUGAHA WHO BROUGHT THAT AYAKASHI IN HERE.

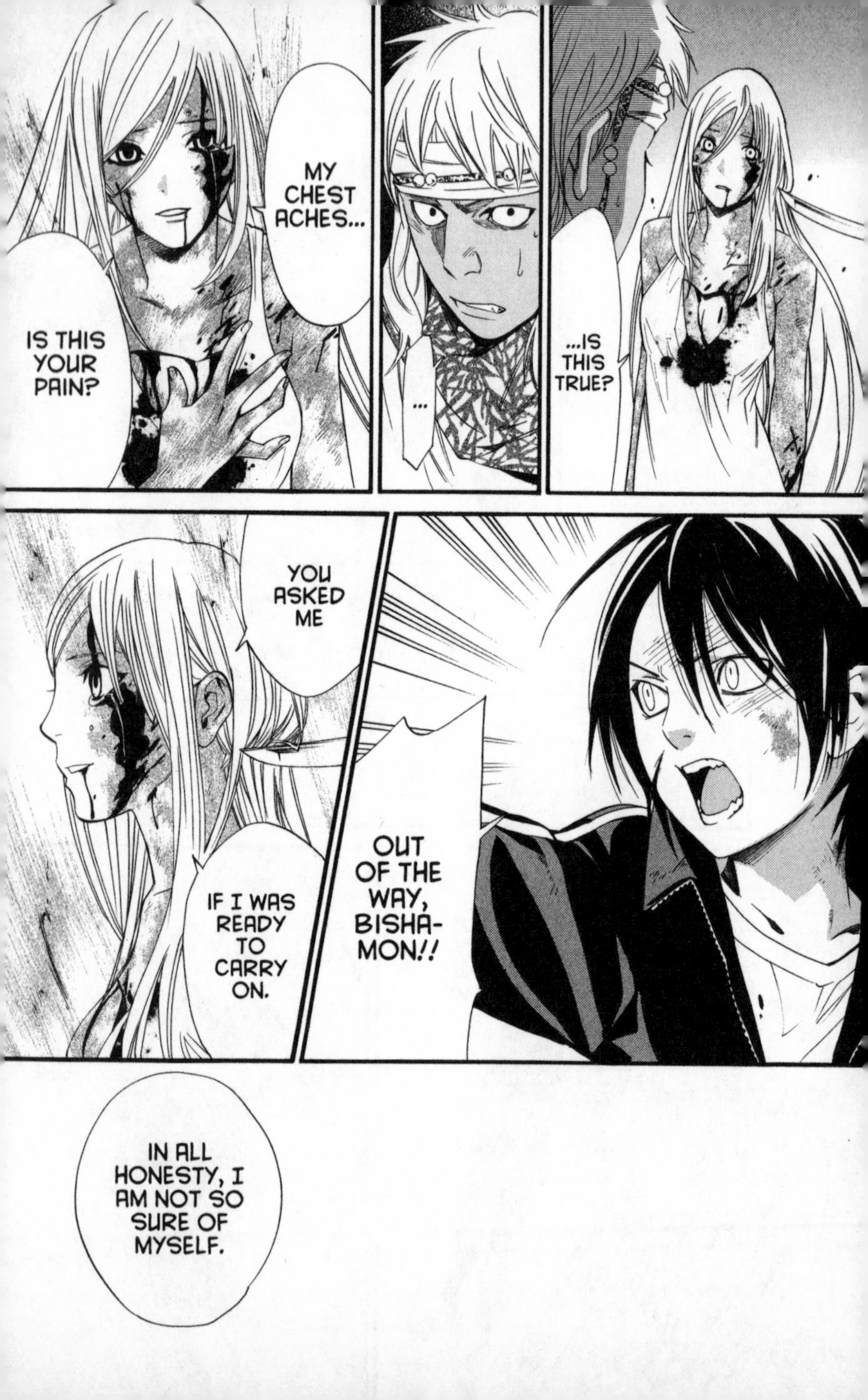
...IS THIS TRUE?
...
MY CHEST ACHES...
IS THIS YOUR PAIN?
OUT OF THE WAY, BISHA-MON!!
YOU ASKED ME
IF I WAS READY TO CARRY ON.
IN ALL HONESTY, I AM NOT SO SURE OF MYSELF.

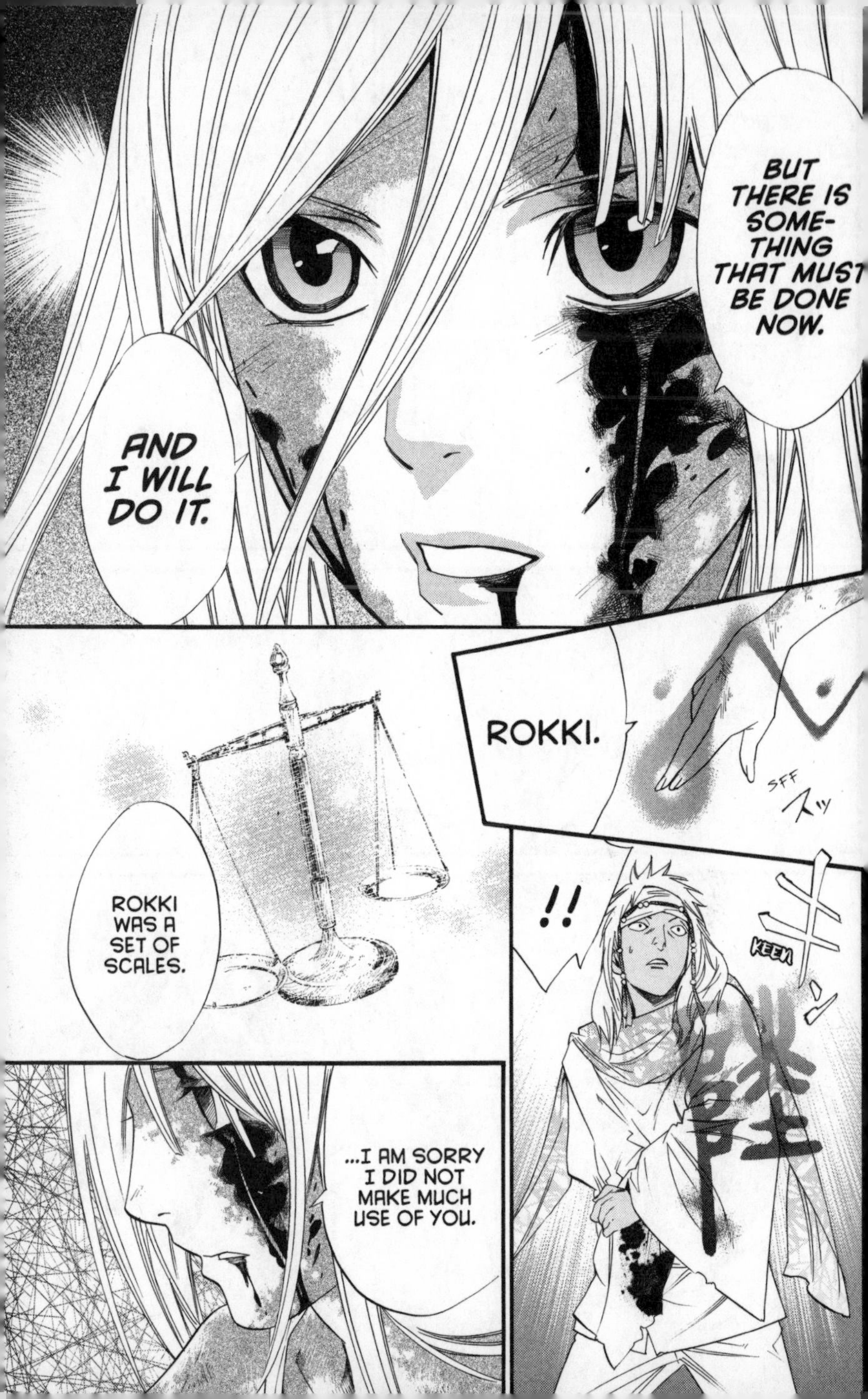
BUT THERE IS SOME- THING THAT MUST BE DONE NOW.
AND I WILL DO IT.
ROKKI.
SFF
ROKKI WAS A SET OF SCALES.
!!
KEEN
...I AM SORRY I DID NOT MAKE MUCH USE OF YOU.

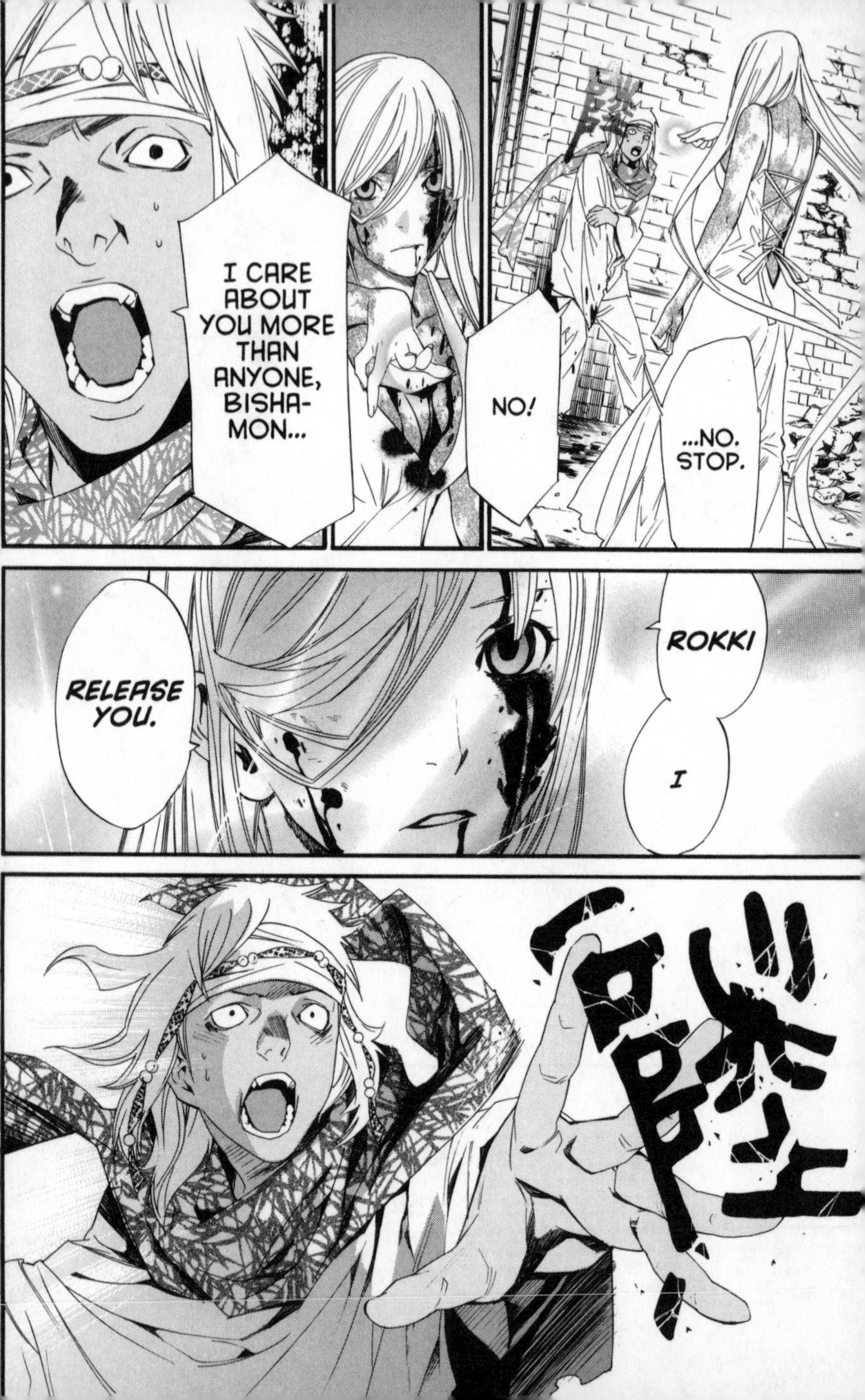
...NO. STOP.
NO!
I CARE ABOUT YOU MORE THAN ANYONE, BISHA-MON...
ROKKI
I
RELEASE YOU.

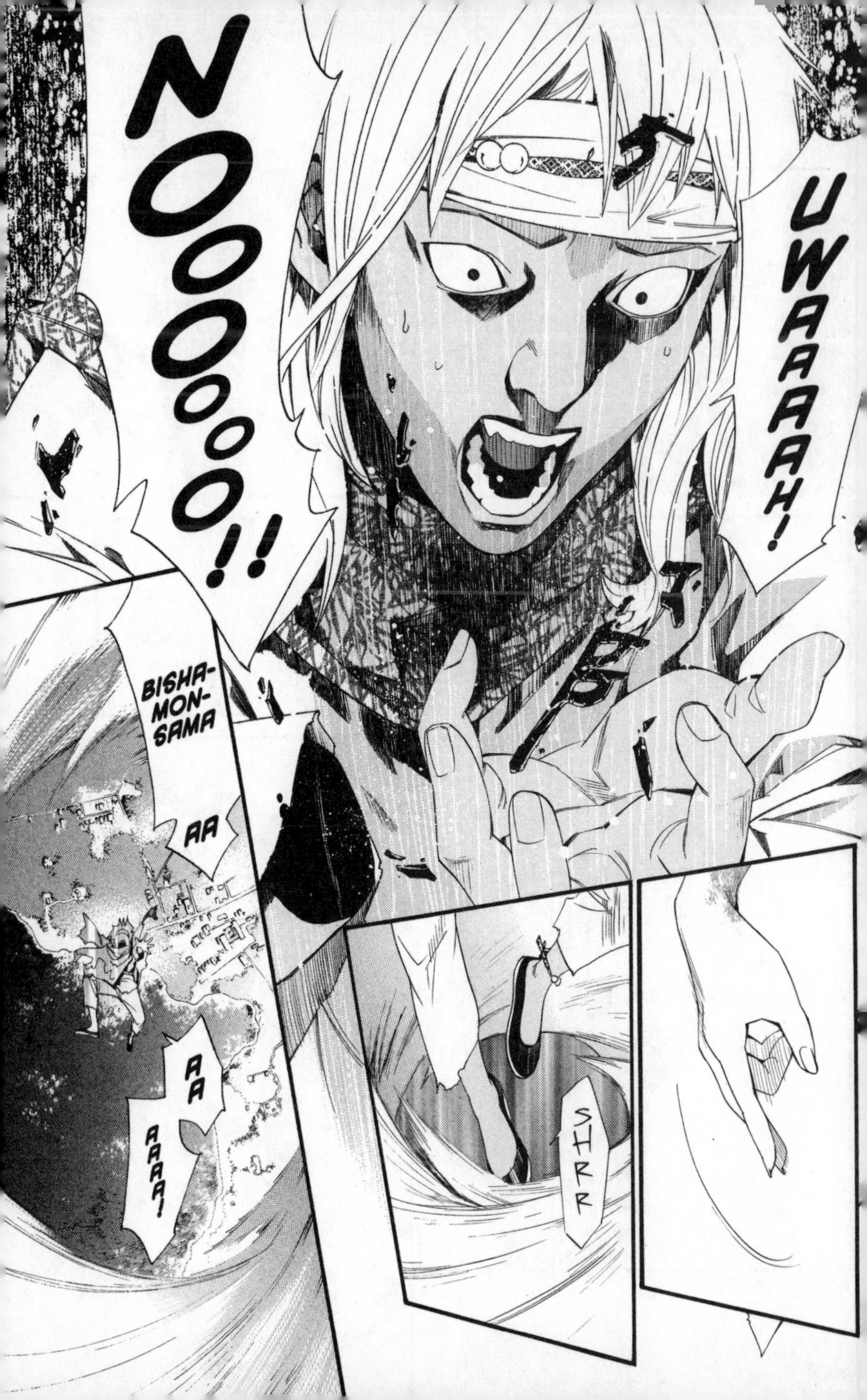
UWAAAAAH!
NOOOOOOO!!
BISHA-MON-SAMA
AA
AA
AAAA!
SHRR

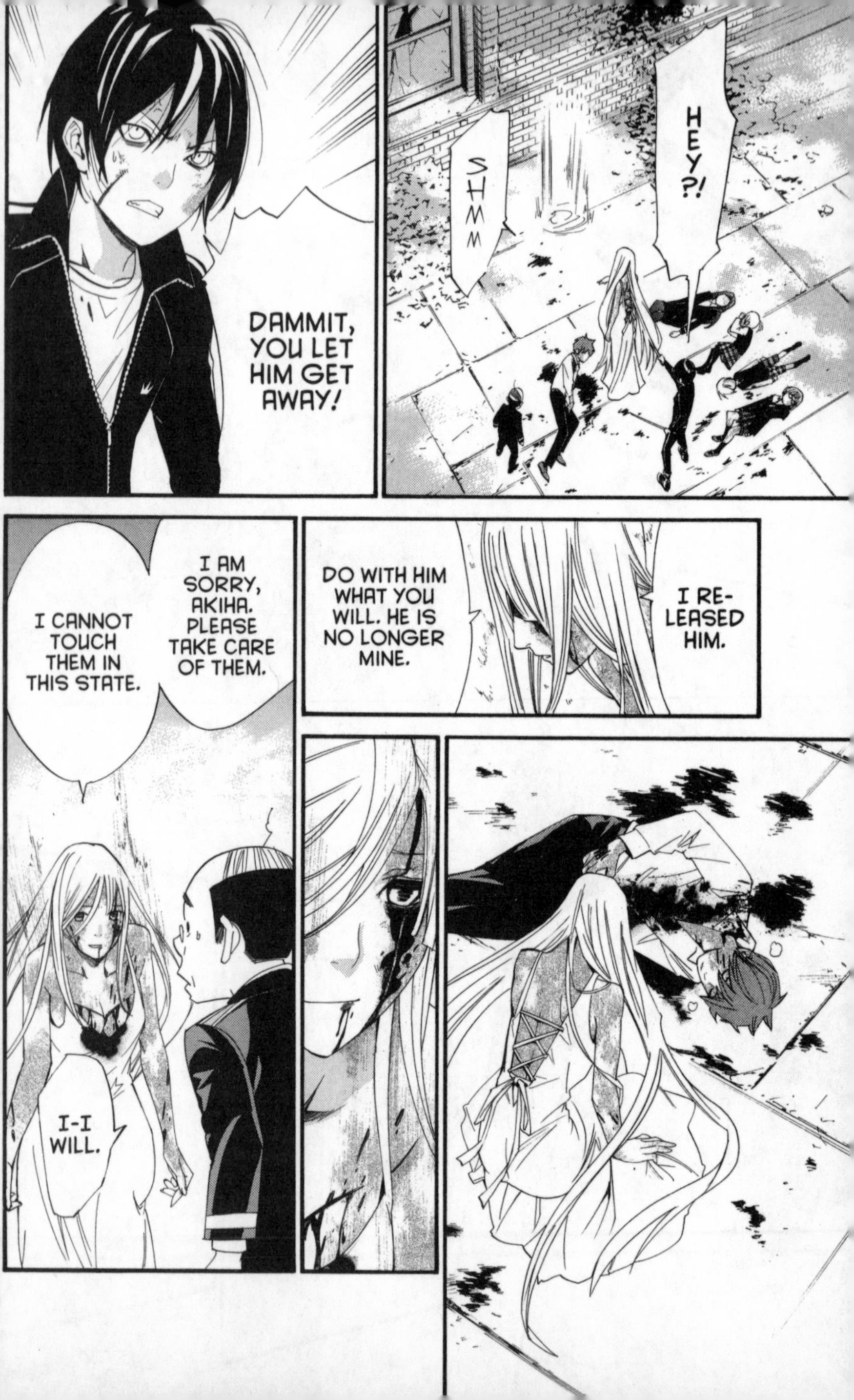
HEY?!
SHMM
DAMMIT, YOU LET HIM GET AWAY!
I RE-LEASED HIM.
DO WITH HIM WHAT YOU WILL. HE IS NO LONGER MINE.
I AM SORRY, AKIHA. PLEASE TAKE CARE OF THEM.
I CANNOT TOUCH THEM IN THIS STATE.
I-I WILL.

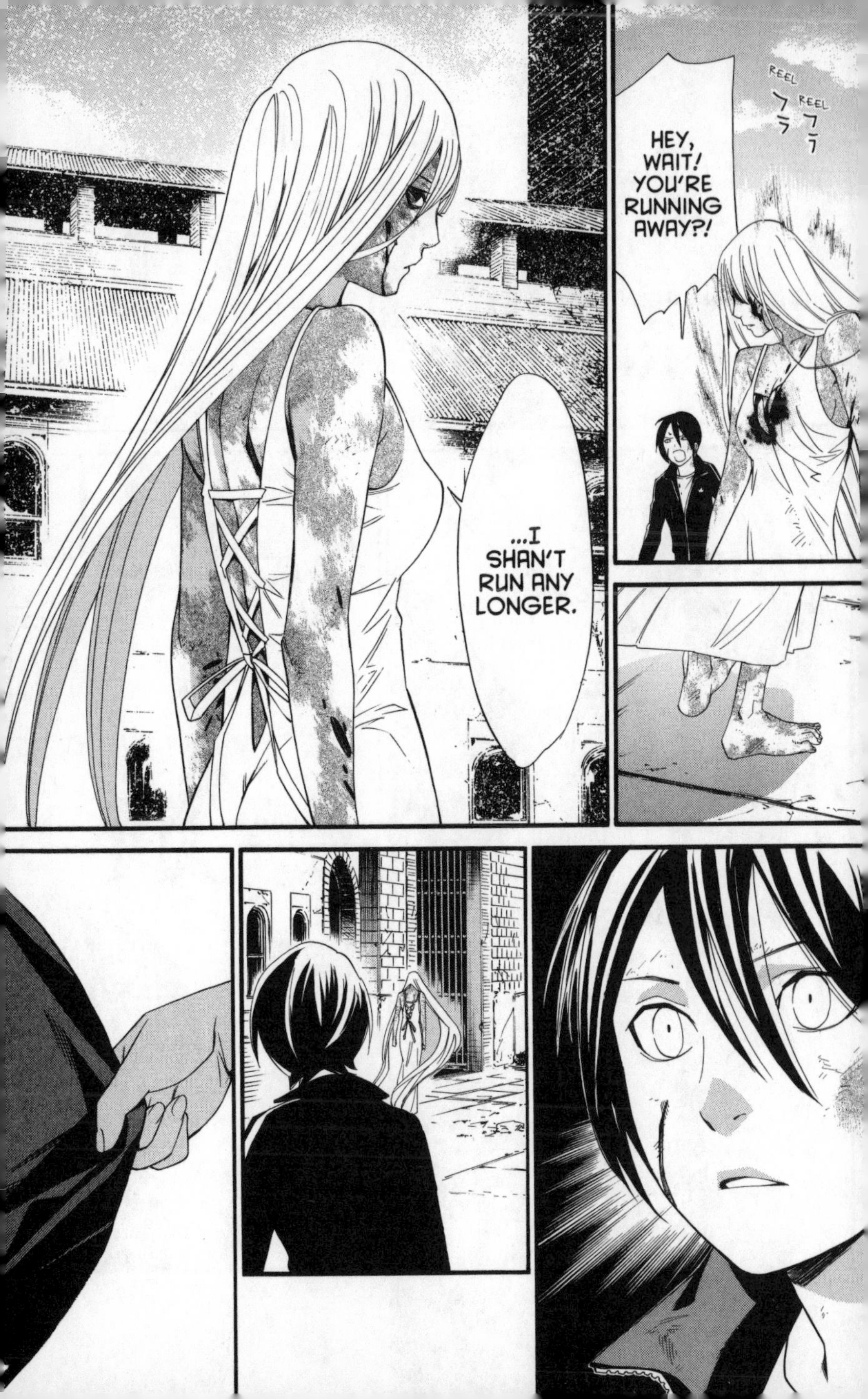
REEL
REEL
HEY, WAIT! YOU'RE RUNNING AWAY?!
...I SHAN'T RUN ANY LONGER.

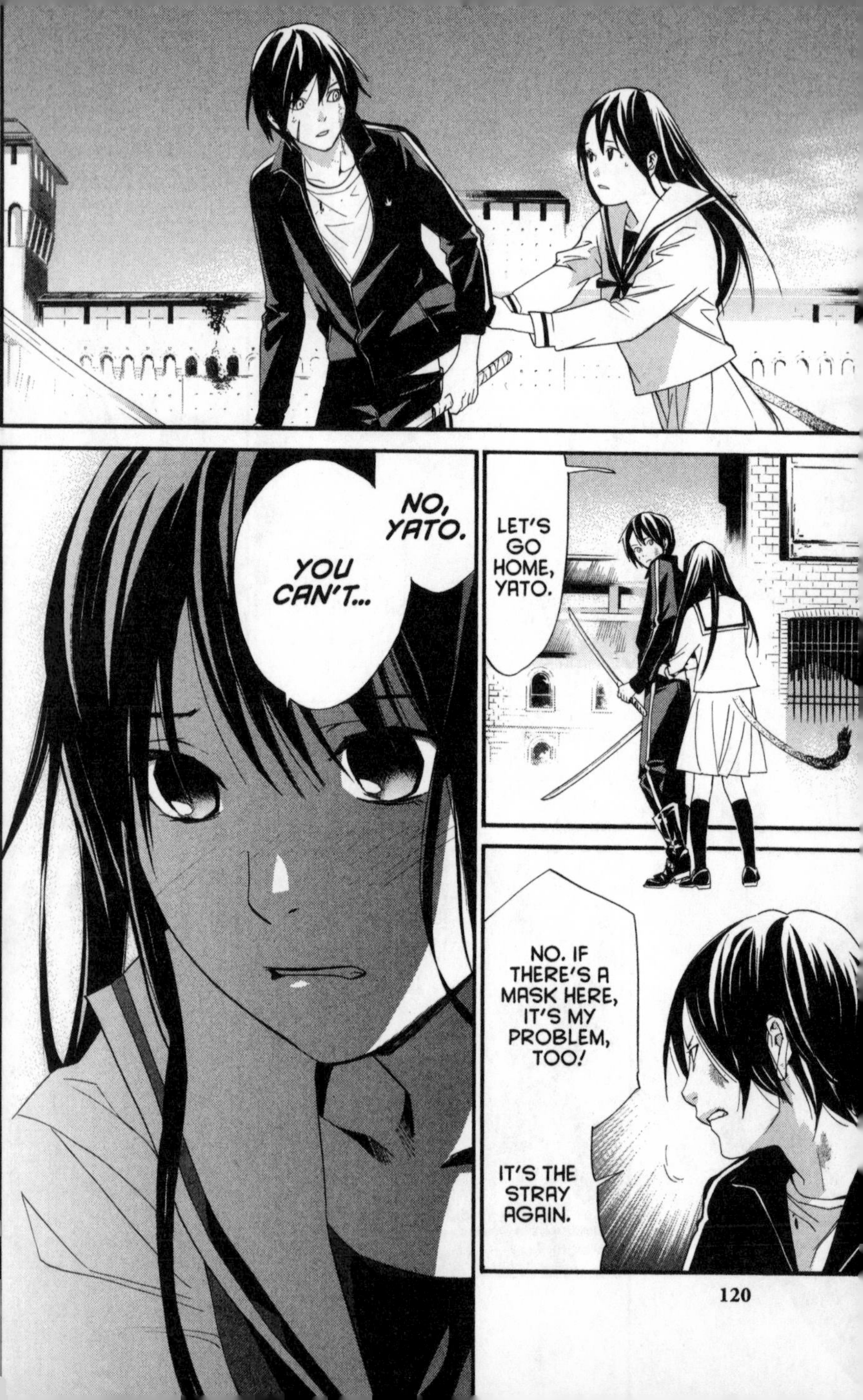
LET'S GO HOME, YATO.
NO. IF THERE'S A MASK HERE, IT'S MY PROBLEM, TOO!
IT'S THE STRAY AGAIN.
NO, YATO.
YOU CAN'T...

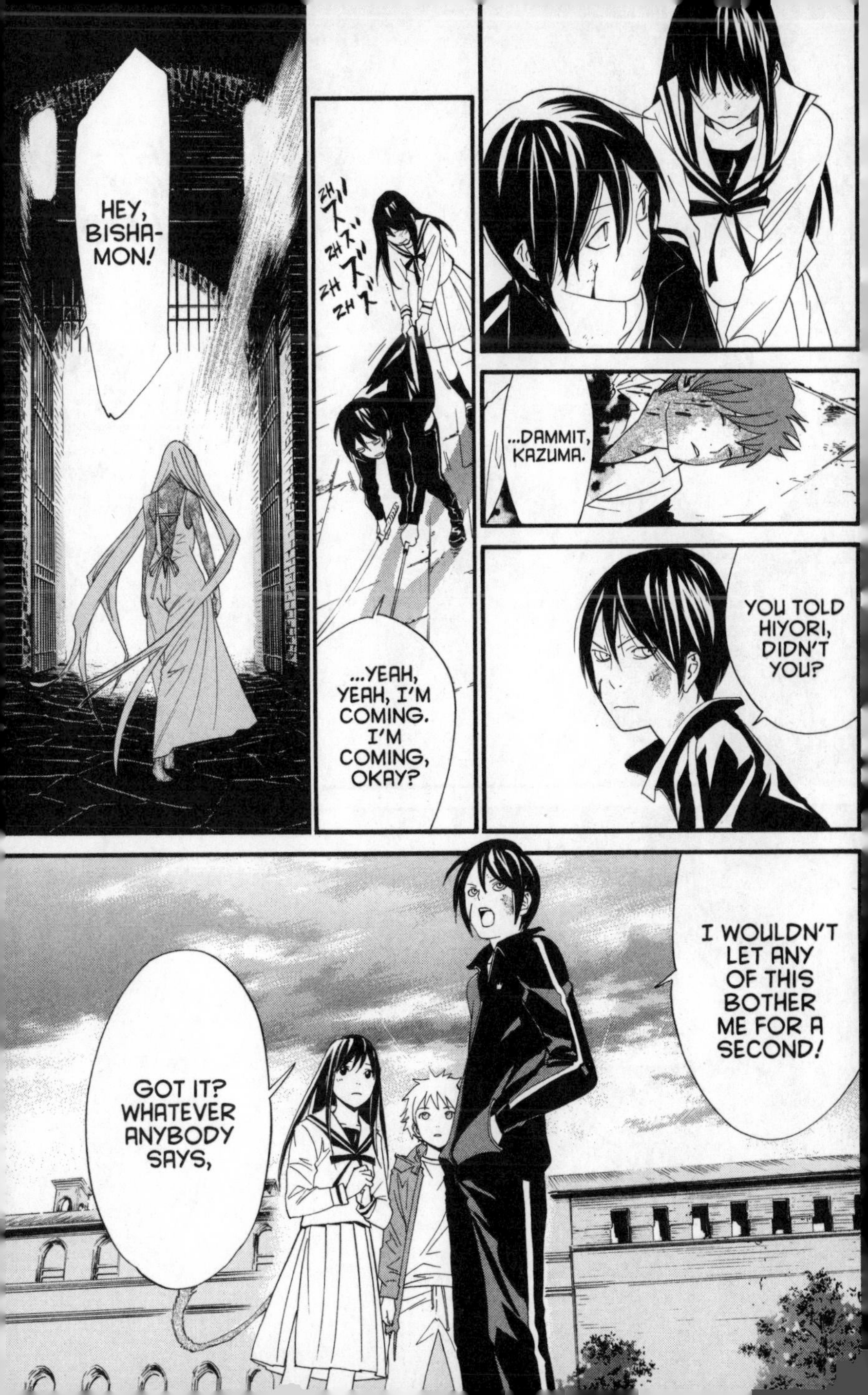
...DAMMIT, KAZUMA.
YOU TOLD HIYORI, DIDN'T YOU?
ズズズズ ZAH ZAH ZAH ZAH
...YEAH, YEAH, I'M COMING. I'M COMING, OKAY?
HEY, BISHA-MON!
I WOULDN'T LET ANY OF THIS BOTHER ME FOR A SECOND!
GOT IT? WHATEVER ANYBODY SAYS,

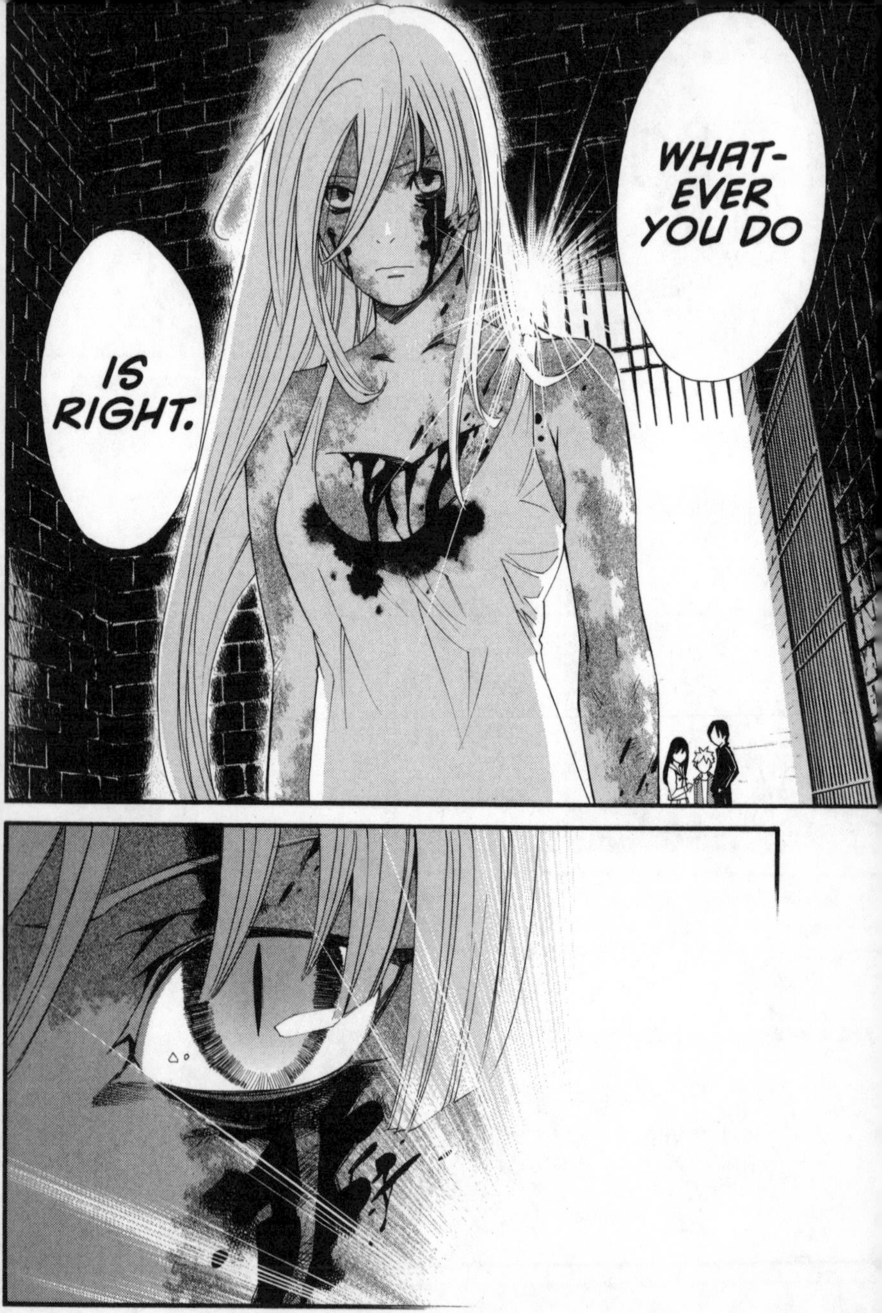
WHAT-EVER YOU DO
IS RIGHT.

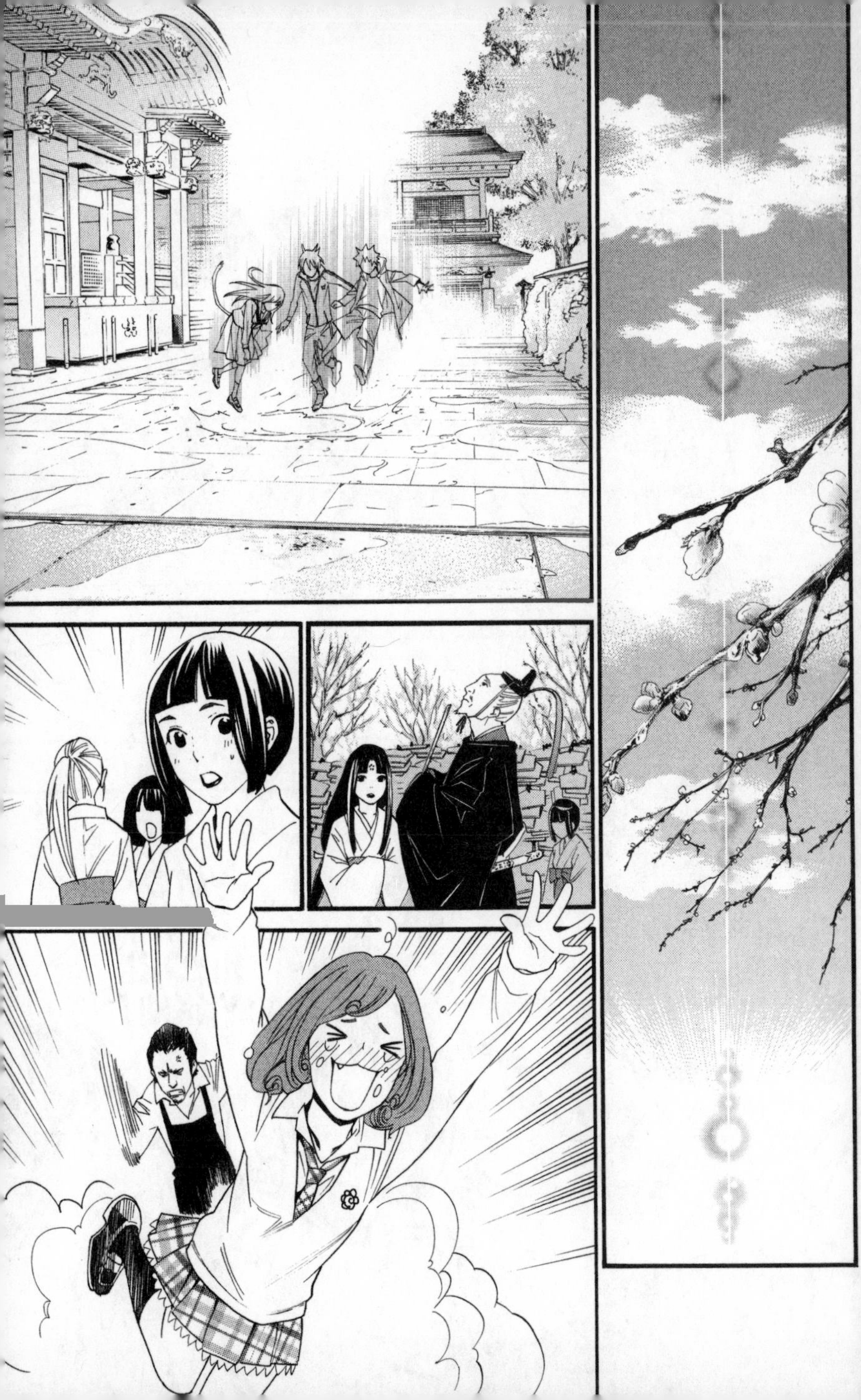

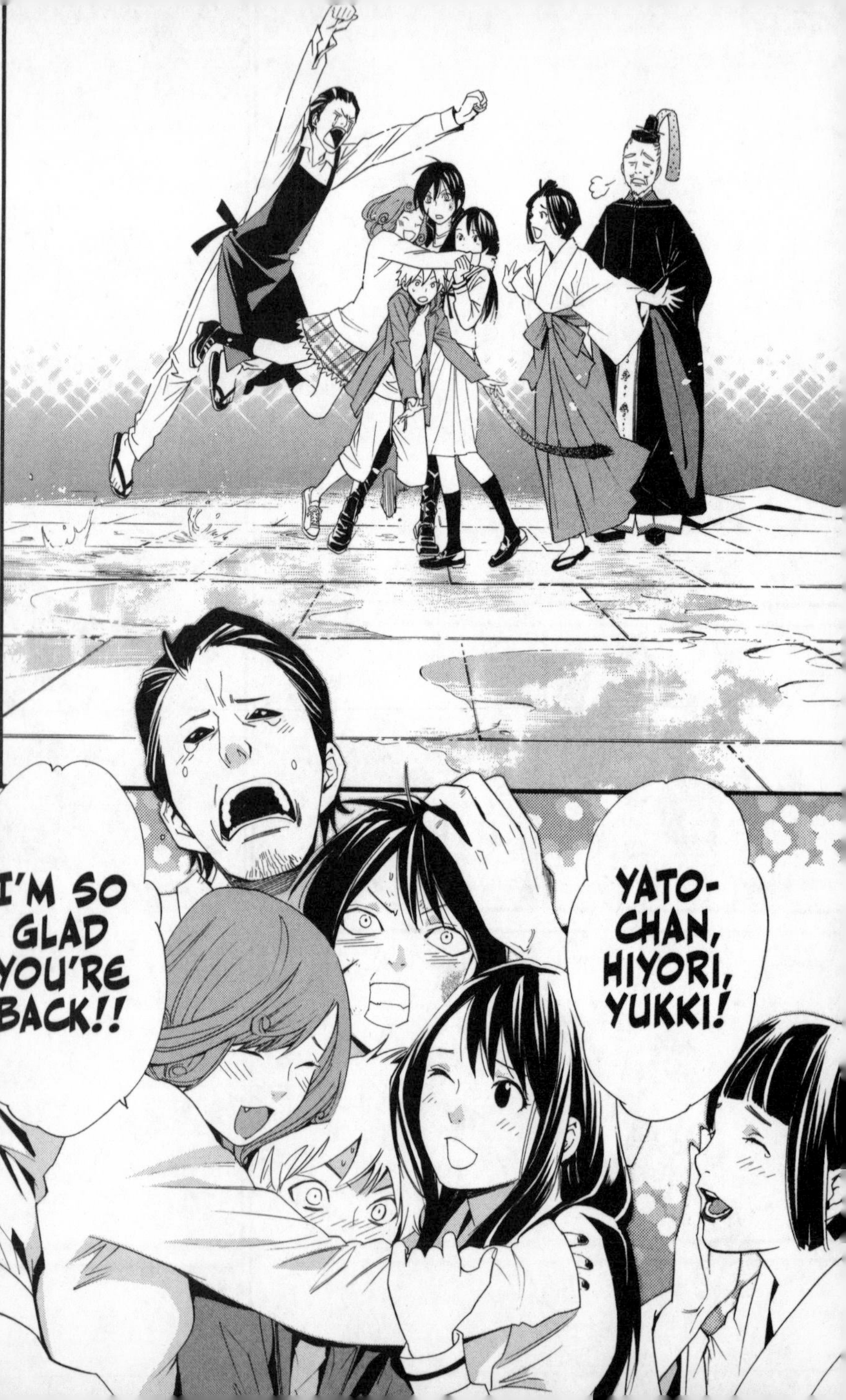
YATO-CHAN, HIYORI, YUKKI!
I'M SO GLAD YOU'RE BACK!!

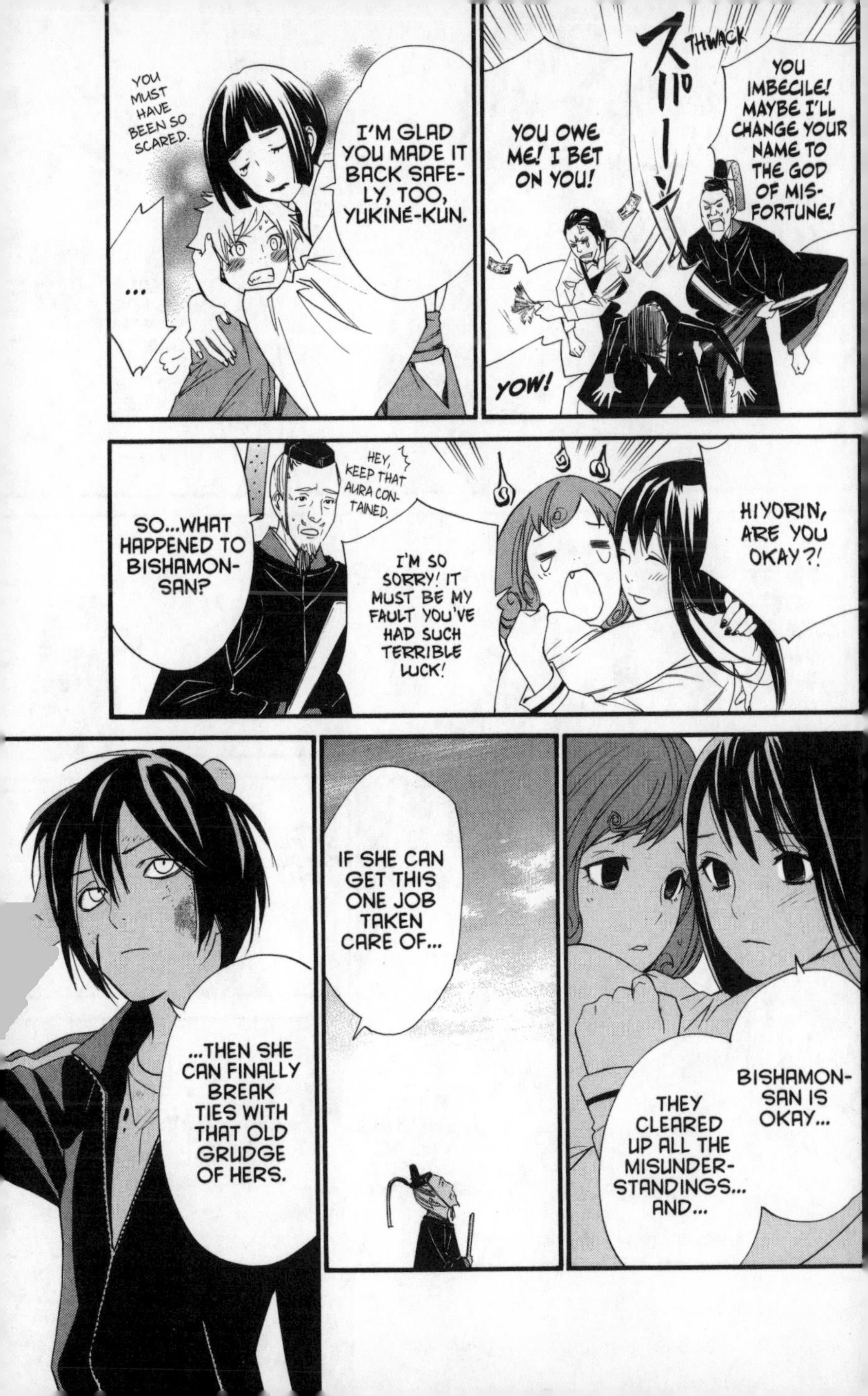
スパーン
THWACK
YOU IMBECILE! MAYBE I'LL CHANGE YOUR NAME TO THE GOD OF MIS-FORTUNE!
YOU OWE ME! I BET ON YOU!
YOW!
I'M GLAD YOU MADE IT BACK SAFE-LY, TOO, YUKINÉ-KUN.
YOU MUST HAVE BEEN SO SCARED.
...
HIYORIN, ARE YOU OKAY?!
I'M SO SORRY! IT MUST BE MY FAULT YOU'VE HAD SUCH TERRIBLE LUCK!
HEY, KEEP THAT AURA CON-TAINED.
SO...WHAT HAPPENED TO BISHAMON-SAN?
BISHAMON-SAN IS OKAY...
THEY CLEARED UP ALL THE MISUNDER-STANDINGS... AND...
IF SHE CAN GET THIS ONE JOB TAKEN CARE OF...
...THEN SHE CAN FINALLY BREAK TIES WITH THAT OLD GRUDGE OF HERS.

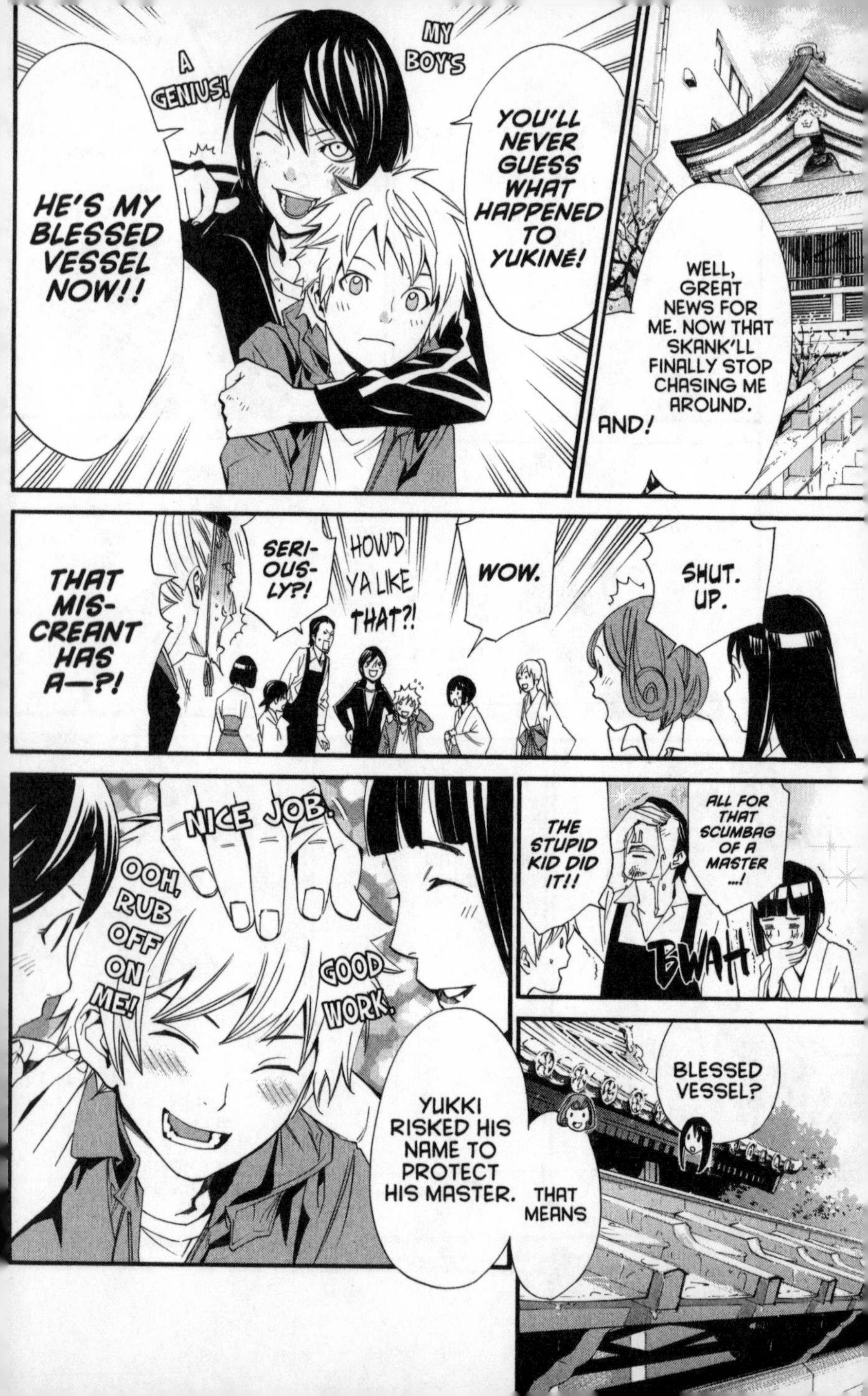
WELL, GREAT NEWS FOR ME. NOW THAT SKANK'LL FINALLY STOP CHASING ME AROUND.
AND!
YOU'LL NEVER GUESS WHAT HAPPENED TO YUKINÉ!
MY BOY'S
A GENIUS!
HE'S MY BLESSED VESSEL NOW!!
SHUT. UP.
WOW.
HOW'D YA LIKE THAT?!
SERI-OUS-LY?!
THAT MIS-CREANT HAS A—?!
ALL FOR THAT SCUMBAG OF A MASTER ...!
THE STUPID KID DID IT!!
BWAH
BLESSED VESSEL?
YUKKI RISKED HIS NAME TO PROTECT HIS MASTER.
THAT MEANS
NICE JOB.
GOOD WORK.
OOH, RUB OFF ON ME!

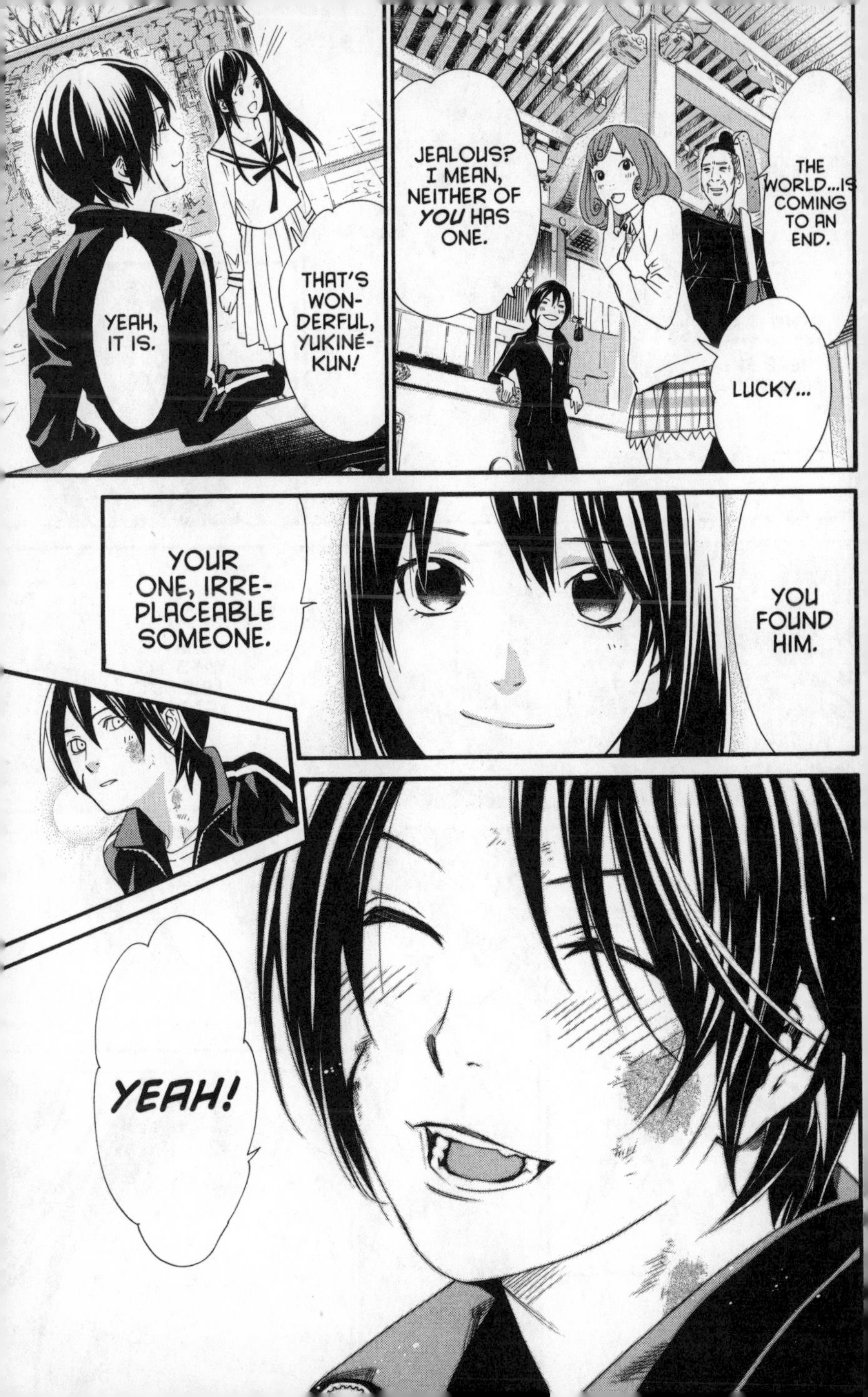
THE WORLD...IS COMING TO AN END.
JEALOUS? I MEAN, NEITHER OF *YOU* HAS ONE.
LUCKY...
THAT'S WON-DERFUL, YUKINÉ-KUN!
YEAH, IT IS.
YOU FOUND HIM.
YOUR ONE, IRRE-PLACEABLE SOMEONE.
YEAH!

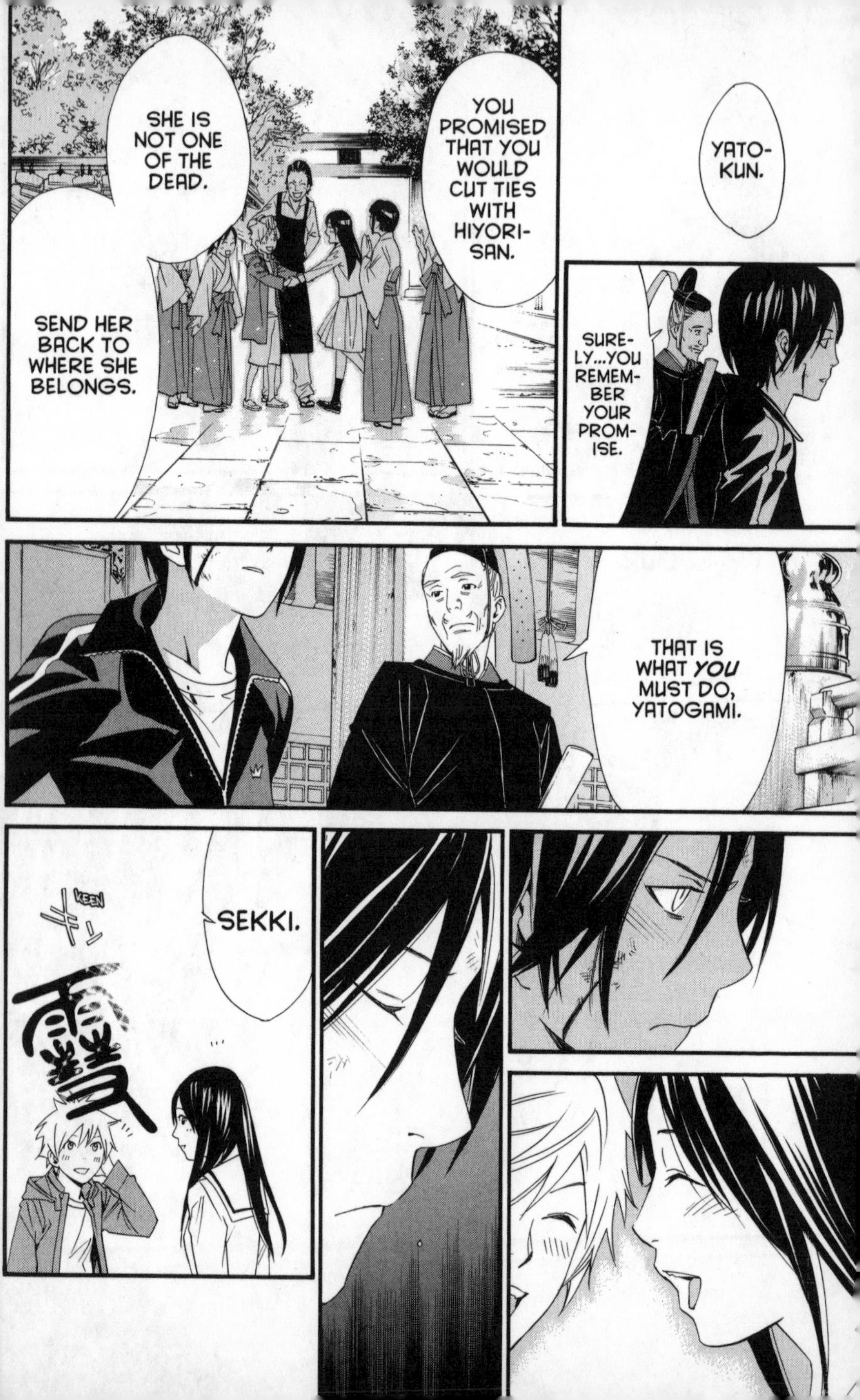
YATO-KUN.
SURELY...YOU REMEMBER YOUR PROMISE.
YOU PROMISED THAT YOU WOULD CUT TIES WITH HIYORI-SAN.
SHE IS NOT ONE OF THE DEAD.
SEND HER BACK TO WHERE SHE BELONGS.
THAT IS WHAT *YOU* MUST DO, YATOGAMI.
SEKKI.
キン
KEEN
...

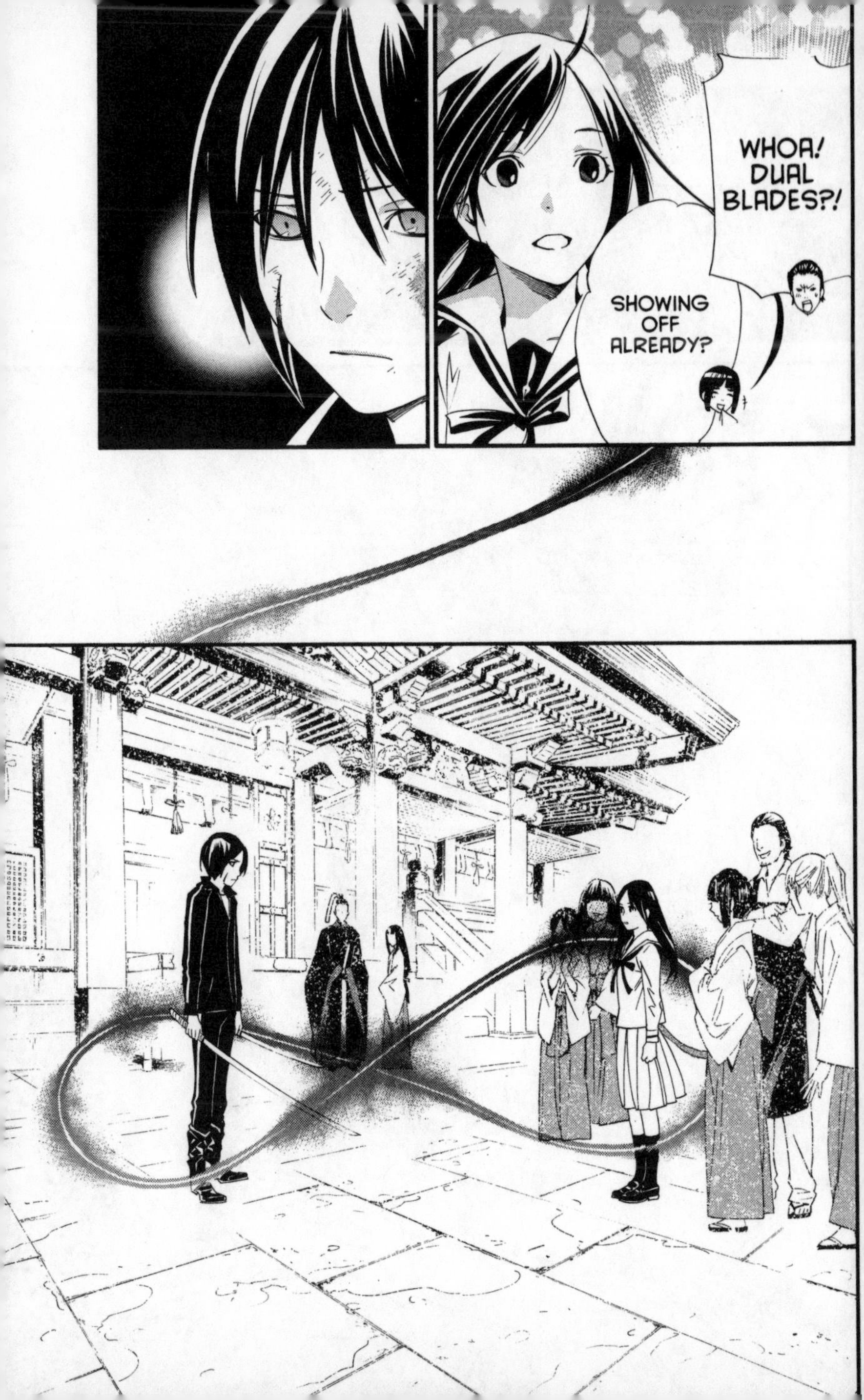
WHOA! DUAL BLADES?!
SHOWING OFF ALREADY?

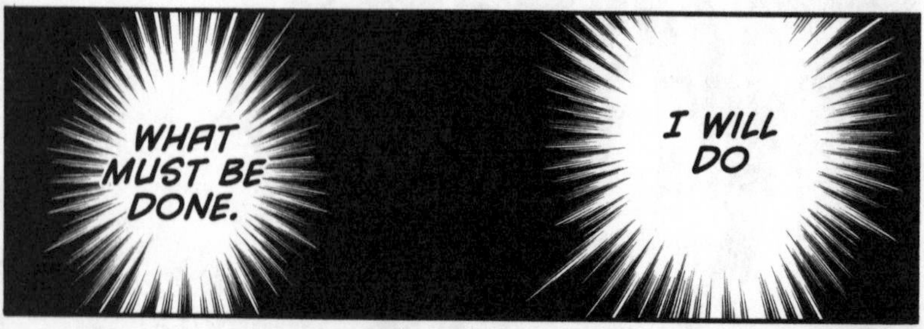
I WILL DO
WHAT MUST BE DONE.
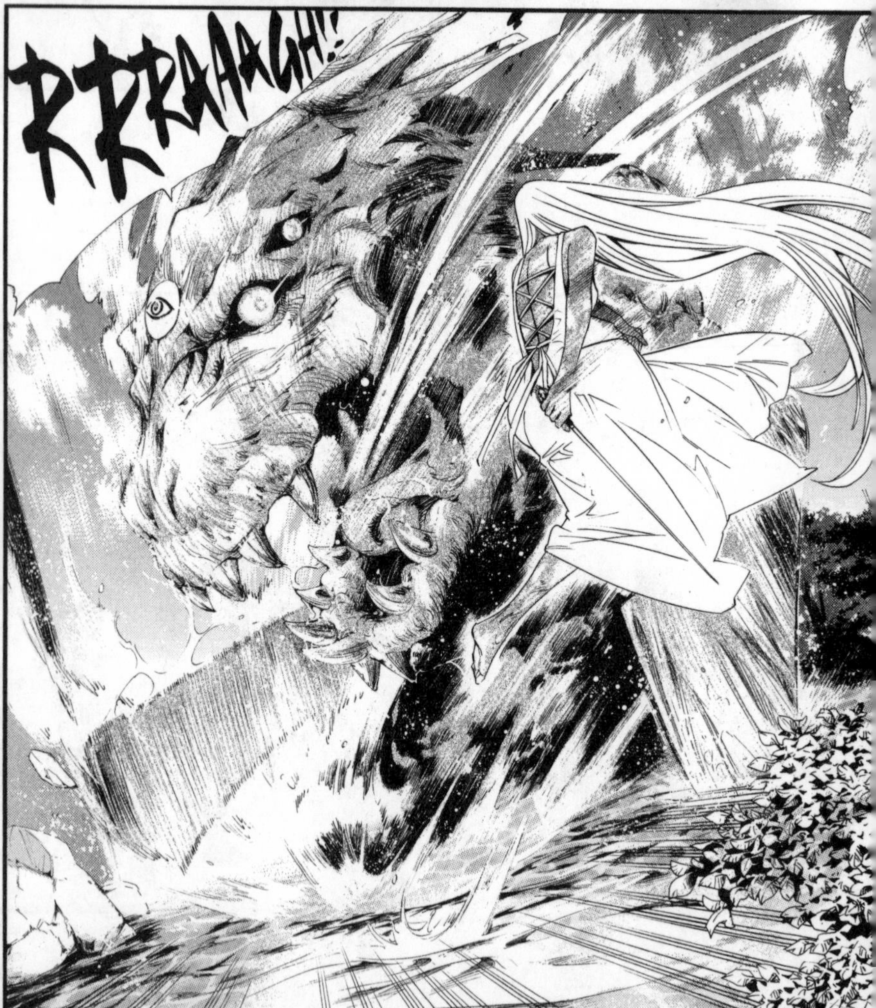
RRRAAAGH!!

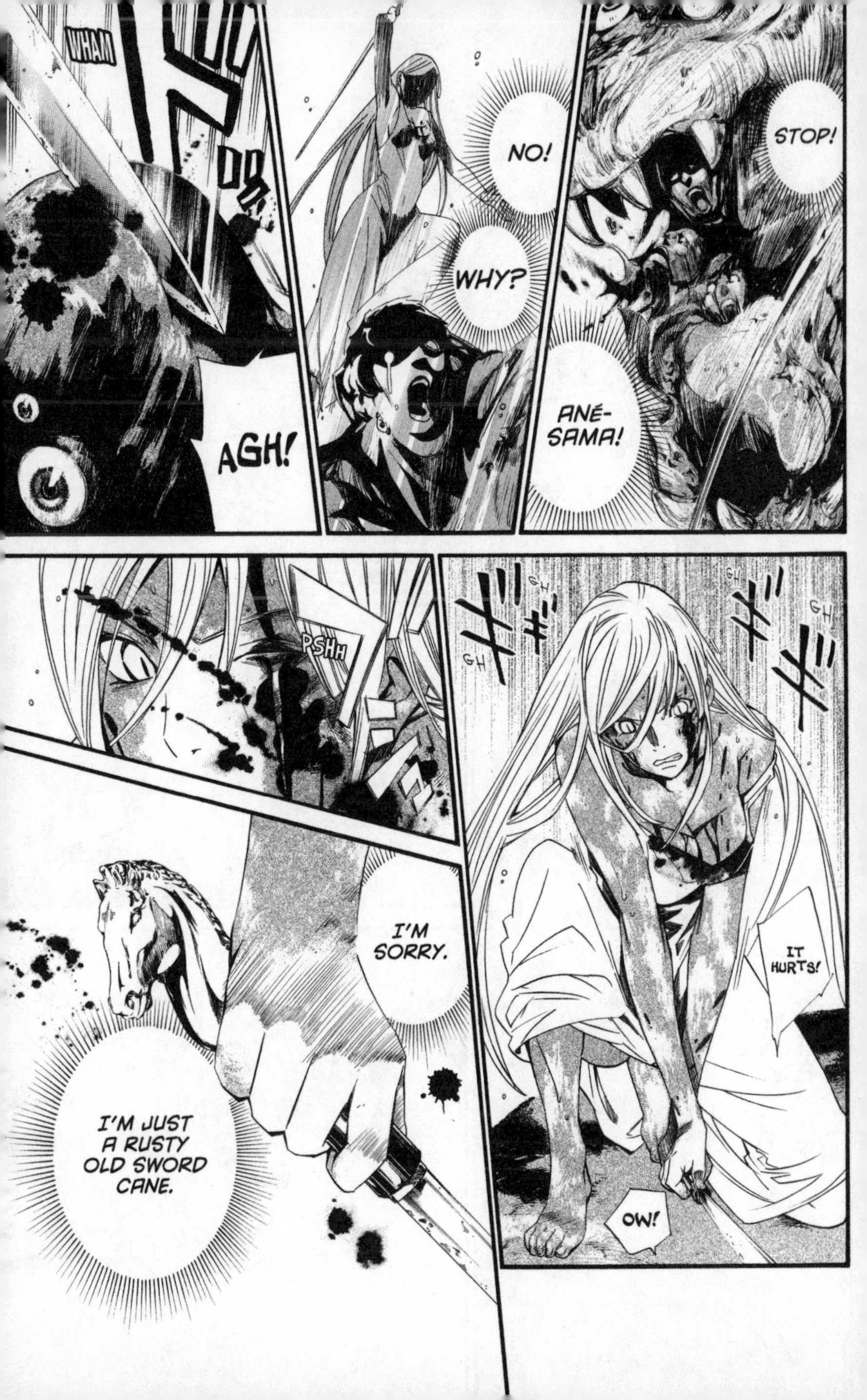
STOP!
ANÉ-SAMA!
NO!
WHY?
WHAM
AGH!
GH
GH
GH
GH
IT HURTS!
OW!
PSHH
I'M SORRY.
I'M JUST A RUSTY OLD SWORD CANE.

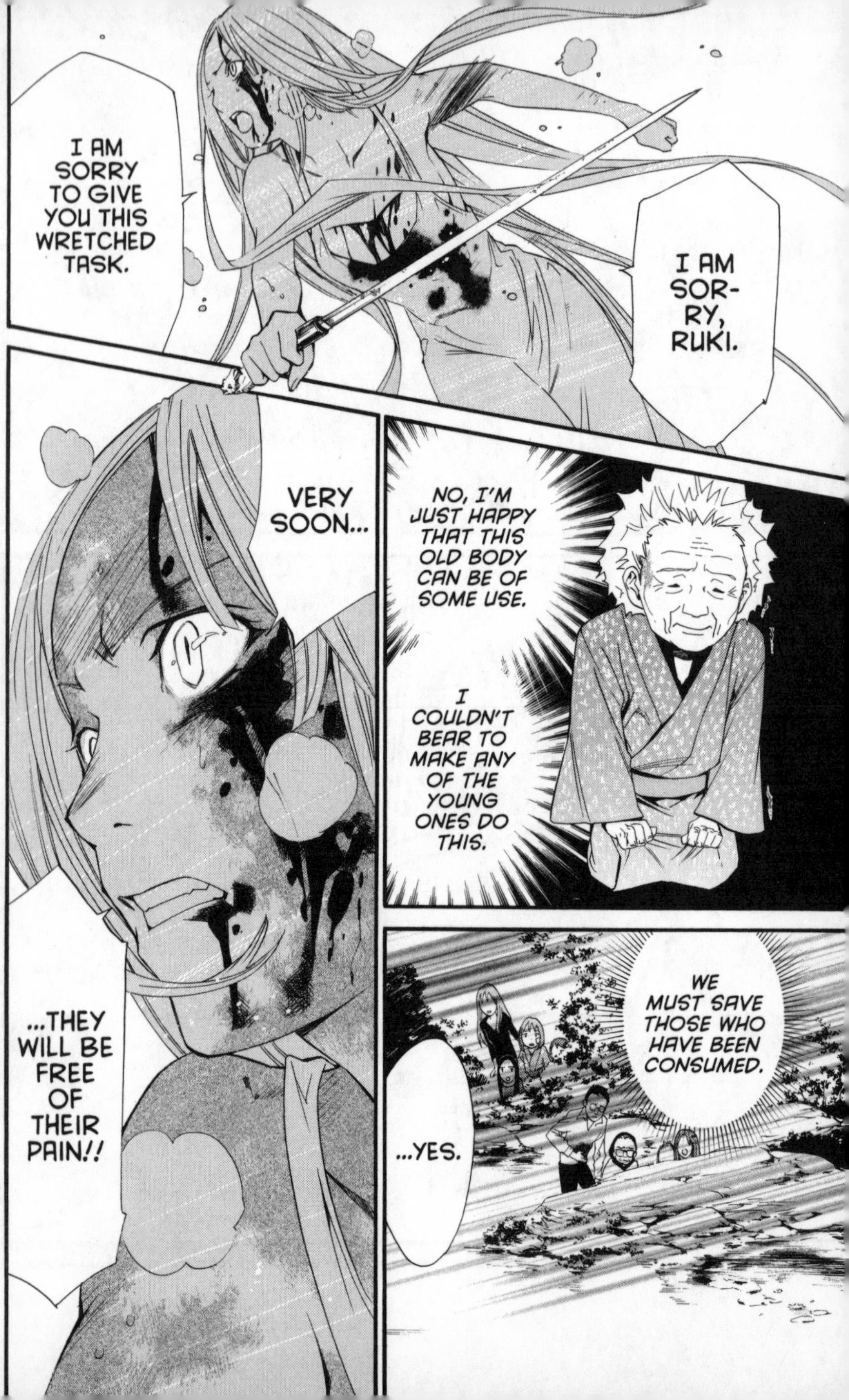
I AM SORRY, RUKI.
I AM SORRY TO GIVE YOU THIS WRETCHED TASK.
NO, I'M JUST HAPPY THAT THIS OLD BODY CAN BE OF SOME USE.
I COULDN'T BEAR TO MAKE ANY OF THE YOUNG ONES DO THIS.
WE MUST SAVE THOSE WHO HAVE BEEN CONSUMED.
...YES.
VERY SOON...
...THEY WILL BE FREE OF THEIR PAIN!!

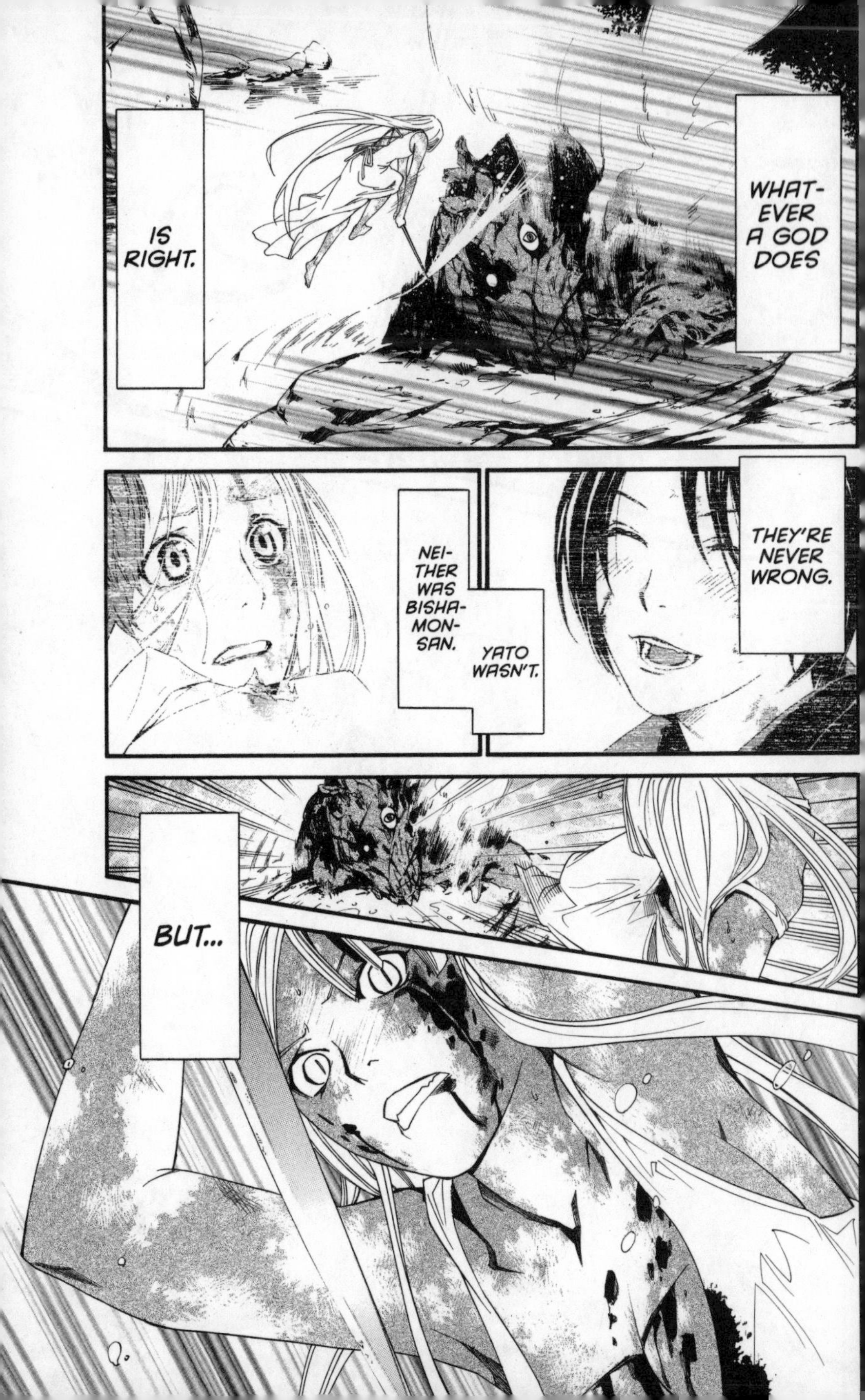
WHATEVER A GOD DOES
IS RIGHT.
THEY'RE NEVER WRONG.
YATO WASN'T.
NEITHER WAS BISHAMON-SAN.
BUT...

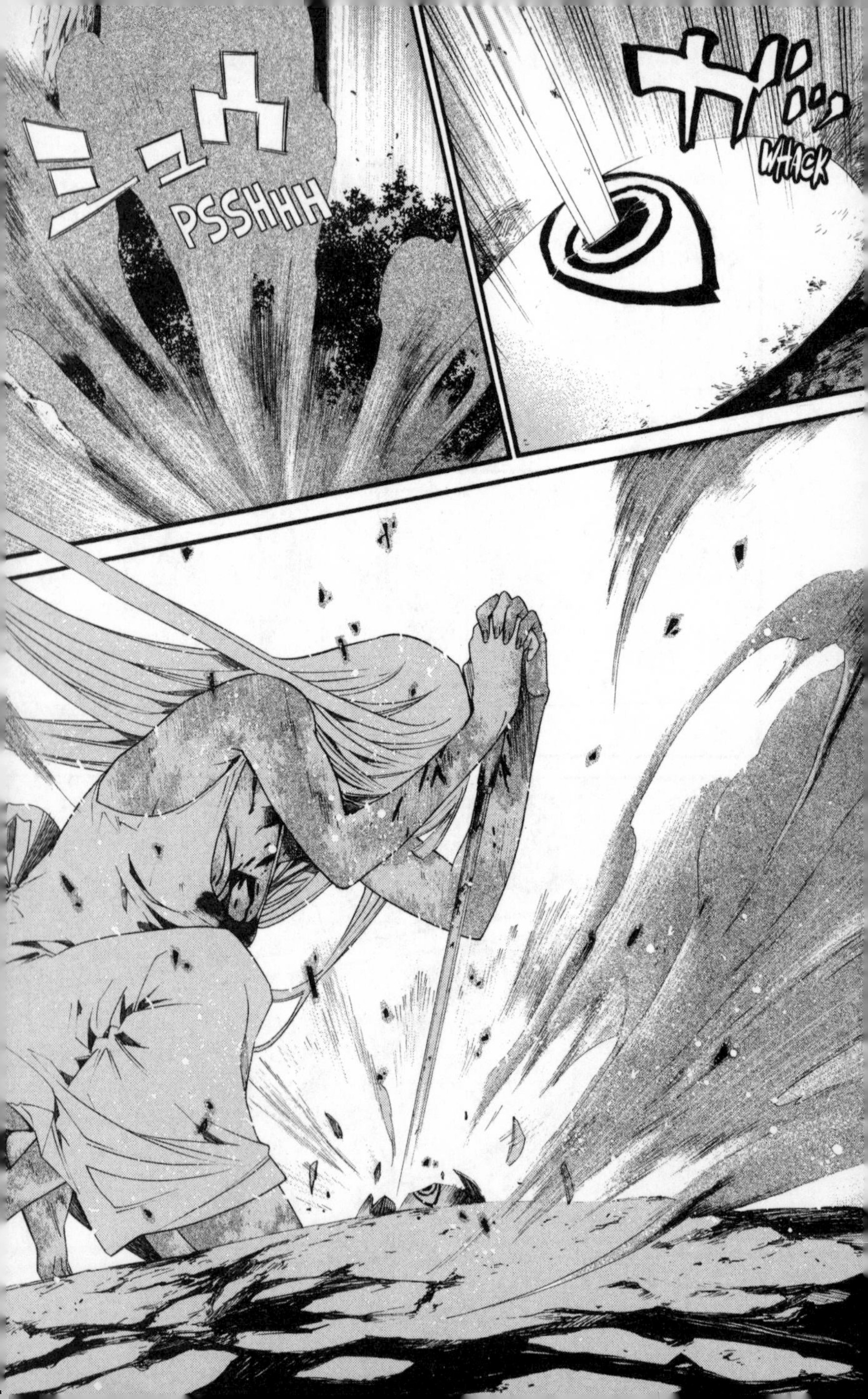
ザクッ
WHACK
シュウ
PSSHHH

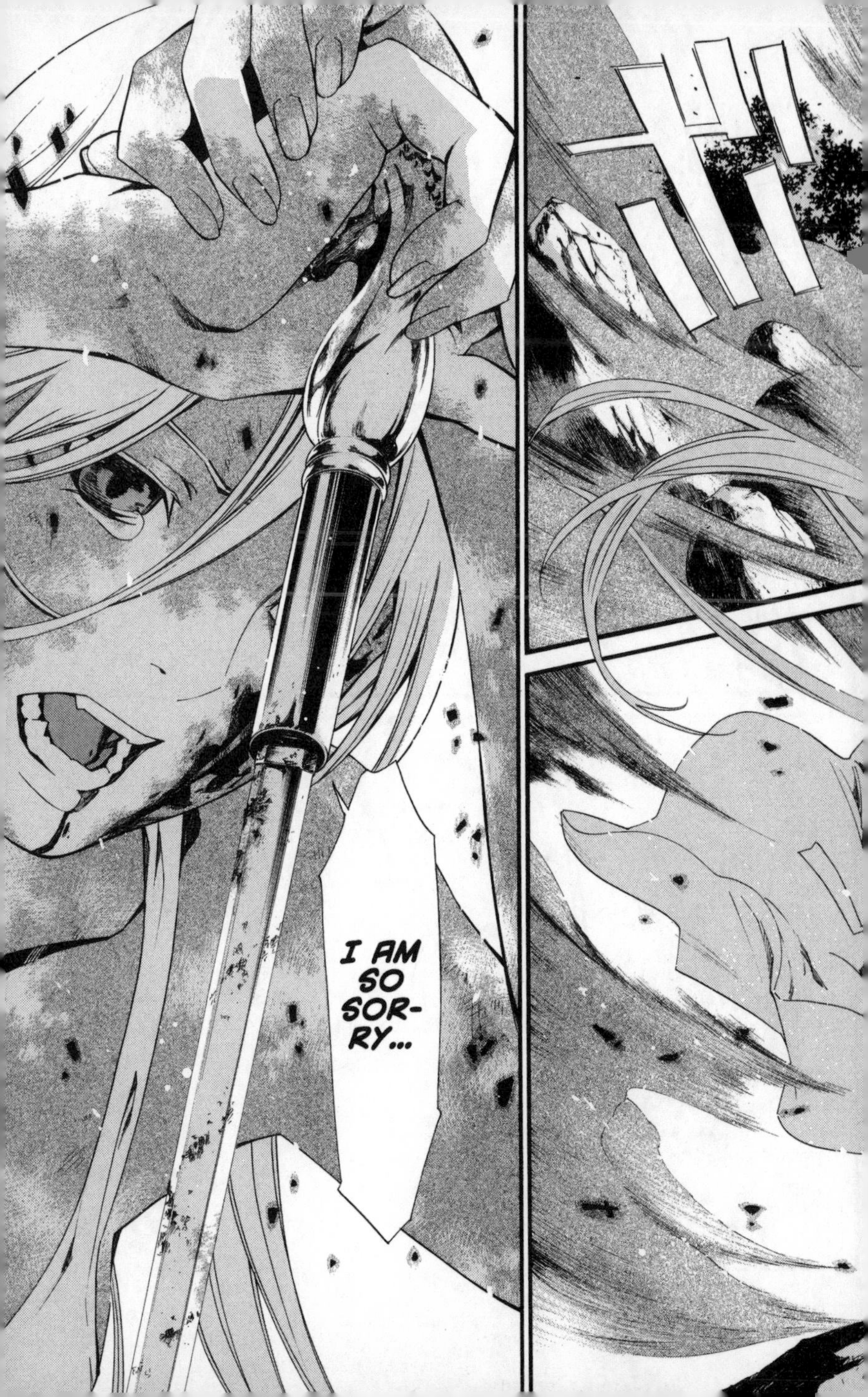
I AM SO SORRY...

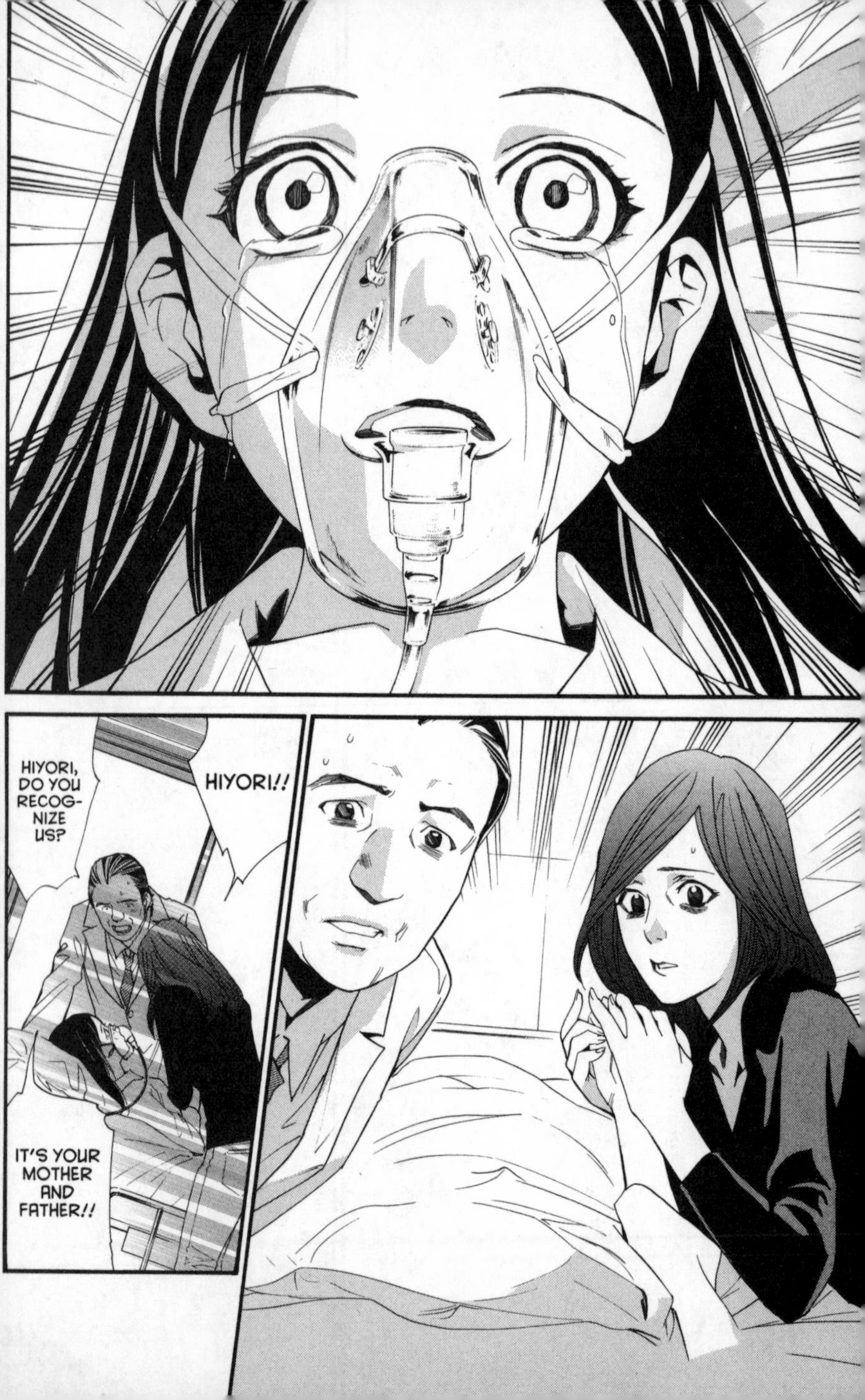
HIYORI!!
HIYORI, DO YOU RECOGNIZE US?
IT'S YOUR MOTHER AND FATHER!!

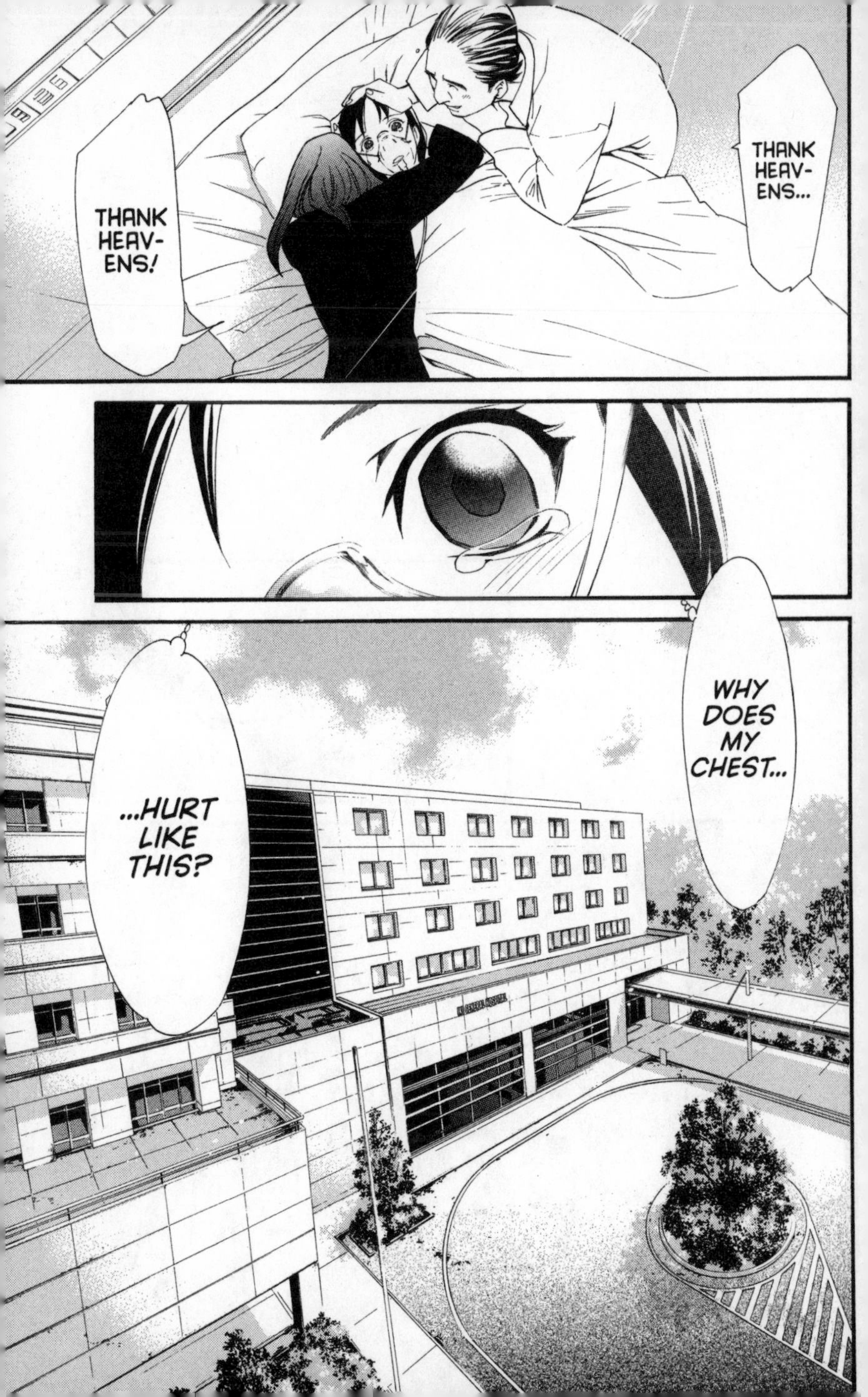
THANK HEAV-ENS...
THANK HEAV-ENS!
WHY DOES MY CHEST...
...HURT LIKE THIS?

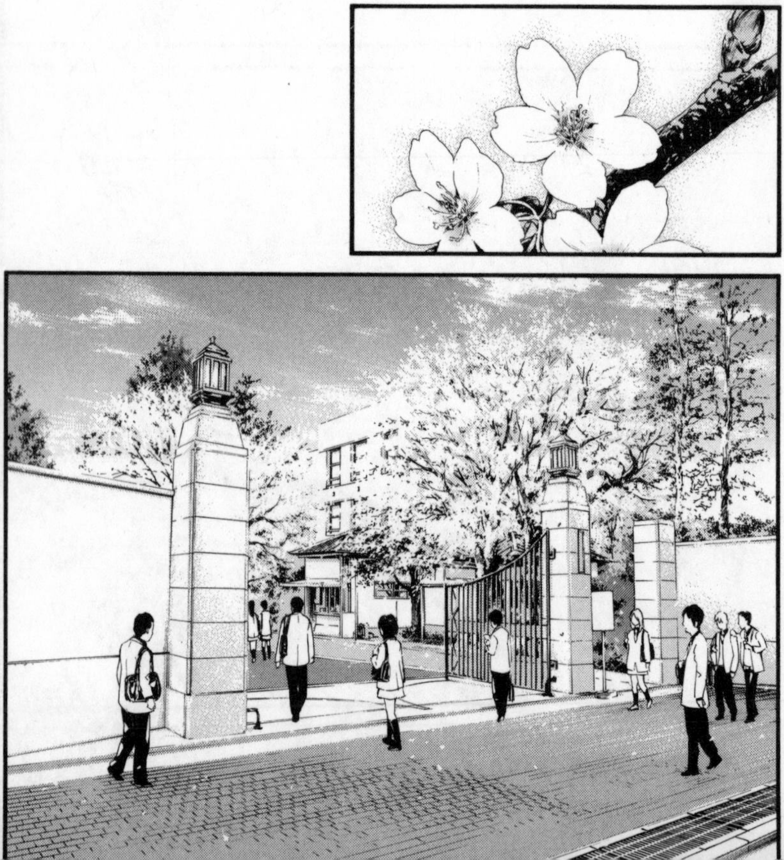

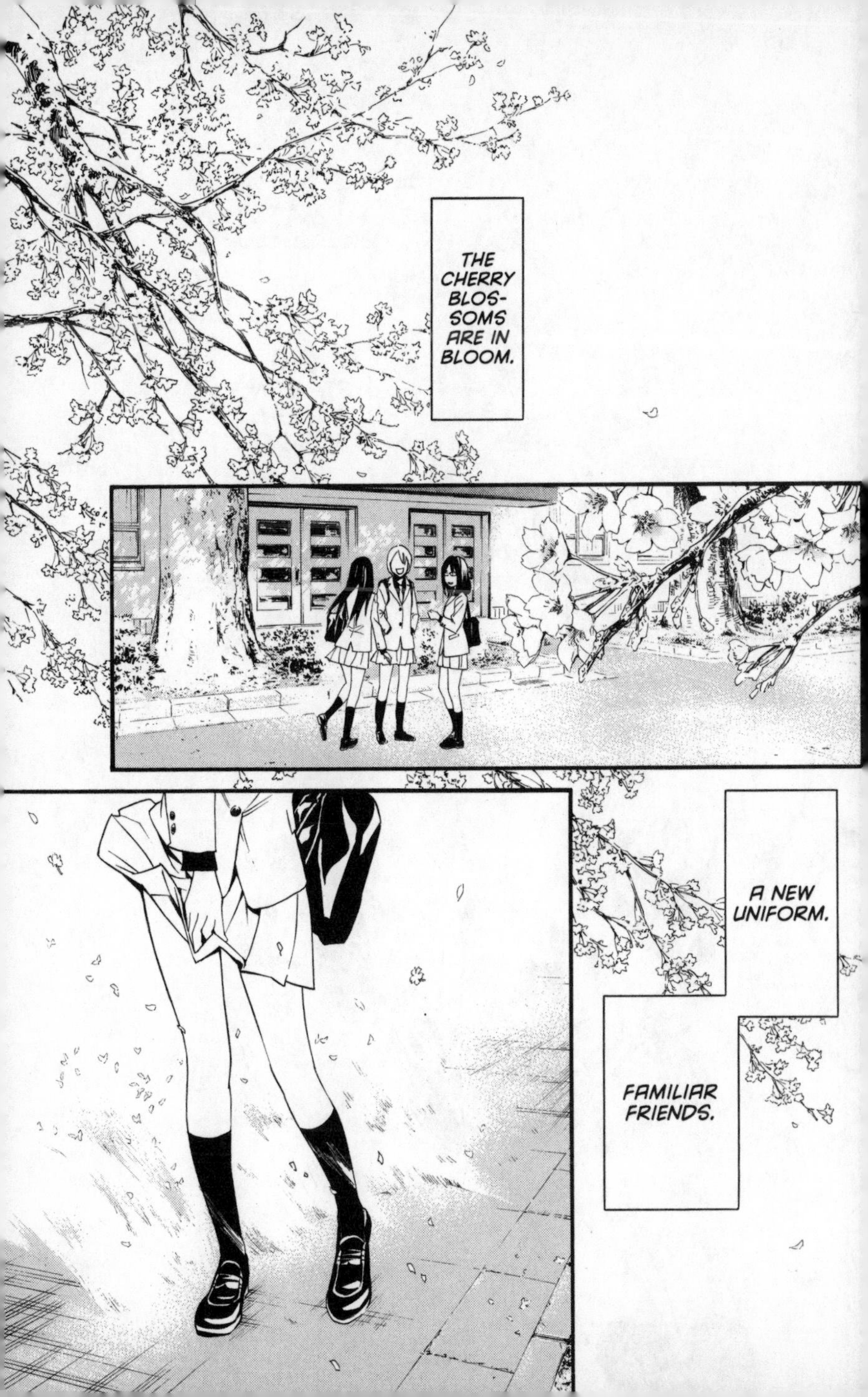
THE CHERRY BLOSSOMS ARE IN BLOOM.
A NEW UNIFORM.
FAMILIAR FRIENDS.

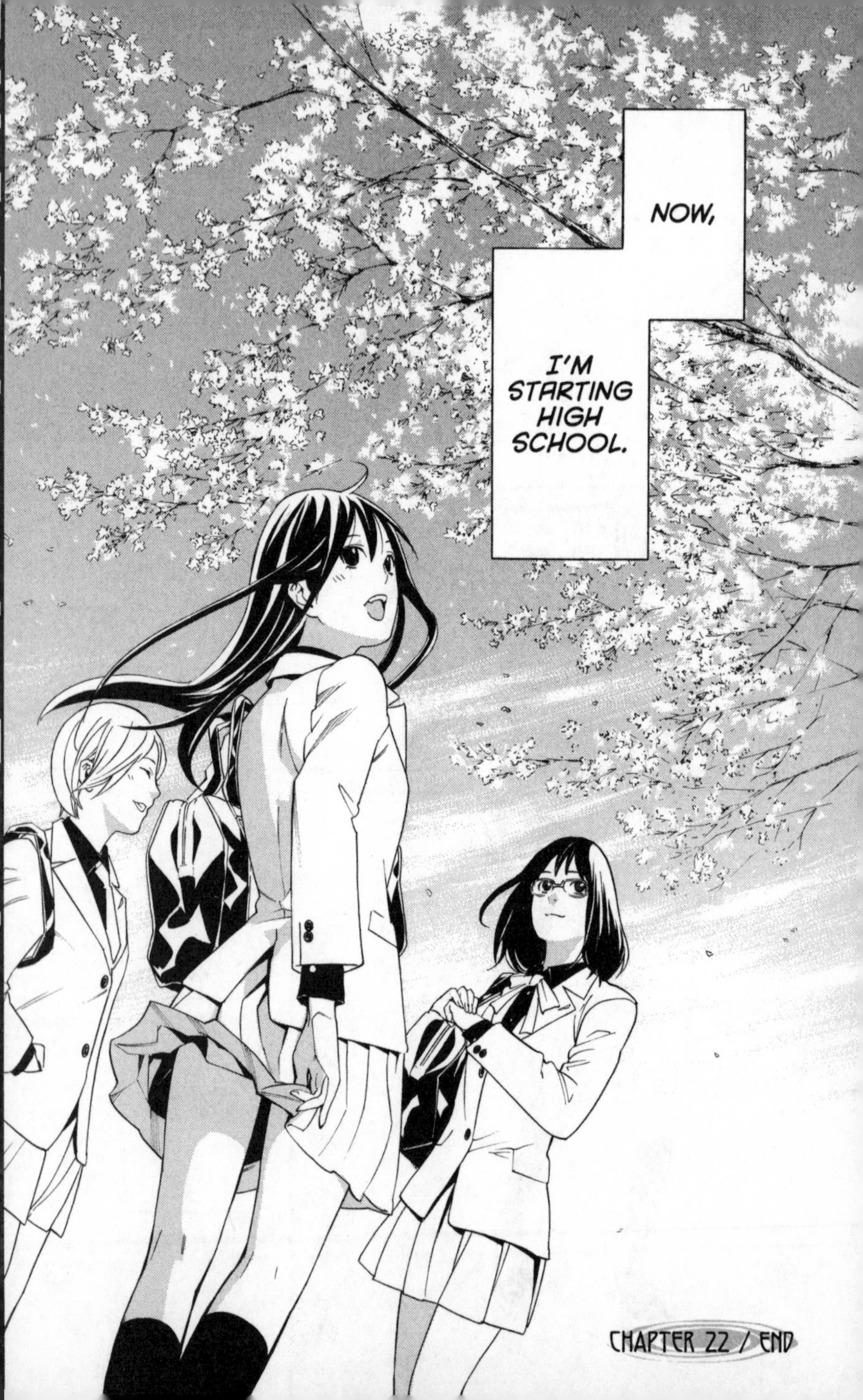
NOW,
I'M STARTING HIGH SCHOOL.
CHAPTER 22 / END

野

豈

神

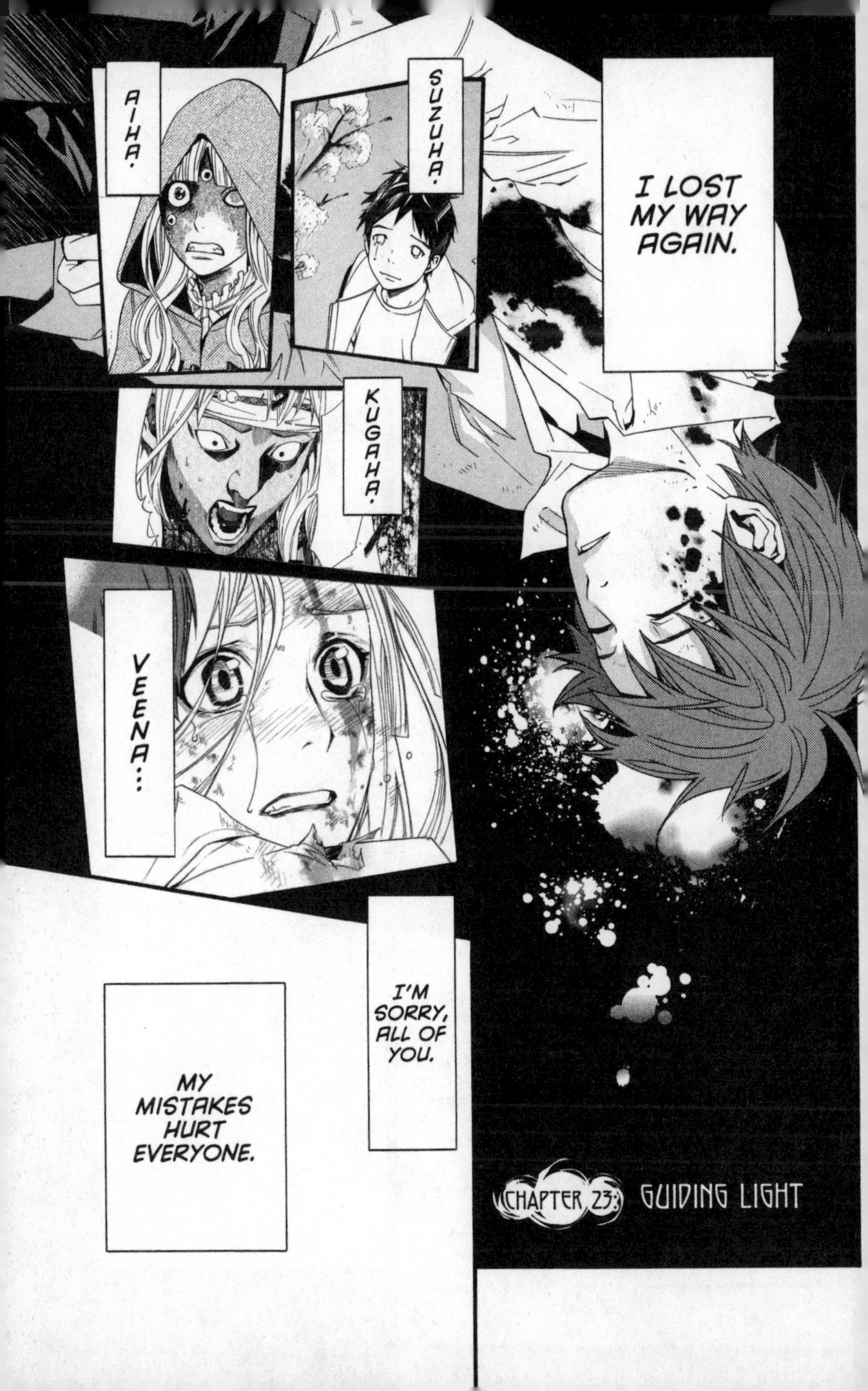

I LOST MY WAY AGAIN.
CHAPTER 23: GUIDING LIGHT
SUZUHA.
AIHA.
KUGAHA.
VEENA...
I'M SORRY, ALL OF YOU.
MY MISTAKES HURT EVERYONE.

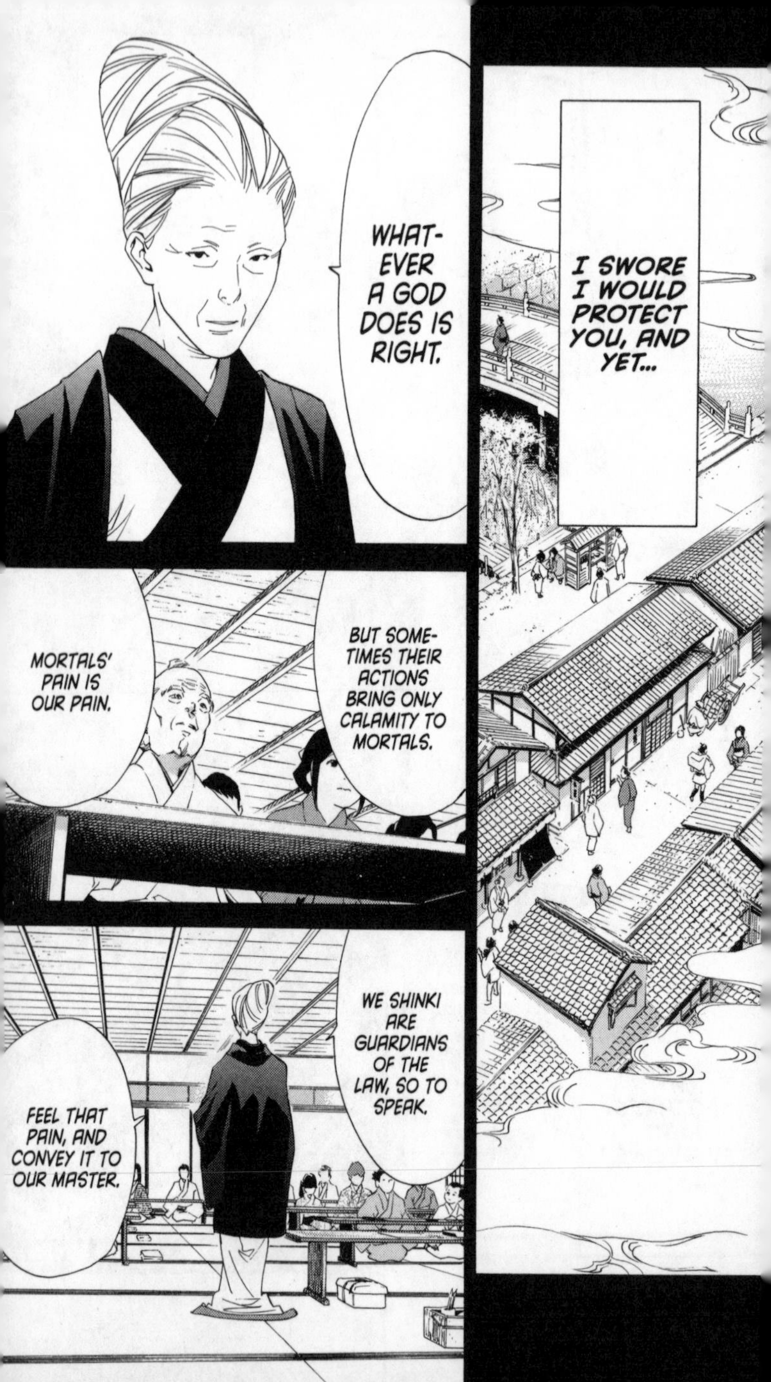
I SWORE I WOULD PROTECT YOU, AND YET...
WHAT-EVER A GOD DOES IS RIGHT.
BUT SOME-TIMES THEIR ACTIONS BRING ONLY CALAMITY TO MORTALS.
MORTALS' PAIN IS OUR PAIN.
WE SHINKI ARE GUARDIANS OF THE LAW, SO TO SPEAK.
FEEL THAT PAIN, AND CONVEY IT TO OUR MASTER.

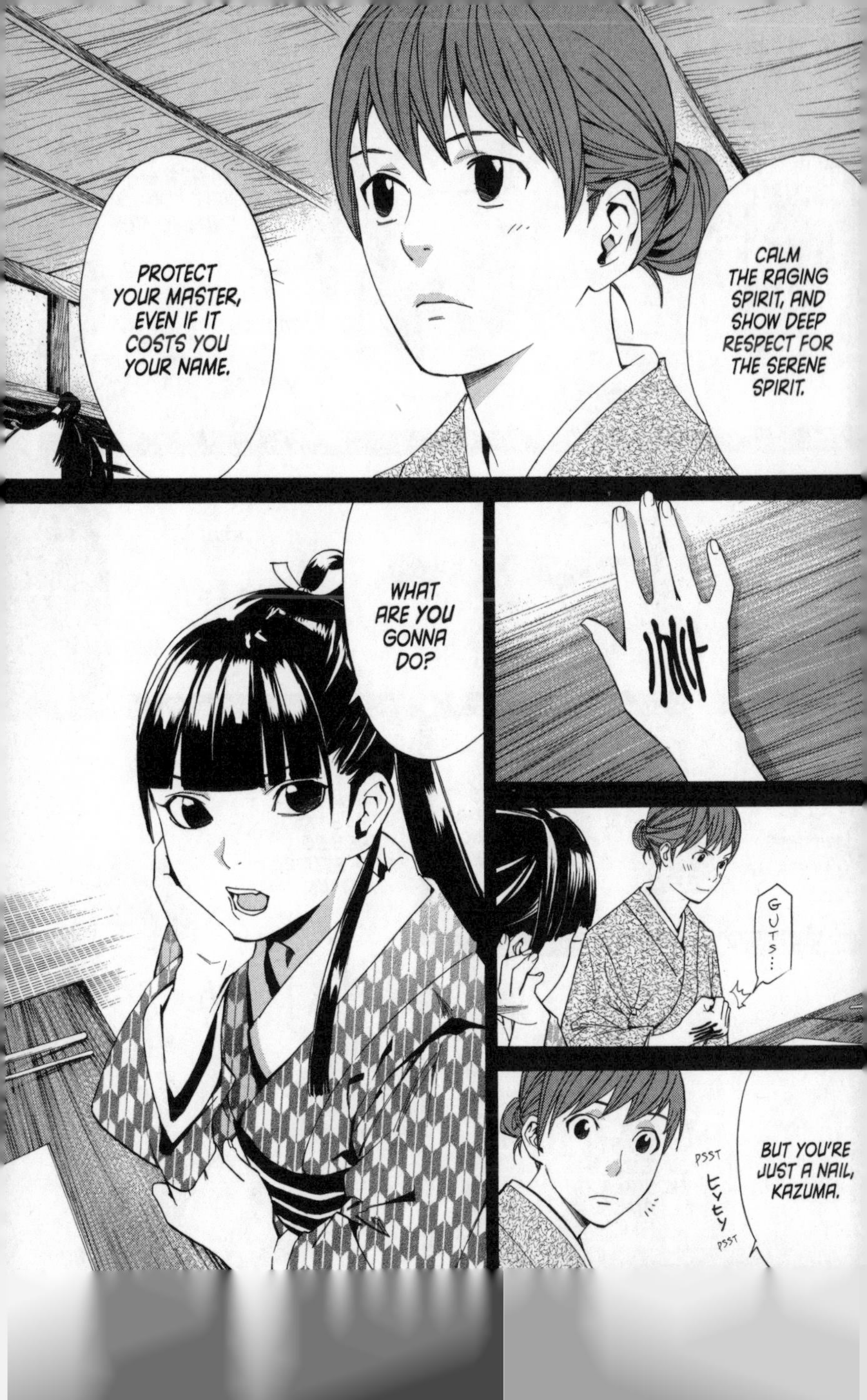
CALM THE RAGING SPIRIT, AND SHOW DEEP RESPECT FOR THE SERENE SPIRIT.
PROTECT YOUR MASTER, EVEN IF IT COSTS YOU YOUR NAME.
GUTS...
BUT YOU'RE JUST A NAIL, KAZUMA.
PSST
ヒソヒソ
PSST
WHAT ARE YOU GONNA DO?

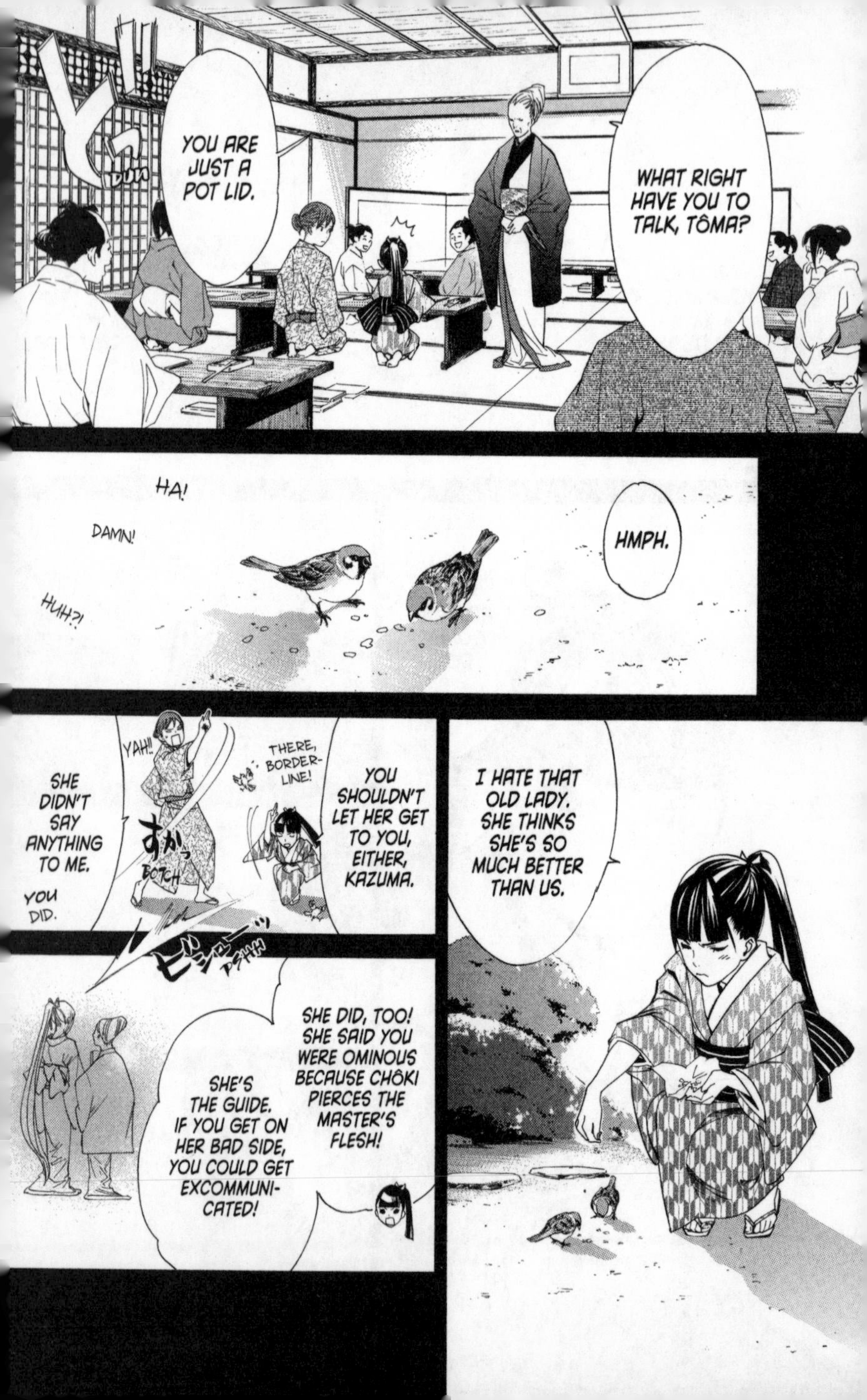
WHAT RIGHT HAVE YOU TO TALK, TÔMA?
YOU ARE JUST A POT LID.
DUN
HMPH.
HA!
DAMN!
HUH?!
I HATE THAT OLD LADY. SHE THINKS SHE'S SO MUCH BETTER THAN US.
YOU SHOULDN'T LET HER GET TO YOU, EITHER, KAZUMA.
THERE, BORDER-LINE!
YAH!!
SHE DIDN'T SAY ANYTHING TO ME.
YOU DID.
BOTCH
PSHH
SHE DID, TOO! SHE SAID YOU WERE OMINOUS BECAUSE CHÔKI PIERCES THE MASTER'S FLESH!
SHE'S THE GUIDE. IF YOU GET ON HER BAD SIDE, YOU COULD GET EXCOMMUNI-CATED!

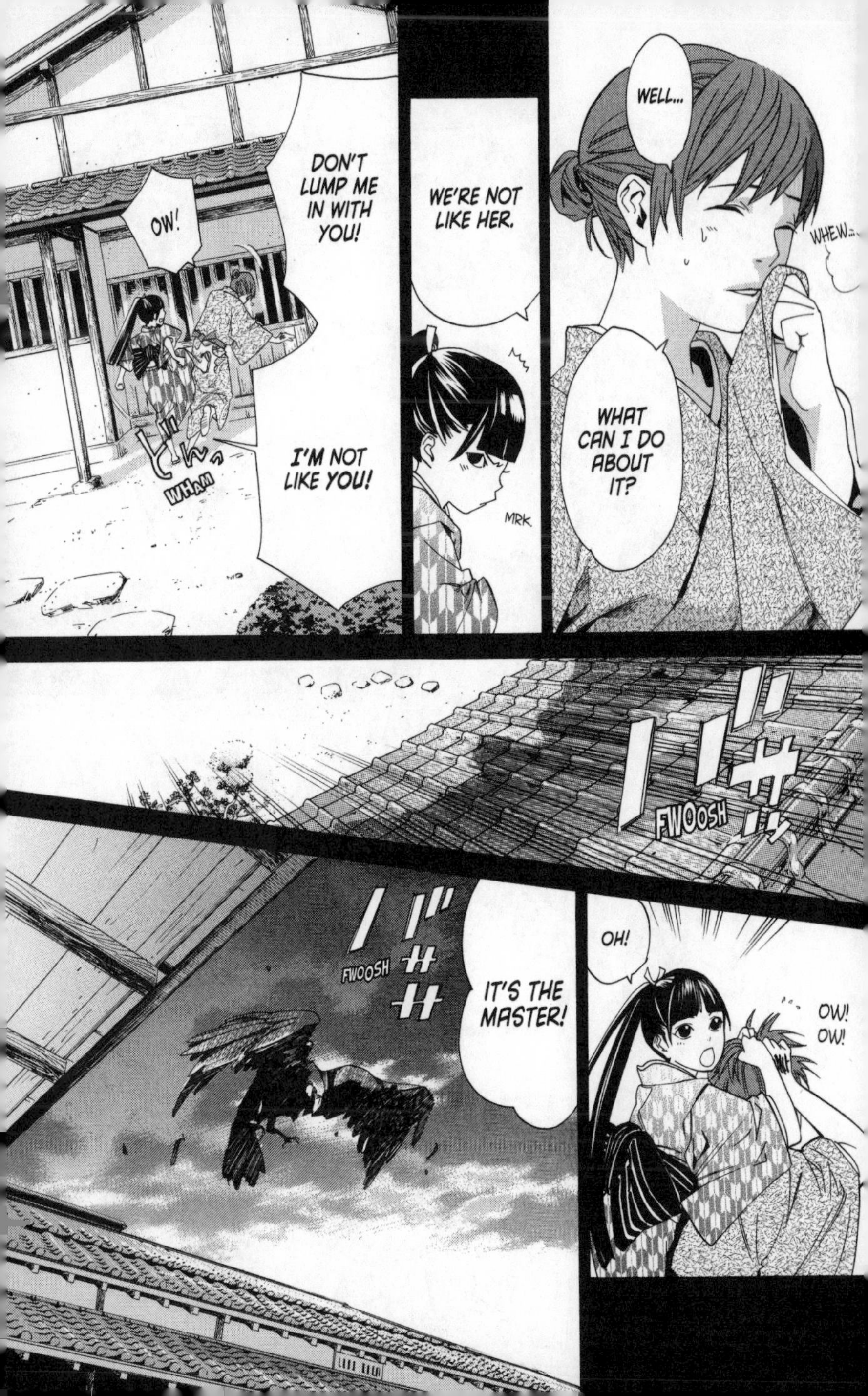
WELL...
WHEW...
WHAT CAN I DO ABOUT IT?
WE'RE NOT LIKE HER.
MRK.
DON'T LUMP ME IN WITH YOU!
OW!
I'M NOT LIKE YOU!
WHAM
FWOOSH
OH!
OW! OW!
IT'S THE MASTER!
FWOOSH

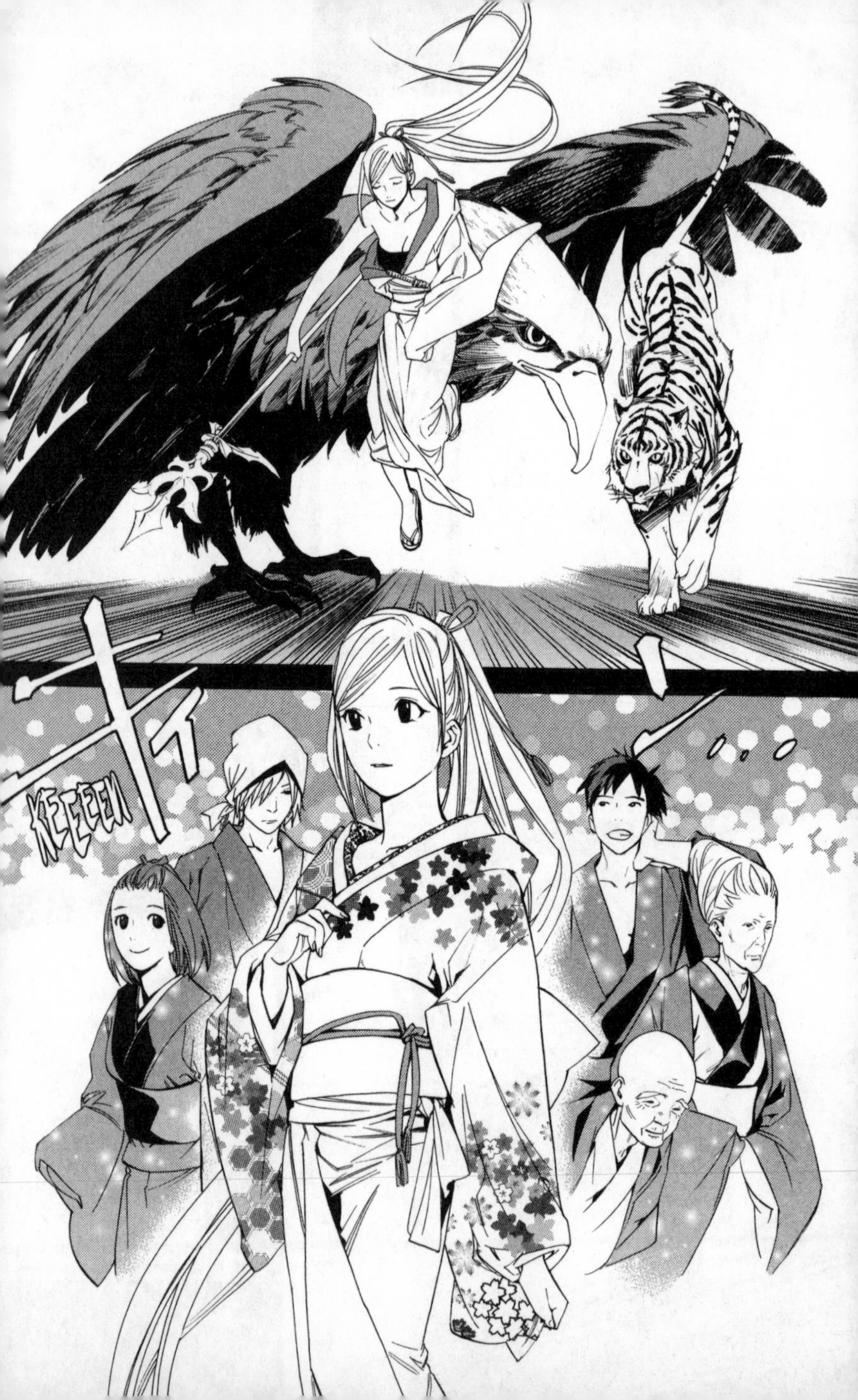
KEEEEN

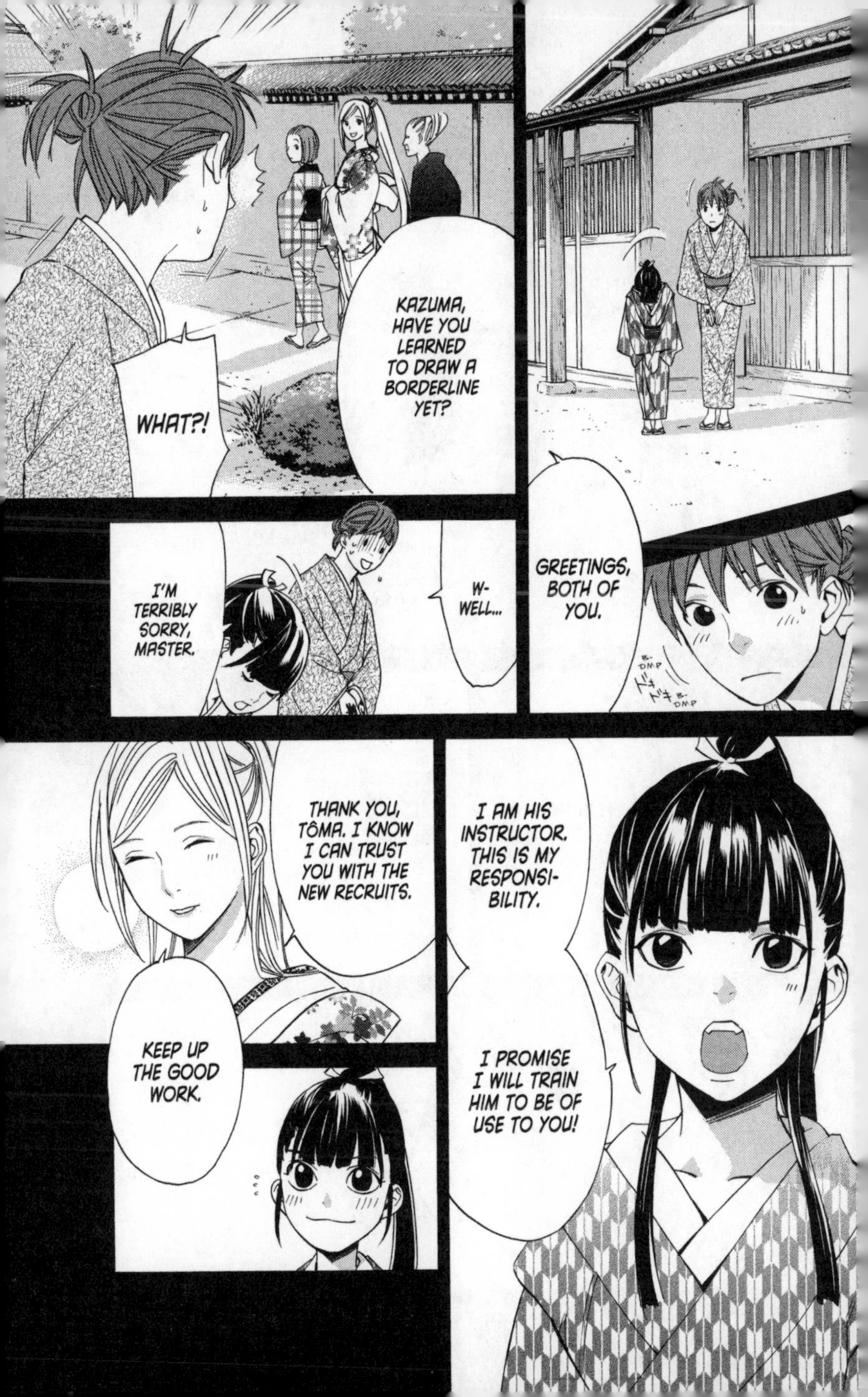
KAZUMA, HAVE YOU LEARNED TO DRAW A BORDERLINE YET?
WHAT?!
GREETINGS, BOTH OF YOU.
B-DMP ドキ ドキ B-DMP
W-WELL...
I'M TERRIBLY SORRY, MASTER.
I AM HIS INSTRUCTOR. THIS IS MY RESPONSI-BILITY.
I PROMISE I WILL TRAIN HIM TO BE OF USE TO YOU!
THANK YOU, TÔMA. I KNOW I CAN TRUST YOU WITH THE NEW RECRUITS.
KEEP UP THE GOOD WORK.

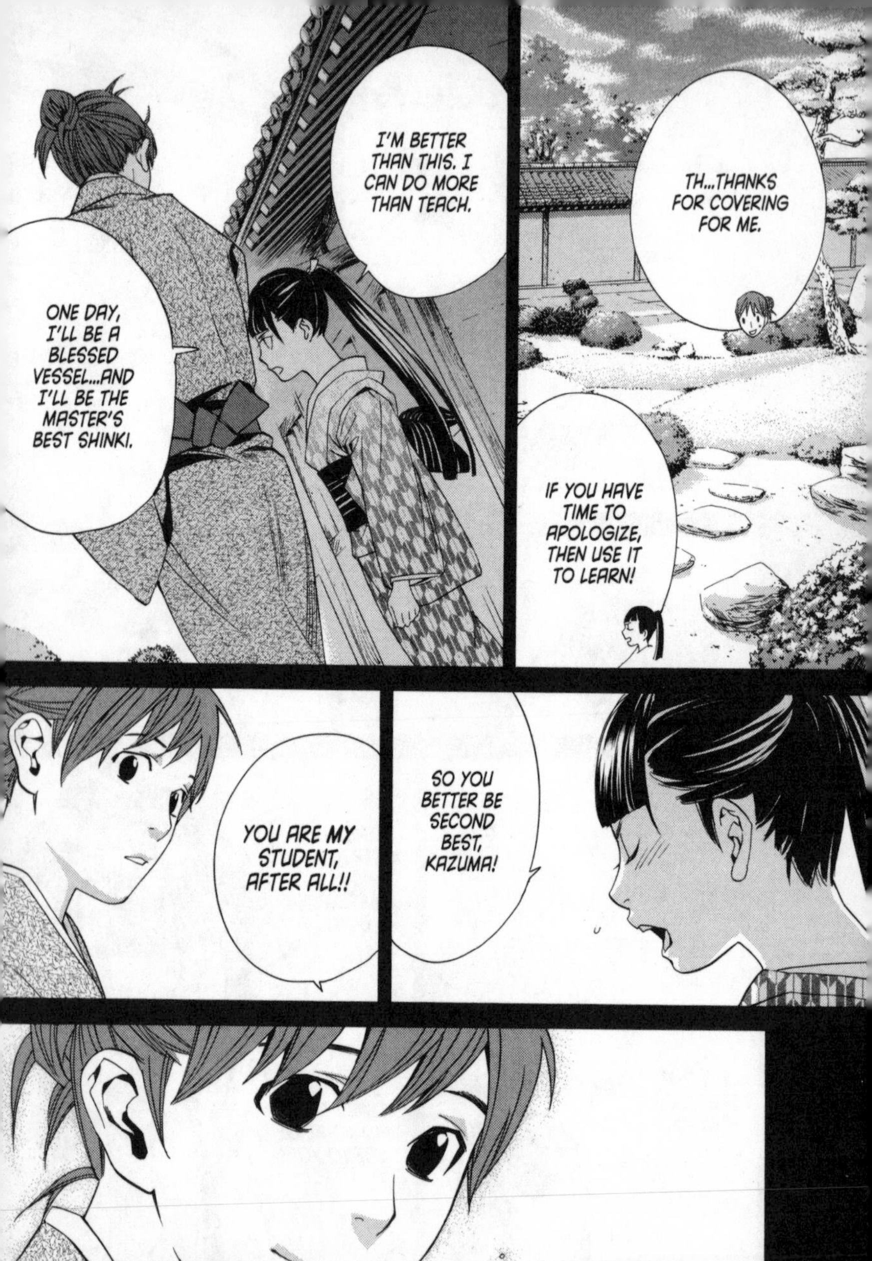
TH...THANKS FOR COVERING FOR ME.
IF YOU HAVE TIME TO APOLOGIZE, THEN USE IT TO LEARN!
I'M BETTER THAN THIS. I CAN DO MORE THAN TEACH.
ONE DAY, I'LL BE A BLESSED VESSEL...AND I'LL BE THE MASTER'S BEST SHINKI.
SO YOU BETTER BE SECOND BEST, KAZUMA!
YOU ARE MY STUDENT, AFTER ALL!!

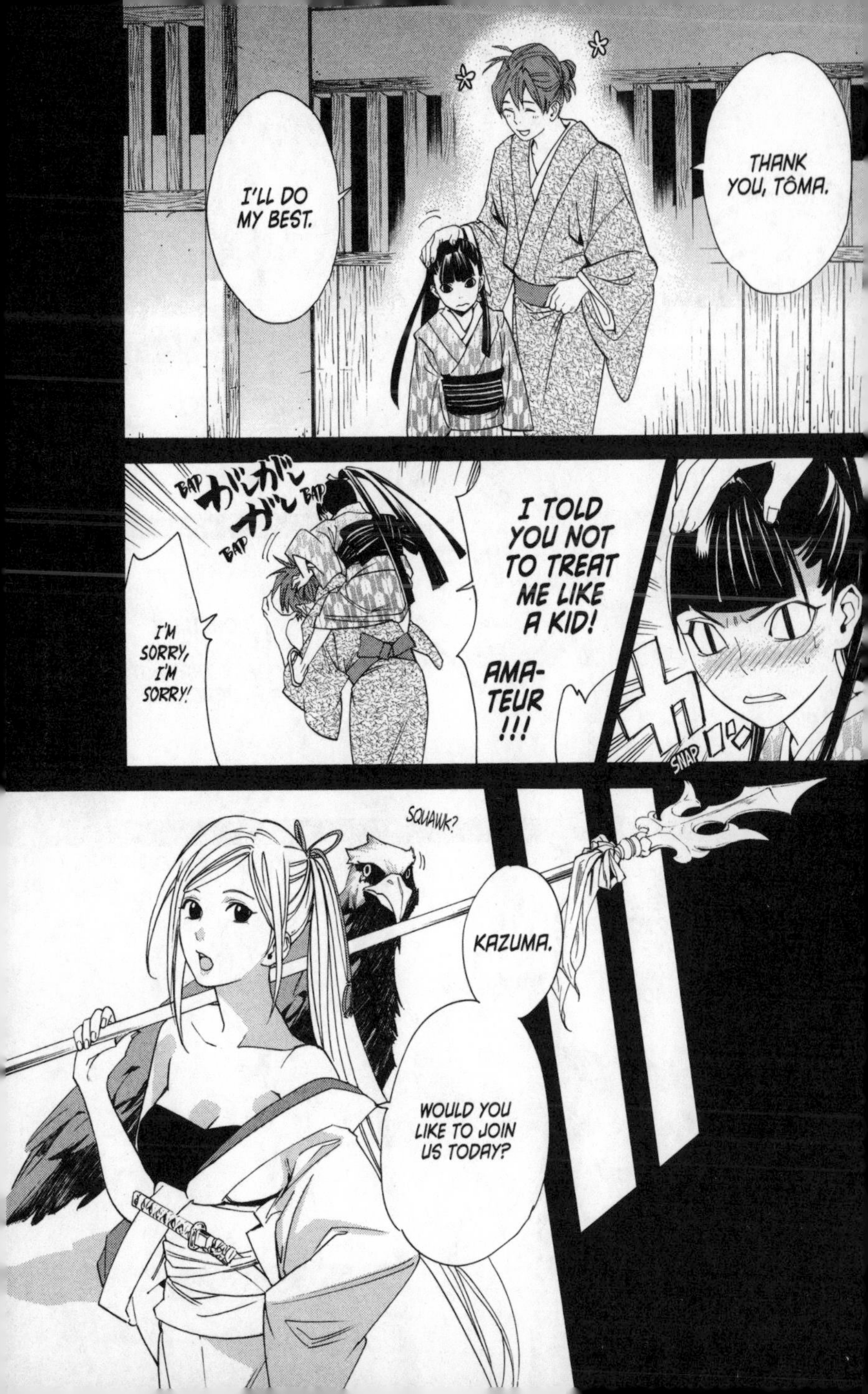
THANK YOU, TÔMA.
I'LL DO MY BEST.
SNAP
I TOLD YOU NOT TO TREAT ME LIKE A KID!
AMA-TEUR!!!
BAP BAP BAP BAP
I'M SORRY, I'M SORRY!
SQUAWK?
KAZUMA.
WOULD YOU LIKE TO JOIN US TODAY?

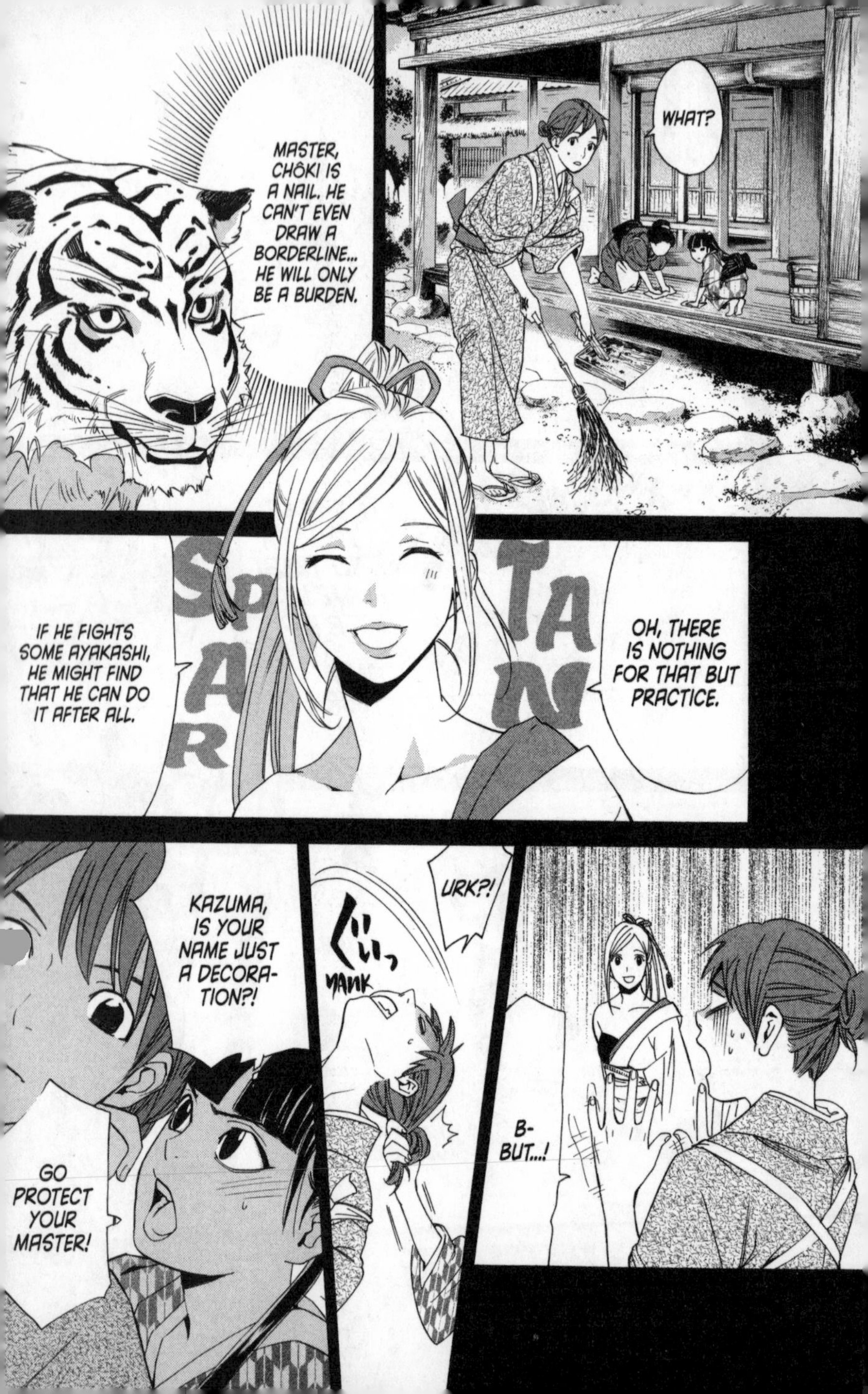
WHAT?
MASTER, CHÔKI IS A NAIL. HE CAN'T EVEN DRAW A BORDERLINE... HE WILL ONLY BE A BURDEN.
OH, THERE IS NOTHING FOR THAT BUT PRACTICE.
IF HE FIGHTS SOME AYAKASHI, HE MIGHT FIND THAT HE CAN DO IT AFTER ALL.
B- BUT...!
URK?!
ぐいっ
YANK
KAZUMA, IS YOUR NAME JUST A DECORATION?!
GO PROTECT YOUR MASTER!

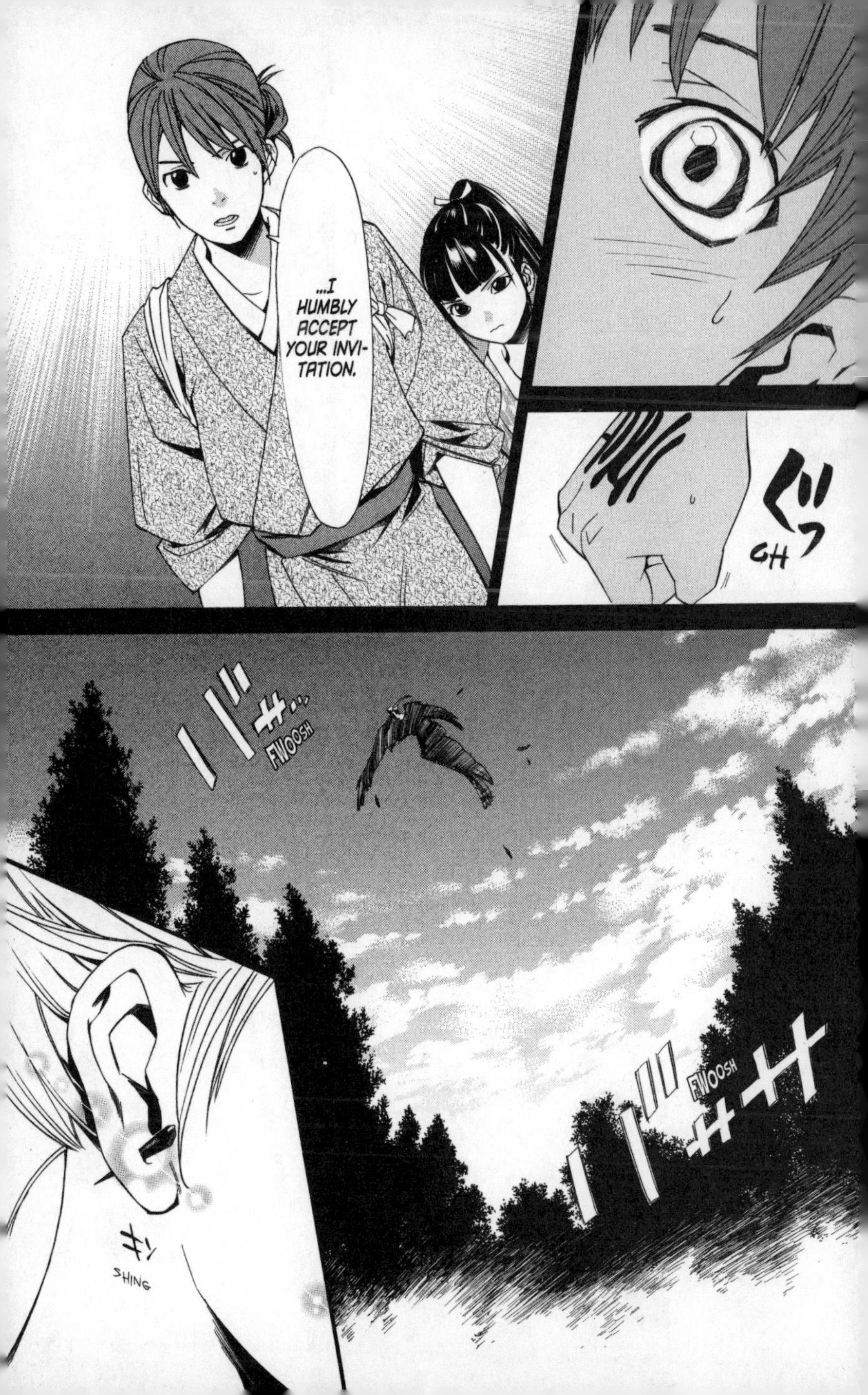
...I HUMBLY ACCEPT YOUR INVITATION.
ぐっ
GH
ザッ...
FWOOSH
ザザザッ
FWOOSH
キン
SHING

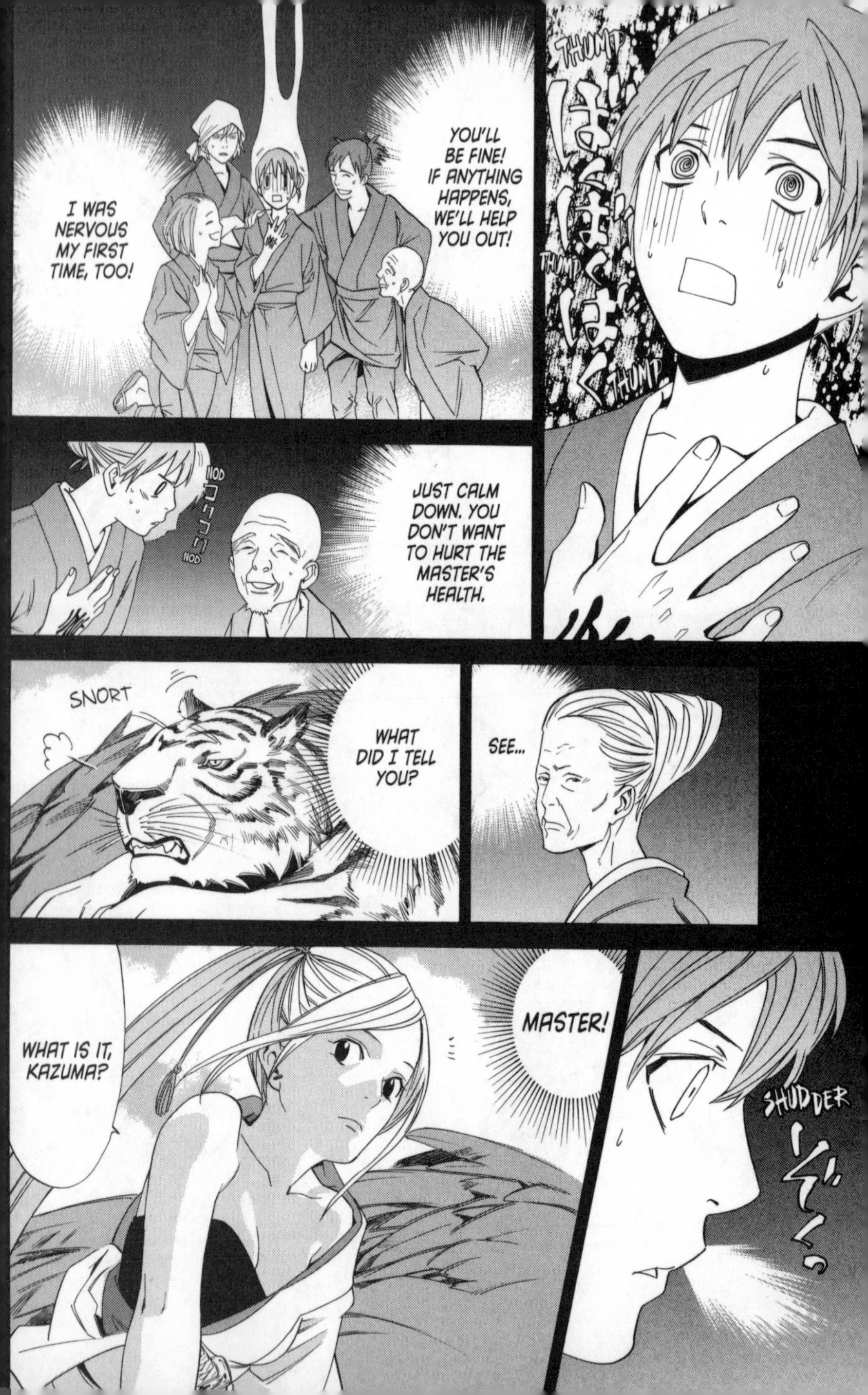
THUMP
THUMP
THUMP
YOU'LL BE FINE! IF ANYTHING HAPPENS, WE'LL HELP YOU OUT!
I WAS NERVOUS MY FIRST TIME, TOO!
JUST CALM DOWN. YOU DON'T WANT TO HURT THE MASTER'S HEALTH.
NOD
NOD
SEE...
WHAT DID I TELL YOU?
SNORT
SHUDDER
MASTER!
WHAT IS IT, KAZUMA?

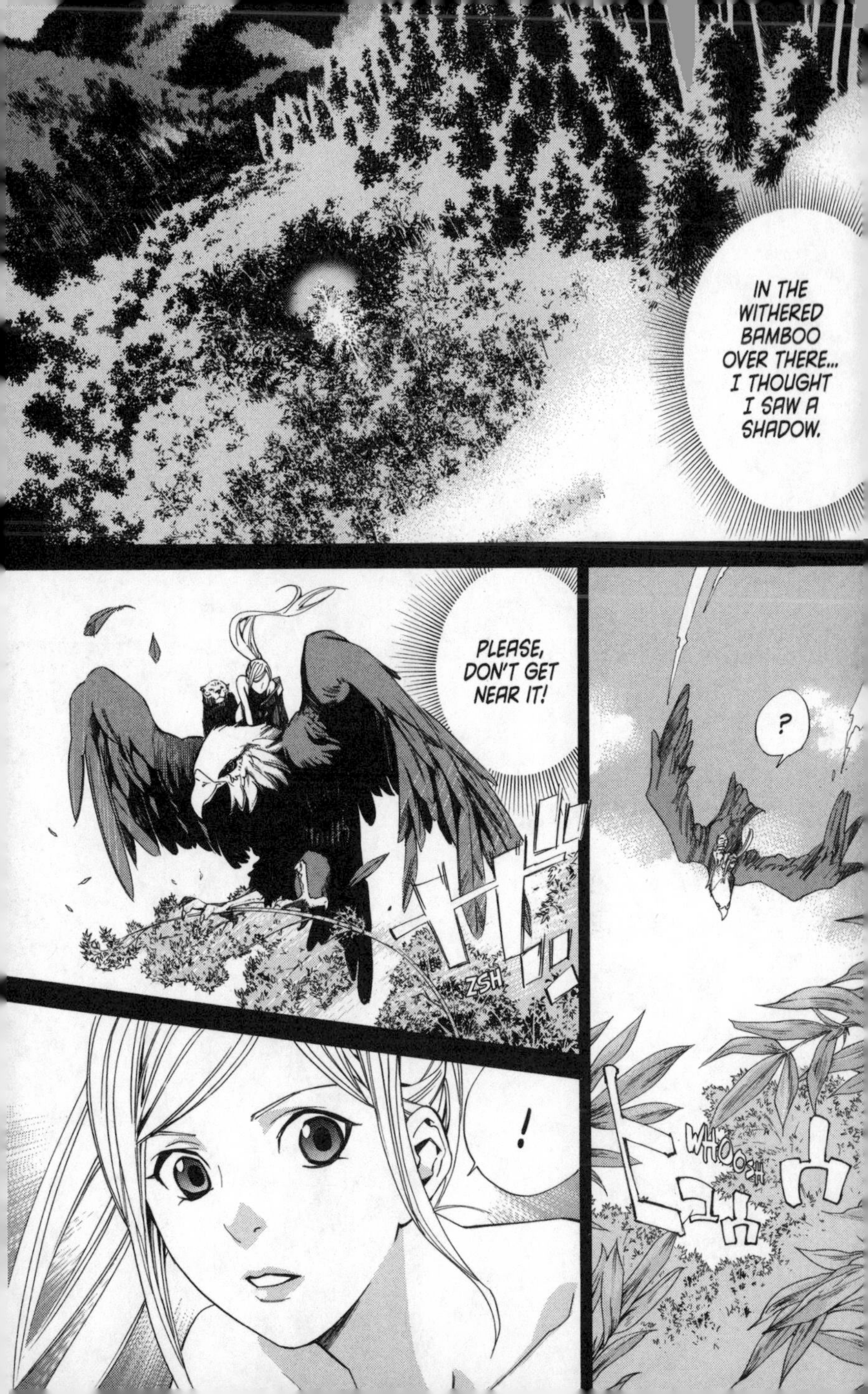
IN THE WITHERED BAMBOO OVER THERE... I THOUGHT I SAW A SHADOW.
?
WHOOSH
PLEASE, DON'T GET NEAR IT!
ZSH
!

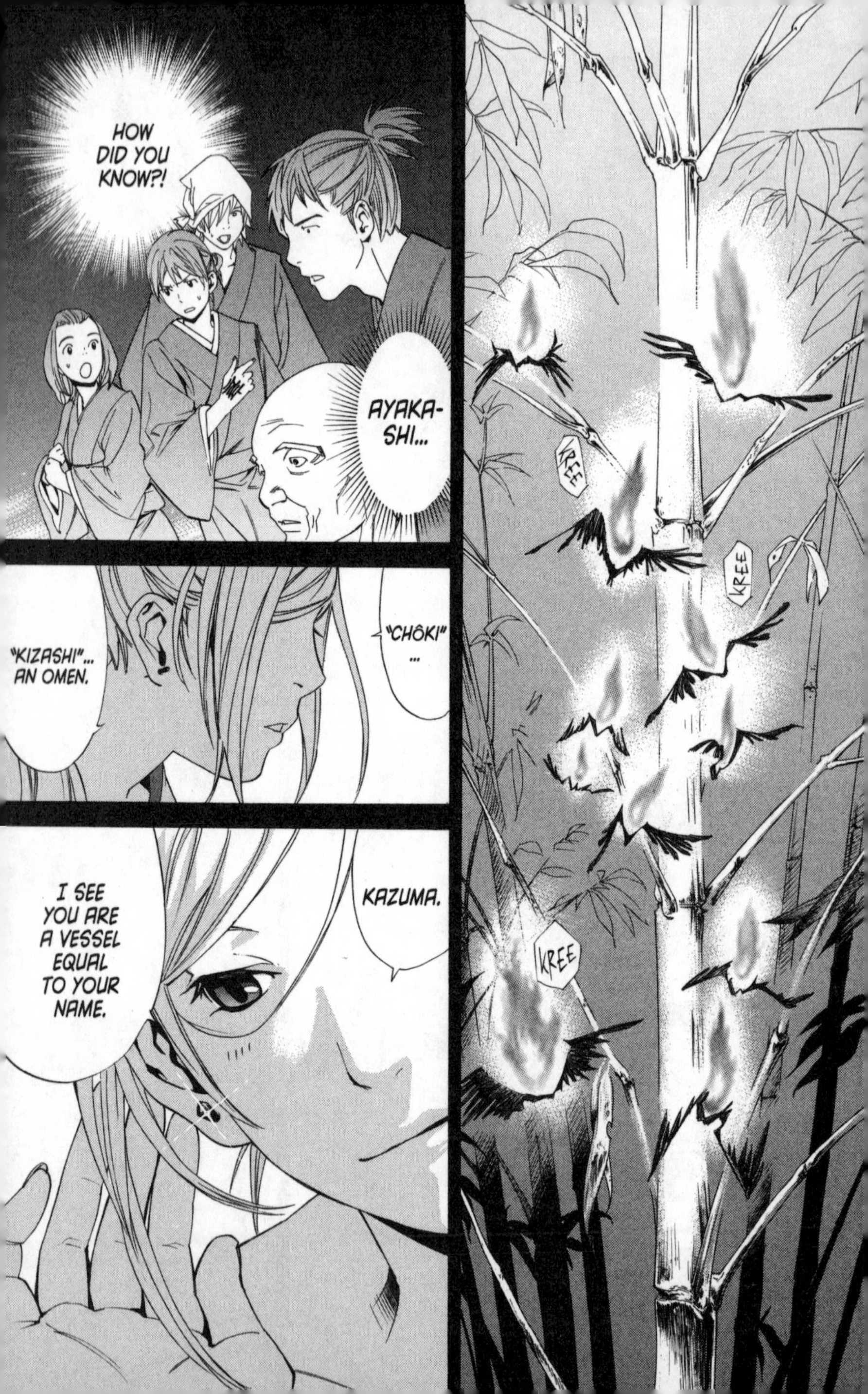

KREE
KREE
KREE
HOW DID YOU KNOW?!
AYAKA-SHI...
"CHÔKI"...
"KIZASHI"... AN OMEN.
KAZUMA.
I SEE YOU ARE A VESSEL EQUAL TO YOUR NAME.

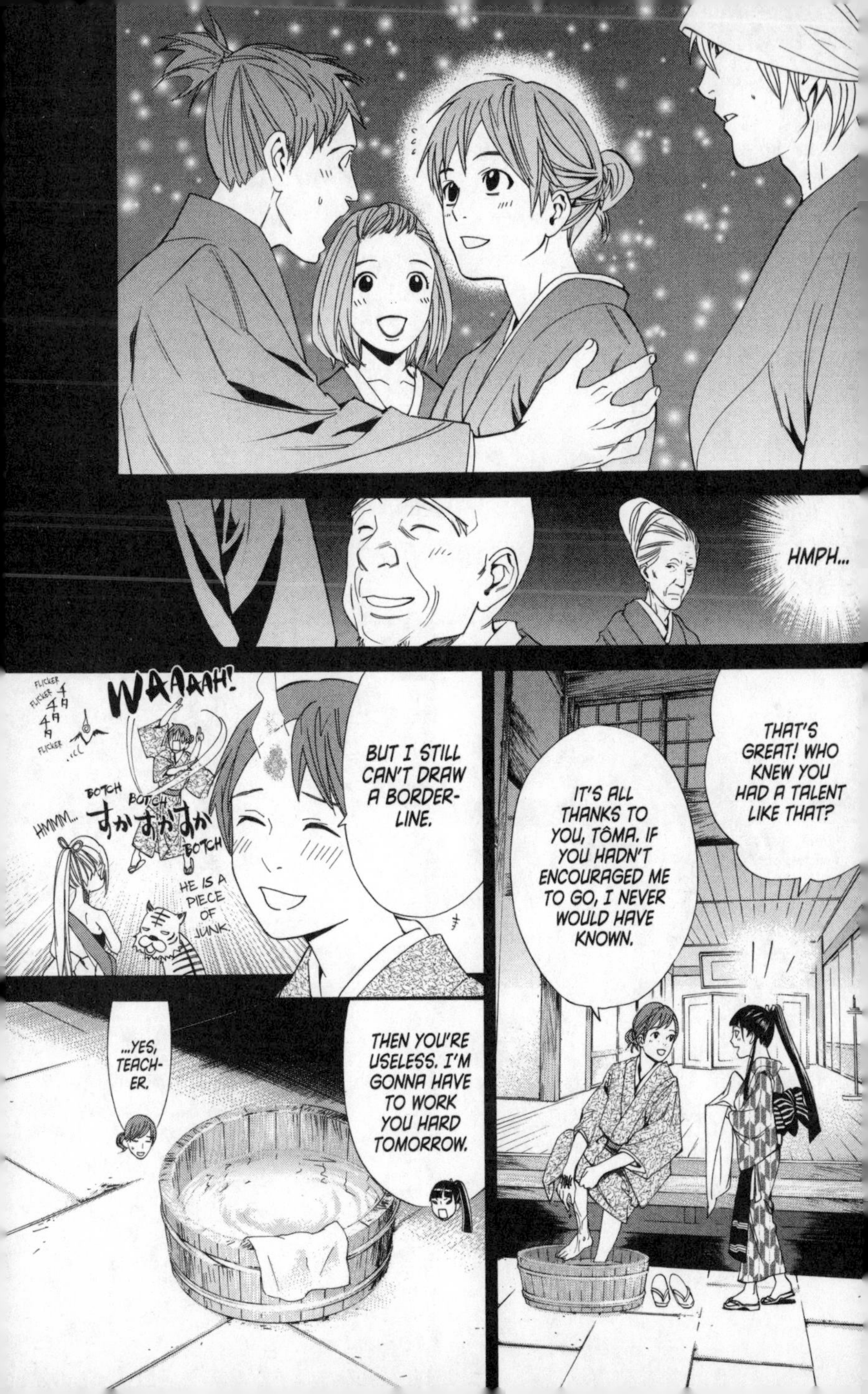
HMPH...
THAT'S GREAT! WHO KNEW YOU HAD A TALENT LIKE THAT?
IT'S ALL THANKS TO YOU, TÔMA. IF YOU HADN'T ENCOURAGED ME TO GO, I NEVER WOULD HAVE KNOWN.
BUT I STILL CAN'T DRAW A BORDER-LINE.
WAAAAH!
FLICKER FLICKER FLICKER
BOTCH BOTCH BOTCH
HMMM...
HE IS A PIECE OF JUNK.
THEN YOU'RE USELESS. I'M GONNA HAVE TO WORK YOU HARD TOMORROW.
...YES, TEACHER.

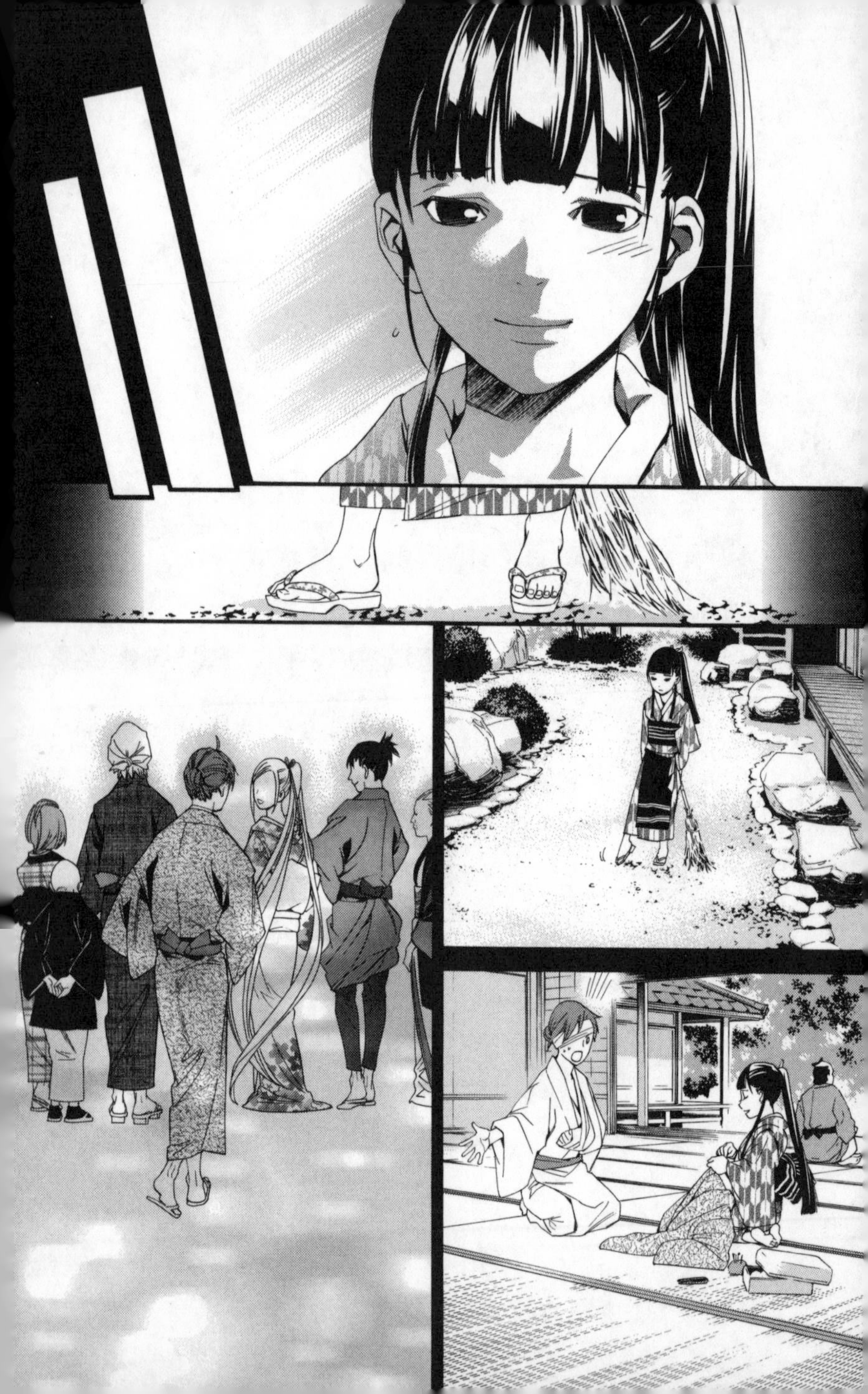

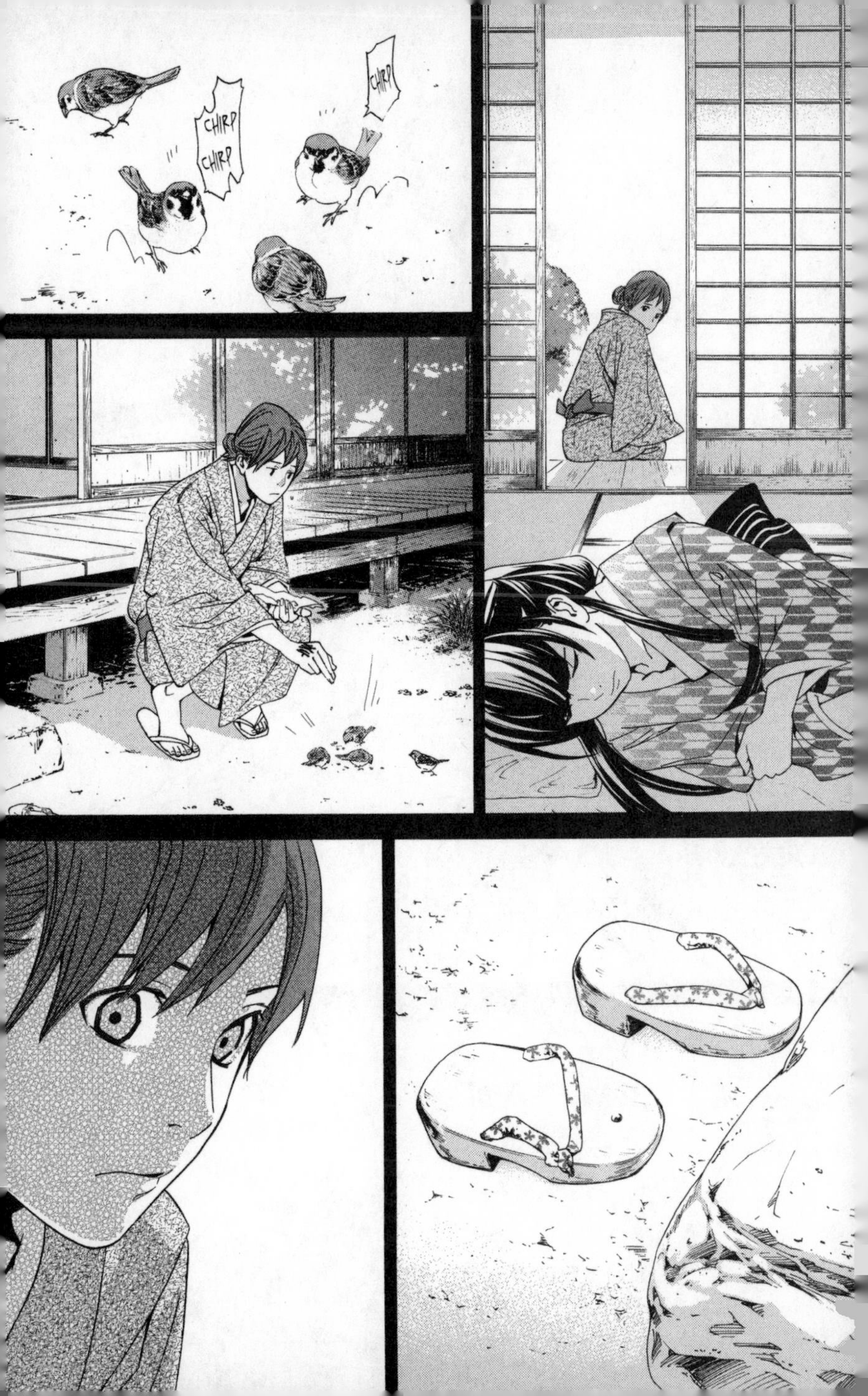
CHIRP
CHIRP
CHIRP

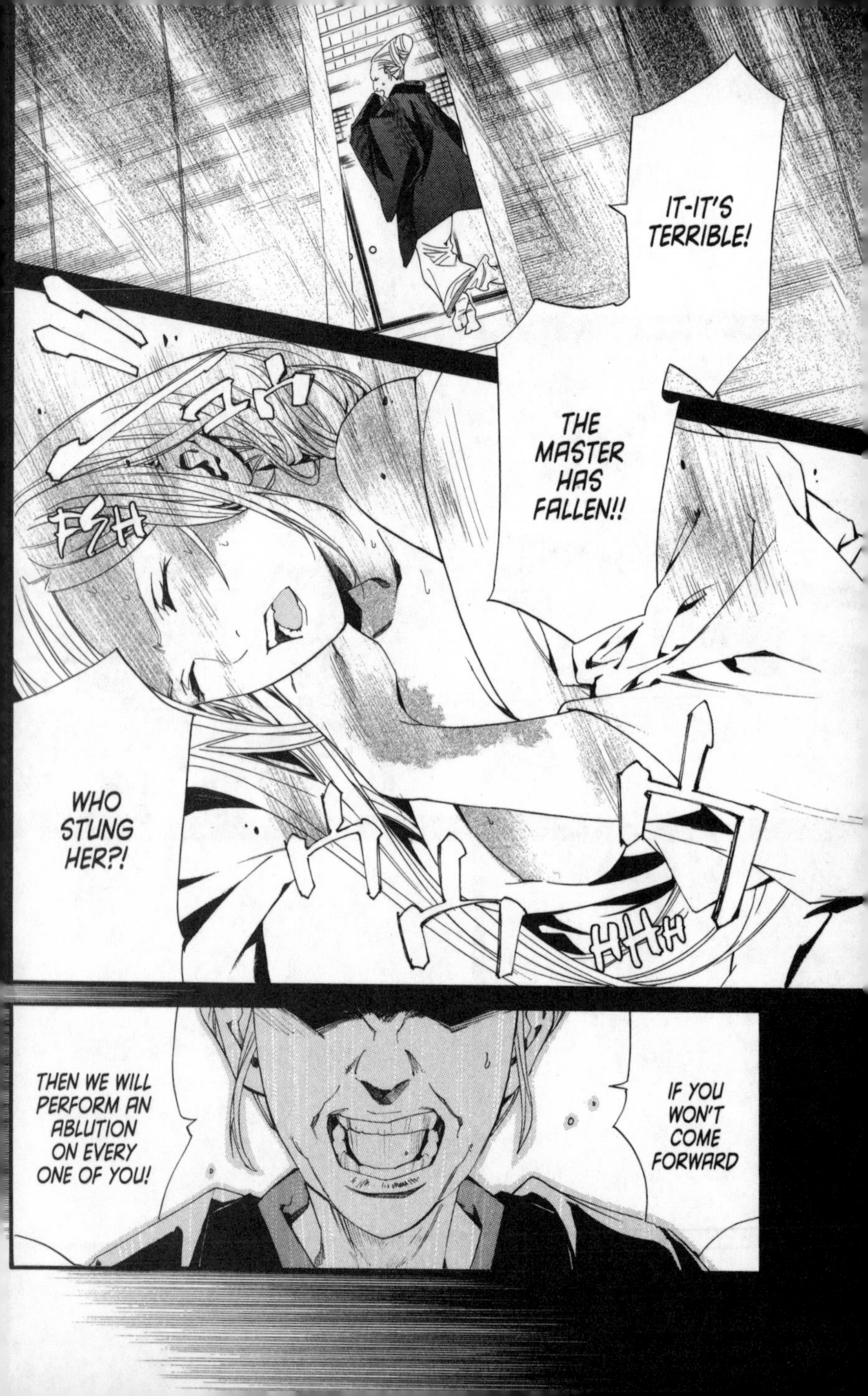
IT-IT'S TERRIBLE!
THE MASTER HAS FALLEN!!
FSH
WHO STUNG HER?!
HHH
IF YOU WON'T COME FORWARD
THEN WE WILL PERFORM AN ABLUTION ON EVERY ONE OF YOU!

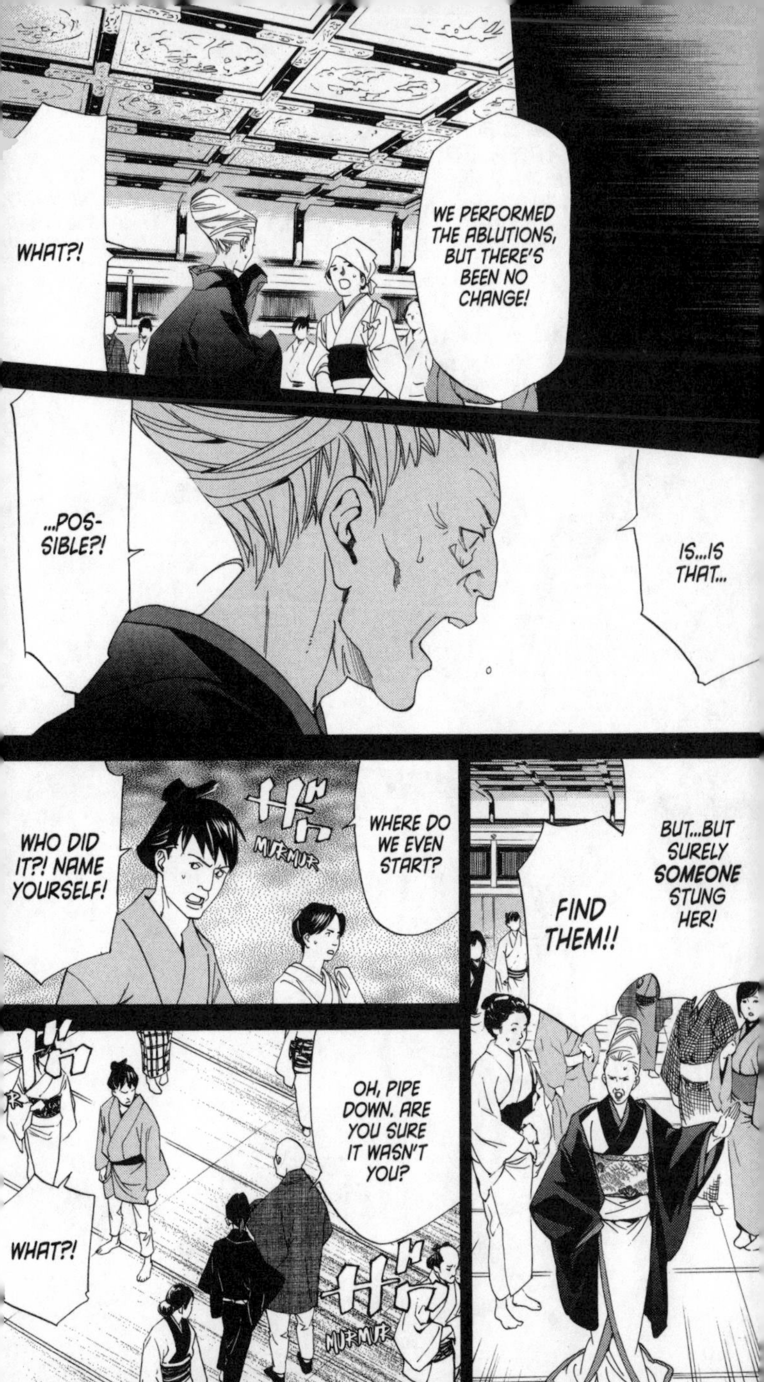
WE PERFORMED THE ABLUTIONS, BUT THERE'S BEEN NO CHANGE!
WHAT?!
IS...IS THAT...
...POS-SIBLE?!
BUT...BUT SURELY SOMEONE STUNG HER!
FIND THEM!!
WHERE DO WE EVEN START?
MURMUR
WHO DID IT?! NAME YOURSELF!
OH, PIPE DOWN. ARE YOU SURE IT WASN'T YOU?
MURMUR
WHAT?!

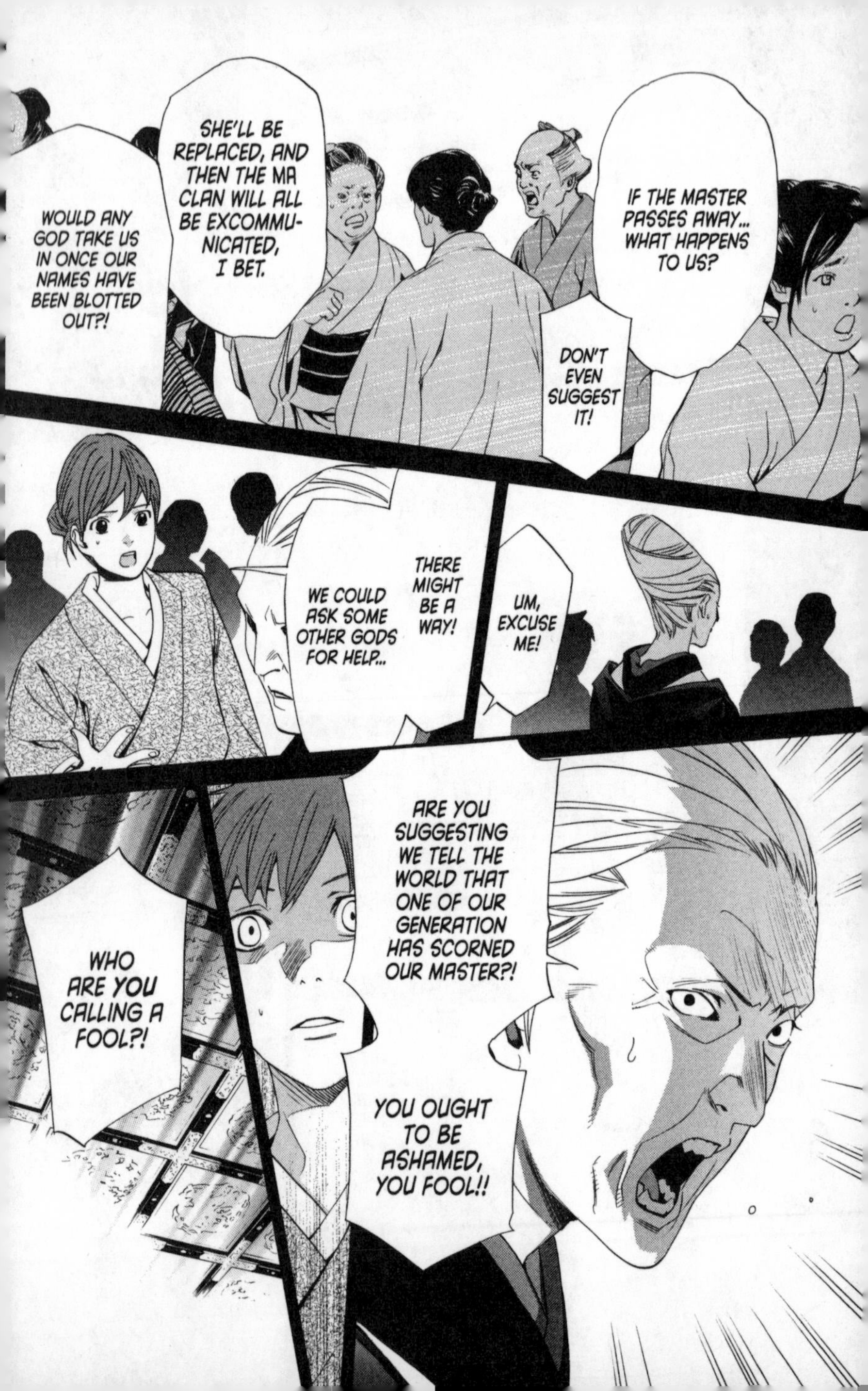
IF THE MASTER PASSES AWAY... WHAT HAPPENS TO US?
DON'T EVEN SUGGEST IT!
SHE'LL BE REPLACED, AND THEN THE MA CLAN WILL ALL BE EXCOMMUNICATED, I BET.
WOULD ANY GOD TAKE US IN ONCE OUR NAMES HAVE BEEN BLOTTED OUT?!
UM, EXCUSE ME!
THERE MIGHT BE A WAY!
WE COULD ASK SOME OTHER GODS FOR HELP...
ARE YOU SUGGESTING WE TELL THE WORLD THAT ONE OF OUR GENERATION HAS SCORNED OUR MASTER?!
YOU OUGHT TO BE ASHAMED, YOU FOOL!!
WHO ARE YOU CALLING A FOOL?!

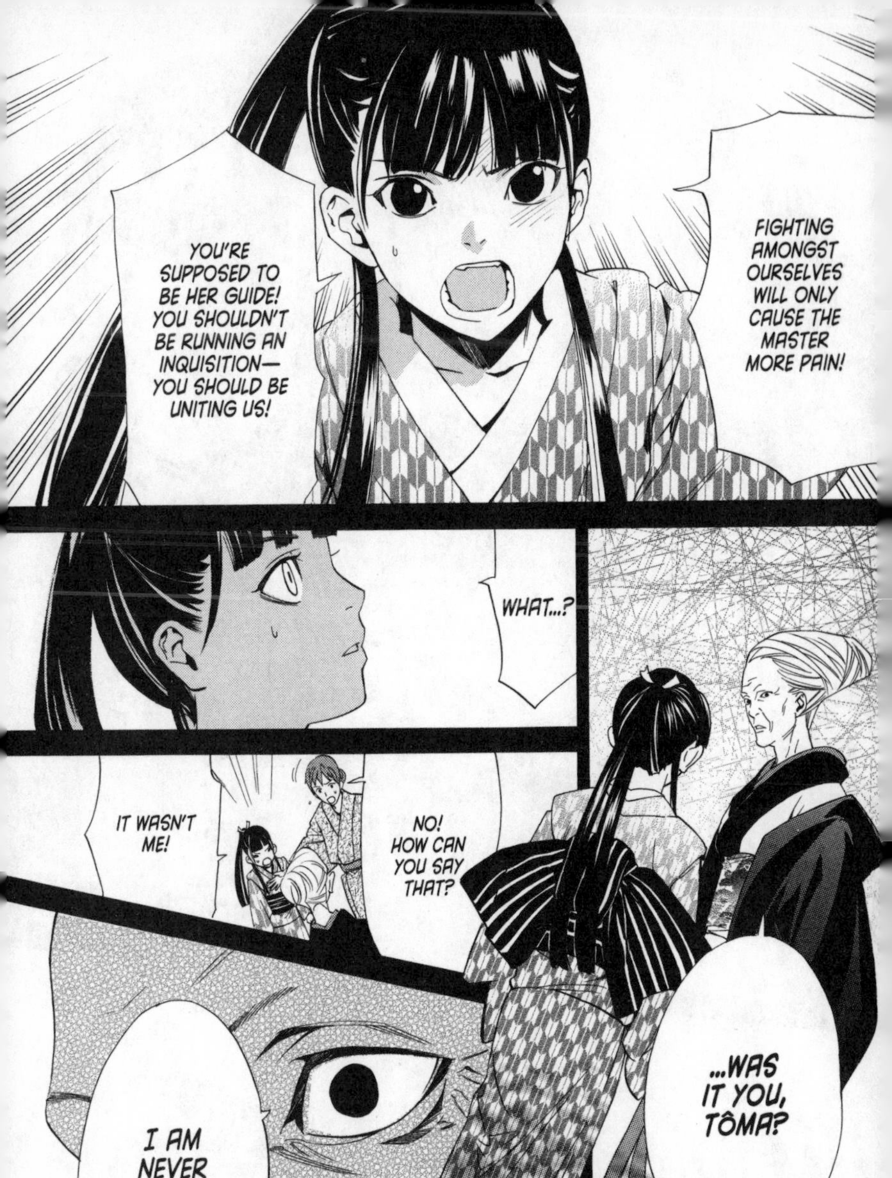
FIGHTING AMONGST OURSELVES WILL ONLY CAUSE THE MASTER MORE PAIN!
YOU'RE SUPPOSED TO BE HER GUIDE! YOU SHOULDN'T BE RUNNING AN INQUISITION— YOU SHOULD BE UNITING US!
...WAS IT YOU, TÔMA?
WHAT...?
NO! HOW CAN YOU SAY THAT?
IT WASN'T ME!
I AM NEVER WRONG.

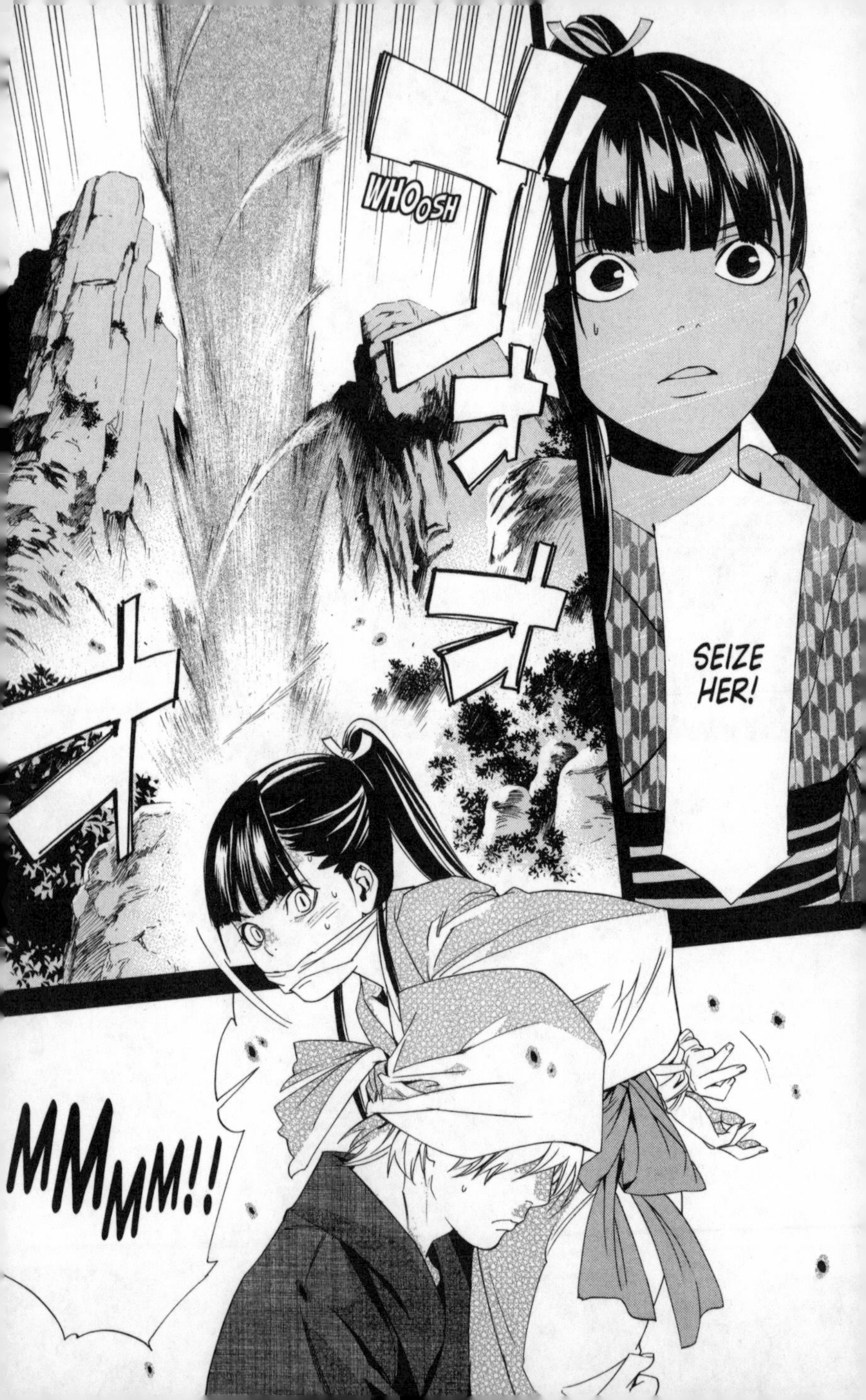
WHOOSH
SEIZE HER!
MMMM!!

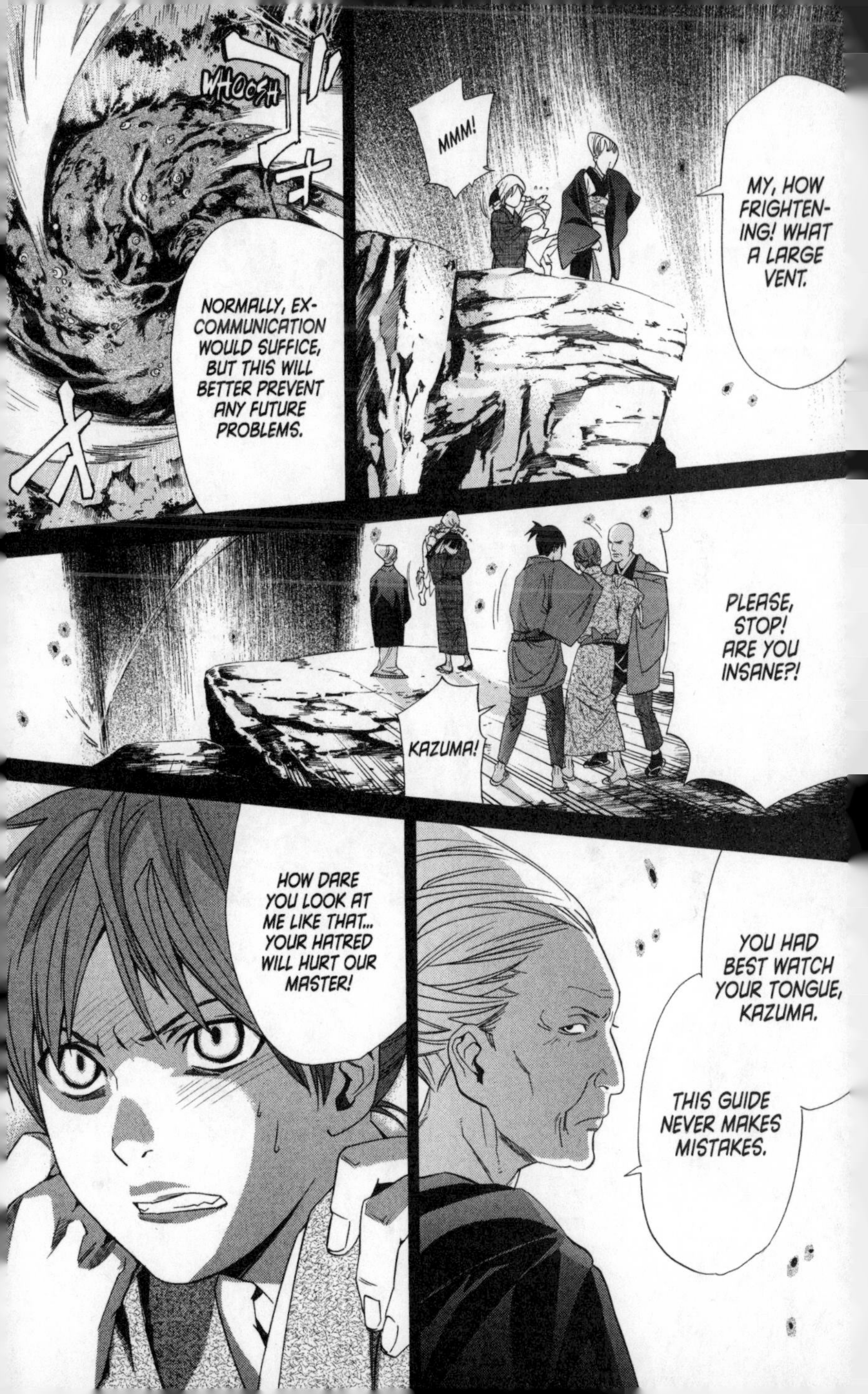
MY, HOW FRIGHTEN-ING! WHAT A LARGE VENT.
MMM!
WHOOSH
NORMALLY, EX-COMMUNICATION WOULD SUFFICE, BUT THIS WILL BETTER PREVENT ANY FUTURE PROBLEMS.
PLEASE, STOP! ARE YOU INSANE?!
KAZUMA!
YOU HAD BEST WATCH YOUR TONGUE, KAZUMA.
THIS GUIDE NEVER MAKES MISTAKES.
HOW DARE YOU LOOK AT ME LIKE THAT... YOUR HATRED WILL HURT OUR MASTER!

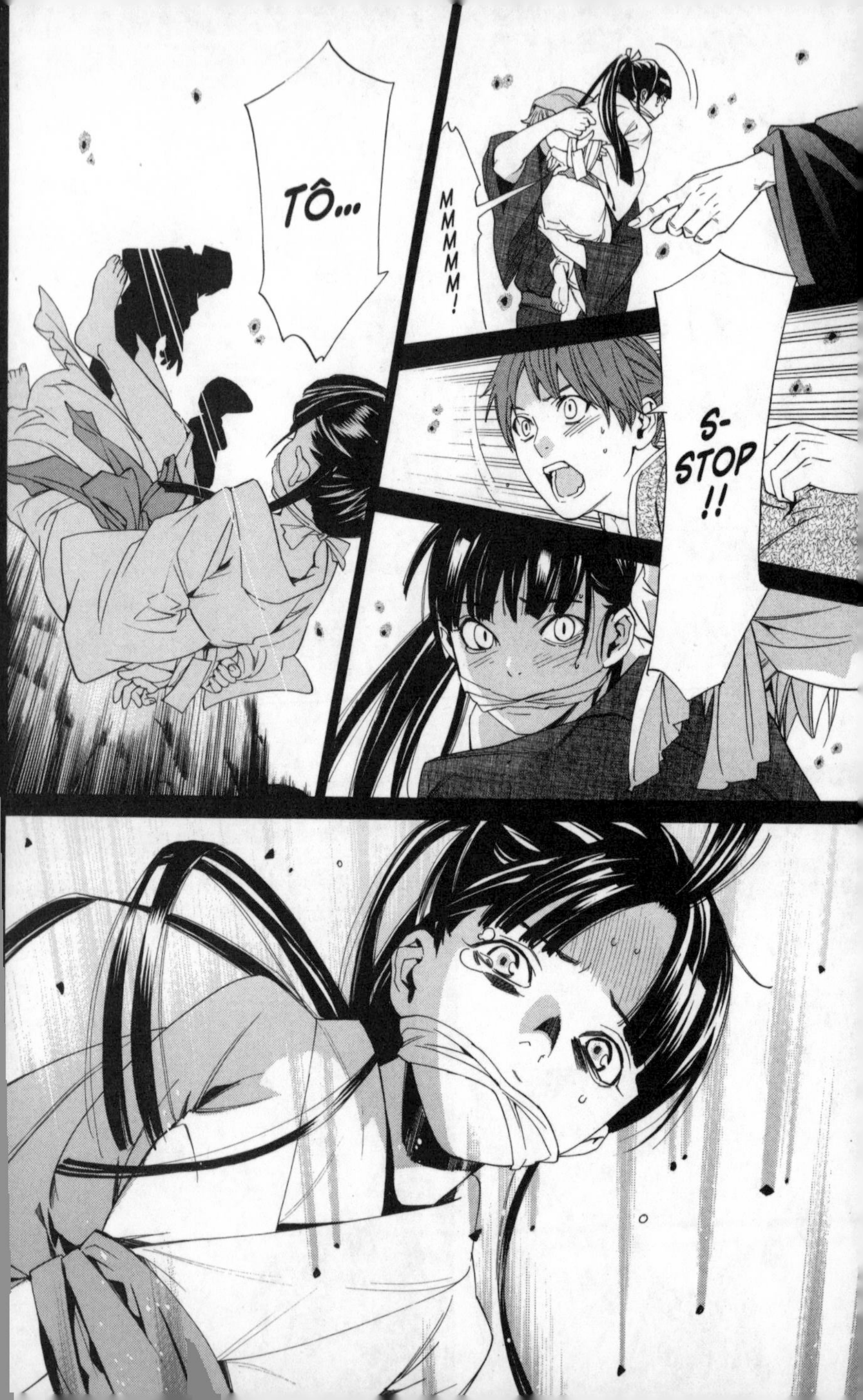
MMMMM!
S-STOP!!
TÔ...

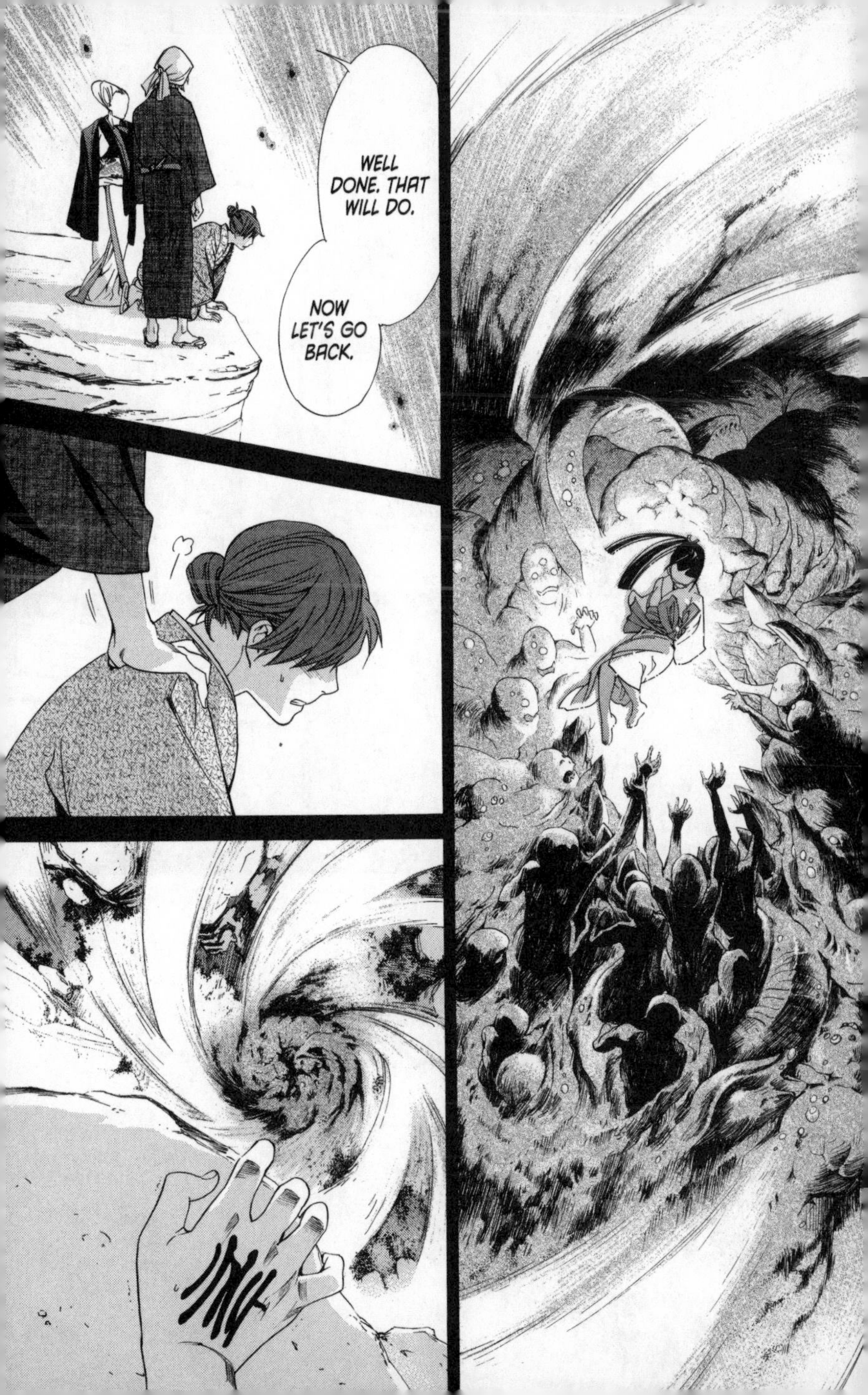
WELL DONE. THAT WILL DO.
NOW LET'S GO BACK.

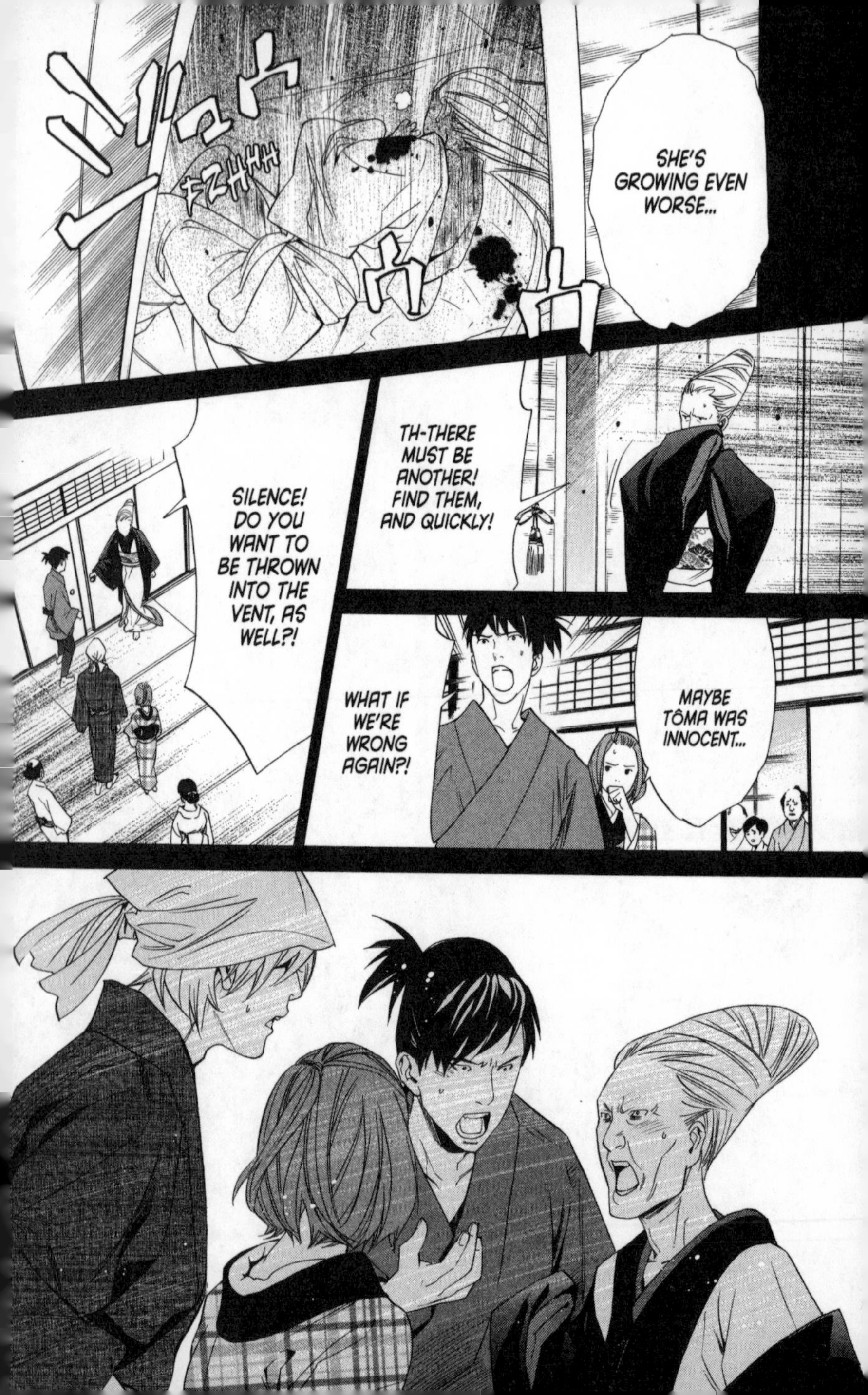
SHE'S GROWING EVEN WORSE...
FZHHH
TH-THERE MUST BE ANOTHER! FIND THEM, AND QUICKLY!
MAYBE TÔMA WAS INNOCENT...
WHAT IF WE'RE WRONG AGAIN?!
SILENCE! DO YOU WANT TO BE THROWN INTO THE VENT, AS WELL?!

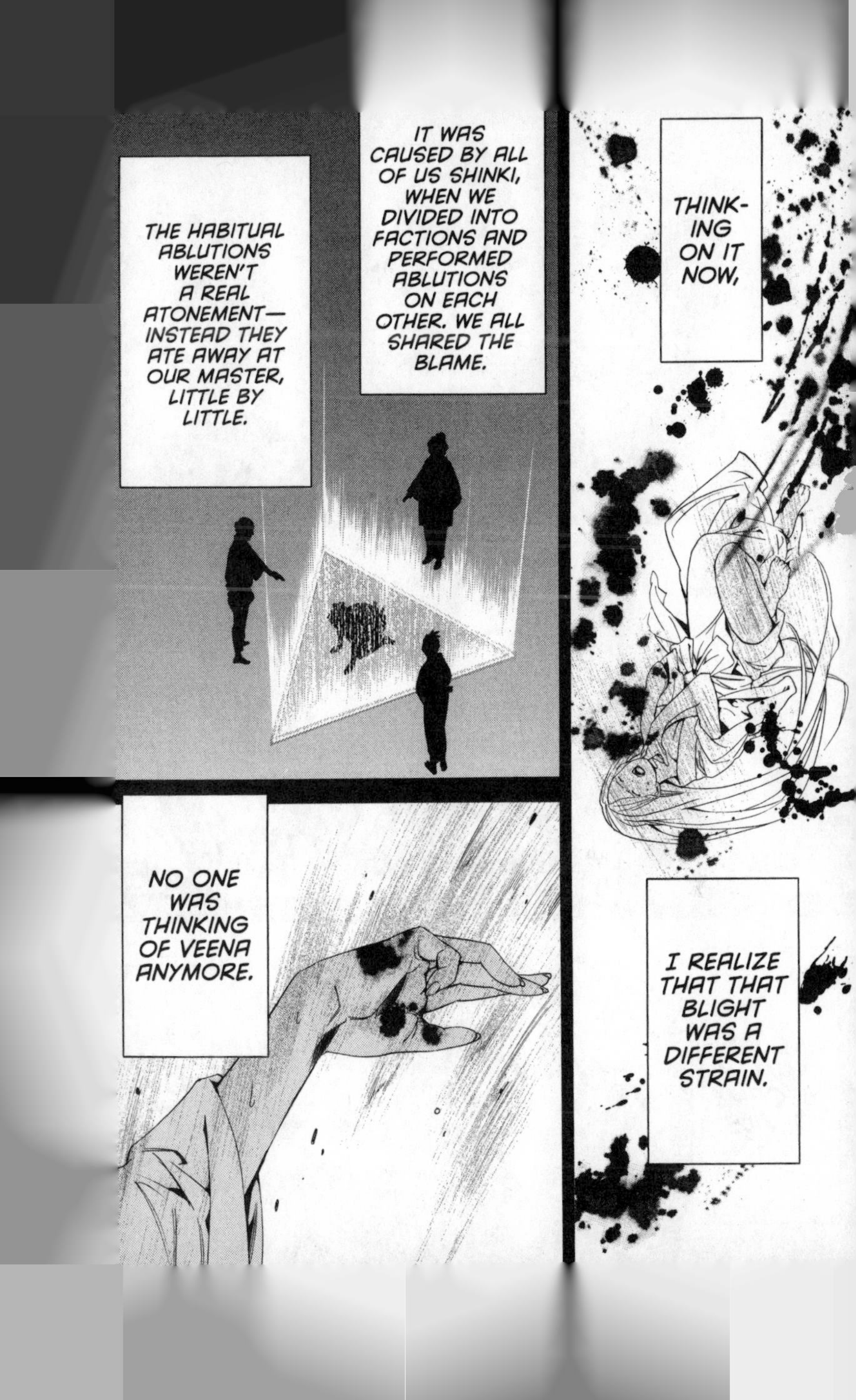
THINK-ING ON IT NOW,
I REALIZE THAT THAT BLIGHT WAS A DIFFERENT STRAIN.
IT WAS CAUSED BY ALL OF US SHINKI, WHEN WE DIVIDED INTO FACTIONS AND PERFORMED ABLUTIONS ON EACH OTHER. WE ALL SHARED THE BLAME.
THE HABITUAL ABLUTIONS WEREN'T A REAL ATONEMENT—INSTEAD THEY ATE AWAY AT OUR MASTER, LITTLE BY LITTLE.
NO ONE WAS THINKING OF VEENA ANYMORE.

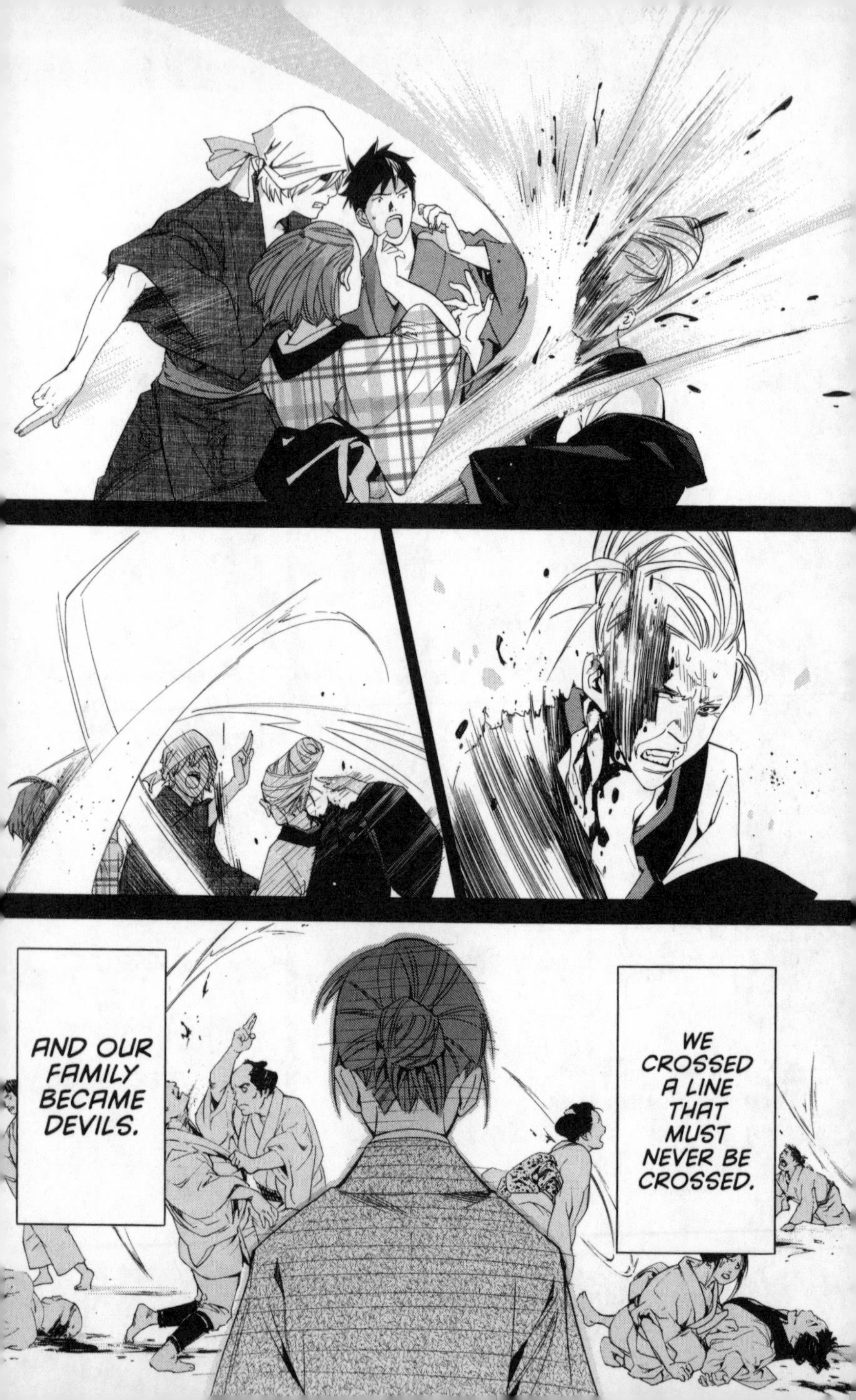
WE CROSSED A LINE THAT MUST NEVER BE CROSSED.
AND OUR FAMILY BECAME DEVILS.

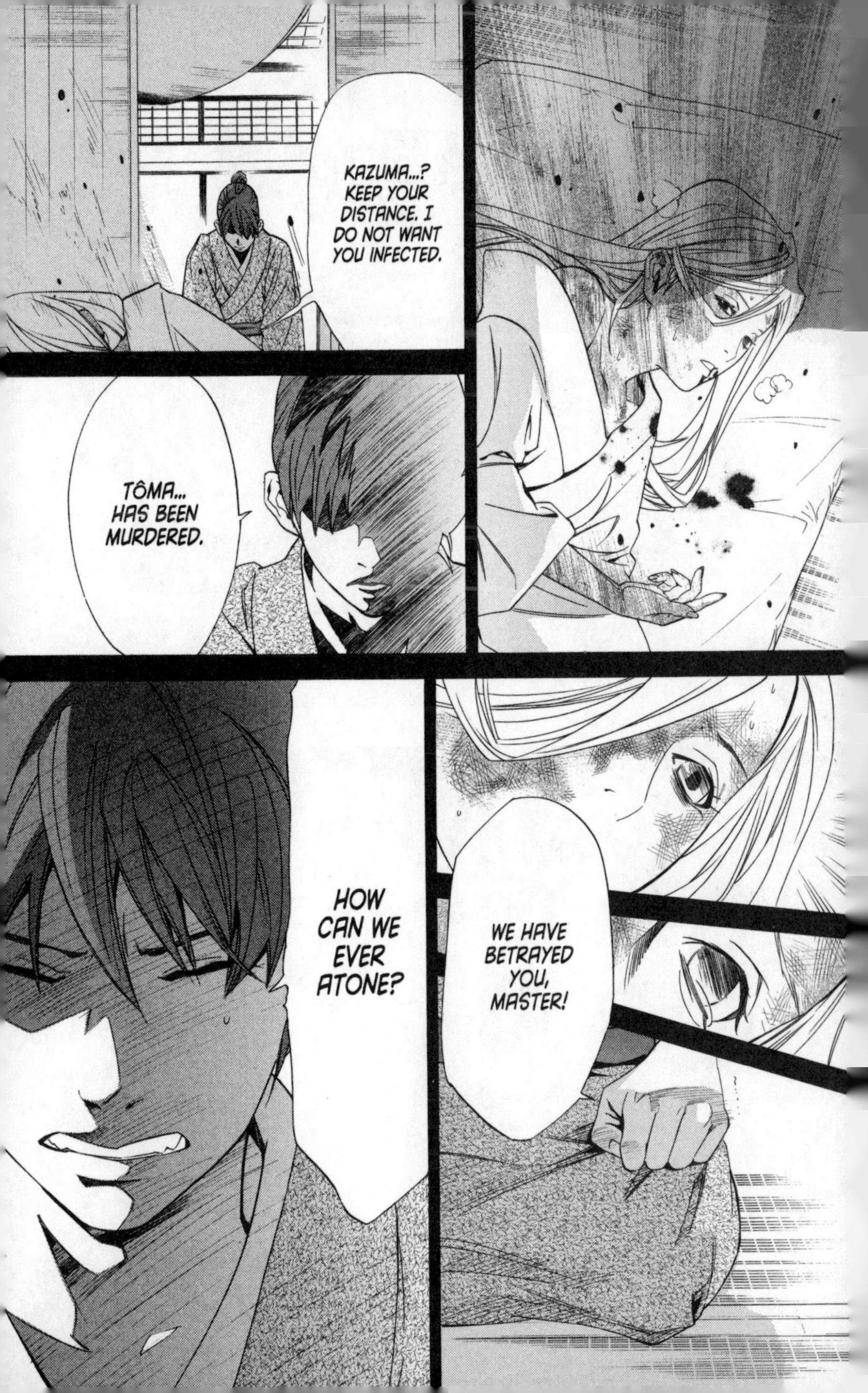
KAZUMA...? KEEP YOUR DISTANCE. I DO NOT WANT YOU INFECTED.
TÔMA... HAS BEEN MURDERED.
WE HAVE BETRAYED YOU, MASTER!
HOW CAN WE EVER ATONE?

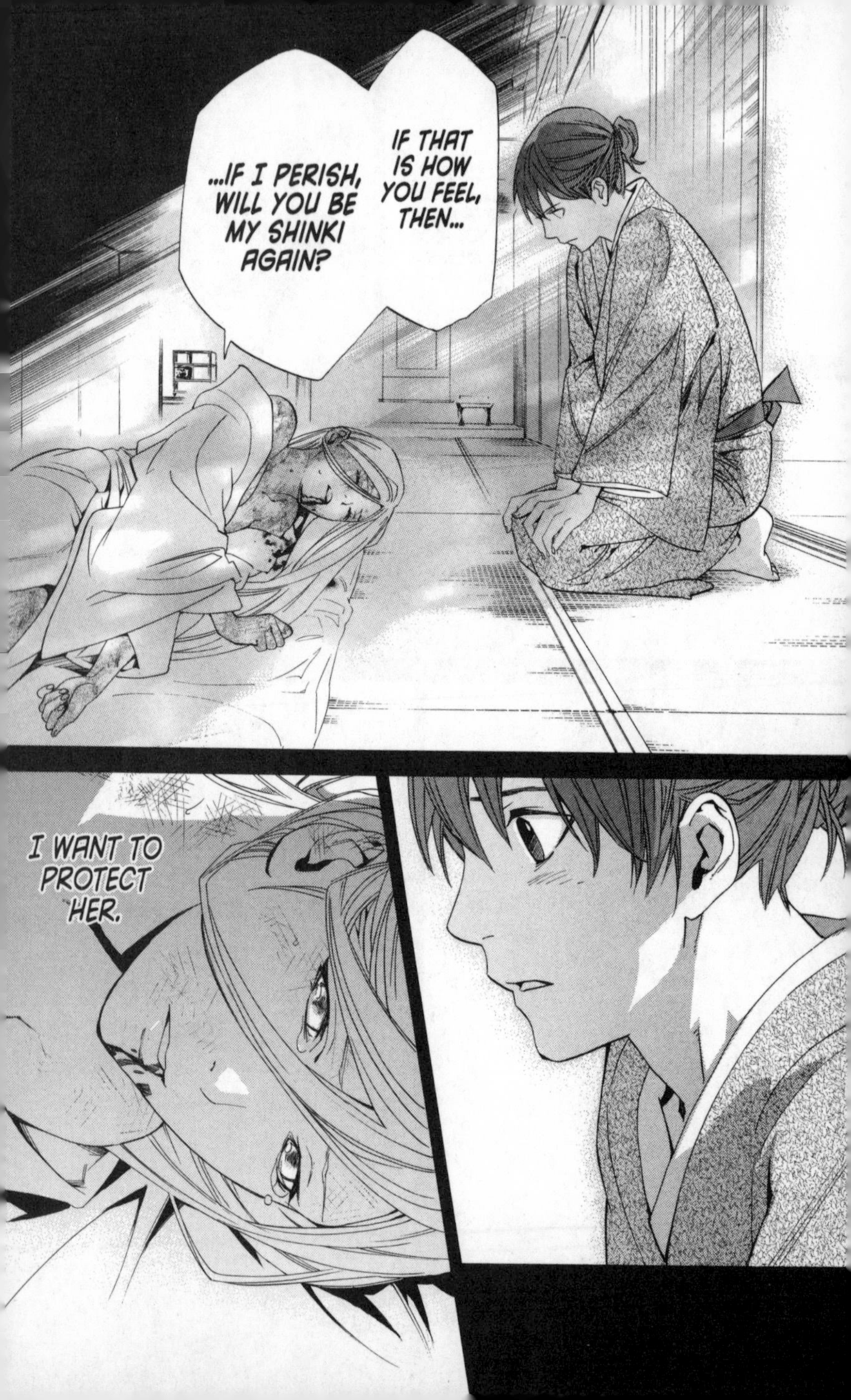
IF THAT IS HOW YOU FEEL, THEN...
...IF I PERISH, WILL YOU BE MY SHINKI AGAIN?
I WANT TO PROTECT HER.

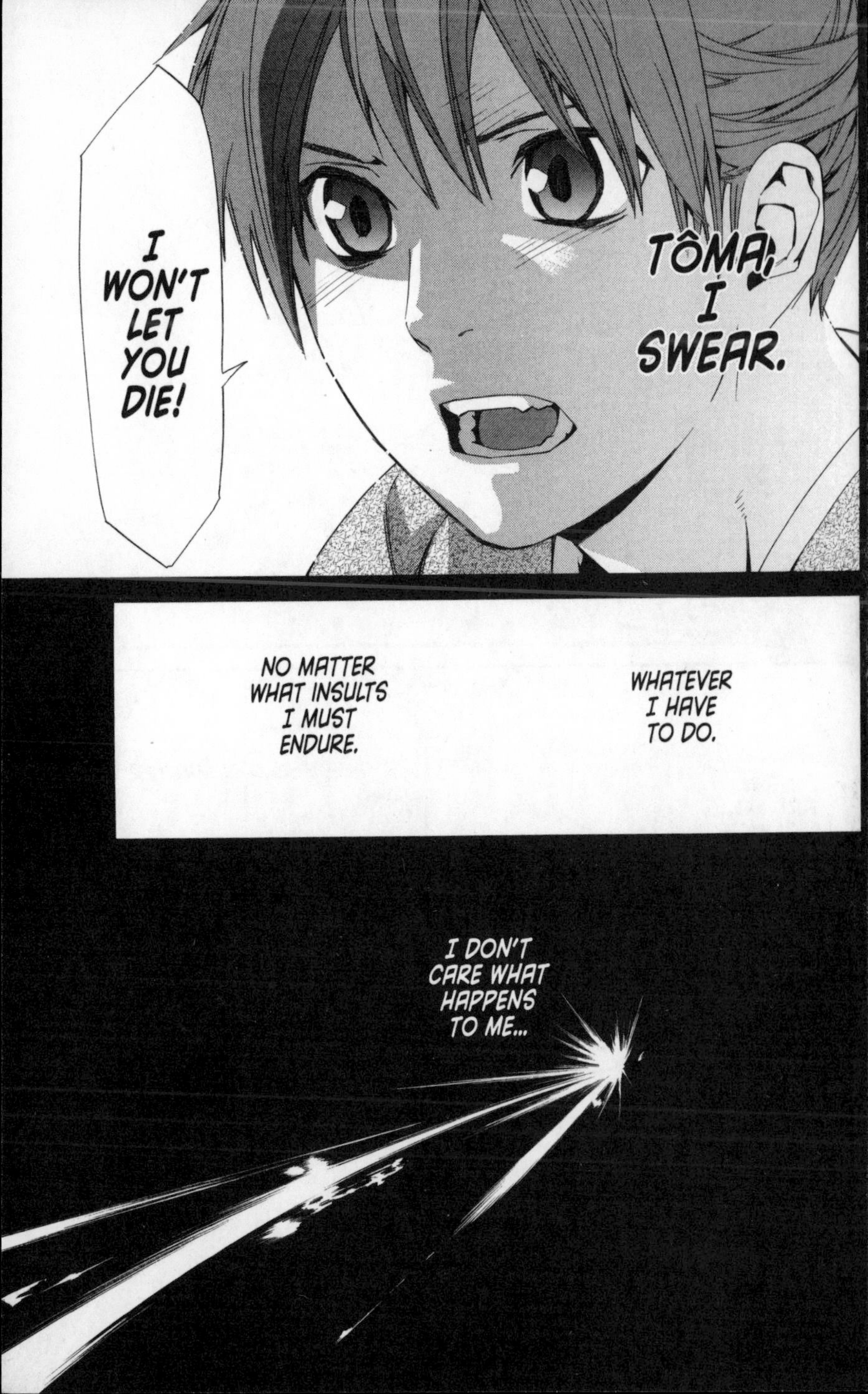
TÔMA, I SWEAR.
I WON'T LET YOU DIE!
WHATEVER I HAVE TO DO.
NO MATTER WHAT INSULTS I MUST ENDURE.
I DON'T CARE WHAT HAPPENS TO ME...

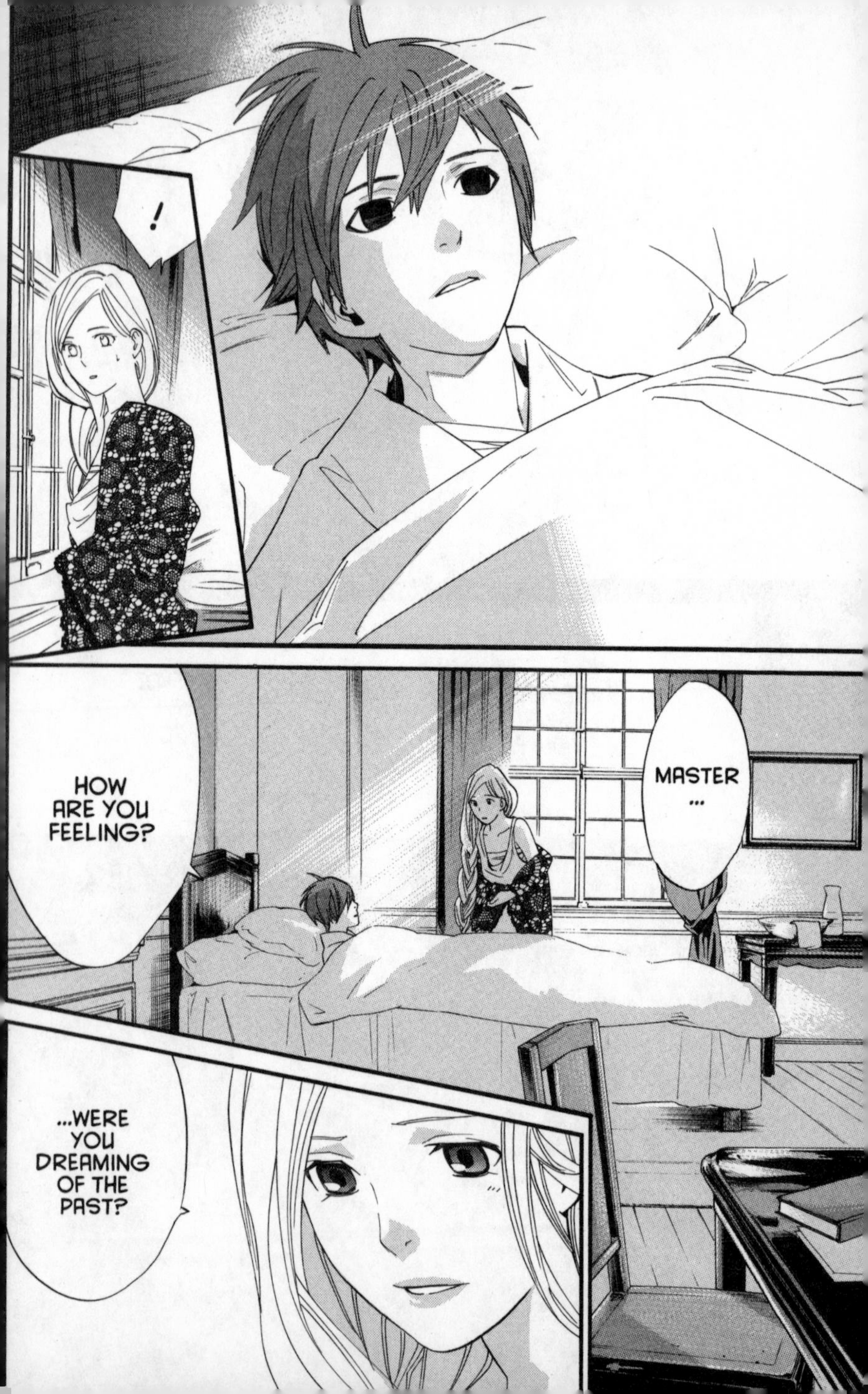
!
MASTER ...
HOW ARE YOU FEELING?
...WERE YOU DREAMING OF THE PAST?

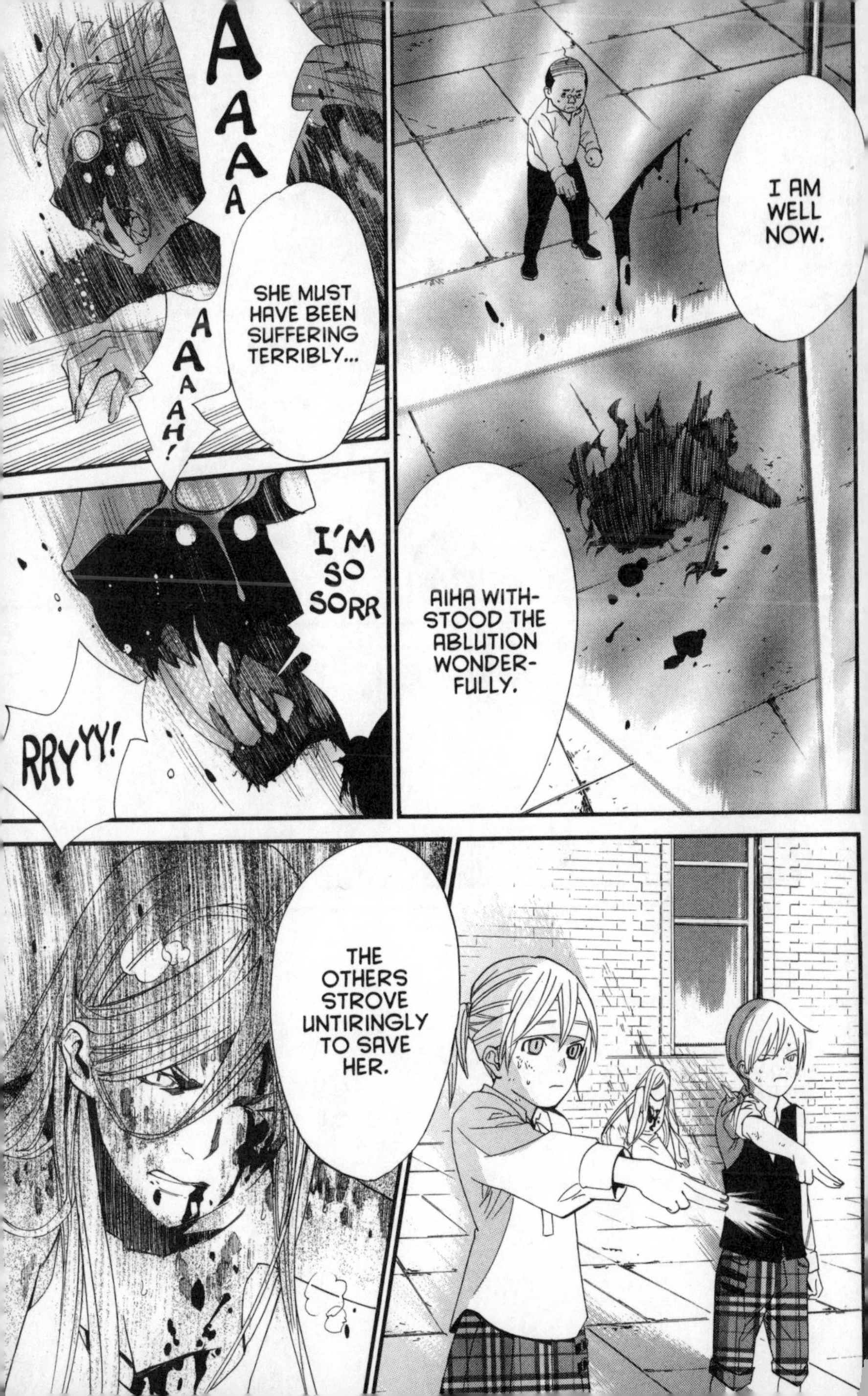
I AM WELL NOW.
AIHA WITH-STOOD THE ABLUTION WONDER-FULLY.
AAAAAAAAH!
SHE MUST HAVE BEEN SUFFERING TERRIBLY...
I'M SO SORR
RRYYY!
THE OTHERS STROVE UNTIRINGLY TO SAVE HER.

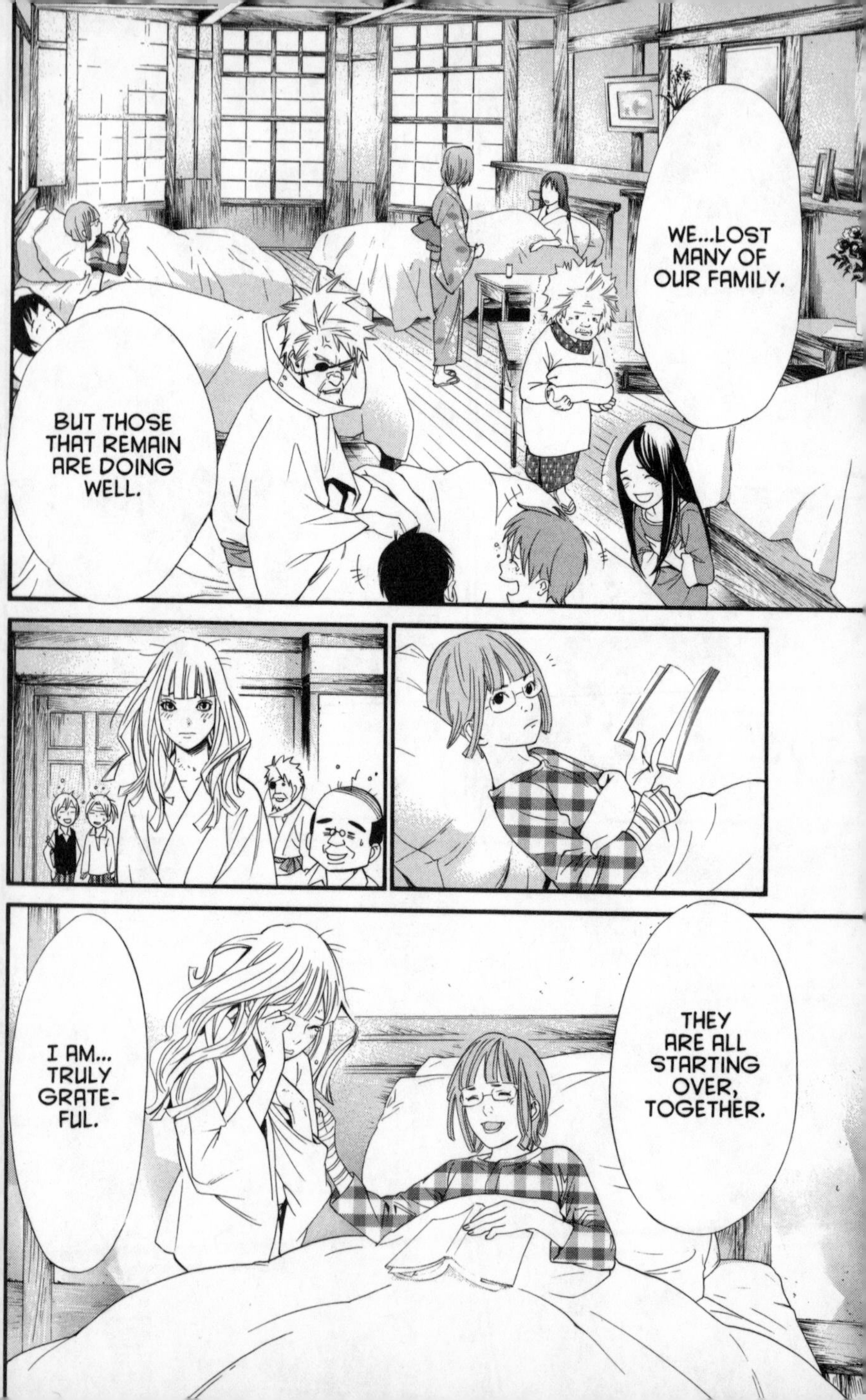
WE...LOST MANY OF OUR FAMILY.
BUT THOSE THAT REMAIN ARE DOING WELL.
THEY ARE ALL STARTING OVER, TOGETHER.
I AM... TRULY GRATE-FUL.

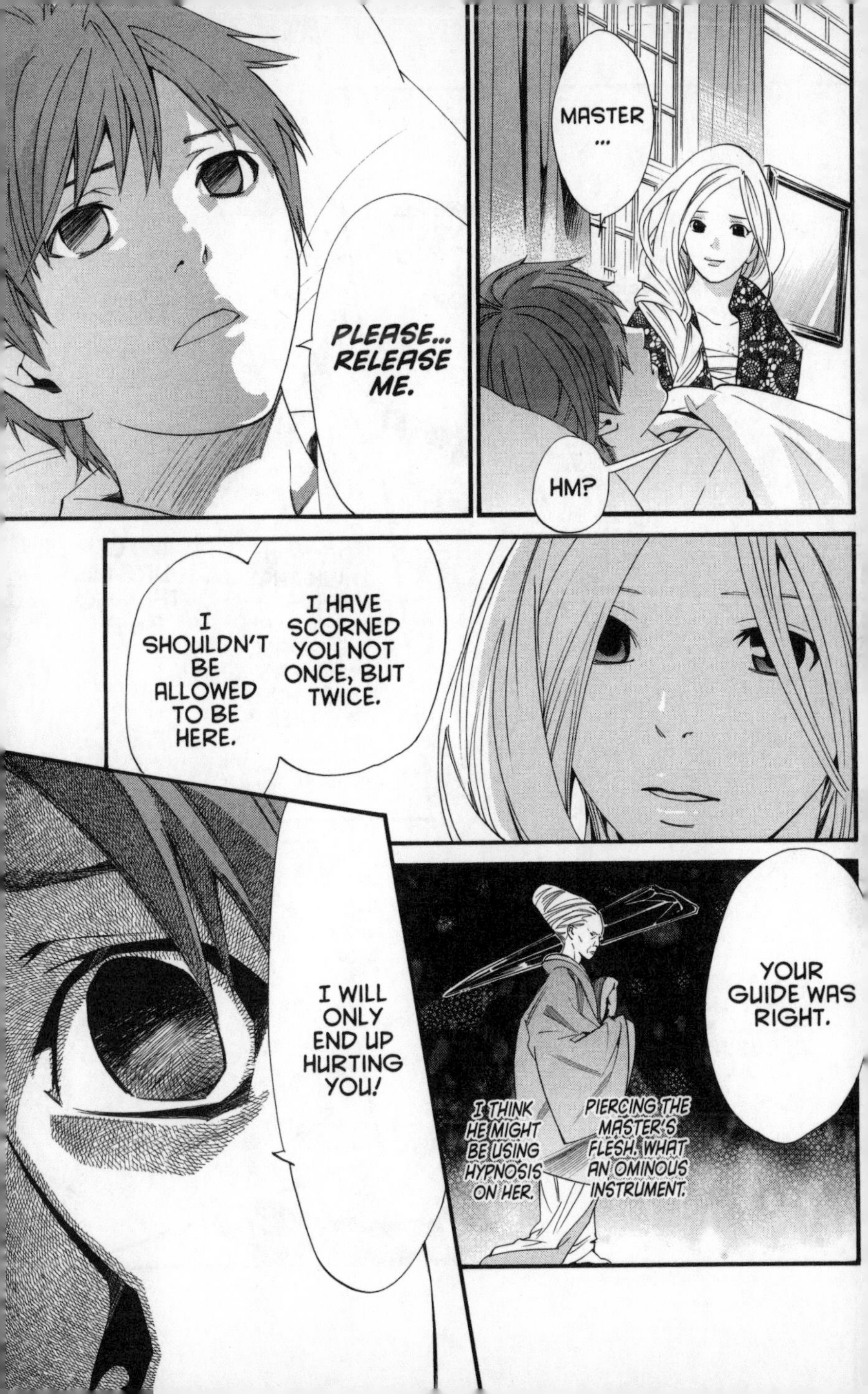

MASTER ...
HM?
PLEASE... RELEASE ME.
I HAVE SCORNED YOU NOT ONCE, BUT TWICE.
I SHOULDN'T BE ALLOWED TO BE HERE.
I WILL ONLY END UP HURTING YOU!
YOUR GUIDE WAS RIGHT.
PIERCING THE MASTER'S FLESH. WHAT AN OMINOUS INSTRUMENT.
I THINK HE MIGHT BE USING HYPNOSIS ON HER.

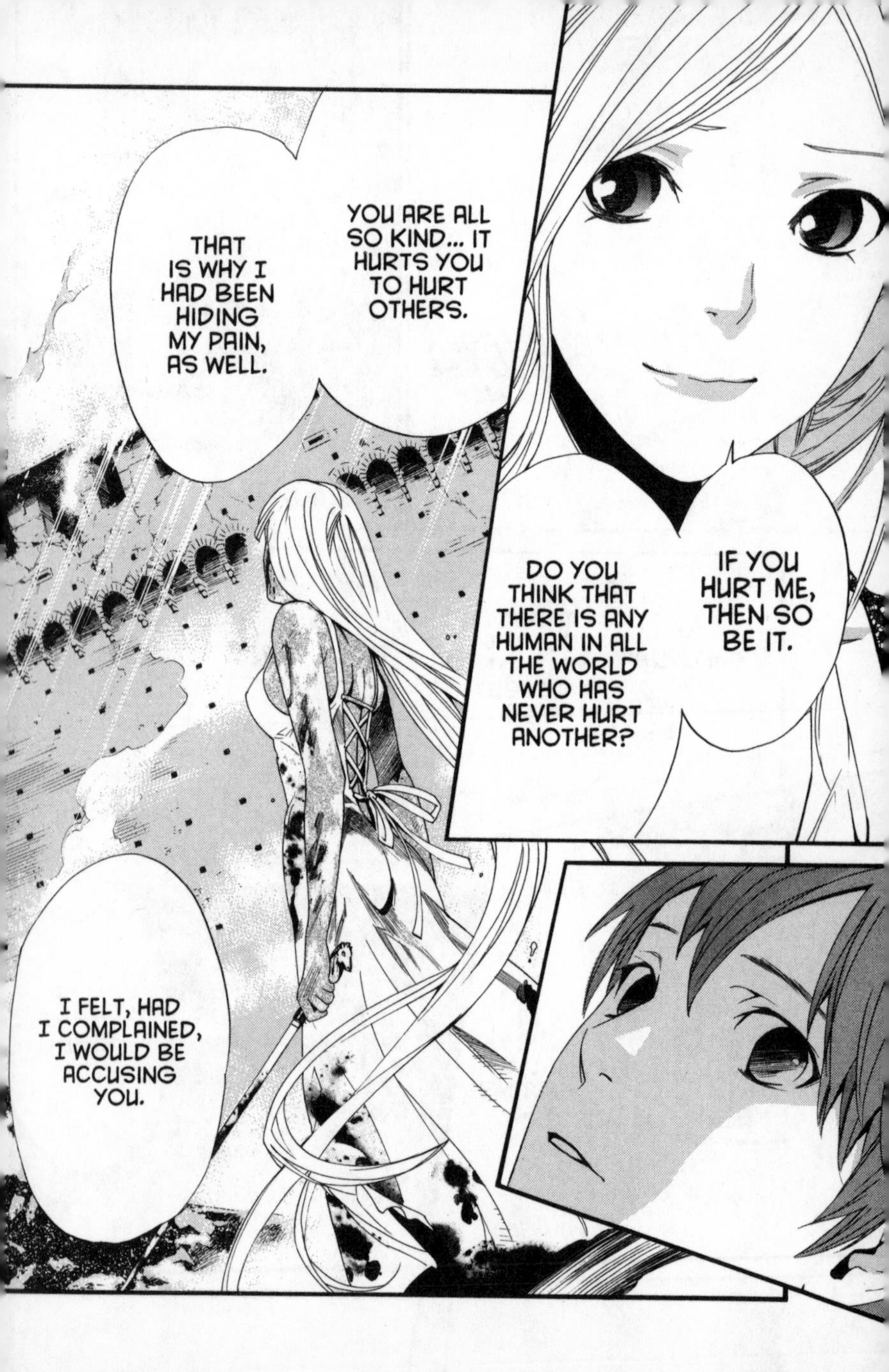
IF YOU HURT ME, THEN SO BE IT.
DO YOU THINK THAT THERE IS ANY HUMAN IN ALL THE WORLD WHO HAS NEVER HURT ANOTHER?
YOU ARE ALL SO KIND... IT HURTS YOU TO HURT OTHERS.
THAT IS WHY I HAD BEEN HIDING MY PAIN, AS WELL.
I FELT, HAD I COMPLAINED, I WOULD BE ACCUSING YOU.

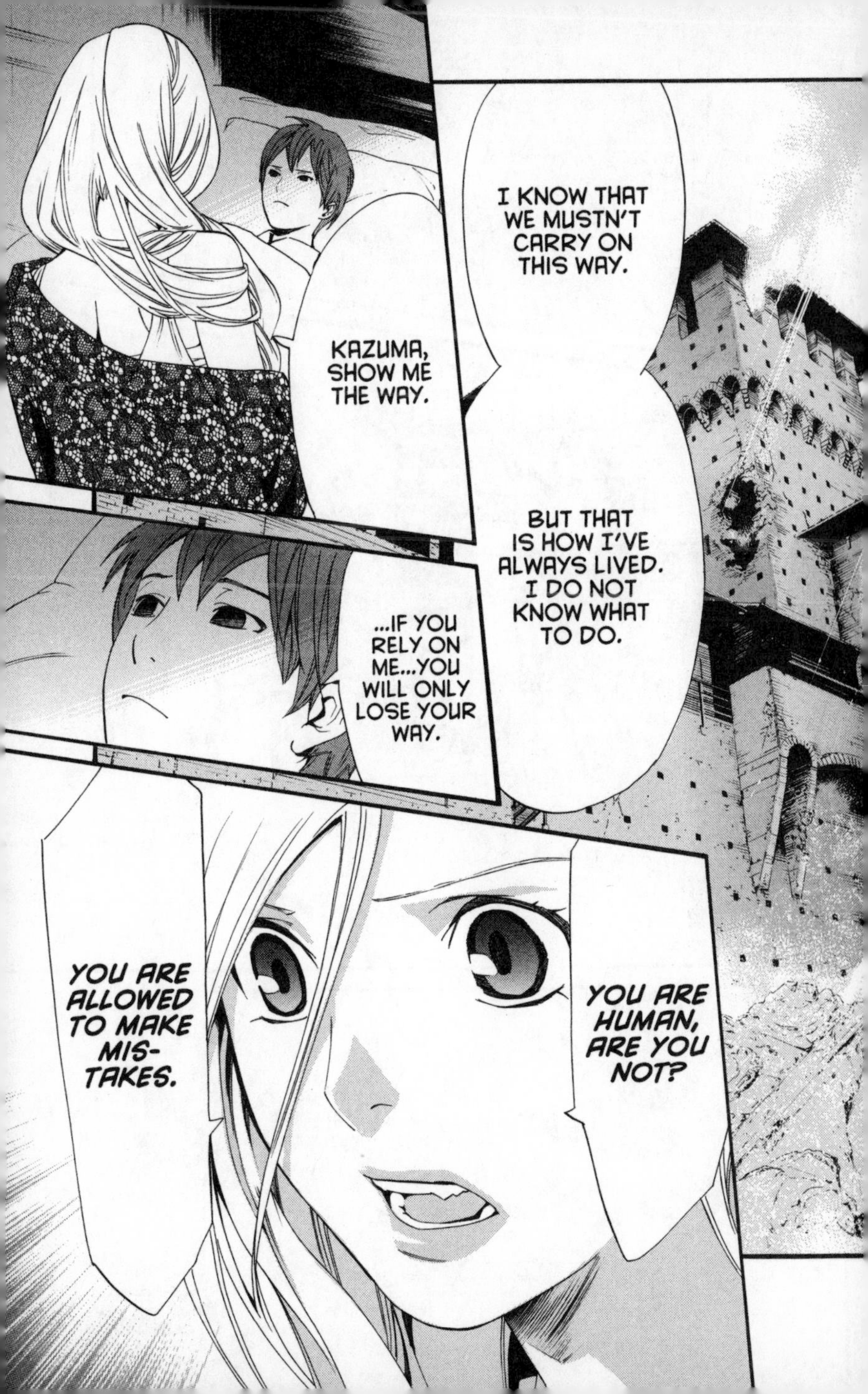
I KNOW THAT WE MUSTN'T CARRY ON THIS WAY.
BUT THAT IS HOW I'VE ALWAYS LIVED. I DO NOT KNOW WHAT TO DO.
KAZUMA, SHOW ME THE WAY.
...IF YOU RELY ON ME...YOU WILL ONLY LOSE YOUR WAY.
YOU ARE HUMAN, ARE YOU NOT?
YOU ARE ALLOWED TO MAKE MIS-TAKES.

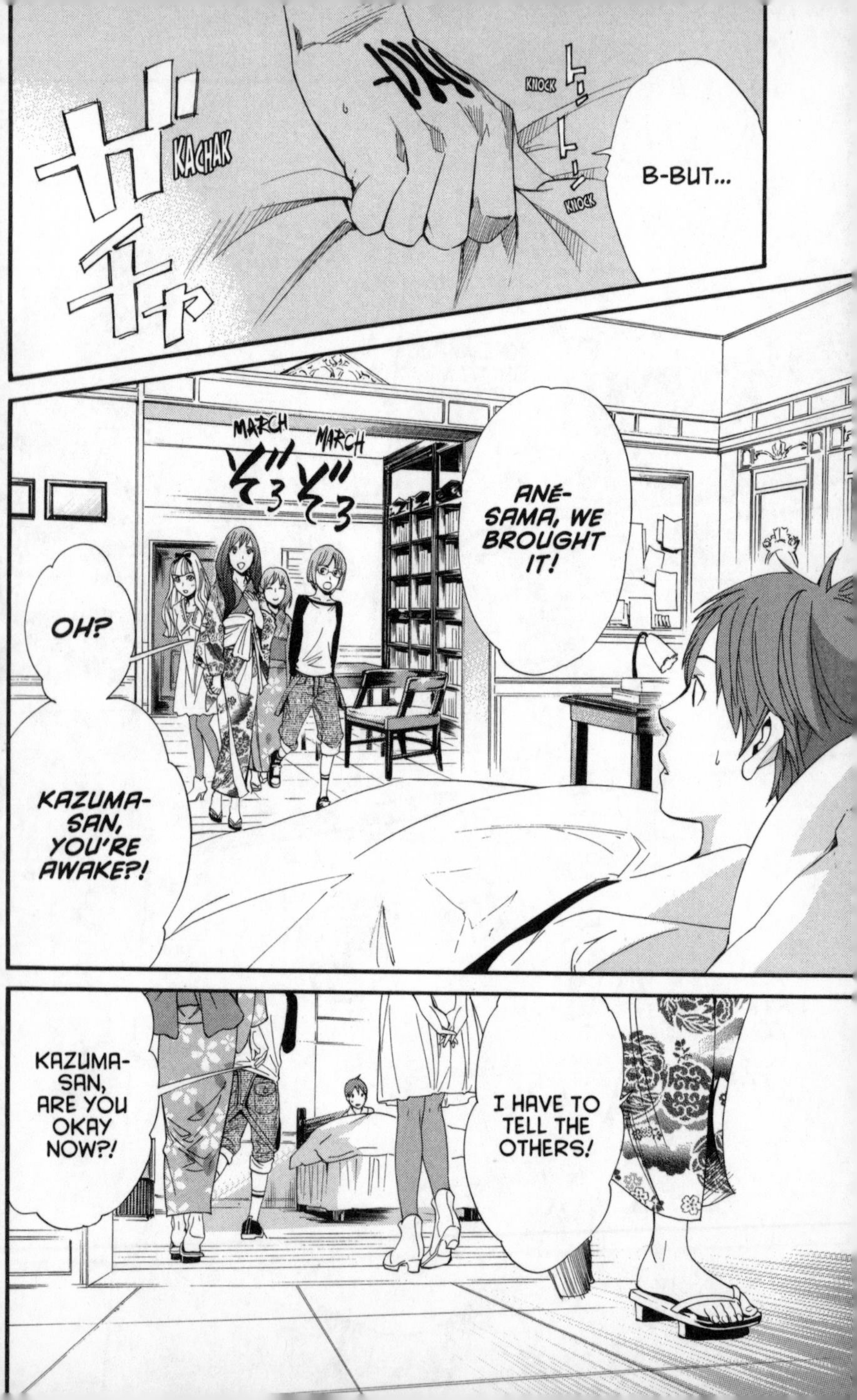
B-BUT...
KNOCK
KNOCK
KACHAK
ANÉ-SAMA, WE BROUGHT IT!
MARCH
MARCH
OH?
KAZUMA-SAN, YOU'RE AWAKE?!
I HAVE TO TELL THE OTHERS!
KAZUMA-SAN, ARE YOU OKAY NOW?!

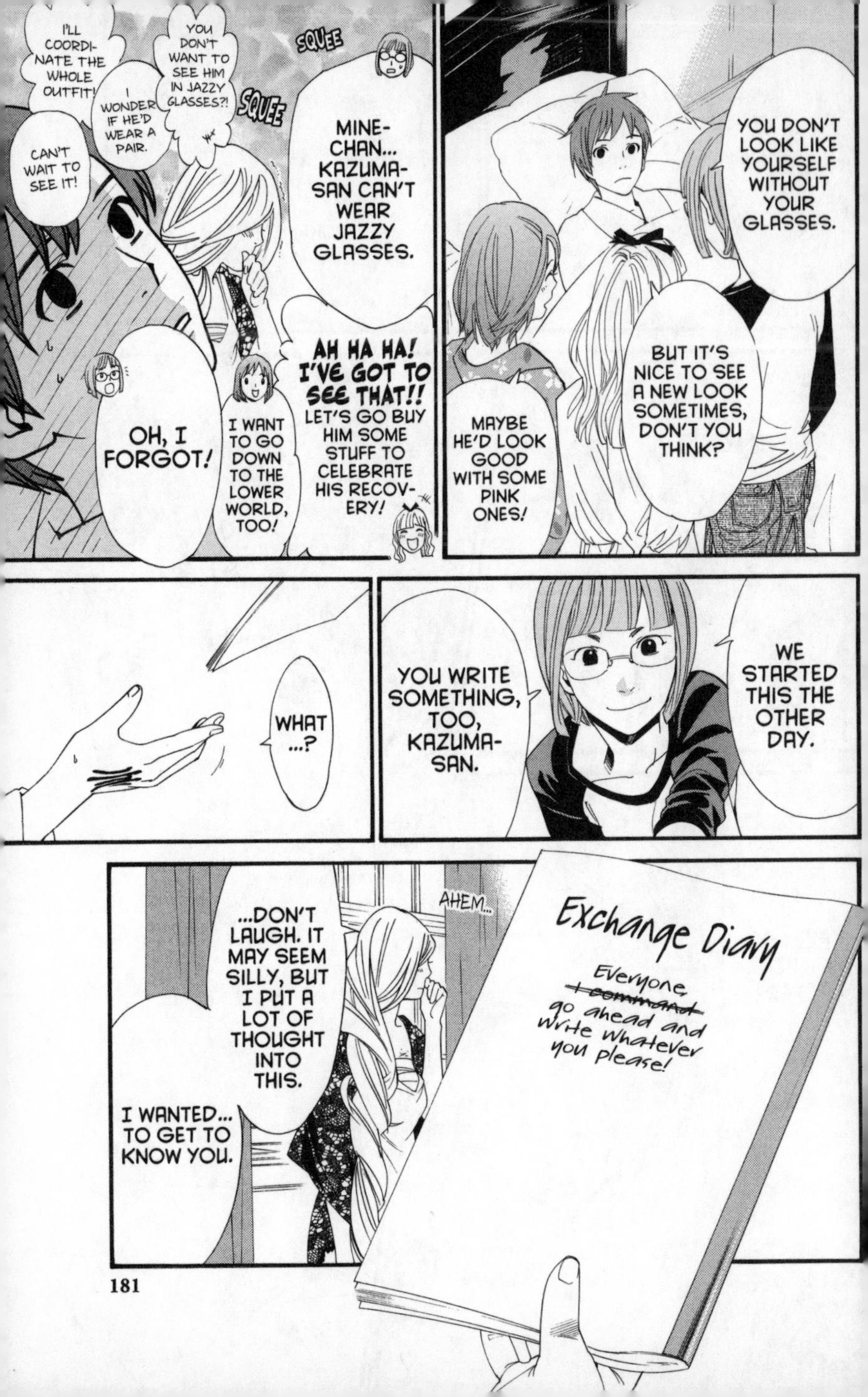
YOU DON'T LOOK LIKE YOURSELF WITHOUT YOUR GLASSES.
BUT IT'S NICE TO SEE A NEW LOOK SOMETIMES, DON'T YOU THINK?
MAYBE HE'D LOOK GOOD WITH SOME PINK ONES!
SQUEE
MINE-CHAN... KAZUMA-SAN CAN'T WEAR JAZZY GLASSES.
SQUEE
YOU DON'T WANT TO SEE HIM IN JAZZY GLASSES?!
I WONDER IF HE'D WEAR A PAIR.
I'LL COORDINATE THE WHOLE OUTFIT!
CAN'T WAIT TO SEE IT!
AH HA HA! I'VE GOT TO SEE THAT!! LET'S GO BUY HIM SOME STUFF TO CELEBRATE HIS RECOVERY!
I WANT TO GO DOWN TO THE LOWER WORLD, TOO!
OH, I FORGOT!
WE STARTED THIS THE OTHER DAY.
YOU WRITE SOMETHING, TOO, KAZUMA-SAN.
WHAT...?
Exchange Diary
Everyone, ~~I command~~ go ahead and write whatever you please!
AHEM...
...DON'T LAUGH. IT MAY SEEM SILLY, BUT I PUT A LOT OF THOUGHT INTO THIS.
I WANTED... TO GET TO KNOW YOU.

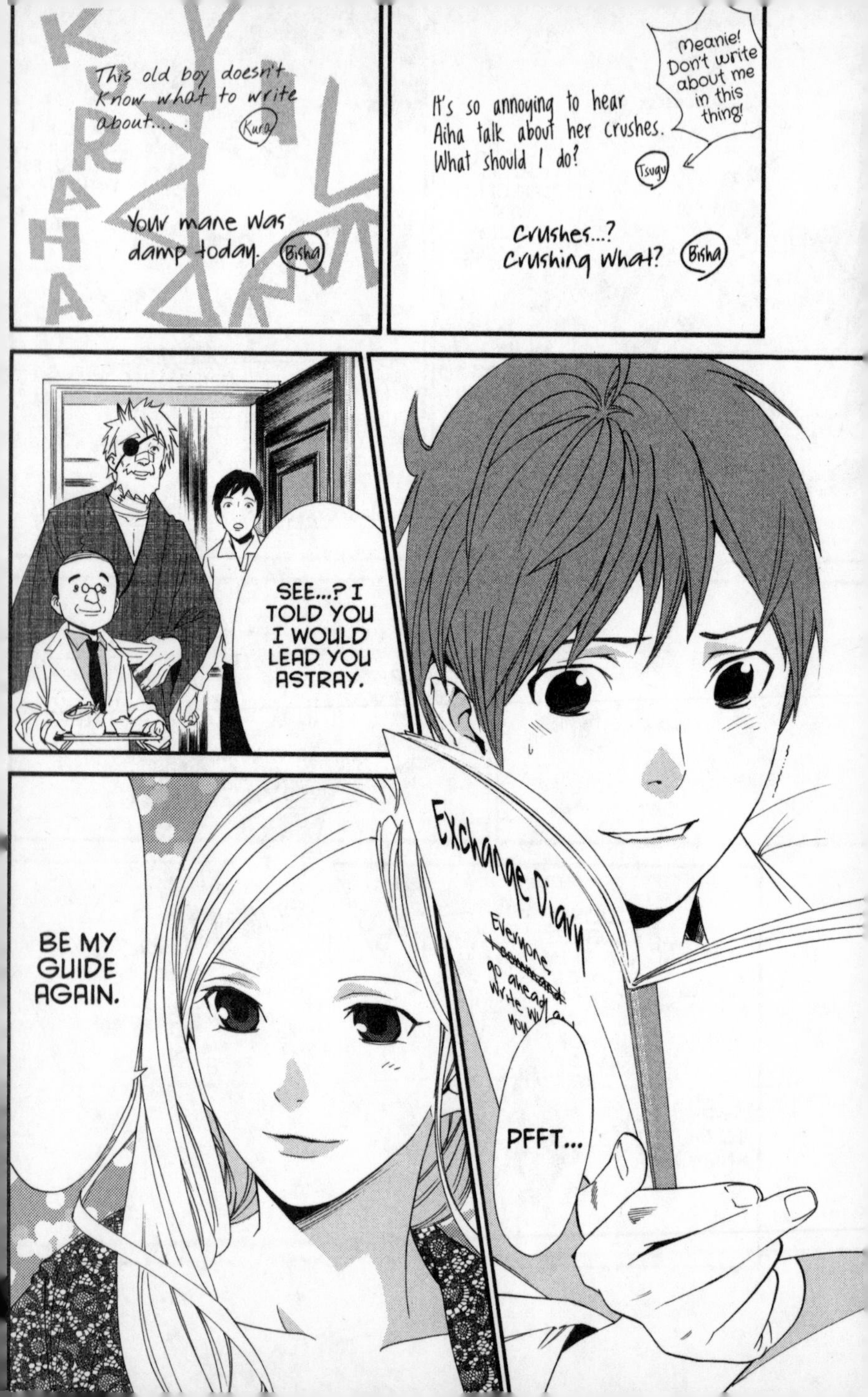
It's so annoying to hear Aiha talk about her crushes. What should I do? Tsugu
Meanie! Don't write about me in this thing!
Crushes...? Crushing what? Bisha
This old boy doesn't know what to write about.... Kura
Your mane was damp today. Bisha
SEE...? I TOLD YOU I WOULD LEAD YOU ASTRAY.
BE MY GUIDE AGAIN.
Exchange Diary
PFFT...

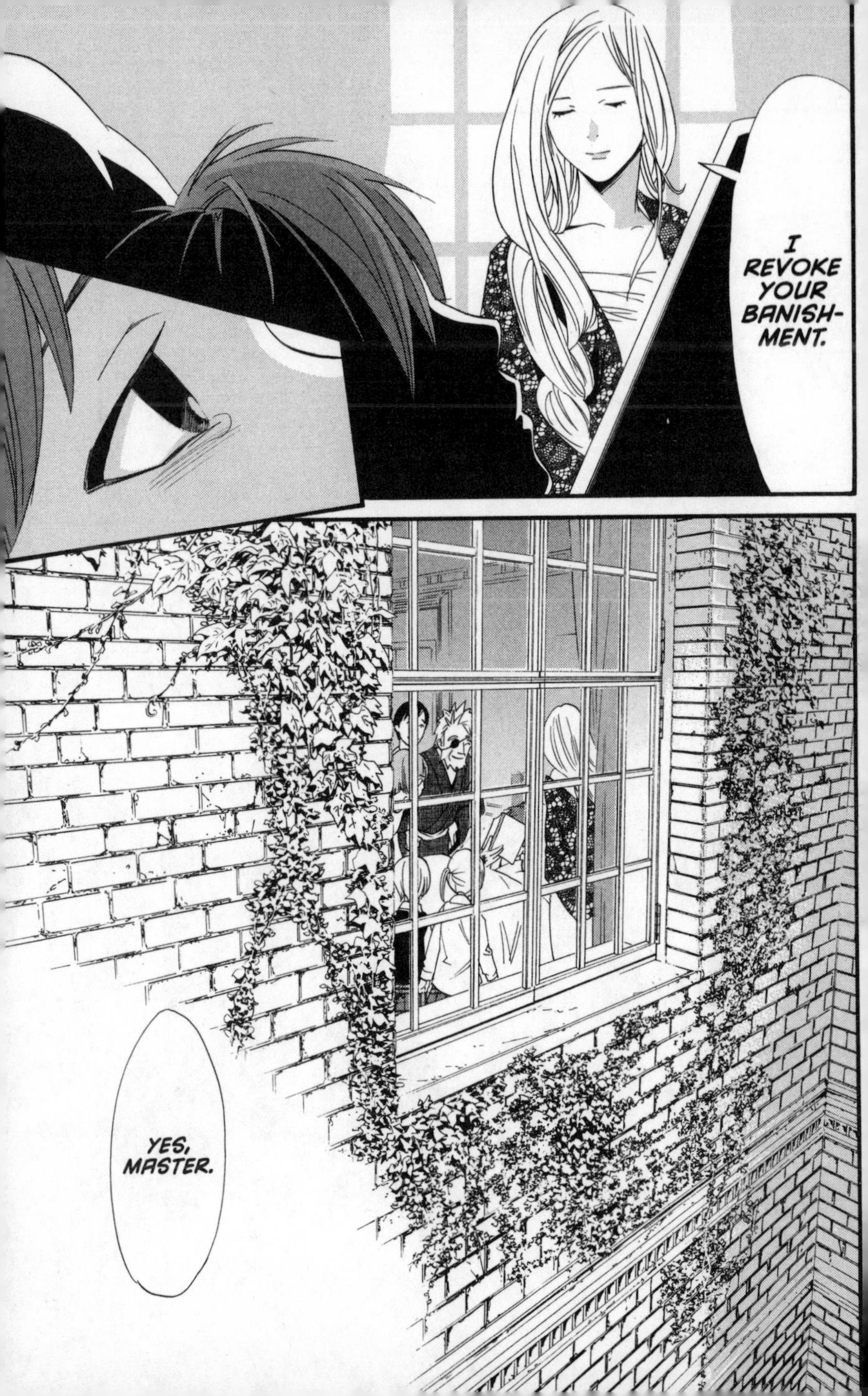
I REVOKE YOUR BANISH-MENT.
YES, MASTER.

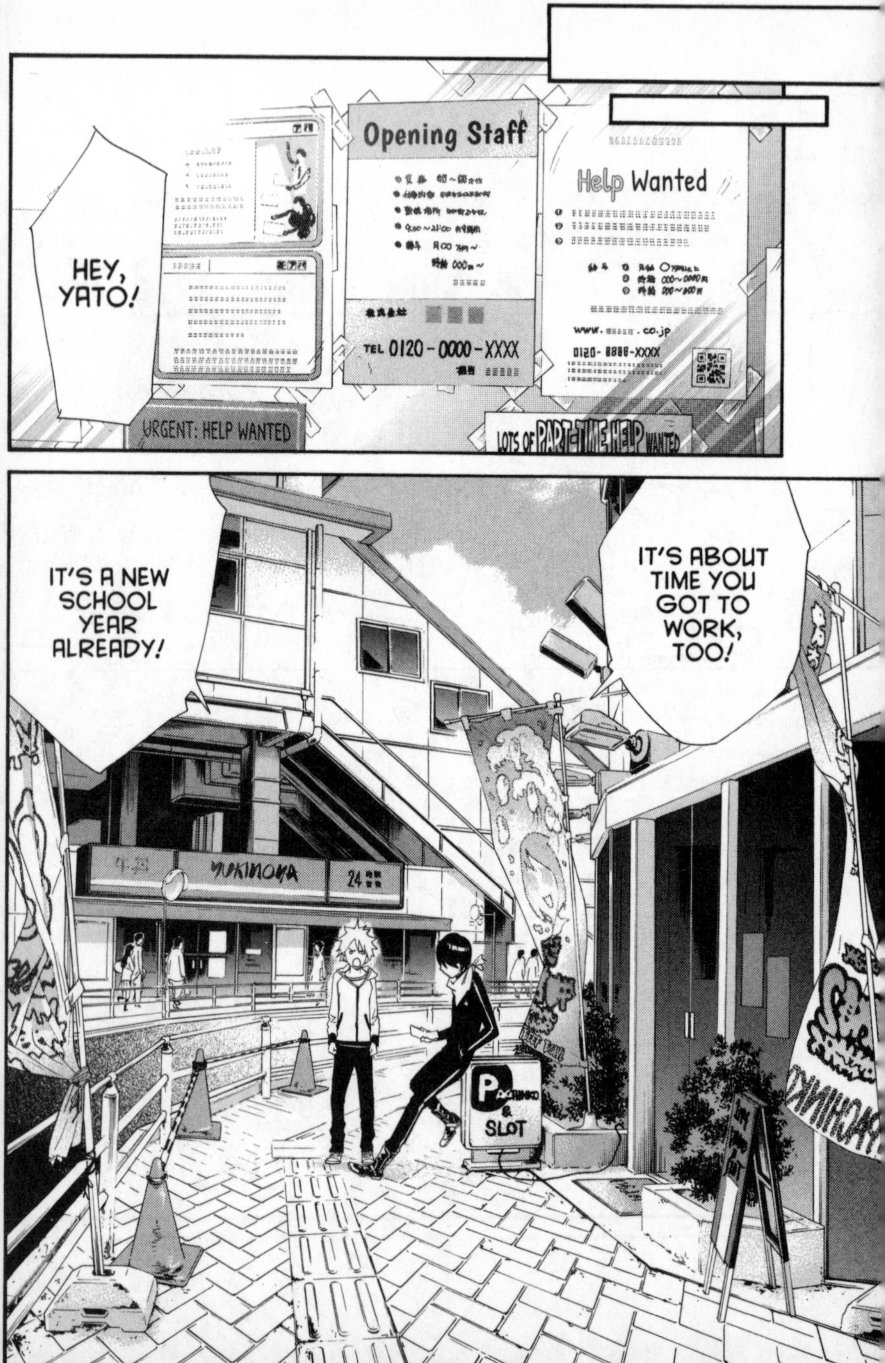
Help Wanted
www. .co.jp
0120-8888-XXXX
Opening Staff
TEL 0120-0000-XXXX
HEY, YATO!
LOTS OF PART-TIME HELP WANTED
URGENT: HELP WANTED
IT'S ABOUT TIME YOU GOT TO WORK, TOO!
IT'S A NEW SCHOOL YEAR ALREADY!
YUKINOYA
24
PACHINKO & SLOT

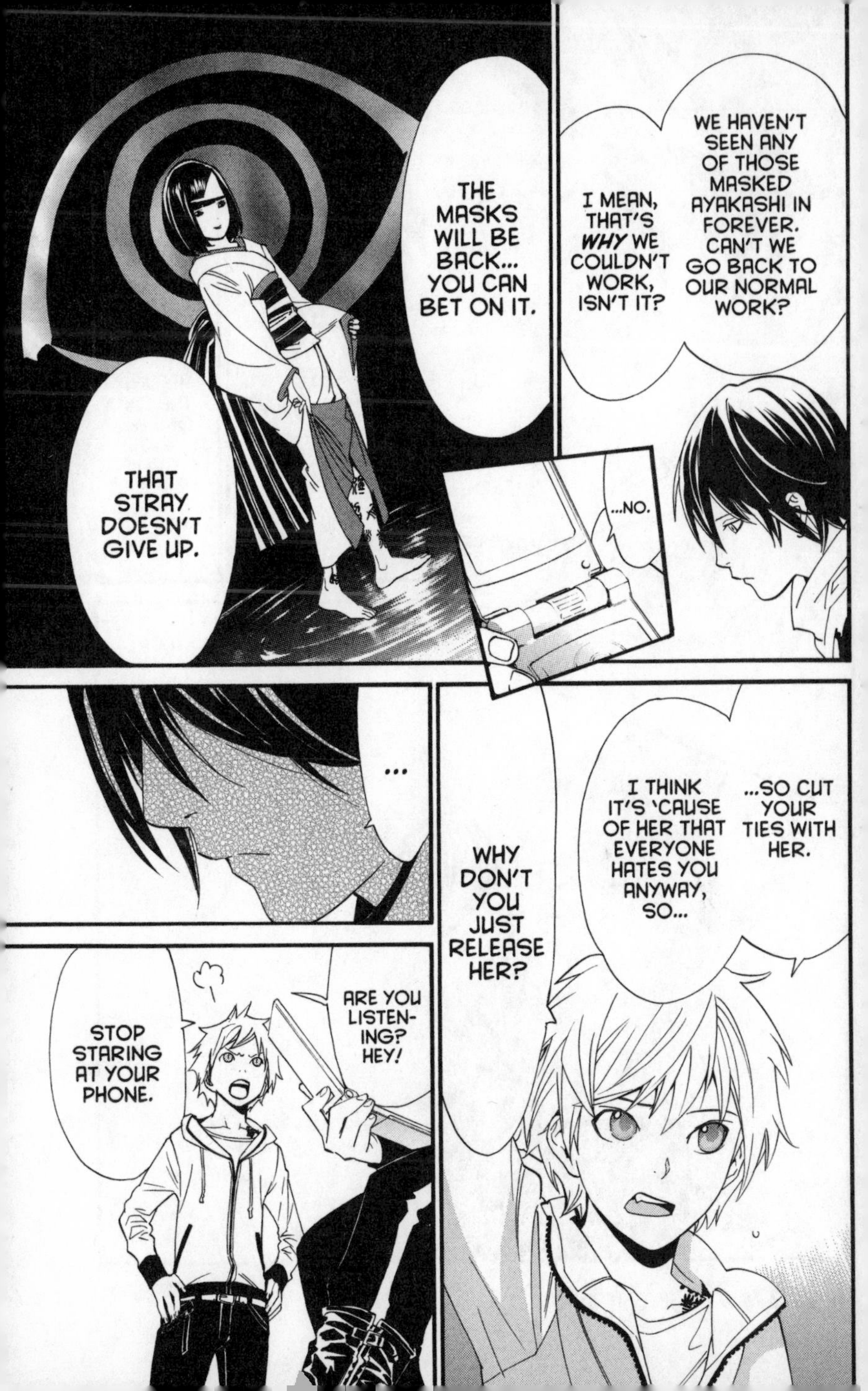
WE HAVEN'T SEEN ANY OF THOSE MASKED AYAKASHI IN FOREVER. CAN'T WE GO BACK TO OUR NORMAL WORK?
I MEAN, THAT'S *WHY* WE COULDN'T WORK, ISN'T IT?
...NO.
THE MASKS WILL BE BACK... YOU CAN BET ON IT.
THAT STRAY DOESN'T GIVE UP.
I THINK IT'S 'CAUSE OF HER THAT EVERYONE HATES YOU ANYWAY, SO...
...SO CUT YOUR TIES WITH HER.
WHY DON'T YOU JUST RELEASE HER?
...
ARE YOU LISTEN-ING? HEY!
STOP STARING AT YOUR PHONE.

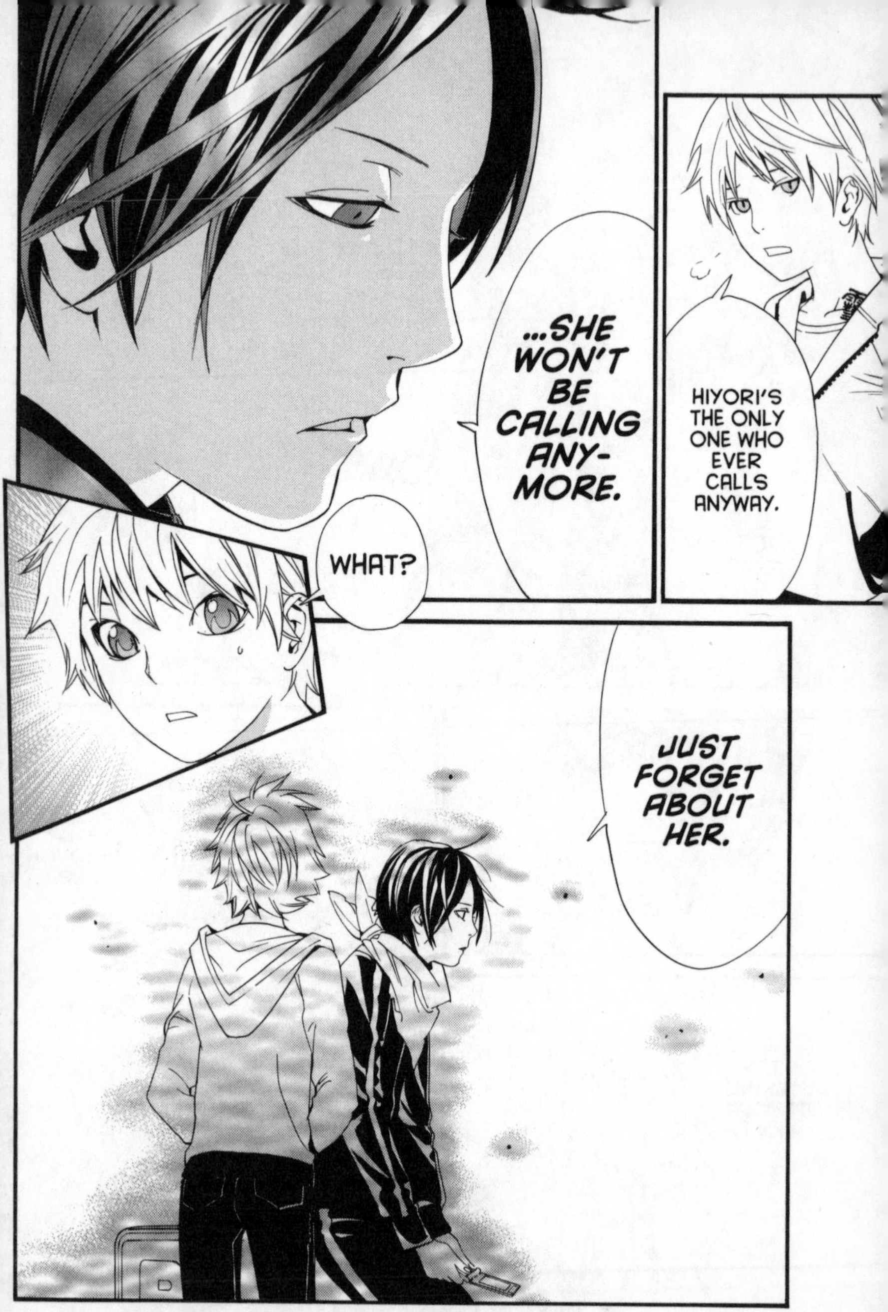
HIYORI'S THE ONLY ONE WHO EVER CALLS ANYWAY.
...SHE WON'T BE CALLING ANY-MORE.
WHAT?
JUST FORGET ABOUT HER.

NORAGAMI / TO BE CONTINUED

野

兒

神

ATROCIOUS MANGA

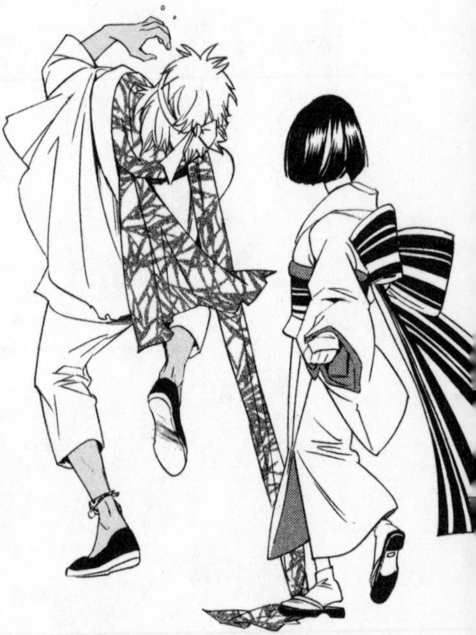

RACE AGAINST TIME!!

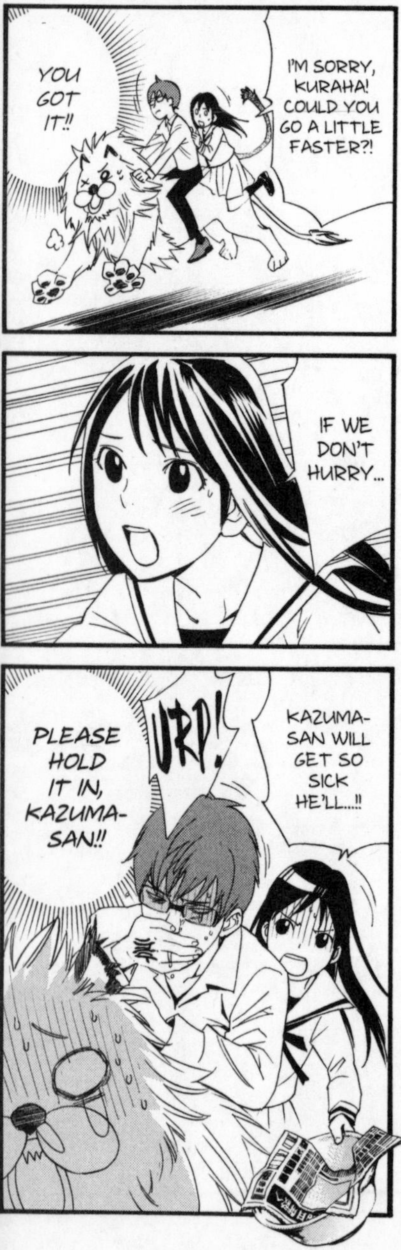

I'M SORRY, KURAHA! COULD YOU GO A LITTLE FASTER?!
YOU GOT IT!!
IF WE DON'T HURRY...
KAZUMA-SAN WILL GET SO SICK HE'LL...!!
URP!
PLEASE HOLD IT IN, KAZUMA-SAN!!

RAISING SIMULATION GAME, PART 1

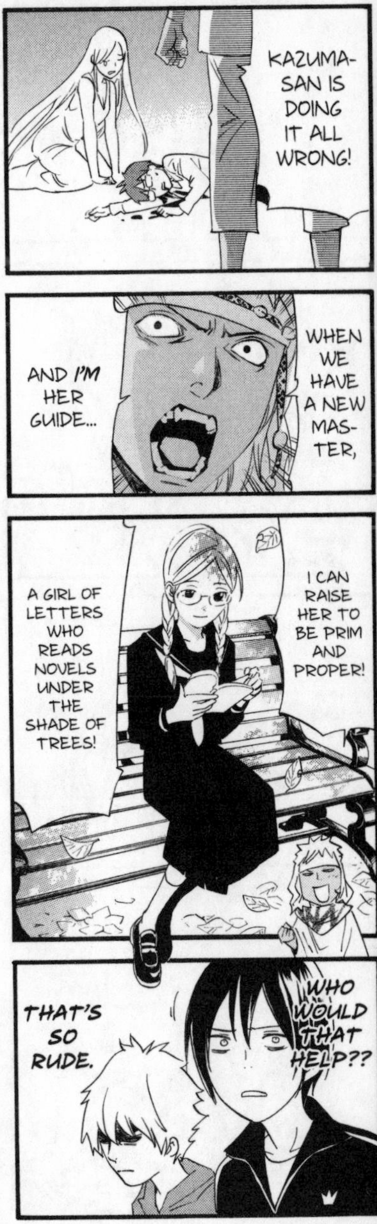
KAZUMA-SAN IS DOING IT ALL WRONG!
WHEN WE HAVE A NEW MASTER,
AND I'M HER GUIDE...
I CAN RAISE HER TO BE PRIM AND PROPER!
A GIRL OF LETTERS WHO READS NOVELS UNDER THE SHADE OF TREES!
WHO WOULD THAT HELP??
THAT'S SO RUDE.

RAISING SIMULATION GAME, PART 2

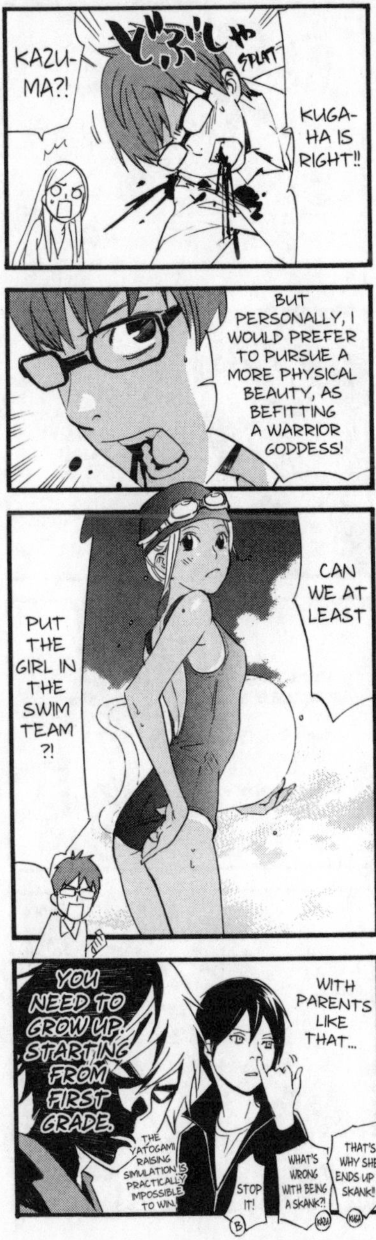
KUGA-HA IS RIGHT!!
どぶしゃ
SPLAT
KAZUMA?!
BUT PERSONALLY, I WOULD PREFER TO PURSUE A MORE PHYSICAL BEAUTY, AS BEFITTING A WARRIOR GODDESS!
CAN WE AT LEAST
PUT THE GIRL IN THE SWIM TEAM?!
WITH PARENTS LIKE THAT...
YOU NEED TO GROW UP. STARTING FROM FIRST GRADE.
THAT'S WHY SHE ENDS UP A SKANK!!
KUGA
WHAT'S WRONG WITH BEING A SKANK?!
KAZU
STOP IT!
B
THE YATOGAMI RAISING SIMULATION IS PRACTICALLY IMPOSSIBLE TO WIN.

REIGNITING OLD FLAMES

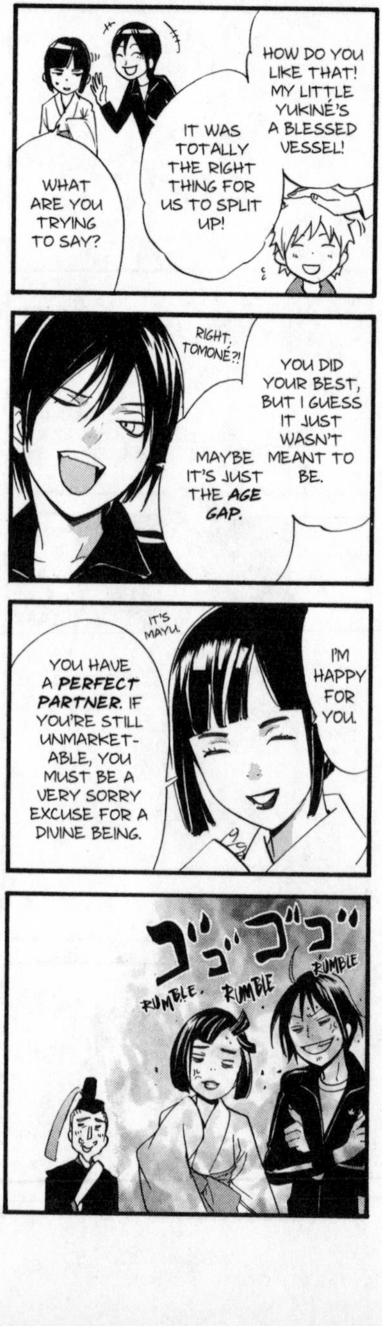
HOW DO YOU LIKE THAT! MY LITTLE YUKINÉ'S A BLESSED VESSEL!
IT WAS TOTALLY THE RIGHT THING FOR US TO SPLIT UP!
WHAT ARE YOU TRYING TO SAY?
YOU DID YOUR BEST, BUT I GUESS IT JUST WASN'T MEANT TO BE.
MAYBE IT'S JUST THE **AGE GAP.**
RIGHT, TOMONÉ?!
I'M HAPPY FOR YOU.
IT'S MAYU.
YOU HAVE A **PERFECT PARTNER.** IF YOU'RE STILL UNMARKET-ABLE, YOU MUST BE A VERY SORRY EXCUSE FOR A DIVINE BEING.
ゴゴゴ
RUMBLE
RUMBLE
RUMBLE

GIFTS

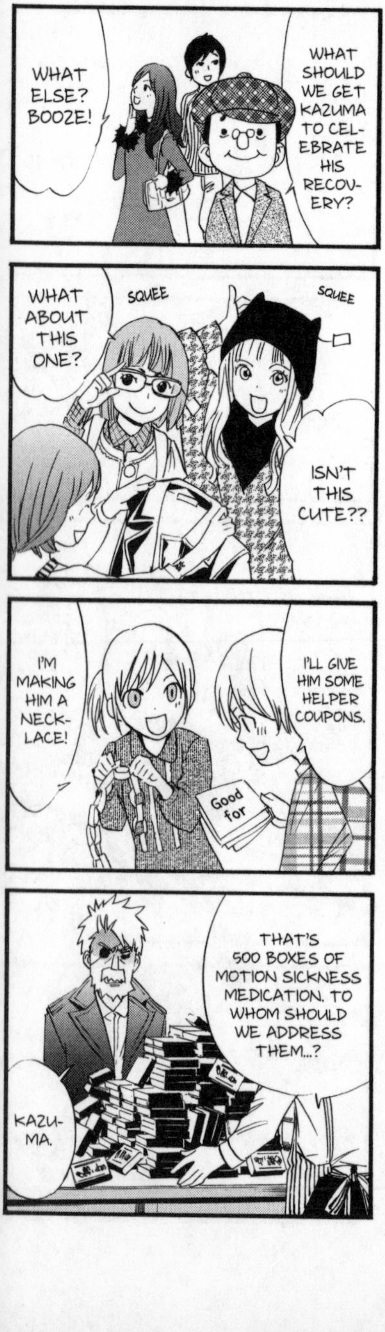
WHAT SHOULD WE GET KAZUMA TO CEL-EBRATE HIS RECOV-ERY?
WHAT ELSE? BOOZE!
SQUEE
ISN'T THIS CUTE??
SQUEE
WHAT ABOUT THIS ONE?
I'LL GIVE HIM SOME HELPER COUPONS.
Good for
I'M MAKING HIM A NECK-LACE!
THAT'S 500 BOXES OF MOTION SICKNESS MEDICATION. TO WHOM SHOULD WE ADDRESS THEM...?
KAZU-MA.

IF WE COULD MEET IN OUR DREAMS

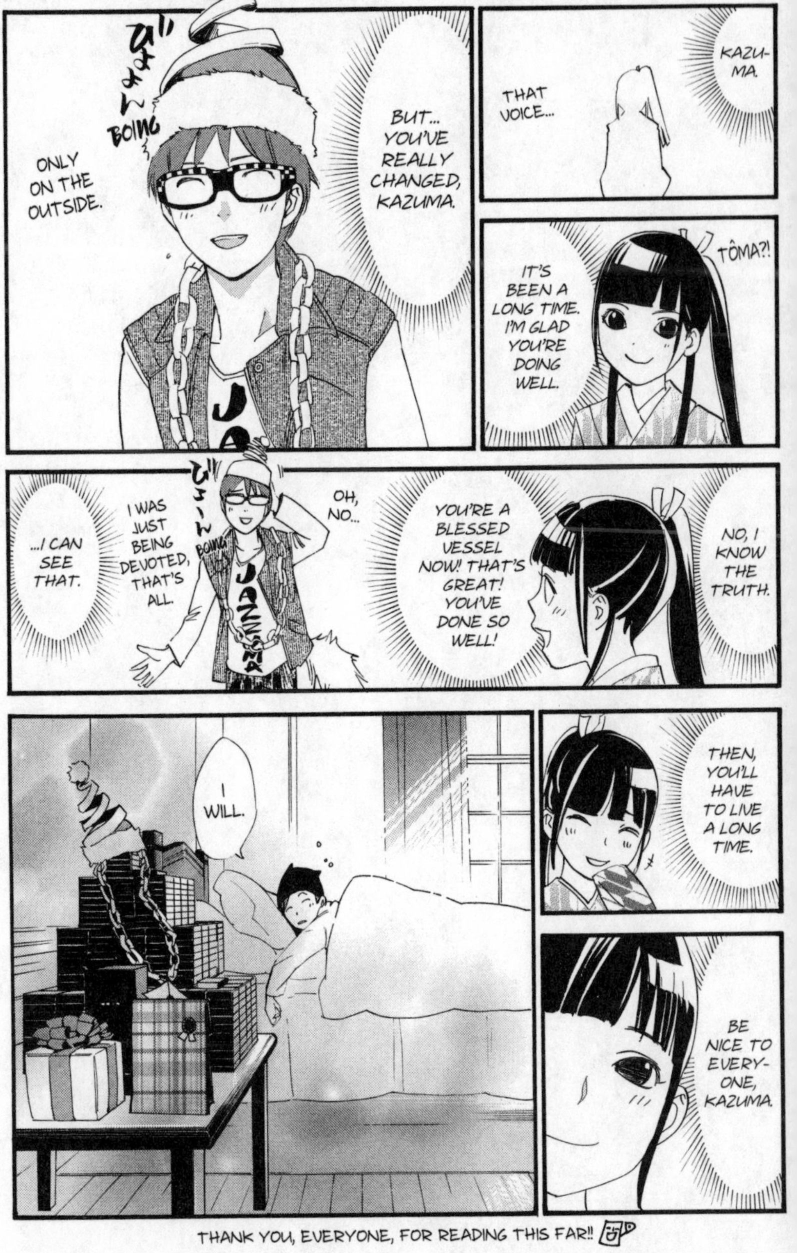
KAZUMA.
THAT VOICE...
TÔMA?!
IT'S BEEN A LONG TIME. I'M GLAD YOU'RE DOING WELL.
BUT... YOU'VE REALLY CHANGED, KAZUMA.
ONLY ON THE OUTSIDE.
びよん
BOING
NO, I KNOW THE TRUTH.
YOU'RE A BLESSED VESSEL NOW! THAT'S GREAT! YOU'VE DONE SO WELL!
OH, NO...
BOING
I WAS JUST BEING DEVOTED, THAT'S ALL.
...I CAN SEE THAT.
THEN, YOU'LL HAVE TO LIVE A LONG TIME.
BE NICE TO EVERYONE, KAZUMA.
I WILL.

THANK YOU, EVERYONE, FOR READING THIS FAR!!

TRANSLATION NOTES

Japanese is a tricky language for most Westerners, and translation is often more art than science. For your edification and reading pleasure, here are notes on some of the places where we could have gone in a different direction in our translation of the work, or where a Japanese cultural reference is used.

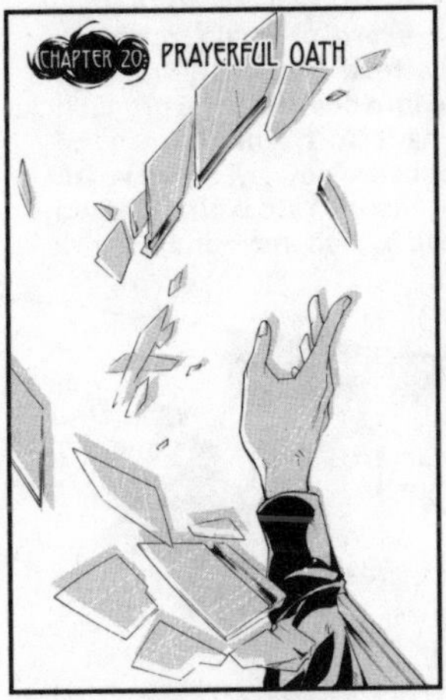
CHAPTER 20: PRAYERFUL OATH

Prayerful Oath, page 5
The Japanese title of this chapter comes from a phrase found in the *Nihon Shoki*, or *The Chronicles of Japan*, which is the oldest book of Japanese history. It includes the mythological story of the creation of Japan, including the famous story of when Amaterasu, the sun goddess, hides in a cave and must be coaxed out so that light can return to the world. Various items were gathered to tempt Amaterasu out, and one deity offered a prayer. The phrase used to tell that the prayer was offered is *kamu hosaki hosakiki*, which is the Japanese title of this chapter.

There are actually two kanji that can be pronounced *hosaki*—one means blessing, and the other means curse. This may be because in Japanese tradition, both blessing and curses come from the gods. So whether someone wants good things to happen to a friend, or bad things to happen to an enemy, that person would pray to the gods. In this chapter, we have characters wishing for both blessings and curses upon other characters.

In an attempt to convey both meanings, the translators have chosen the word "oath," which can refer to a solemn appeal to deity (made out of determination to keep a promise), or a blasphemous use of the name of a god, often referred to in English as "cursing."

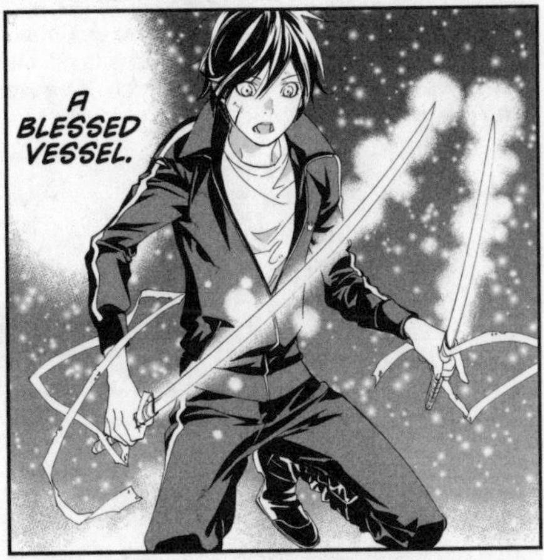
A BLESSED VESSEL.

Blessed vessel, page 10
This is a more or less literal translation of *hafuri no utsuwa*, but there are some things worth noting about the word *hafuri*. First, a *hafuri* (using the same *kanji*) is a type of Shinto priest who would assist in worship rituals. Second, according to Classical Japanese pronunciation rules, the characters written as *hafu* are pronounced together as *hô*, and the Japanese *R* can also be pronounced as an *L*, so the word translated as "blessed" can be pronounced as "holy."

Girl gone wild, page 37

What Yato yelled in the Japanese version was *onna-mata-jikara*, which is likely a reference to an erotic Japanese variety show called *Tsutomu-kun*. In the TV show referenced, women compete in a "sexy athletic meet," which is filmed at various risque angles. The *kanji* characters for *tsutomu* are the same as in *onna-mata-jikara*, meaning roughly "woman double effort," and when the three *kanji* are merged into one, it can be pronounced *tsutomu*, meaning "effort." The *jikara* in the phrase can also mean "power," which would be one of many reasons Yato would make the connection between Bishamon and the girls in that program.

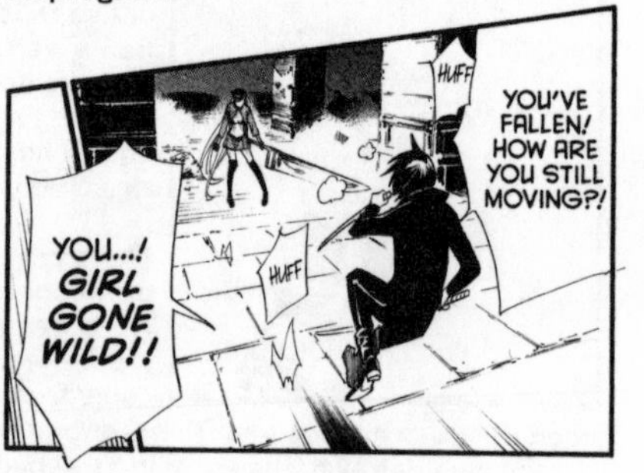
HUFF
YOU'VE FALLEN! HOW ARE YOU STILL MOVING?!
YOU...! GIRL GONE WILD!!
HUFF

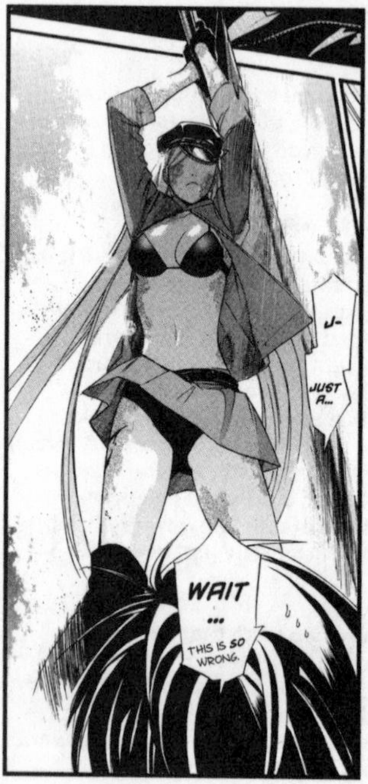
J-
JUST A...
WAIT ...
THIS IS SO WRONG.

Ew, yuck, page 70

What Kugaha said in the Japanese text was *engacho*. This word is usually used by children to identify someone who is infected with dirtiness, such as a friend who stepped in something gross. Until the *engacho* is lifted, the person so identified is to be avoided, so that no one else will catch the dirtiness. It's a little like cooties. In this case, Kugaha is probably referring to the blood that is getting splattered everywhere, which, if he were to get on himself, would infect him with dirtiness as well.

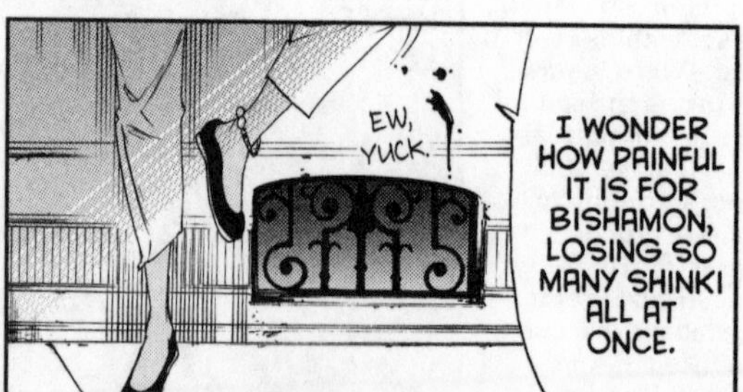
I WONDER HOW PAINFUL IT IS FOR BISHAMON, LOSING SO MANY SHINKI ALL AT ONCE.
EW, YUCK.

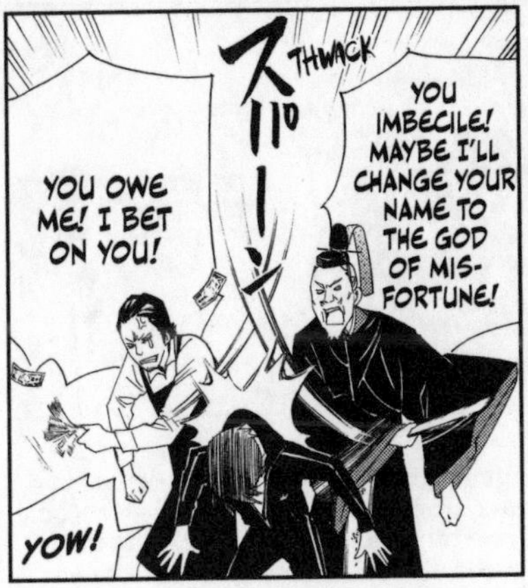
THWACK
YOU IMBECILE! MAYBE I'LL CHANGE YOUR NAME TO THE GOD OF MIS-FORTUNE!
YOU OWE ME! I BET ON YOU!
YOW!

God of Misfortune, page 125

Specifically, Tenjin suggests changing Yato's name to *Yakubyôgami*, which literally means "God of Pestilence." In modern times, however, the term is used to describe any person, divine or otherwise, who brings any form of bad luck or misfortune, pestilent or otherwise, to all in his or her vicinity—in other words, a jinx.

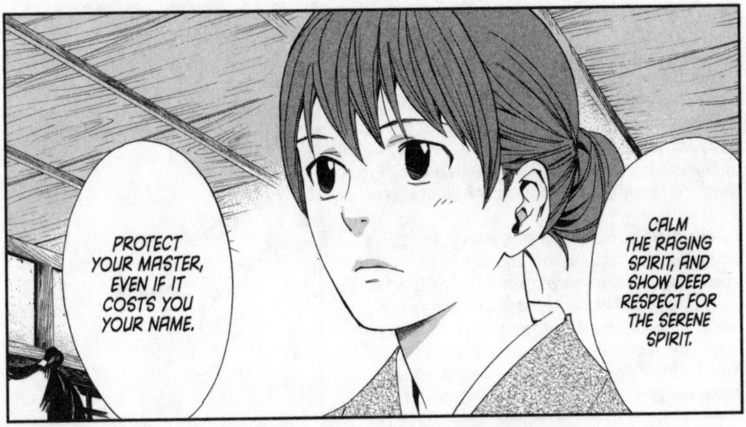
CALM THE RAGING SPIRIT, AND SHOW DEEP RESPECT FOR THE SERENE SPIRIT.
PROTECT YOUR MASTER, EVEN IF IT COSTS YOU YOUR NAME.

The raging spirit and the serene spirit, page 145

Some readers may recall that in the previous volume of *Noragami*, Bishamon addressed Yato as a "raging spirit," or *ara-mitama*. The "raging spirit" of an angry god is only one aspect of that god. When not enraged, the god will be found in a more harmonious aspect, the *nigi-mitama*, or "serene spirit." This is the aspect of the god that brings blessings such as rain and sunshine.

IF THE MASTER PASSES AWAY... WHAT HAPPENS TO US?
DON'T EVEN
SHE'LL BE REPLACED, AND THEN THE MA CLAN WILL ALL BE EXCOMMUNICATED, I BET.
WOULD ANY GOD TAKE US IN ONCE OUR NAMES HAVE BEEN BLOTTED OUT?!

Names blotted out, page 162

The shinki are wondering what would happen if they were released, or excommunicated by a new Bishamon and the *imina* (true names) they were given become *imina* (avoided names). In an effort to retain the nuance without slowing the readers down, the translators referred to the Biblical phrase that tends to be used when someone is excommunicated—that person's name is "blotted out" of the church records. The shinki are unsure that any god would accept a shinki that has been excommunicated by another god.

Exchange diary, page 182

Exchange Diary
PFFT...

An exchange diary, or *kôkan nikki*, is a diary shared between friends or lovers. Each person sharing the diary will take turns writing down their thoughts or feelings, knowing full well that other people will read it—kind of like Facebook without the internet. Like Facebook, all of the writer's friends who are in a position to read the "feed" can comment on posts/entries.

As for the first post in this diary, Tsuguha may not necessarily be complaining only about Aiha's crushes. Apparently Aiha likes to talk about romantic stories in general, which may or may not be about her personally. The word Tsuguha uses for this is *koibana*, short for *koibanashi*, which means "tale of romantic love". The abbreviation is fairly recent slang, and Tsuguha didn't use a *kanji* character for it, which would have given away the meaning. That being the case, Bishamon, who is not up on all the modern lingo, is a little confused by the term. The best she can come up with is that maybe *bana* is related somehow to bananas.

Meanie! Don't write about me in this thing!
It's so annoying to hear Aiha talk about her crushes. What should I do?
Tsugu
Crushes...? Crushing what?
Bisha

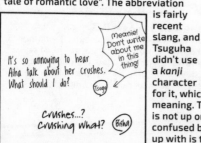

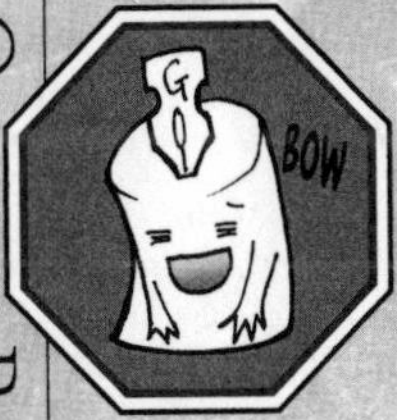
BOW

Generally, when I draw color pictures in the winter, the paper tears. So I tried using some durable paper, and this time, the artist tape broke. ...So that's how you're gonna play it!

Adachitoka

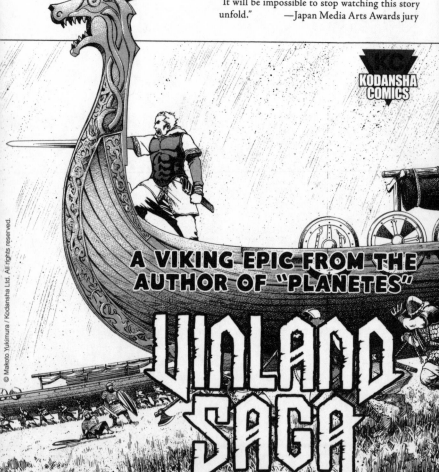

NO.6

A PERFECT LIFE IN A PERFECT CITY

For Shion, an elite student in the technologically sophisticated city No. 6, life is carefully choreographed. One fateful day, he takes a misstep, sheltering a fugitive his age from a typhoon. Helping this boy throws Shion's life down a path to discovering the appalling secrets behind the "perfection" of No. 6.

KODANSHA COMICS

Noragami: Stray God volume 6 is a work of fiction. Names, characters, places, and incidents are the products of the author's imagination or are used fictitiously. Any resemblance to actual events, locales, or persons, living or dead, is entirely coincidental.

A Kodansha Comics Trade Paperback Original.

Published in the United States by Kodansha Comics, an imprint of Kodansha USA Publishing, LLC, New York.

Publication rights for this English edition arranged through Kodansha Ltd., Tokyo.

First published in Japan in 2013 by Kodansha Ltd., Tokyo, as *Noragami*, volume 6.

ISBN 978-1-61262-996-4

Printed in the United States of America.

www.kodansha.us

9 8 7 6 5

Translator: Alethea Nibley & Athena Nibley
Lettering: Lys Blakeslee